Introduction to Acting

Laurence Olivier as Hamlet in the film. (Culver Pictures, Inc.)

Introduction to Acting

SECOND EDITION

Stanley Kahan

California State University
Long Beach

Allyn and Bacon, Inc.

Boston   London   Sydney   Toronto

Library of Congress Cataloging in Publication Data

Kahan, Stanley, 1931–
　　　Introduction to acting.

　　Includes index.
　　1. Acting.　I. Title.
PN2061.K3　1985　　　792′.028　　　84–16799
ISBN 0–205–08204–1

Printed in the United States of America

10　9　8　7　6　　　　　　　89　88

CREDITS

Cover photo:　Commedia dell'arte—Zanni—Jacques Callot, National Gallery of Art, Washington, Rudolf L. Baumfeld
Collection.

Chapter opening photos:
CHAPTER 1　*The Playboy of the Western World* by J. M. Synge
Stanford University. Directed by James Haran.

CHAPTER 2　*Oedipus Rex* by Sophocles
Catholic University. Directed by James D. Waring.

CHAPTER 3　*Come Back, Little Sheba* by William Inge
California State University, Long Beach. Directed by Stanley Kahan.

CHAPTER 4　*Chemin de Fer* by Georges Feydeau
Wayne State University. Directed by Anthony Schmitt.

CHAPTER 5　*The Country Wife* by William Wycherly
University of Minnesota. Directed by Ken Bryant.

CHAPTER 6　*Long Day's Journey into Night* by Eugene O'Neill
Indiana University. Directed by Howard Jensen.

Credits continue on page 350

Contents

Preface

This edition of *Introduction to Acting* is a completely revised version of the text that was in general use for almost two decades. It includes significant material and exercises from *An Actor's Workbook,* which also was extensively used up to a few years ago. As was true of the original edition, first published in 1962, it is designed to serve the needs of the beginning student in acting. As then, it is intended as a textbook for college acting classes and the working actor in community and amateur theatre.

The teacher of acting is well aware that all students are not alike. They do not come into the classroom with the same level of training or experience, nor do they have the same psychological or mental makeup. They have different problems and different questions to be answered. Much of this responsibility is certainly that of the instructor: this text has been organized to serve as a practical tool to help clarify many of these areas. The book takes an *eclectic* approach for the beginning actor and general student, some of whom may never take another acting class. Therefore, there has been no attempt in this book to require the actor to follow any absolutely rigid or dogmatic system for developing his or her ability. It serves as a major adjunct to the teacher's work in the classroom or studio. The book stresses the point that the student should find the approach most meaningful for his or her own expressiveness.

Several additional sections have been added since the last edition. The volume begins by anticipating the beginning actor's most frequent questions, and introduces the background necessary to come to grips with the basic problems common to all actors. The text then proceeds to a new comprehensive chapter dealing with the history of acting, which the general student should find useful. It begins with the acting of the Greeks and looks at a wide variety of acting theories, with particular attention given to the contribution of Stanislavski. The third chapter deals exclusively with the use of improvisation, including extensive materials for large groups, small groups of two or more actors, and for the single actor. The text then proceeds to provide a basis for work in vocal and stage techniques, which may be conveniently categorized as the "external" fundamentals of stage work. This is followed by an examination of the development of a character, preparing a role, and putting the role on stage, an approach that is essentially subjective or "internal." A detailed look at the problems of playing comedy, farce, tragedy, and period plays in general is included in Chapter 8.

The final chapters deal with television and parenthetically "screen" acting, as well as radio acting—which has been making a sporadic comeback in recent years, particularly on public radio. These materials have been placed in separate chapters so that the instructor may choose not to utilize them with the remainder of the text which deals with the fundamentals of stage acting. This division, however, should not imply any serious dichotomy between stage and "media" acting; it is clear that the well-equipped actor in the theatre is prepared to handle the development of a role for radio and the screen as well.

One of the most useful features of this book is the inclusion of over forty complete scenes for actors, with particular emphasis on twentieth-century "realistic" plays. Scenes from plays by Neil Simon, Joe Orton, Eugene O'Neill, Arthur Miller, Howard Pinter, Noel Coward, Tennessee Williams, G. Bernard Shaw, Shakespeare, Lillian Hellman, Moliére, Anton Chekhov, Jean Anouilh, and others are included.

Grateful acknowledgment is made to those colleagues in the profession who have been kind enough to provide photographs of productions from their institution's and theatre's productions for inclusion in the text. I am indebted to the performance faculty of California State University, Long Beach, who helped to develop some of the material dealing with the development of character. Particular note should be made of the help given by Professor Libby Appel in coalescing these ideas with the performance faculty as they were being organized.

Mr. Kenneth Rugg supplied me with several of the "ambiguous dialogue" exercises that originated in his playwriting class. Personal use of these unique exercises has shown them to be an excellent means of stimulating the actor's imagination in developing character, situation, and motivation.

A particular note of appreciation is due to Professor Herbert L. Camburn for design renderings, and particularly Professor T. William Smith for preparing the line drawings. Both of my colleagues at California State University, Long Beach, were most generous of their time and talents.

As was noted in the original edition to the book, only this author can fully appreciate the invaluable contribution of his wife in the editorial preparation of the manuscript. To the many inquiring and stimulating students who posed the questions and challenges that first prompted consideration of the first edition, and to those who have used the original edition over the years and revealed its strengths and weaknesses, I owe the greatest obligation of all.

Stanley Kahan

List of Scenes

CHAPTER ONE

Some Questions Answered

If the sight of the blue skies fills you with joy, if a blade of grass springing up in the fields has power to move you, if the simple things of nature have a message that you understand, rejoice, for your soul is alive; and then aspire to learn that other truth, that the least of what you receive can be divided. To help, to continually help and share, that is the sum of all knowledge; that is the meaning of art.

The artist-actor gives the best of himself; through his interpretations he unveils his inner soul. By these interpretations only should he be accepted and judged. When the final curtain falls between him and his audience, nothing can be said or done, add or detract from his performance. His work is done, his message is delivered.

Eleonora Duse

Why Act?

One need only watch a group of children in the midst of their games to discover the universality of acting. Ask a child, or even an adult, to compose a sonata, carve a statue, or paint a landscape and the response would almost certainly be, ''But I don't know enough about music, or sculpture, or painting, to do what you ask.'' If one were then to inquire whether or not that person would like to act in a play, the adult might hesitate a moment, claim not to be a really *good* actor, but offer to give it a try if his or her fellow performers possessed the same level of ability. The great number of thriving community theatres in the country today testifies to the continued interest in the theatre among those whose livelihood and profession lie in different areas. Children, of course, would find no challenge in the suggestion. After all, they act all the time with their friends—at ''cowboys and Indians,'' ''playing house,'' and ''cops and robbers.''

All human beings possess, to some degree, what may be termed the *mimetic instinct*, a compulsion to imitate other human beings. It is this mimetic instinct that is directly responsible for the infant's and young child's developmental learning of language and social behavior. As children grow older, they project creative activities into games with fantasy and role playing. By late adolescence, such activities are usually subordinated to the requirements of adult society. Nevertheless, we never lose our impulse to dramatize situations, to alter in our imaginations unpleasant experiences, or to synthesize new ones. For example, how many of us have not personally fantasized ourselves into positions of authority, even inventing ''dialogue'' we might use in a given situation?

Yet acting is much more than this. At its best it is a creative force in our lives and in our culture, requiring as much competence as any creative or recreative art. Although the theatre is a collection of many arts—poetry; dance; music; scenic, costume, and lighting design; literary and philosophical thought—it is the actor who makes the theatre come to life. It is the actor who gives the written drama its vitality and its reason for existence. It is the actor who takes the ideas and dreams of the playwright and gives them shape, substance, and, above all, life.

The intangible rewards of acting may explain the irrepressible surge of young men and women to the theatre and their dedication to it despite the most overwhelming handicaps. The odds against security and financial reward are high; yet this fact deters few. In our conservatories, in college, university, and community theatres, we find a large number of dedicated men and women whose interest in the theatre has produced work of very high caliber indeed. Local, state, regional, and national theatre festivals surely point to the undiminished vitality of the young artists who will make up the theatre of tomorrow. As long as theatre continues to provide an artistic opportunity for those whose creativity must find a meaningful means of expression, the question ''Why act?'' should not be difficult to answer. Acting provides rewards measurable by the satisfaction derived from all creative endeavors when the job is well done. In the long run, this may be the most meaningful reward of all.

FIGURE 1.1 *Timon of Athens* by Shakespeare. Yale Repertory Theatre, directed by Lloyd Richards. James Earl Jones as Timon and James Greene as Flavius. (Photo by Gerry Goodstein)

Is There an Ideal Actor?

One of the most misleading comments heard about actors and acting is that certain physical and vocal attributes automatically ensure success. This belief is quite widespread, and its results are seen not only in the theatre but also in television and film, where attractive but otherwise unqualified youngsters hope for quick success. It is certainly true that physical attractiveness is an essential ingredient in the portrayal of *certain types* of roles. It is also true that occasionally a particular type may be in demand and can find suitable employment—until the fashion changes. Many years ago the film industry was particularly on the lookout for attractive sex-symbols, regardless of the actor's or actress's ability to act. There followed, in the 1960s and 1970s, the period of the antihero, where a certain insouciance and rebelliousness were deemed more important than simply looking pretty. Errol Flynn and Tyrone Power have given way to Dustin Hoffman, Woody Allen, and Jean-Paul Belmondo. Who can say what tomorrow will bring?

The belief that physical attractiveness alone provides a sure road to success, to the exclusion of other attributes, is damaging to the realization that there is no substitute for training and an understanding of the essentials of good acting.

Physical Standards

There is no specific type of physique required for good acting. The belief that one type of body is suited to acting in all roles is contradicted both by the evidence of history and by the variety of roles found in almost every play. Some of the great roles in Shakespeare's plays provide an interesting array of character types. Let us consider just two such roles, Cassius in *Julius Caesar* and the immortal comic creation Falstaff, found in three of Shakespeare's plays. Cassius is very carefully described as having a "lean and hungry look." As admirable an actor as Orson Welles is, he would have difficulty in giving a truly realistic portrait of this character. This in no way detracts from his ability as an actor. Consider also Falstaff, who throughout the plays in which he appears is referred to as "fat Jack," "this huge hill of flesh," "that swollen parcel of dropsies, that huge bombard of sack." One can think of any number of fine actors who, because of their physical makeup alone, would be unable to undertake the portrayal of this delightful character, even with the aid of padding!

Nor do seemingly restrictive physical characteristics always serve to limit the quality or range of the intelligent actor. In the long history of the English-speaking theatre, Thomas Betterton, David Garrick, Edmund Kean, Edwin Booth, and John Barrymore stand among the giants of the acting profession. Betterton was the unexcelled actor of the English Restoration in the seventeenth century; Garrick was the most notable actor of the eighteenth century; Kean was the finest of all nineteenth-century romantic actors; Booth is still generally regarded as the greatest of American actors; and John Barrymore's remarkable performances as Hamlet and Richard III are yet another proud part of the American theatre's heritage. All were versatile and exciting actors who overcame seemingly great physical limitations to rise to the pinnacle of their profession. Betterton was short and stout; he had a pair of beady eyes set in a huge face marked by the ravages of smallpox. Yet he was universally admired for his portrayals of the great heroes of Shakespeare's plays and the dignified gentlemen of Restoration comedy. In the commentary of biographers and observers of the other great actors, we find the constant reminder that such a possible limitation as short stature in no way affected the quality of their acting or their success in a wide range of leading and character roles.

It was said of David Garrick:

FIGURE 1.2 David Garrick. (Culver Pictures, Inc.)

His short stature (he was five feet four inches according to his measurements) proved an irritating handicap. Nevertheless, no other English actor of his standing has been better equipped for his calling. When he held the stage for a prologue or a soliloquy, his slight build gave the illusion of average height, and as soon as the action began, he moved about the stage rapidly and added so much new and ingenious byplay that the audience forgot to make comparisons. . . . Every muscle in his lithe young body was in perfect control. . . .[1]

And Playfair wrote of Edmund Kean:

This is what impressed his admirers most—his ability to make them forget that he was really an undersized little man with an unmelodious voice. Perhaps he was particularly suited to Richard [III] or Shylock or Iago. . . . Yet as Hamlet . . . he revealed beauties before undreamed of. . . . 'By God he is a Soul,' said Byron.[2]

---

1. Margaret Barton, *Garrick* (New York: Macmillan Co., 1949), p. 41.
2. Giles Playfair, *Kean* (London: Reinhardt and Evans, 1950), p. 116.

Otis Skinner wrote about Edwin Booth:

> Although a small, even a frail man, I could swear at times in *Othello* and in *Macbeth* he was seven feet tall.[3]

John Barrymore was barely five feet nine inches tall, and one might note that Al Pacino and Dustin Hoffman, who are among today's best young actors, are remarkably short in height.

If there is any physical standard that should be used to evaluate either the ability or potentiality of an actor, it is the level of *control* that the actor maintains over his or her body. Actors must learn to use their physical apparatus expressively and with economy of motion. The great actors just referred to refused to permit any physical limitations to interfere with their careers; rather, they accepted the challenge to utilize existing elements to make their acting even more exciting and vital. The only true physical limitation is an actor's inability or refusal to use physical equipment with intelligence and imagination.

Vocal Standards

The same qualifications discussed in relation to physical standards might just as easily be applied to the voice. There is no type of voice best suited to the theatre. We may hear the suggestion that a particularly beautiful or striking voice is a definite asset for an actor. It is true that an attractive voice may be useful in the portrayal of certain roles, and a voice that is well pro-

FIGURE 1.3a John Barrymore as Hamlet. (Culver Pictures, Inc.)

---

3. Otis Skinner, *Footlights and Spotlights* (New York: Bobbs-Merrill Company, Inc., 1924), p. 93.

FIGURE 1.3b Laurence Olivier as
Hamlet in the film. (Culver Pictures,
Inc.)

duced and free of annoying habits should be of great value to an actor. John
Dolman, Jr. has clearly defined the requirements of the good stage voice.

> It need not be a supremely beautiful voice in the musical sense; it will, in fact,
> be more useful if not too beautiful, since an excessively beautiful voice may
> hypnotize an audience into admiring the tones rather than listening to the
> play. . . . What the actor needs to develop is a voice that is highly adaptable to
> a variety of uses, and so managed as to withstand fatigue, and even abuse.[4]

*The first and most important function of the voice in the theatre is that it be
heard and understood.* This indicates a primary responsibility on the part of
any actor to develop proper projection and articulation. No matter how expressive or how lively, the voice that cannot be heard and understood is a
meaningless tool of communication for the actor. It is of course true that the
voice must also be used in the projection of shades of meaning, nuances,
and subtleties. This may be accomplished by the development of flexibility
and variety in pitch, rate, and volume.

It is obvious that the voice can be an important asset to any actor. One
of the famous legends of the theatre tells of the wonderful vocal ex-

---

4. John Dolman, Jr., *The Art of Acting* (New York: Harper and Brothers, 1949), pp.
187–88.

pressiveness of the great Polish actress Helena Modjeska. Once at a dinner party, when asked to perform one of her famous scenes for the assembled guests, the actress complied by giving a very brief monologue. Many onlookers were moved to tears by the gripping effect of Modjeska's eloquence, despite the fact the she performed the ''scene'' in Polish! After she had finished she was asked which great and touching selection she had chosen to move her audience so deeply. It must have been with a sly wink that she confided that in fact she had recited the Polish alphabet. Such effectiveness was made possible not only by her sense of the dramatic but by a supple and expressive voice, delicately tuned with a great versatility to the needs of every occasion.

Can Actors Be Classified?

There are many kinds of actors, just as there are many philosophies on how to act or how to train actors. Although many students of the theatre have tried to systematize acting into a set of rules applicable to all occasions, it is clear that such an approach is impractical when one deals with human beings. Theoretically, it should be possible to arrive at a universal set of rules, useful to all actors at all times. However, the diversity of acting styles and techniques in the theatre shows that fine acting may be, and is, achieved by more than one means.

Interviews with many actors have shown that there are several different roads leading to the final goal, to make the actor and actress as expressive and creative as possible. However the work is approached, there should be no mistaking the fact that it is hard work. No matter how an actor undertakes this work, it is worth bearing in mind the words of Charlton Heston. Talking about his preparation for a play under the direction of Laurence Olivier, Heston noted in his diary

> I've never felt such an overwhelming sense of the *difficulty* of acting. . . . who said it was supposed to be easy?[5]

There are a number of ways by which one may classify actors—in reference to their styles, personal characteristics and idiosyncrasies, philosophy, temperament, technique or lack of it, successful repetition of one type of role, and so on. It may be useful to examine some of these distinctions that tend to suggest how actors differ and why. However, a word of warning is in order. We can no more pigeonhole all actors into definite classifications than we can indicate a universal formula for suc-

---

5. Charlton Heston, *The Actor's Life: Journals 1956–1976,* ed. Hollis Alpert (New York: Pocket Books, 1979), p. 112.

cessful acting. Many performers do not fall neatly into any specific classification and on certain occasions may depart sharply from their usual style or technique. If we are prepared to accept these classifications as not too rigid, it is possible to point to three areas that help illustrate distinctive differences in acting.

Emotional vs. Technical Acting

> If he does not really feel the anguish of the betrayed lover or the dishonored father, if he does not temporarily escape from the dullness of his existence in order to throw himself wholeheartedly into the most acute crises, he will move nobody. How can he convince another of his emotion, of the sincerity of his passions, if he is unable to convince himself to the point of actually becoming the character that he has to impersonate?[6]

Sarah Bernhardt here summarizes very clearly the point of view of the actor who believes it is necessary to feel the role during the performance. All actors face the elemental problem of deciding whether or not they should feel emotion in the playing of a role, and to what degree they should feel it. We shall look carefully at this important problem in Chapter 2, but at this point let us consider how actors may be evaluated on the matter of emotion and technique in their acting.

Many performers give themselves over entirely to the character they are enacting. They literally *become* that individual, feeling his or her emotions and passions and often losing themselves entirely in the role. The emotional actor usually is not concerned with techniques of acting in relation to the voice or body. One interesting study of emotionalism in acting has suggested that "gesture, movement, and performance of stage business are likely to be impromptu, unstudied and haphazard."[7] The emotional actor relies on impulse and the springs of inspiration, to make a character's reactions and feelings meaningful. Such acting may often produce exciting and admirable performances, but its very nature suggests that it will lack consistency. Estelle Parsons, a multiple winner of acting awards, including two Off-Broadway Obies, two Tony nominations, and an Academy Award, has little respect for this kind of acting. She states quite clearly:

> An actress is someone who's able to use herself, not just lose control. That would be self-indulgence; that wouldn't be acting.[8]

---

6. Sarah Bernhardt, *The Art of the Theatre* (London: G. Bles, Ltd., 1924), p. 104.
7. Garff B. Wilson, "Emotionalism in Acting," *Quarterly Journal of Speech* 42 (February 1956): 44.
8. Estelle Parsons, quoted in Joanmarie Kalter, *Actors on Acting* (New York: Sterling Publishing Co., Inc., 1979), p. 226.

It is not uncommon to encounter actors and actresses who are so overcome by a role they may be playing that the effect lingers upon them long after they have left the stage.

On the other hand, the actor who eliminates all feeling from acting relies completely on the principles of stage technique and internal honesty to make a character meaningful to an audience. The actor will have the details of a performance carefully planned, with nothing left to chance or to sudden whims for unplanned emotional outbursts onstage. Raymond Massey indicated that this was his fundamental philosophy of acting. He has written:

> If he [the actor] allows his emotion to dominate the performance, he will lose all unity, all power of reproducing the character. . . . Personally, I have not "felt the part" before an audience in twenty years. Acting, to me, is always a case of "outside looking in." Without that detachment it is impossible for me to maintain the control necessary to keep the performance at proper pitch.[9]

There are, of course, a great number of actors who seek the middle ground, combining elements of both emotionalism and technique. Some lean more heavily toward one procedure than the other. It is evident, nevertheless, that an individual's approach to "feeling the part" is one legitimate way of differentiating among actors. Obviously it can be difficult to determine the level of emotionalism or technique used in any given performance. Very often the successful technical actor may so perfectly perform a role with all its emotional nuances that the audience will be certain they have witnessed emotional acting. A story is told in theatre circles about one of the most respected actors of our time. Another fine actor, watching him perform from the wings, was astonished to see him exit, after a deeply moving sequence (which had held even his fellow-actors in awe), and ask as he entered the wings, with tears streaming down his face, how the poker game was going backstage. The distinction between emotionalism and technique is a difference in the means rather than in the end, which in this case is a living performance.

Personality vs. Character Acting

It might seem on first consideration that personality and character acting are simply extensions of the two approaches discussed as emotional and technical acting. This is not true, however, in the sense in which these terms are used here. Nor, it must be added, does the term "character acting"

---

9. Raymond Massey, "Acting," from *The New Theatre Handbook and Digest of Plays,* ed. Bernard Sobel. Copyright 1940, 1948, 1959 by Crown Publishers, Inc. Used by permission of the publisher.

carry the connotation that is usually attached to it. We often hear the term applied to an actor who consistently plays a general character type in a large portion of the plays, films, or television series in which he or she appears. In the present practice of type casting, such actors continue successfully to portray the same basic character over and over again. This is not, however, character acting in the most meaningful sense.

In some ways this use of the term "type casting" is misleading. During the 1930s three of the most famous gangster actors in the Warner Brothers "stable" were Edward G. Robinson—"The Little Caesar"; James Cagney—"The Public Enemy"; and Humphrey Bogart—"A Gangster for All Seasons." Yet in real life these actors were quite different from their screen images. Robinson was a soft-spoken art collector and reflective pipe smoker, Bogart an excellent chess player and avid yachtsman, and Cagney (in his early days) an effective song-and-dance man.

The true character actor alters his or her personality to fit the demands of any role. This type of actor eliminates those features of his or her own personality that audiences would recognize and seeks to emphasize the personality of the role being undertaken. There are many fine actors of this type, of whom Laurence Olivier, Peter Sellers, Helen Hayes, and Alec Guinness are among the best known. One splendid example of this type of acting was the work of Alec Guinness in the English film *Kind Hearts and Coronets*. In this droll comedy Guinness played *eight* roles, each with a specific and well-defined personality and character. He also played a Japanese widower in *A Majority of One*; Hitler in *Hitler, The Last Ten Days*; Obi-Wan Kenobe in *Star Wars*; and a blind butler in *Murder by Death*. Much of the career of Marlon Brando has been built on his desire to "stretch" himself in this way, sometimes more successfully in some roles than others.

True character acting, then, requires great flexibility in the projection of age, social status, manners, and temperament. There are, however, two conclusions that should not be drawn from this appraisal of character acting. First, *the character actor does not necessarily feel the role.* Submergence of one's own personality in a character may be done either internally or externally. The distinction is this: how successfully does the actor eliminate his or her own personality in the playing of a role? It may be a very studied and carefully thought-out transition, or it may come almost entirely from the inner resources of the performer. Neither manner is directly related to character acting. The second conclusion often drawn is a qualitative evaluation of the two types of acting: *the character actor is not always a better actor than the noncharacter, or personality, actor.* We shall now see why this is so.

The personality actor creates a role within the framework of his or her own personality and mannerisms. In this type of acting the actor makes the role over in his or her own image, using personal characteristics to illustrate facets of the role being played. This does not suggest that the personality actor distorts the role. It does mean, however, that the actor comments on the character through his or her own personality. Charlton Heston is an excellent example of an actor whose personality permeates all the roles in which he appears. This certainly does not lessen his ability to create exciting characterizations, but it should be clear that his approach is fundamentally different from that of Alec Guinness and Ms. Hayes. Nor should it be assumed that Mr. Heston or other personality actors, such as James Stewart, or the late Henry Fonda, or the late Gary Cooper were less able than their colleagues whose approach to a role is somewhat different. We often hear this comment about a given actor: ''He is the same in every role he plays.'' Such criticism implies indifferent or inexperienced acting, but the comment may be somewhat misleading. John Mason Brown found this type of acting, in many respects, the more admirable.

> Then there are those precious few, standing at the top of their profession, whose high gift it is to act themselves, to adapt their spirits to the spirits of the parts they are playing, to possess and then to be possessed by the characters they project, and to give them the benefit of their beauty and their intelligence, their sympathy and their virtuosity, their poetry and their inner radiance, their imagination and their glamour.[10]

It should be apparent here, as in the previous discussion of emotionalism, that there are likely to be performers who fall between these two poles, combining distinctive characterizations with the use of their own personality. There is a need for both types of acting in the theatre, both on the amateur and professional level.

Representational vs. Presentational Acting

On many occasions, the type of play in which the actor is performing will affect his or her approach to a role and the manner of presentation. Although a number of stylistic distinctions can be made among numerous plays, the most fundamental differences in acting styles relate specifically to those plays that may be characterized as either *representational* or *presentational*. The representational style derives its name from the fact that the actors give the illusion that the audience is watching a *representation* of life. The acting suggests that the audience does not exist, by proceeding on the assumption that the invisible ''fourth wall'' of the setting separates actor and audience. The audience is given the impression that they are peeking in on human beings who are unaware of the existence of observers sitting in the house. Acting in this style is required in realistic plays[11] which constitute a large por-

---

10. John Mason Brown, *The Art of Playgoing* (New York: W. W. Norton Co., 1936), p. 194.

11. This style will, on occasion, also be used in plays that are not realistic. A fantasy, for example, would not be classified as a realistic play, yet an attempt to suggest the illusion of a fourth wall may still be used. It is this factor that distinguishes the representational style of acting.

tion of contemporary drama, and may also be found as the fundamental approach in contemporary motion-picture and television drama.

Representational acting should not be confused with the absence of any of the usual techniques of acting. The representational actor artfully conceals many of the important techniques in order to be seen and heard by the audience and maintain the illusion that he or she is simulating life. However, this concealment of the actor's art does not eliminate the need for the basic techniques of acting.

Presentational acting, on the other hand, is frankly theatrical, with little attempt to disguise the fact that the actor is performing on a stage before an audience. Speeches are often spoken directly to the audience; movement and action will attempt not necessarily to suggest life but to heighten it and sharpen its salient features. The presentational style is to be found in most of the dramas of the past: the tragedies of the Greeks, the dramas of Shakespeare and his contemporaries, and the great seventeenth-century comedies of the English Restoration and Molière. Today musical comedy frequently uses this technique. The actor, in fact, is telling the audience, ''Look, I know you are there, and I'm performing for you, so let us enjoy it together.''

FIGURE 1.4 *The Imaginary Invalid* by Molière. Brandeis University, directed by Daniel Gidron.

The clearest distinction between presentational and representational acting is in the focus of the actor's attention. In general, *representational acting is centered on the other actors in the play* and within the area of the stage setting itself. *Presentational acting tends to be audience centered*, with a continual awareness of the existence of the audience as the focal point of the action. As we shall see later, there are other subtle distinctions relating to the projection of these concepts, but they all are directed toward the fundamental goals just suggested. Many actors are adept at both styles of playing; others seem to find one style more harmonious with their training and temperament. It should be obvious that factors of emotionalism-technique and personality-character are not directly related to the use of either the presentational or the representational style.

What Should the Actor Know?

The good actor is an *intelligent* human being. He or she knows the techniques and conventions of the theatre, is usually well read, knows the great books and plays, has studied historical manners and customs, and is a generally well-informed individual. It is perfectly clear that the wider the range of experience and knowledge upon which an actor can draw, the finer actor he or she is likely to be. The world's great novels and plays depict a panorama of human emotions, motives, and personalities. This alone would be reason enough to enrich the mind with the views of the most observant students of human nature. Serving as a storehouse of our heritage, great literature provides the sensitive actor with an elemental source to tap for his or her own enrichment as a human being, and therefore as an actor as well.

There are also more practical considerations. The drama encompasses the entire range of human history. Princes, thieves, vagabonds, philosophers, and adventurers are found among the characters of thousands of plays. The actor undertaking such roles as these will find it literally impossible to draw on first-hand information. Yet the actor must understand the motives of such individuals, the customs and habits of their times, and their ambitions and their conflicts, in order to realize truly meaningful characterizations. Dedicated actors have long realized the necessity to broaden their viewpoints and knowledge. Directly on this point, the great Italian actor Tommaso Salvini wrote:

> By familiarizing myself with great writers, I formed a fund of information which was the greatest assistance to me in the pursuit of my profession. I made comparisons between the heroes of ancient Greece and those of Celtic races; their characters, their passions, their manners, their tendencies, to such pur-

pose that when I had occasion to impersonate one of these types I was able to study it in its native atmosphere.[12]

Salvini's comment represents by no means an isolated viewpoint. It stems from the very heart of the problem of intelligent and purposeful acting. Sarah Bernhardt expressed very much the same thing when, after a life spent in the theatre, she wrote:

Consequently the actor must become familiar with the entire past of humanity . . . the manners, the customs, and the passions of different peoples and of different times. It is certain that love does not reveal itself in every age in the same forms, and that the expressions of hate vary from century to century, and from people to people. . . . Now how can these sentiments be embodied without dipping into books—for the past—and into the current of life—for the present. . . .[13]

The actor who strives to improve the range of experience upon which to draw in the preparation of a role needs to be aware that all that he or she chooses to read, or is able to observe, serves to strengthen and nourish his or her acting ability.

What Is "The Illusion of the First Time"?

One of the most difficult critical problems in the theatre is that of evaluating the work of actors and actresses from one performance to another. Why did one actor succeed in making a character come to life where another failed, and why may an actor at a given performance fall below the level of the night before? There are any number of standards relating to the technical competence of an actor by which we may evaluate a specific performance. There is one element, however, that serves as a basis of the study of acting as discussed in this text. This factor has been described by actors in countless ways, but the description by the American actor William Gillette (the theatre's first Sherlock Holmes) is perhaps the most precise. He spoke of the actor's duty to maintain for the audience the "illusion of the first time." By this he meant that the members of the audience must sense that the character in the play is experiencing and reacting to the varied situations not for the tenth or twentieth or hundredth time, as the actor is likely to do after numerous rehearsals and performances, but for the first time. Sidney Poitier calls this "refuelling." Specifically, he says "With me—as with other

---

12. *Leaves from the Autobiography of Tommaso Salvini* (New York: The Century Co., 1893), p. 65.

13. Sarah Bernhardt, op. cit., pp. 88–89.

actors, I believe—it's quite a job to prevent the work from becoming mechanical. You have to find ways to keep refuelling the impulse.''[14]

Often audiences will be hard put to specify the exact nature of a weak performance, sensing, however, that they have witnessed a stale repetition of something that had been done many times before. The element of spontaneity is essential to all good performances. This spontaneity is as meaningful in plays of a poetic and presentational style as in the most realistic dramas. Gillette was insistent on this point.

> Each successive audience before which [the presentation] is given must feel—not think or reason about, but *feel*—that it is witnessing, not one of a thousand weary repetitions, but a life episode that is being lived just across the magic barrier of the footlights. That is to say, the whole must have that indescribable life-spirit or effect which produces the Illusion of the First Time.[15]

Gillette's essay is perhaps the most articulate expression of this important facet of good acting. John Barrymore said much the same thing during an interview: "Acting is the art . . . of doing and saying the thing as spontaneously as if you were confronted with the situation in which you were acting, for the first time.''[16]

David Belasco wrote eloquently of the last public performance of Edwin Booth:

> The last time that ever I heard Booth speak Hamlet's immortal soliloquy on life and death was the last time that ever he spoke it in public, at the old Academy of Music, in Brooklyn, April 4, 1891. In the preceding fifteen years I had heard him speak that speech probably forty times; he was then old, worn and frail, yet the familiar words seemed to come from his lips for the first time, to utter thoughts then first formulated.[17]

And yet again Henry Fonda has said almost the same thing as Gillette. In referring to his multiple-year run on Broadway as Mister Roberts, and to the film version as well, he commented:

> The pitfall you get into in most long runs is you stop listening. . . . It never happened in *Mister Roberts*. The thing I try to do onstage is to create the illusion that it's happening for the first time. In two years, not a performance got by of all the performances we did that the audience didn't get what it came for; for them it was happening for the first time. I never got tired of it.[18]

---

14. Sidney Poitier, quoted in Lillian Ross and Helen Ross, *The Player: A Profile of an Art* (New York: Simon and Schuster, 1962), p. 110.

15. William Hooker Gillette, ''The Illusion of the First Time in Acting,'' in *Papers in Acting*, ed. Brander Matthews (New York: Hill and Wang, Inc., 1958), p. 133.

16. Helen Ten Broeck, ''From Comedy to Tragedy: An interview with John Barrymore,'' *Theatre*, July 1916, p. 23.

17. David Belasco, ''About Acting,'' *Saturday Evening Post*, 24 September 1921, pp. 11 ff.

18. Henry Fonda, quoted in Ross and Ross, op. cit., pp. 89–90.

For many actors this is an unconscious part of their art, grasped intuitively and made meaningful by experience. Every effort devoted to the expansion of the actor's dramatic potential must incorporate this element. Whatever is likely to become artificial, stilted, or stale can only detract from the projection of the essence of life upon the stage. It must be rejected—from whatever source it may come. It is through the actor's own personality that these techniques and ideas can be molded to find proper expression on the stage. The goal is that moment on stage when the audience will feel the essence that means "I believe it"—not because it is necessarily realistic but because it is *true and right*.

QUESTIONS AND EXERCISES

Questions for Discussion

1. Is acting a creative art or is it an interpretive art? How much that is original does the actor contribute to the playing of a role?
2. How does the acting of the silent film differ from the acting in films today? How does the acting in the early talking films of the 1930s vary from film and television acting today? Why have there been such distinctive changes in acting styles within a period of only half a century?
3. Classify the following actors and actresses as either "character" or "personality" performers: (a) Marlon Brando, (b) Jon Voight, (c) Shirley MacLaine, (d) Bette Davis, (e) Dustin Hoffman, (f) Cecily Tyson, (g) Katharine Hepburn, (h) Burt Reynolds, (i) Ben Vereen, (j) Ed Asner, (k) Al Pacino, (l) Jane Fonda. Compare your conclusions with the conclusions of other people in class and discuss your differences of opinion.
4. Is it possible to tell when an actor is "feeling" the role?
5. Is there any value in attempting to classify types of actors? Is anything to be learned in studying other actors' means of approaching a role?
6. (a) Which actor whom you have seen on the stage, in film, or in television has the most expressive and versatile voice? (b) Which actor whom you have seen on the stage, in film, or in television has made the most expressive use of his or her body?
7. What qualities should a human being possess before entering a study of acting? Can anyone become a competent actor?
8. Read a portion of the biography of any actor of the past or present. Try to uncover the reason that made that individual turn to the stage as a career. Compare notes with other people in the class.

Exercises

Select one of the following monologues, or use one of your own choosing as a warmup round. Examine the meaning of the speech and its relationship to the character and the play by reading the play in which the monologue occurs.

Monologues

1. Monologue from *The Glass Menagerie,* by Tennessee Williams.

Amanda is speaking to her daughter Laura. She dreams of a fine marriage for her daughter who is, however, crippled and shy. They are poor, but this does not stop Amanda from dreaming, and she has many dreams for her children. In this speech she remembers her own girlhood in the South.

AMANDA: Possess your soul in patience—you will see! Something I've resurrected from that old trunk! Styles haven't changed so terribly much after all. . . . Now just look at your mother! (*feverishly*) This is the dress in which I led the cotillion. Won the cakewalk twice at Sunset Hill, wore one spring to the Governor's ball in Jackson! See how I sashayed around the ballroom, Laura? (*She raises her skirt and does a mincing step around the room.*) I wore it on Sundays for my gentlemen callers! I had it on the day I met your father—I had malaria fever all that spring. The change of climate from East Tennessee to the Delta—weakened resistance—I had a little temperature all the time—not enough to be serious—just enough to make me restless and giddy!—Invitations poured in—parties all over the Delta!—"Stay in bed," said Mother, "you have fever!"—but I just wouldn't.—I took quinine but kept on going, going!—Evenings, dances!—Afternoons, long, long rides! Picnics—lovely!—So lovely, that country in May.—All lacy with dogwood, literally flooded with jonquils!—That was the spring I had the craze for jonquils. Jonquils became an absolute obsession. Mother said "Honey, there's no more room for jonquils." And still I kept on bringing in more jonquils. Whenever, wherever I saw them, I'd say, "Stop! Stop! I see jonquils!" I made the young men help me gather the jonquils! It was a joke, Amanda and her jonquils! Finally there were no more vases to hold them, every available space was filled with jonquils. No vases to hold them? All right, I'll hold them myself! And then I—met your father!

2. Monologue from *Long Day's Journey into Night,* by Eugene O'Neill.

In this very autobiographical play, young Edmund Tyrone is based on the character of Eugene O'Neill. Here Edmund reflects on the days he spent on a variety of ships, a time when he was free in body and in spirit. O'Neill's love of the sea is also reflected in Paddy's speech from *The Hairy Ape,* which has a similar ring of something remembered and something lost.

EDMUND: You've just told me some high spots in your memories. Want to hear mine? They're all connected with the sea. Here's one. When I was on the Squarehead square rigger, bound for Buenos Aires. Full moon in the

Trades. The old hooker driving fourteen knots. I lay on the bowsprit, facing astern, with the water foaming into spume under me, the masts with every sail white in the moonlight, towering high above me. I became drunk with the beauty and singing rhythm of it, and for a moment I lost myself—actually lost my life. I was set free! I dissolved in the sea, became white sails and flying spray, became beauty and rhythm, became moonlight and the ship and the high dim-starred sky! I belonged, without past or future, within peace and unity and a wild joy, within something greater than my own life, or the life of Man, to Life itself! To God, if you want to put it that way. Then another time, on the American Line, when I was lookout on the crow's nest in the dawn watch. A calm sea, that time. Only a lazy ground swell and a slow drowsy roll of the ship. The passengers asleep and none of the crew in sight. No sound of man. Black smoke pouring from the funnels behind and beneath me. Dreaming, not keeping lookout, feeling alone, and above, and apart, watching the dawn creep like a painted dream over the sky and sea which slept together. Then the moment of ecstatic freedom came. The peace, the end of the quest, the last harbor, the joy of belonging to a fulfillment beyond men's lousy, pitiful, greedy fears and hopes and dreams! And several other times in my life, when I was swimming far out, or lying alone on a beach, I have had the same experience. Became the sun, the hot sand, green seaweed anchored to a rock, swaying in the tide. Like a saint's vision of beatitude. Like the veil of things as they seem drawn back by an unseen hand. For a second you see—and seeing the secret, are the secret. For a second there is meaning! Then the hand lets the veil fall and you are alone, lost in the fog again, and you stumble on toward nowhere, for no good reason! (*He grins wryly.*) It was a great mistake, my being born a man, I would have been much more successful as a sea gull or a fish. As it is, I will always be a stranger who never feels at home, who does not really want and is not really wanted, who can never belong, who must always be a little in love with death!

3.   Monologue from *Long Day's Journey into Night*, by Eugene O'Neill.

The Tyrone family has exhausted itself this day in recriminations, alcholic abuses, and self-torture. Each character sinks into his or her own escape from the pain of living after their "long journey." Mary, the mother, is a drug addict, and, finding temporary peace, she stares dreamily ahead, her face looking "youthful and innocent." She begins to talk aloud to herself. None of the other members of her family is listening.

MARY: I had a talk with Mother Elizabeth. She is so sweet and good. A saint on earth. I love her dearly. It may be sinful of me but I love her better than my own mother. Because she always understands, even before you say a word. Her kind blue eyes look right into your heart. You can't keep any secrets from her. You couldn't deceive her, even if you were mean enough to want to. (*She gives a little rebellious toss of her head—with girlish pique.*) All the same, I don't think she was so understanding this time. I told her I wanted to be a nun. I explained how sure I was of my vocation, that I had prayed to the Blessed Virgin to make me sure, and to find me worthy. I told Mother I had had a true vision when I was praying in the shrine of Our Lady of Lourdes, on the little island in the lake. I said I knew, as surely as I knew I was kneeling there, that the Blessed Virgin had smiled and blessed me with her consent. But Mother Elizabeth told me I must be more sure than that, even, that I must prove it wasn't simply my imagination. She said, if I was so sure, then I wouldn't mind putting myself to a test by going home after I graduated, and living as other girls lived, going out to parties and dances and enjoying myself; and then if after a year or two I still felt sure, I could come back to see her and we would talk it over again. (*She tosses her head—indignantly.*) I never dreamed Holy Mother would give me such advice! I was really shocked. I said, of course, I would do anything she suggested, but I knew it was simply a waste of time. After I left her, I felt all mixed up, so I went to the shrine and prayed to the Blessed Virgin and found peace again because I knew she heard my prayer and would always love me and see no harm ever came to me so long as I never lost my faith in her. (*She pauses and a look of growing uneasiness comes over her face. She passes a hand over her forehead as if brushing cobwebs from her brain—vaguely.*) That was in the winter of senior year. Then in the spring something happened to me. Yes, I remember. I fell in love with James Tyrone and was so happy for a time.

4.   Monologue from *Antigone,* by Jean Anouilh.

Antigone and Ismene are sisters whose brothers have just died fighting on opposite sides in a war. Antigone insists on giving her rebel brother a decent burial, but Ismene is terrified that Creon, King of Thebes, will exact a terrible retribution for such an act against the state. Ismene expresses that fear in the following speech.

ISMENE: His mob will come running, howling as it runs. A thousand arms will seize our arms. A thousand breaths will breathe into our faces. Like one single pair of eyes, a thousand eyes will stare at us. We'll be driven in a tumbrel through their hatred, through the smell of them and their cruel, roaring laughter. We'll be dragged to the scaffold for torture, surrounded by guards with their idiot faces all bloated, their animal hands clean-washed for the sacrifice, their beefy eyes squinting as they stare at us. And we'll know that no shrieking and no begging will make them understand that we want to live, for they are like slaves who do exactly as they've been told, without caring about right or wrong. And we shall suffer, we shall feel pain rising in us until it becomes so unbearable that we *know* it must stop. But it won't stop, it will go on rising and rising, like a screaming voice. Oh, I can't, I can't, Antigone!

5.   Monologue from *Death of a Salesman,* by Arthur Miller.

Willy Loman, a broken-down salesman in his mid-sixties, has come to ask his young boss Howard for a job in the home office. Willy is too tired to continue working for commissions on the road. Meeting resistance from Howard, Willy begins to reminisce about how selling has changed since the wonderful days of his youth.

WILLY: Oh, yeah, my father lived many years in Alaska. He was an adventurous man. We've got quite a little streak of self-reliance in our family. I thought I'd go out with my older brother and try to locate him, and maybe settle in the North with the old man. And I was almost decided to go, when I met a salesman in the Parker House. His name was Dave Singleman. And he was eighty-four years old, and he drummed merchandise in thirty-one states. And old Dave, he'd go up to his room, y'understand, put on his green velvet slippers—I'll never forget—and pick up his phone and call the buyers, and without ever leaving his room, at the age of eighty-four, he made his living. And when I saw that, I realized that selling was the greatest career a man could want. 'Cause what could be more satisfying than to be able to go, at the age of eighty-four, into twenty or thirty different cities, and pick up a phone, and be remembered and loved and helped by so many different people? Do you know? when he died—and by the way he died the death of a salesman, in his green velvet slippers in the smoker of the New York, New Haven and Hartford, going into Boston—when he died, hundreds of salesmen and buyers were at his funeral. Things were sad on a lotta trains for months after that. (*He stands up.* HOWARD *has not looked at him.*) In those days there was personality in it, Howard. There was respect, and comradeship, and gratitude in it. Today, it's all cut and dried, and there's no chance for bringing friendship to bear—or personality. You see what I mean? They don't know me any more.

6. Monologue from *Death of a Salesman*, by Arthur Miller.

Linda is the hardworking, loyal wife of salesman Willy Loman. She speaks from despair as she explains to her two thirty-year-old sons why they must continue to love and respect him. She knows Willy plans suicide and fights the thought in her mind. Her defense of Willy is compassionate but filled with an anger which is directed at her sons.

LINDA: I don't say he's a great man. Willy Loman never made a lot of money. His name was never in the paper. He's not the finest character that ever lived. But he's a human being, and a terrible thing is happening to him. So attention must be paid. He's not to be allowed to fall into his grave like an old dog. Attention, attention must be finally paid to such a person. . . . A small man can be just as exhausted as a great man. He works for a company thirty-six years this March, opens up unheard-of territories to their trademark, and now in his old age they take his salary away. . . . When he brought them business, when he was young, they were glad to see him. But now his old friends, the old buyers that loved him so and always found some order to hand him in a pinch—they're all dead, retired. He used to be able to make six, seven calls a day in Boston. Now he takes his valises out of the car and puts them back and takes them out again and he's exhausted. Instead of walking he talks now. He drives seven hundred miles, and when he gets there no one knows him any more, no one welcomes him. And what goes through a man's mind, driving seven hundred miles home without having earned a cent? Why shouldn't he talk to himself? Why? When he has to go to Charley and borrow fifty dollars a week and pretend to me that it's his pay? How long can that go on? How long? You see what I'm sitting here and waiting for? And you tell me he has no character? The man who never worked a day but for your benefit? When does he get the medal for that?

7. Monologue from *The Sea Gull*, by Anton Chekhov, translated by Stark Young.

Nina left home to find success on the stage but found failure instead. She was attracted to a successful playwright, but in this scene she unburdens herself to a young, sensitive writer who still loves her deeply. She has just entered his study, ill and tired.

NINA: Why do you say you kiss the ground I walk on? I ought to be killed. I'm so tired. If I could rest—rest. I'm a sea gull. No, that's not it. I'm an actress. Well, no matter. He didn't believe in the theatre, all my dreams he'd laugh at, and little by little I quit believing in it myself, and lost heart. And there was the strain of love, jealousy, constant anxiety about my little baby. I got to be small and trashy, and played without thinking. I didn't know what to do with my hands, couldn't stand properly on the stage, couldn't control my voice. You can't imagine the feeling when you are acting and know it's dull. I'm a sea gull. No, that's not it. Do you remember, you shot a sea gull? A man comes by chance, sees it, and out of nothing else to do, destroys it. That's not it—(*Puts her hand to her forehead.*) What was I—? I was talking about the stage. Now I'm not like that. I'm a real actress, I act with delight, with rapture, I'm drunk when I'm on the stage, and feel that I am beautiful. And now, ever since I've been here, I've kept walking about, kept walking and thinking, thinking and believing my soul grows stronger every day. Now I know, I understand, Kostya, that in our work—acting or writing—what matters is not fame, not glory, not what I used to dream about, it's how to endure, to bear my cross, and have faith. I have faith and it all doesn't hurt me so much, and when I think of my calling I'm not afraid of life.

8. Monologue from *The Hairy Ape*, by Eugene O'Neill.

Paddy is an old sailor, traveling the seas as a stoker in the stokehold of an ocean liner. But he remembers a happier day, when the sea was conquered by the great four-masters with full sail in the breeze.

PADDY: (*Who has been sitting in a blinking, melancholy daze—suddenly cries out in a voice full of old sorrow*) We belong to this, you're saying? We make the ship to go, you're saying? Yerra then, that Almighty God have pity on us! Oh, to be back in the fine days of my youth, ochone! Oh, there was fine beautiful ships them days—clippers wid tall masts touching the sky—fine strong men in them—men that was sons of the sea as if 'twas the mother that bore them. Oh, the clean skins of them, and the clear eyes, the straight backs and full chests of them! Brave men they was, and bold men surely! We'd be sailing out, bound down round the Horn maybe. We'd be making sail in the dawn, with a fair breeze, singing a chanty song wid no care to it. And astern the land would be sinking low and dying out, but we'd give it no heed but a laugh, and never a look behind. For the day that was, was enough, for we was free men—and I'm thinking 'tis only slaves to be giving heed to the day that's gone or the day to come—until they're old like me. (*with a sort of religious exaltation*) Oh, to be scudding south again wid the power of the Trade Wind driving her on steady through the nights and the days! Full sail on her! Nights and days! Nights when the foam of the wake would be flaming wid fire, when the sky'd be blazing and winking wid stars. Or the full moon maybe. Then you'd see her driving through the gray night, her sails stretching aloft all silver and white, not a sound on the deck, the lot of us dreaming dreams, till you'd believe 'twas no real ship at all you was on but a ghost ship like the *Flying Dutchman* they says does be roaming the seas forevermore widout touching a port. And there was the days, too. A warm sun on the clean decks. Sun warming the blood of you, and wind over the miles of shiny green ocean like strong drink to your lungs. Work—aye, hard work—but who'd mind that at all? Sure, you worked under the sky and 'twas work wid skill and daring to it. And wid the day done, in the dog watch, smoking me pipe at ease, the lookout would be raising land maybe, and we'd see the mountains of South Americy wid the red fire of the setting sun painting their white tops and the clouds floating by them! (*His tone of exaltation ceases. He goes on mournfully.*) Yerra, what's the use of talking? 'Tis a dead man's whisper.

9. Monologue from *There Shall Be No Night*, by Robert E. Sherwood.

Miranda is the American wife of Dr. Kaarlo Valkonen, Finnish Nobel Prize winner. Valkonen, a life-long pacifist, finally realized that at some point a man must fight for what he believes in, and he gave his life for the ideal of freedom. Miranda is reading his last letter, written just after he received news of the death of his only son in defense of his homeland against the Russian invasion.

MIRANDA: (*reading*) "In this time of our own grief it is not easy to summon up the philosophy which has been formed from long study of the sufferings of others. But I must do it, and you must help me." You see—he wanted to make me feel that I'm stronger—wiser. "I have often read the words which Pericles spoke over the bodies of the dead, in the dark hour when the light of Athenian democracy was being extinguished by the Spartans. He told the mourning people that he could not give them any of the old words which tell how fair and noble it is to die in battle. Those empty words were old, even then, twenty-four centuries ago. But he urged them to find revival in the memory of the commonwealth which they together had achieved; and he promised them that the story of their commonwealth would never die, but would live on, far away, woven into the fabric of other men's lives. I believe that these words can be said now of our own dead, and our own commonwealth. I have always believed in the mystic truth of the Resurrection. The great leaders of the mind and the spirit—Socrates, Christ, Lincoln—were all done to death that the full measure of their contribution to human experience might never be lost. Now—the death of our son is only a fragment in the death of our country. But Erik and the others who give their lives are also giving to mankind a symbol—a little symbol, to be sure, but a clear one—of man's unconquerable aspiration to dignity and freedom and purity in the sight of God. When I made that radio speech''—you remember? . . . ''I quoted from St. Paul. I repeat those words to you now, darling: 'We glory in tribulations; knowing that tribulation worketh patience; and patience, experience; and experience, hope.' There are men here from all different countries. Fine men. Those Americans who were at our house on New Year's Day—and that nice Polish officer, Major Rutkowski—they are all here. They are waiting for me now, so I must close this, with all my love.''

10.   Monologue from *After the Fall*, by Arthur Miller.

In this play Miller makes use of flashbacks and stream-of-consciousness passages which provide a very fluid means of telling his story. In this speech, Quentin, a man in his forties, addresses the Listener, ''who, if he could be seen, would be sitting beyond the edge of the stage itself.''

QUENTIN: You know, more and more I think that for many years I looked at life like a case at law, a series of proofs. When you're young you prove how brave you are, or smart; then, what a good lover; then, a good father; finally, how wise, or powerful or what-the-hell-ever. But underlying it all, I see now, there was a presumption. That I was moving on an upward path toward some elevation, where—God knows what—I would be justified, or even condemned—a verdict anyway. I think now that my disaster really began when I looked up one day—and the bench was empty. No judge in sight. And all that remained was the endless argument with oneself—this pointless litigation of existence before an empty bench. Which, of course, is another way of saying—despair. And, of course, despair can be a way of life; but you have to believe in it, pick it up, take it to heart, and move on again. Instead, I seem to be hung up. (*Slight pause.*) And the days and the months and now the years are draining away. A couple of weeks ago I suddenly became aware of a strange fact. With all this darkness, the truth is that every morning when I awake, I'm full of hope! With everything I know—I open my eyes, I'm like a boy! For an instant there's some—unformed promise in the air. I jump out of bed, I shave. I can't wait to finish breakfast—and then, it seeps in my room, my life and its pointlessness. And I thought—if I could corner that hope, find what it consists of and either kill it for a lie, or really make it mine . . .

11.   Monologue from *After the Fall*, by Arthur Miller.

Also see the preceding monologue from this play. In this scene, Quentin tries to create an image of his father in his memory, but the image is mingled with the voice of Quentin's mother, who remembers the father with great affection.

MOTHER: To this day he walks into a room you want to bow! (*Warmly.*) Any restaurant—one look at him and the waiters start moving tables around. *Because,* dear, people know that this is a *man*. Even Doctor Strauss, at my wedding he came over to me, says, "Rose, I can see it looking at him, you've got a wonderful man," and he was always in love with me, Strauss. . . . Oh, sure, but he was only a penniless medical student then, my father wouldn't let him in the house. Who knew he'd end up so big in the gallstones? That poor boy! Used to bring me novels to read, poetry, philosophy, God knows what! One time we even sneaked off to hear Rachmaninoff together. (*She laughs sadly; and with wonder more than bitterness.*) That's why, you see, two weeks after we were married; sit down to dinner and Papa hands me a menu and asks me to read it to him. Couldn't *read!* I got so frightened I nearly ran away! . . . Why? Because your grandmother is such a fine, unselfish woman; two months in school and they put him into the shop! That's what some women are, my dear—and now he goes and buys her a new Packard every year. (*With a strange and deep fear.*) Please, darling, I want you to *draw* the letters, that scribbling is ugly, dear; and your posture, your speech, it can all be beautiful! Ask Miss Fisher, for years they kept my handwriting pinned up on the bulletin board; God, I'll never forget it, valedictorian of the class with a scholarship to Hunter in my hand . . . (*A blackness flows into her soul.*) And I came home, and Grandpa says, "You're getting married!" I was like—like with small wings, just getting ready to fly; I slept all year with the catalogue under my pillow. To learn, to learn everything! Oh darling, the whole thing is such a mystery!

CHAPTER
TWO

A Brief History of Acting and Acting Theories

Many of the questions commonly asked about acting have been the concern of actors from the earliest days of the theatre. If we look at the work of the great actors of the past and read what they have written about their craft, we find a continual concern about certain persistent questions, indeed, the same questions we still ask today: *Does the actor feel the part? Does the actor completely subordinate his or her personality in playing various roles? What form should the actor's training take?*

Perhaps the most difficult question pondered over the years is that of the essential nature of the actor: *Is he or she a creative artist with a singular creative responsibility or simply an adept interpreter of the intention of the playwright or even of the director?* Each actor will undoubtedly find individual answers to these problems, but it is reassuring to know that the same questions have long been discussed by the great actors and critics.

It will be of value to examine the past to see what if any light it sheds on these persistent questions. We shall find little uniformity of opinion, but we shall discover that serious attention has always been paid to the art of the theatre and acting. In this one regard most actors are similar. They are truly concerned about the nature of their medium. Although final answers to these questions will not be found here, the ideas raised by the following discussion should help each actor think more carefully about his or her own acting.

The First Actors

The first actor was very likely a hunter in prehistoric times who described to his fellow tribesmen his adventures of that day. He gesticulated, exaggerated his cunning and resourcefulness, and described how the animal had fought valiantly against the hunter's guile. He was impersonating, imitating, and recalling previous events. He may even have used the tusks, antlers, or skin of the animal to enliven his impersonation. Enhanced by firelight and performing before an audience that shared his concerns, he probably did not realize that, in one sense, he was starting a tradition that would persist to the present day. Unfortunately neither this prehistoric hunter nor any of his viewers and listeners left a record of how he went about his performance. However, contemporary evidence indicates that such impromptu accounts of hunting stories involved masks and costumes and grew into intricate performances of long-standing myths. Eventually speech, dance, makeup, costume, music, pantomime, and the audience all contributed to the ''production.'' It was a means of fulfilling the primitive society's need to understand the essential considerations of their group, from the stability of their food supply to their concern about the supernatural. Remnants of these rituals still exist in certain societies today. A concern about humanity's place in the universe has been a part of all the great ages of the theatre, from the Greek tragic playwrights to the existential and absurdist playwrights of today.

What the Ancients Tell Us

Theatre in the western world had its origins in Greece around the sixth century B.C. Religious festivals in honor of the god Dionysus were held every year with choral chants called *dithyrambs* and probably animal sacrifices. Dionysus was a nature god, a god of wine, fertility, and spring, and he was reborn every year. These choral chants, held in large outdoor arenas (see Figure 2.1), were essentially undramatic until an individual by the name of Thespis had the inspiration to include in the rituals a ''responder'' to the head of the chorus of priests. With this idea Western drama was born. Two individuals responding to each other permitted conflict, action, and

FIGURE 2.1 Greek Theatre at Epidaurus.

perhaps even the germ of a plot. The first "responder" or *protagonist* became the first actor. Regular Dionysian festivals were held annually as a form of competition for the writing of dithyrambs and tragedies, and Thespis was the winner of the first contest, held in Athens in 534 B.C. The name Thespis has been linked with the art of acting ever since. Gradually the form of these contests permitted greater freedom in the writing and performance of the plays.

Viewing the Greek drama of the past in broad perspective, certain perceptions we have about Greek acting become clearer. The theatres were vast open areas, with a circle for dancing by the chorus and with seating in a semicircle on the hillside for the spectators. This *theatron,* as it was called, often seated up to seventeen thousand spectators. The stone remnants of these theatrons can still be found in and around Greece. Clearly such huge outdoor arenas required *presentational* acting of a highly exaggerated style. The actors wore boots (*cothurni*) to add to their height and used masks which served to identify their characters from great distances, as well as to help amplify their voices. There were no more than three main actors on the stage at any one time, and the same actors could play many roles in a tragedy simply by changing masks and costumes. All roles were played by men, including the great female characters of Greek tragedy.

The information we have concerning the Greek actor's approach to his role is quite meager, but scattered clues suggest some interesting conclusions. Not only did the Greek actor need to be an able dancer and singer, but he had to possess a beautiful and well-managed speaking voice. Aristotle, in fact, defined acting as "the proper management of voice to express several emotions." Obviously a well-managed and well-placed voice was essential in the huge outdoor theatres in which the Greek actor was required to perform.

It is likely that the Greeks believed that great acting was a matter of inspiration rather than technique and that only through inspiration could the actor achieve his effects. Plato gives us a clue to this view in one of his dialogues. In it Socrates is questioning the actor Ion.

> SOCRATES: I wish you would frankly tell me, Ion, what I am going to ask of you: When you produce the greatest effect upon the audience in the recitation of some striking passage . . . are you in your right mind? Are you not carried out of yourself, and does not your soul in an ecstasy seem to be among the persons or the places of which you are speaking . . .
>
> ION: . . . I must frankly confess that at the tale of pity my eyes are filled with tears, and when I speak of horrors, my hair stands on end and my heart throbs.[1]

FIGURE 2.2   Greek Theatre at Delphi.

---

1. Plato, "Ion," *Dialogues*, tr. Benjamin Jowett (New York: Oxford University Press, 1892), vol. 1, pp. 497–504.

We have other clues to support the belief that the Greek actor identified himself emotionally with his role. One famous anecdote reinforces this point and illustrates the lengths to which an actor might go to produce an effect. The Greek tragedian Polus, who had achieved notable success in portraying many tragic roles, lost a son whom he loved dearly. After his son's death Polus was called on to play the role of Electra in the play by Sophocles. In one scene Electra was required to mourn the death of her brother while carrying an urn supposedly holding his ashes. Polus carried in an urn holding the ashes of his own son and played the grief-stricken Electra with a genuine grief that evidently was startling. We are told that Polus "filled the arena, not with the appearance and suggestion of misery, but with true sorrow and grief. Although it seemed to some that a play was being performed it was indeed a real enactment of grief."[2]

Although the contemporary actor may gain little from the general approach of the Greeks to acting, it is of value to note two important points. First, acting was a matter of emotion and inspiration, evidently little concerned with any systematic approach; second, great reliance was placed upon the voice as a means of conveying those emotions.

The Decline of the Theatre

After Greece's decline as a major power in the ancient world, the vacuum in theatre was filled by the Romans. During the period of the Roman republic, in the second and third centuries B.C., the comedies of Plautus and Terence attained some prominence, as did some Roman tragedies, which are now generally forgotten. Gradually Roman entertainments moved to massive spectacles which included gladiatorial combats, the massacre of hundreds of animals in a single day, and realistically staged sea battles in which criminals and captured enemies fought to the death. Indeed, the best gladiators and pseudosailors were those who could die well, with some dignity. Unfortunately, these performances did not lend themselves to repeat engagements. If one did not die "well," the state could take a number of unpleasant measures against the bad "actor." With the construction of the huge amphitheatre completed during the reign of Titus Flavius in 80 A.D., spectacles of this sort completely superceded interest in acted drama. This amphitheatre, popularly known as the Colosseum, celebrated its opening by having nine to ten thousand animals slaughtered for sport during its first one hundred days. Other events held there were equally staggering to the imagination. It was probably the most "interesting" grand opening in history. Clearly, an audience that became satiated seeing animals and humans slaughtered in a variety of ingenious

---

2. Reported in *Attic Nights* by the Roman grammarian Aulus Gellius.

ways found traditional theatre fare rather pale entertainment. Several factors were at work, which would ultimately bring an end to the last semblance of theatre in the Roman Empire. Internal decay, the attacks of barbarians from without, the acceptance of Christianity, and the church's opposition to the theatre all contributed to the decline and demise of theatre in Rome. For all intents and purposes, in fact, the theatre and drama all but vanished from the Western world for almost a thousand years.

The Commedia dell'Arte

Sometime in the late fifteenth or early sixteenth century, the *commedia dell'arte* (comedy of professional players) evolved in Italy. When the Roman Empire finally dissolved, in the sixth century, actors dispersed, or "took to the road." They moved from one locale to another, performing at festivals, in little towns or in castles, for whatever they could earn. The traditions of

FIGURE 2.3 Jacques Callot, *Il Capitano* or *L'Innamorato*. Rudolf L. Baumfeld Collection, National Gallery of Art, Washington.

FIGURE 2.4 Jacques Callot,
Pantalone. Rudolf L. Baumfeld
Collection, National Gallery of Art,
Washington.

early Greek and Roman farces were preserved, but they also underwent
changes. Nevertheless, the character of Capitano, for example, a *commedia*
figure of the sixteenth century, is a direct descendant of the braggart warrior
in a comedy by the Roman Plautus.

By the time Italy moved into its great humanistic period, which we
now call the Renaissance, the actors were ready to return. The *commedia
dell'arte* was a theatre of improvisation, using stock plots, stock characters,
and stock bits of business. It is in the *commedia* that we find the characters of
Pantalone, Scaramouche, and Capitano, as well as Pierrot, Harlequin, and
Columbine.

Each actor became an expert in playing a certain type of role and frequently played that one stock character all of his (or her) life. The plots were
typical farces, dealing with deceived husbands, mistaken identity, romantic
intrigue, old husbands and young wives, loud-mouthed pseudointelligent
buffoons, and clever servants.

The characters were permanently established by tradition, and each
actor knew his or her bits of business. Thus, when a simple outline of a play
was posted for the actors, they could fall back on their favorite dialogue,

FIGURE 2.5 Commedia dell'Arte character Pantalone in *The Servant of Two Masters* by Goldoni. California State University, Long Beach, directed by W. David Sievers.

business, and gags, which they had refined over a lifetime of playing the same characters. Often they indulged in extensive pantomime and acrobatic tricks. They were travelling players, playing on crude wooden stages, or in town squares and market places (see Figure 2.6). Many etchings of the *commedia* players' work which have survived not only show them in their habitual costumes but also in their surroundings. Such acting was clearly broad, presentational, highly exaggerated, and little given to subtlety. The *commedia* actors took great pride in their improvisational ability, even though it tended to become standardized over the years. One writer of many *commedia* scenarios insisted that at the end of the seventeenth century

> . . . when a comedy which is improvised is produced by good actors it is as successful as a completely written play. . . . Any actor who knows how to improvise, which is most difficult, will find it easy to act in a written play, which is not as difficult.[3]

We may not necessarily completely agree with Andrea Perrucci, who was evidently involved in a bit of self-conceit, but we would agree that the

———————

3. Andrea Perruci, *Dell'arte rappresentativa, premeditata ed all'improviso* (Naples, 1699).

FIGURE 2.6 Commedia characters in *Androcles and the Lion* by Aurand Harris. California State University, Long Beach, directed by Ken Rugg.

commedia actors brought a rich and meaningful tradition back to Europe. Another observer writing a few years later insisted that the *commedia* actors also worked from a sense of nature, at least as well as the term was understood at that time. Luigi Riccoboni, who also wrote *commedia* scenarios, gave this advice to *commedia* actors in 1728:

> The principal idea for the actor is to show that he does not evade the truth, for only in this manner can he convince an audience that what he is doing is not false, and in this manner he can truly please them. In order to produce a natural effect, the actor should use not just his four limbs, but a fifth as well, that is his head, for he must feel what he acts . . . passion, rage, jealousy . . . The actor must act in proper proportion and not overstep the truth.[4]

---

4. Luigi Riccoboni, *Advice to Actors* (Florence, Italy: 1728).

Although the *commedia dell'arte* has passed away, its tradition is still found in modern puppet shows, the Punch of Punch and Judy, and the yearly English Christmas pantomimes. Many of the best comics of American vaudeville, burlesque, and television were and are the spiritual heirs of the *commedia dell'arte*.

Shakespeare and His Actors

With the return of humanism in the Renaissance, following the so-called "dark" ages, the professional theatre also flourished, notably in England during the age of Queen Elizabeth I (1533–1603). The Elizabethan Age followed a two-hundred-year period of invigorating dramas performed by amateurs in the churches, streets, fields, and schools of England. In particular, the period between 1585 and 1620 brought forth one of the most concentrated bursts of energy in the history of the theatre. It included certainly the greatest playwright of the late Renaissance, and possibly of all time, William Shakespeare. Shakespeare was the finest of the many playwrights of this time, but he had able colleagues and competitors in such men as Christopher Marlowe, Ben Jonson, Thomas Kyd, John Ford, John Webster, John Marston, George Chapman, Robert Greene, William Rowley, Thomas Dekker, Francis Beaumont, John Fletcher, and many others. It's a safe guess that such an outpouring of new plays meant there were both audiences willing to view and actors able to perform them.

Without doubt William Shakespeare (1564–1616) was one of the greatest playwrights who ever lived and the most important influence on the theatre of his time. Although it is 400 years since his birth, his plays are regularly performed by professional companies in every English-speaking country in the world and most of the other nations of the world as well. Surprisingly, Shakespeare may very well have begun his career as an *actor*, gradually developing his talents as playwright and poet and continuing to act for many years with his own company.

From what we can surmise about Shakespeare's career, we know he was the member of a permanent acting company called, during much of its existence, the Lord Chamberlain's Men. The company consisted of many permanent members (as well as bit players called in on special occasions for large casts and apprentices), with only a moderate turnover of actors. These facts are important if we are to understand how Shakespeare wrote for actors and his intentions regarding their work.

It is interesting to note that women did not appear on the Elizabethan stage and that young boys played the roles of women. It is possible that older men may have played such roles as the Nurse in *Romeo and Juliet* and the Witches in *Macbeth*, but it is a matter of record that Shakespeare wrote many of his greatest female roles—Juliet, Desdemona, Rosalind, Ophelia,

FIGURE 2.7 *The Merry Wives of Windsor* by Shakespeare. California State University, Long Beach, directed by David MacArthur.

and even Cleopatra—for young boys whose voices had not yet changed and whose acting training was at best somewhat limited.

Most of the performances of his plays took place out of doors, in large wooden buildings that were either leased or owned by the acting company. Inasmuch as Shakespeare was a shareholder in the company, it was important that the plays be performed as successfully as possible, even under the moderately difficult conditions of noise, inclement weather (London is not noted as a health resort), and the general restlessness among people standing in the pit of an outdoor theatre (the groundlings). At first Shakespeare's company performed in a theatre aptly called the Theatre, owned in large part by the Burbage family, but by 1599, the beginning of Shakespeare's most creative and inspired period, a new theatre was constructed on the south bank of the Thames (Bankside). This theatre was called the Globe, and its name is forever linked with this most important playwright who wrote his plays to be performed in a large, thatched, outdoor theatre.

It seems to have been a moderately stable company. We might liken it to an ensemble troupe today, which may stay together over a period of years. In such a group one gets to know the strengths and weaknesses of one's fellow actors. We know that there were many fine actors in Shakespeare's company; in fact most of the roles in his plays were created for specific actors. One such actor, Richard Burbage, was the leading actor of his day. It is very likely that the roles of Richard III, Hamlet, King Lear, Romeo, Othello, Macbeth, and Coriolanus were written for him. If Shakespeare had not had an actor of this magnificent range, the legend of Shakespeare's plays might have been very different indeed. At the same time, as the kinds of comic actors changed in Shakespeare's company, so did the kind of comic characters who appeared in his plays.

When we attempt to evaluate Elizabethan acting, however, we are dealing with a difficult and controversial subject. It is debatable whether Elizabethan acting was *presentational* or *representational*. Current criticism tends to suggest that it was *presentational* and that unusual attention was paid to the voice. This is not surprising, for the great and vigorous poetry and prose of the Elizabethan playwrights required a sensitive and well-modulated speaking voice. It is interesting to note the similar dependence on the voice in the Greek theatre.

Unfortunately we have very little direct testimony on how actors approached their roles or on their manner of presentation during this period. Shakespeare left no *direct* comment or criticism about the production of his plays. What little we know about Burbage's acting, for example, suggests that he moved gracefully and was "natural" in style. However, as we will continue to see, what was "natural" in one age was considered artificial in the next. Interestingly enough, one scrap of evidence describes Shakespeare as an actor, probably as Adam in *As You Like It.* In his old age, the playwright's brother vaguely remembered seeing Shakespeare

> . . . act a part in one of his own comedies, wherein being to personate a decrepit old man, he wore a long beard, and appeared so weak and drooping and unable to walk, that he was forced to be supported and carried by another person to a table, at which he was then seated among some company who were eating, and one of them sung a song.[5]

This description, if completely accurate, would suggest that *Shakespeare himself* utilized a high degree of what we would today call "natural" acting.

Some clues to the nature of Elizabethan acting may be gathered from the direct evidence of the plays themselves. The most helpful material of this kind comes from Shakespeare's *Hamlet.* At one point in the play, Hamlet speaks to a group of actors on the proper means of playing their roles. It is almost a detailed manual, and it is undoubtedly Shakespeare himself speaking to all actors on the responsibilities of their profession. He was concerned with certain important techniques and goals of acting, and we may note in this speech the following important points:

---

5. Reported in Bernard Grebanier's *Then Came Each Actor* (New York: David McKay Co., Inc., 1975).

1. Good articulation is an essential ingredient of acting.
2. Overacting is to be avoided.
3. The good actor finds the proper balance between overacting and underacting.
4. The good actor projects a reasonable suggestion of what we may call "truth" or "nature."
5. The good actor does not act simply for the approval of the majority of his audience. Honesty in acting will be clear to the more discriminating members of the audience.

> HAMLET: Speak the speech, I pray you, as I pronounced it to you,
> *Point 1* trippingly on the tongue. But if you mouth it, as many of your players do, I had as lief the town crier spoke my lines. Nor do not
> *Point 2* saw the air too much with your hand, thus, but use all gently. For in the very torrent, tempest, and, as I may say, whirlwind of your passion, you must acquire and beget a temperance that may give it smoothness. Oh, it offends me to the soul to hear a robustious periwig-pated fellow tear a passion to tatters, to very rags, to split the ears of the groundlings, who for the most part are ca-
> *Point 3* pable of nothing but inexplicable dumb shows and noise. . . . Be not too tame neither but let your own discretion be your tutor. Suit the action to the word, the word to the action, with this spe-
> *Point 4* cial observance, that you o'erstep not the modesty of nature. For anything so overdone is from the purpose of playing, whose end, both at the first and now, was and is to hold as t'were the mirror up to Nature—to show Virtue her own feature, scorn her own image, and the very age and body of the time his form and pres-
> *Point 5* sure. Now this overdone or come tardy off, though it make the unskillful laugh, cannot but make the judicious grieve, the censure of the which one must in your allowance o'erweigh a whole theater of others. . . .

Certainly these are important suggestions—as meaningful today in their actual application as they were in the age of Elizabeth I. We must continue to remember that "nature" did not necessarily mean natural or realistic acting in the sense in which we use it today. Theatre conventions change as do acting styles. The comments, nevertheless, indicate a serious concern on Shakespeare's part for the proper performance of his plays. It is one of the first detailed discussions on the art of acting that has validity for our own time as well.

The Seventeenth Century

From the period 1642 to 1660, during the Puritan Commonwealth, the theatres in England were closed or torn down and stage performances were forbidden by order of Parliament. After 1660 when the monarchy was restored, hence the name the Restoration, Charles II was an avid theatregoer. Partly following the tradition of the past, but breaking new ground as well, the Restoration theatre began a line of continuity that extends to the present British and American theatre. Several noteworthy changes took place during the period of Restoration drama, generally in the last portion of the seventeenth century.

1. Theatres were permanently established indoors.
2. Theatres were artificially lit, primarily by candlelight, though also by oil lamps.
3. A theatre remained lit during the entire performance. If a candle sputtered, either in the house or on stage, an attendant or candle snuffer, "invisible" to the audience by the convention of the day, walked to the appropriate place and attended to the sputtering candle.
4. Women appeared on the English stage.
5. Visiting professional companies (primarily French theatre companies and *commedia* troupes) visited England.
6. Extensive scenery was used in the professional theatre, with wings on either side of the stage and flats that could be moved along grooves in the back.

This type of theatre was one that would seem to lend itself to a *presentational* style of acting, keeping the attention of playgoers even as "orange girls" and sellers of wine, and other foods plied their "trade" during performances. In newly enclosed indoor theatres, lit and heated for hours by candles; in an era when bathing was minimal; with constant eating and hawking of food; spectators coming in late for half price and wearing heavy clothing; fops who often poked the feet of actors with their rapiers for amusement—the delights of theatre attendance in the English Restoration can be imagined. Many of the plays written during the Restoration were either overblown tragedies or comedies of manners which prortrayed a world of money, elegance, rakes, and dandies. The plots dealt with adultery, attempts at seduction, opportunistic marriage alliances, vanity, flirtation, backbiting, scandals, and general useless frivolity. In this theatre world, a new generation of actors rose to ply their craft.

The most famous, and the best, actor of the Restoration theatre was Thomas Betterton (1635–1710), who not only played most of the roles originally performed by Burbage but also acted in the new plays of the age. Betterton dominated the English theatre until the early eighteenth century and trained many actors and actresses in the craft of acting. Indeed, he is an early and important exponent of rigid actor training. He was known as an actor of great dignity and sincerity and gave his audiences the appearance of being "natural," as opposed to other actors of his day who had a tendency to shout, rant, and "tear a passion to tatters." Samuel Pepys, whose diary gives invaluable first-hand information on Restoration performances and productions, said of Betterton that he had

. . . a great head, a short thick neck . . . fat short arms, . . . his actions very few, but just. . . . His voice was low and grumbling, yet he could tune it by an artful climax which enforc'd universal attention even from the fops and orange girls.[6]

Betterton, himself, had strong ideas about acting, and in comments ascribed to him, spoke about the importance of characterization in acting.

He [the actor] must adjust every action; he must perfectly express the quality and manners of the man, whose person he assumes . . . A patriot, a prince, a beggar, a clown, etc., must each have their propriety, and distinction in action as well as words and language. An actor therefore . . . must transform himself into every person he represents . . .[7]

Such comments about, and by, Betterton suggest that even in an age when highly rhetorical and bombastic acting was in vogue, used by most performers, an actor who still followed Shakespeare's ideal of holding the "mirror up to nature" was respected as using the ideal approach to the art of acting. However, there were all too few Bettertons in the seventeenth century.

David Garrick: An Actor Speaks

In the two hundred years that followed the Elizabethan age, two names led the honor roll of great actors. Besides Thomas Betterton, who carved for himself one of the most successful careers in the history of acting, the second was David Garrick (1717–1779), undoubtedly the greatest actor of the eighteenth century and the most famous in the long tradition of the English-speaking theatre.

The most consistent comment about Garrick was his "naturalness" as an actor. "Naturalism" in Garrick's day, of course, meant something quite different from what it means now. Today we would probably consider Garrick's acting too stylized for our tastes. In the mid-eighteenth century, however, Garrick ushered in a refreshingly new style, diametrically opposed to the older, formalistic school, which required actors and actresses to intone their speeches in a deliberate monotone and in statuesque poses. Garrick brought variety back to acting: his characters differed one from the other, and he actually responded to what was happening on the stage around him. Today we take this all for granted, but in Garrick's time it was a distinct break with tradition. The earlier style had persisted since the mid-

---

6. Samuel Pepys, *Diary and Correspondence*, 4 vols. (New York: n.d.).

7. Charles Giddon, *The Life of Thomas Betterton* (London: Printed for Robert Gosling, 1710).

seventeenth century in imitation of French declamatory acting. To the great roles Garrick brought a new vitality and energy; in some ways he seemed to create a tradition that has extended to our own day.

Those who had the opportunity to watch Garrick have left ample evidence of his effectiveness as an actor. Early in his career he chose to perform in a play with his great rival James Quin, the champion of the older, declamatory style. Quin was first on stage: the fat and aging actor recited the dialogue in a sing-song oratorical manner punctuated by a few mechanical gestures and stilted poses. A schoolboy in the audience, later to become a noted playwright himself, watched the exciting duel of personalities. Richard Cumberland wrote of that evening: "I beheld little Garrick, young and light and alive in every muscle and every feature, come bounding on the stage—heavens, what a transition!—it seemed as if a whole century had been stepped over in the transition of a single scene!"[8]

One of the most penetrating appraisals of David Garrick's acting came from the novelist Henry Fielding in his novel *Tom Jones*. During a performance of Garrick in *Hamlet*, the actor's projected terror at seeing the ghost of Hamlet's father almost made the audience forget they were watching a stage performance. In the novel, the unsophisticated Partridge, however, saw little to commend in the performance. "Why," he said, "I could act as well as he myself. I am sure if I had seen a ghost, I should have looked in the very same manner and done just as he did." To Henry Fielding and his contemporaries, Garrick was an outstanding "naturalistic" actor.

Garrick knew, however, that there was no short cut to acting. All the great moments so admired by others in his performances were the result of concentrated study and attention paid to the most exacting detail. Fortunately we have some of Garrick's own words concerning the art of acting; they remain highly instructive. He consistently returns to the idea that study, observation, and integrity are the paths which lead to a successful stage career.

> The only way to arrive at great excellence in characters of humor, is to be very conversant with human nature, that is the noblest and best study, by this way you will more accurately discover the workings of spirit (or what other physical term you please to call it) upon the different modifications of matter.[9]

To a fellow actor Garrick gave this advice:

> Study hard, my friend, for [several] years, and you may play the rest of your life. I would advise you to read at your leisure other books besides plays in which you are concerned . . .[10]

---

8. Richard Cumberland, *Memoirs*, 2 vols. (London: Lockington, Allen, 1807).
9. David Garrick, *An Essay on Acting* (London: Printed for W. Beckerton, 1744), p. 2.
10. David Garrick, *The Private Correspondence of David Garrick with the Most Celebrated Persons of His Times*, ed. James Boaden (London: Henry Colburn and Richard Bentley, 1831), vol. 1, p. 178.

Garrick believed strongly in the integrity of the good actor, and we find a distinct echo of Hamlet's advice to the players when Garrick also wrote:

Do not sacrifice your taste and feelings to the applause of the multitude; a true genius will convert an audience to his manner, rather than be converted by them to what is false and unnatural . . .[11]

A dedicated actor and reformer of the stage and acting, David Garrick is surely one of the great figures in the long and colorful history of the theatre.

The Great Debate—Emotion vs. Reason

One of the most persistent questions debated by actors everywhere is: "Should an actor actually feel the emotions of the character he or she is portraying?" It would be simple to take a poll of any group of actors to discover just how diversified the views on this subject are. Perhaps the most controversial book ever written on the subject was Denis Diderot's *The Paradox of Acting*, which served as the major argument of the antiemotionalists and the prime target of the emotionalists.

Diderot—The Paradox of Acting

Although Diderot never acted professionally, he was nevertheless deeply interested in the theatre. He brought to his examination of the problem the same meticulous care shown in his labors on the *Encyclopédie*, the most prodigious work of scholarship of the eighteenth century. His short book *The Paradox of Acting* was not published until 1830, forty-six years after his death. It made a profound impression on actors at the time and is still stimulating and vital reading for anyone seriously interested in the art of acting.

It was because of a meeting with Garrick when the great English actor visited France in 1773 that Diderot set about to develop his famous paradox. Even before this time Diderot believed that the French stage needed greater vitality and energy through the use of emotional acting.

Garrick's success and technique were especially interesting to Diderot's enquiring mind. Here was an actor who planned every movement and response carefully and seemed to leave nothing to chance. His most startling and moving effects were achieved entirely by technique. In-

---

11. Ibid.

deed, Garrick's comment that a good actor could as easily make love to a wooden table as to a beautiful woman gave Diderot food for thought. He was aware that many actors and actresses acted by impulse. A performance might be electrifying one day and lackluster the next.

Diderot's contention, in his *Paradox*, was that the actor should never "feel" the role. The actor must be an "unmoved and disinterested onlooker. He must have, consequently, penetration and no sensibility." [12] The reason for this, Diderot indicated, was the actor's responsibility to sustain a performance night after night. He wrote:

> If the actor were full, really full, of feeling, how could he play the same part twice running with the same spirit and success? Full of fire at the first performance, he would be worn out and cold as marble at the third . . . what confirms me in this view is the unequal acting of players who play from the heart. From them you must expect no unity. . . . On the other hand, the actor who plays from thought . . . will be one and the same at all performances, will be always at his best mark; he has considered, combined, learnt and arranged the whole thing in his head. [13]

To the objection that feeling the role often produces a moving experience for both actor and audience, Diderot responded with a pointed illustration which is also a plea for a well-developed technique of acting.

> You give a recitation in a drawing room; your feelings are stirred . . . you burst into tears . . . you were carried away, you surprised and touched your hearers, you made a great hit. All this is true enough. But now transfer your easy tone, your simple expression, your everyday bearing, to the stage, and I assure you, you will be paltry and weak. You may cry to your heart's content, and the audience will only laugh. [14]

To make sure that no one missed his point, Diderot summed up the case as concisely as possible. "I hold to my point, and I tell you this: Extreme sensibility makes middling actors; middling sensibility makes the ruck of bad actors; in complete absence of sensibility is the possibility of a sublime actor." [15]

Naturally, when Diderot's *Paradox* was published, actors supported or denounced its thesis vigorously. Some insisted that, because he himself had never been an actor, Diderot was unaware of the means by which many actors achieved great moments on the stage.

---

12. Denis Diderot, "The Paradox of Acting" (1830) from *The Paradox of Acting—Masks or Faces* (New York: Hill and Wang, Inc., 1957), p. 14.
13. Ibid., pp. 14–15.
14. Ibid., pp. 20–21.
15. Ibid., p. 20.

Constant Coquelin

The most celebrated defender of Diderot's *Paradox* was Constant Coquelin (1841–1909), the French actor for whom Edmond Rostand wrote *Cyrano de Bergerac*—the play in which Coquelin achieved his greatest success in a long and illustrious career. Coquelin was an actor of persevering attention to detail and intellectual control.* In his comments about the use of emotion on the stage, Coquelin suggested that the actor had a dual personality, one self being the player, the second self the instrument. The first self, or the one that sees, should be the master over the second self, or the one that executes. The more absolute the subjugation to the first self, the supreme ruler or ruling intellect, the greater is the artist. Coquelin clearly believed in Diderot's doctrine of the rule of the intellect over feeling, as his following comment indicates:

> The actor should remain master of himself. Even when the public, carried away by his action, conceives him to be abandoned to his passion, he should be able to see what he is doing, to judge of his effects, and to control himself—in short, he should never feel the shadow of the sentiments to which he is giving expression at the very instant that he is representing them with the utmost power and truth. . . . The actor ought never to let his part "run away" with him—if you have no more consciousness where you are and what you are doing—you have ceased to be an actor; you are a madman.[16]

Just as Diderot's *Paradox* had created a stir among actors, so too did Coquelin's views when they were published. Sir Henry Irving, the celebrated English contemporary of Coquelin, and an "emotionalist," answered Coquelin in print with withering sarcasm, and the argument continued in the leading journals of the day.

Tommaso Salvini

The most eloquent rebuttal, however, came from the greatest of Italian actors, Tommaso Salvini (1829–1915). Salvini projected such vitality and energy in his performances that fellow actors as well as audiences were deeply moved. Salvini's acting was an important factor in stimulating Constantin Stanislavski to develop his well-known system of acting, of which we shall say more shortly. Salvini firmly believed that the actor must *feel* a role in order to move the audience. Without this feeling, the actor could not

---

*American drama critic George Jean Nathan noted that Coquelin was "the only actor who ever lived who proved that he had a critical mind in the appraisal of acting."

16. Benoit Constant Coquelin, "Acting and Actors," *Harper's New Monthly Magazine*, May 1887, pp. 891–909.

expect to recreate the same sentiments in the audience. On this point Salvini wrote:

> I believe, then, that every great actor ought to be and is, moved by the emotion he portrays; that not only must he feel this emotion once or twice, or when he is studying the part, but that he must feel it in a greater or less degree—and to just that degree will he move the hearts of his audiences—whenever he plays the part, be it once or a thousand times.[17]

Salvini was well aware of Coquelin's philosophy of emotion on stage, and, although he admired the French actor, he believed that his great weakness was his refusal or inability to feel his role. Salvini attacked Coquelin directly on this issue.

> Accomplished and versatile an artist as he is [Coquelin], I have been struck more than once, as I enjoyed the pleasure of his performance, with the thought that something amid all the brilliancy of execution was lacking. . . . The actor who does not feel the emotion he portrays is but a skillful mechanician, setting in motion certain wheels and springs which may give his lay figure such an appearance of life that the observer is tempted to exclaim, 'How marvelous! Were it only alive it would make me laugh or weep.'[18]

Salvini, however, did not believe that actors should lose themselves in the role. He believed that the actor must feel the emotions of the character but that there must always be the element of *restraint* to help the actor keep the ultimate objective in mind—not only to feel but to make the audience feel as well.

This great debate is not ended. It continues in the green room, in newspapers and magazines, and, of course, in the classroom. One conclusion we may reach is that actors have been able to express themselves successfully despite differing views on this point. Each actor synthesizes some technique in a manner that suits his or her personality and emotional makeup. Some actors feel a great deal, some feel only a little, and some do not feel at all. For those who believe that somewhere there must be a compromise, a middle ground between the "emotionalists" and the "rationalists" in acting, there are the reassuring words of Joseph Jefferson. His famous comment was brief but to the point—and he meant to refer only to himself, without attempting to indoctrinate anyone. It is the perfect compromise and a good starting point for any actor: "For myself, I know that I act best when the heart is warm and the head is cool."

---

17. Tommaso Salvini, "Some Views on Acting," *Theatre Workshop*, October 1936, pp. 73–78.
    18. Ibid.

The Contribution of Stanislavski

Constantin Stanislavski (1863–1938) was one of the most important theorists as well as one of the most practical men of the theatre. His work has profoundly influenced acting in the twentieth century. His name is known to those both in and out of the theatre, not only for his important contributions but as the focal point of the continuing debate about the actor and the question of emotional identification with a role.

Unfortunately the work of Stanislavski is misunderstood by many who believe that he advocated feeling the role to the point of ignoring conventional stage training and technique. Because the work of Stanislavski should be understood by all actors, whether they subscribe to his theories or not, some consideration of it will be undertaken here. It is dangerous to attempt to synthesize all of Stanislavski's work in a few pages; this will not be attempted here. His work should be placed in proper perspective, however, and such a discussion may serve to stimulate further investigation.

Stanislavski was one of the most successful actors on the Russian stage during the late nineteenth and early twentieth century. In 1898 he established, with his Russian colleagues, the Moscow Art Theatre. Here he acted in and produced dramas of international origin, although special attention was given to his fellow countrymen Anton Chekhov and Maxim Gorki. (Much of Stanislavski's early career and the development of the Moscow Art Theatre may be traced in his autobiography, *My Life in Art*.) It was at this point in his career that he began to put into practice many of the theories that had stimulated him for years.

The fact that Stanislavski was a producer and director as well as an actor gave him a broader view of the problem of creating successful theatrical characterizations. For years he had been dissatisfied with his own acting; he had fallen more and more into the habit of using artificial tricks and devices rather than finding the basic truth in his characterizations. He felt this failing as a director as well, for too often he simply had imposed his will on other actors without permitting them the freedom of their own imagination and creative impulses. He was convinced that there must be a means by which the actor could avoid the tyranny of stage habits and conventionalized external devices.

As an actor Stanislavski was aware that some performances were better than others: that on a certain night he would give a truly memorable performance, only to follow it the next evening with an uneven or a poor one. Merely feeling the part was not enough, for there would be some evenings when he might feel physically better than others, and some evenings when that "magic spark" would come and some evenings when it might not. We can see how his thinking in one way parallels that of Diderot—who insisted, however, that emotion should be ruled out of the actor's performances entirely. Stanislavski's approach to the problem was quite different. Certainly, he believed, the actor must feel, but how can the actor be sure of feeling just the right thing at the right time on any given night, and would that feeling be truthful?

His solution was to develop a course of study, or a "system," that required more mental and physical discipline than most actors had ever experienced before. Although this system was originally designed for actors who already knew all the basic techniques of stage movement, composition, and the essential controls of body and voice, it has since developed into a complete method for actors on all levels of proficiency. The important fact that has been so often overlooked in Stanislavski's system is that the entire method should be studied, with proper attention devoted to *all* the important elements.

The Stanislavski system may be divided into two equal parts. The first concerns the *External,* or the development of proper stage technique and correct management of body and voice. This area includes ballet, acrobatics, stage movement, voice placement, diction, relaxation, and other related elements. The second part concerns the *Internal,* or such areas as concentration, observation, imagination, and the use of emotional memory to help create a character from the inside as well as from the outside.

Stanislavski expounded his system in three books, *An Actor Prepares* (1936), *Building a Character* (1949), and *Creating a Role* (1961). The first deals with the internal aspects of his method and the second with the external, whereas the more recent publication, posthumously edited from his notes, is a working manual helpful in the actual creation of a role on the stage. It serves to put his basic principles to the test of the living performance. Unfortunately the books were not published together, and until *Building a Character* was published the Stanislavski system was represented only by the book that dealt with internal acting. It is no wonder that confusion over Stanislavski's system developed and continues even to this day. The two parts of the system should be used together, with equal emphasis on internal and external elements during the early stages. The system, in order to be used properly, requires many years of work and concentration, and even then it may not prove successful for all actors. Stanislavski said, "If it works for you, fine; if not—throw it away."

There is little that is really new in the Stanislavski system. It is an orderly compilation of the ideas and techniques that actors have always used, consciously or unconsciously. It was the sifting and organizing of these ideas that made Stanislavski's contribution so important. Stanislavski has written:

> You would be as justified to call a system any method of study that provides the ways and means to real creative work if only they are dealt with in a consistent manner. In my system we apply ourselves to the study of the powers and feelings which are inherited in man.[19]

19. Quoted in David Margarshack, *Stanislavsky on the Art of the Stage* (London: Faber and Faber, 1950).

Just What Is the "Method"?

We have heard a good deal in recent years of the Method and Method actors. Associated with Method acting are such well-known and successful performers as Marlon Brando, Shelley Winters, Anthony Franciosa, Karl Malden, Ben Gazzara, Al Pacino, and Robert DiNiro. The term "Method" as used in this context is synonymous with "system," or more specifically, the Stanislavski system. A Method actor, therefore, is one who has studied and is utilizing the Stanislavski system. There are many advocates of the Stanislavski training system in the United States but perhaps the best-known American training school devoted to teaching this system has been the Actor's Studio. More recently the late Lee Strasberg and Stella Adler have worked effectively in utilizing aspects of the system in their teaching.

In the 1930's the Group Theatre in New York became the first American professional theatre organization to use the Stanislavski system in the producing of its plays. Born of the depression, the Group Theatre disbanded in the forties, but its actors carried its spirit to other parts of the theatrical world. Luther Adler, Franchot Tone, John Garfield, Lee J. Cobb, Morris Carnovsky, Elia Kazan, Harold Clurman, and others continued to be vital influences in our theatre and encouraged those interested in learning more about the system they had used so successfully.

In 1947 Elia Kazan, Robert Lewis, and Cheryl Crawford started the Actor's Studio in order to provide a training ground for actors incorporating the principles that had guided the acting of the Group Theatre. Among those who attended classes the first year at the Actor's Studio were Marlon Brando, Montgomery Clift, Tom Ewell, John Forsythe, Mildred Dunnock, Karl Malden, and Maureen Stapleton.

Unfortunately there are those who have made of the Method something of a fetish. There are those who, misunderstanding the basic dogma of Stanislavski's teachings, complain, "I can't do it this way—I don't feel it," and there are those who have justly been classified as mumblers. This has produced a humorous picture in the public mind of some Method performers which is unfortunate, if not wholly undeserved. However, we must not lose sight of the fact that serious and exhaustive work on the Stanislavski system *as a whole* has given the theatre some of its finest actors. The Stanislavski Method is really one technique of acting. As Estelle Parsons, another student of the Actor's Studio, has commented:

> For a person like me—and I suspect for anyone who is any good—the material itself is inspiring enough to create its own emotions.[20]

---

20. Estelle Parsons in Joanmarie Kalter, *Actors on Acting* (New York: Sterling Publishing Co., Inc., 1979), p. 212.

Clearly Miss Parsons has her own way of working, as do all fine performers. There are many approaches to making the actor aware of his or her potential, and none is an end; each is only a means toward developing effective expression on the stage.

The Director and Freedom for the Actor

The actor must ultimately work with a director who will assume responsibility for the fundamental approach to any production. Some directors control the production to the extent that they feel it necessary to dictate every movement and gesture of the actor; they will insist that lines be read in exactly the manner that they indicate. The most articulate defender of this point of view is Gordon Craig, who has gone so far as to suggest that the human actor could give way to the "super-marionette," which would be able to execute a role perfectly without any of the failings of a human competitor: under no circumstances would the actor be permitted to create for him- or herself. Such directors feel that only one individual should be responsible for the total design and execution of the play. This type of director-actor relationship, they believe, should exist not only for the beginning actor but for the most experienced actor as well. "The finer the actor," said Craig, "the finer his intelligence and taste, and therefore the more easily controlled."

Opposed to this point of view are many directors who believe that the actor must collaborate in the creative process with the director. Such a view is certain to be shared by actors who feel confident in their ability to utilize their training and imagination. Representing this school of thought was the eminent American director Arthur Hopkins. We are all creative, Hopkins believed, and the director who continually stifles the actor and shuts off the actor's creative impulse is guilty of wiring false fruit to a tree that has never flowered. "The highest function of the stage director," he wrote, "is to help the seeker open the door to his own riches."[21]

Every actor will work with directors of varying viewpoints and philosophies. They may belong to different schools of thought and have diametrically opposed plans of directing the actor. Whatever relationship develops between the actor and director, and whatever approach to acting the actor takes, there is one goal upon which many of them agree: "We must always realize that the chief mission of the theatre is to reveal to ourselves, and to others, the inner riches that are the only surviving essence of all of us."[22]

---

21. Arthur Hopkins, *Reference Point* (New York: Samuel French, 1948), p. 50.
22. Ibid., p. 53.

Noted actors and actresses of the past

Thespis (6th century B.C.)
  Greek

Roscius (d. 62 B.C.)
  Roman

Will Kemp (1579–1600)
  English

Richard Burbage (d. 1619)
  English

Edward Alleyn (1566–1626)
  English

Thomas Betterton (1635?–1710)
  English

Molière (1622–1673)
  French (also playwright)

Anne Bracegirdle (1673–1748)
  English

Charles Macklin (1697?–1797)
  English

David Garrick (1717–1779)
  English

Peg Woffington (1714–1760)
  English

Sarah Siddons (1755–1831)
  English

John Philip Kemble (1757–1823)
  English

François Joseph Talma (1763–1826)
  French

Edmund Kean (1787–1833)
  English

Edwin Forrest (1806–1872)
  American

Joseph Jefferson (1829–1905)
  American

Tommaso Salvini (1829–1915)
  Italian

Edwin Booth (1833–1893)
  American

Henry Irving (1838–1905)
  English

Constant Coquelin (1841–1909)
  French

Sarah Bernhardt (1844–1923)
  French

Ellen Terry (1848–1928)
  English

William Gillette (1855–1937)
  American

Otis Skinner (1858–1942)
  American

Eleonora Duse (1859–1924)
  Italian

Constantin Stanislavski (1863–1938)
  Russian

John Barrymore (1882–1942)
  American

SUGGESTIONS FOR FURTHER READING

Archer, William. *Masks or Faces? A Study in the Psychology of Acting.* New York: Hill and Wang Dramabook, 1957.

Brown, John Russell. *Shakespeare's Plays in Performance.* Baltimore: Penguin Books, 1969.

Cole, Toby, and Chinoy, Helen Krich, eds. *Actors on Acting.* New rev. ed. New York: Crown Publishers, Inc., 1970.

Eustis, Morton. *Players at Work.* New York: Theatre Arts Books, 1937.

Funke, Lewis, and Booth, John E. *Actors Talk About Acting.* New York: Random House, 1961.

Grebanier, Bernard. *Then Came Each Actor.* New York: David McKay Co., Inc., 1975.

Hethman, Robert H., ed. *Strasberg at the Actor's Studio.* New York: The Viking Press, 1965.

Joseph, Bertram. *Elizabethan Acting.* London: Oxford University Press, 1951.

Joseph, Bertram. *Acting Shapespeare.* New York: Theatre Arts Books, 1969.

Joseph, Bertram. *The Tragic Actor.* New York: Theatre Arts Books, 1959.

Kalter, Joanmarie. *Actors on Acting.* New York: Sterling Publishing Co., Inc., 1979.

Lewis, Robert. *Method or Madness.* New York: Samuel French, Inc., 1958.

Marowits, Charles. *The Method as Means.* London: Herbert Jenkins, 1961.

Marowits, Charles. *Stanislavsky and the Method.* New York: Citadel Press, 1964.

Nicoll, Allardyce. *Masks, Mimes and Miracles.* New York: Harcourt, Brace, Jovanovich, 1931.

Redgrave, Michael. *The Actor's Ways and Means.* London: William Heinemann; New York: Theatre Arts Books (HEB Paperback), 1979.

Renault, Mary. *The Mask of Apollo.* New York: Pantheon, 1966. (Fictionalized but accurate story of a typical Greek actor, told extremely well.)

Ross, Lillian, and Ross, Helen. *The Player: A Profile of an Art.* New York: Simon and Schuster, 1962.

Smith, Winifred. *The Commedia dell'Arte: A Study in Italian Popular Comedy.* New York: Benjamin Blom, 1965.

Sprague, A. C. *Shakespeare and the Actors.* Cambridge, Mass.: Harvard University Press, 1945.

Sprague, A. C. *Shakespearean Players and Performances.* Cambridge, Mass.: Harvard University Press, 1953.

Stanislavski, Constantin. *An Actor Prepares.* Translated by Elizabeth Reynolds Hapgood. New York: Theatre Arts Books, 1936.

Stanislavski, Constantin. *Building a Character.* Translated by Elizabeth Reynolds Hapgood. New York: Theatre Arts Books, 1949.

Stanislavski, Constantin. *Creating a Role.* Translated by Elizabeth Reynolds Hapgood. Edited by Hermine Isaacs Popper. New York: Theatre Arts Books, 1961.

Webster, Margaret. *Shakespeare Without Tears.* Greenwich, Conn.: Fawcett World Library, 1955.

Webster, T. B. L. *Greek Theatre Production.* London: Oxford University Press, 1956.

CHAPTER THREE

Using Improvisation

Improvisation has many practical uses, including developing and improving the actor's imagination, creativity, and concentration on objects and fellow actors, as well as helping the actor deal with the actual preparation of a specific role in a play. Sometimes improvisations utilize only physical actions and the use of the actor's space or environment; on other occasions they may be quite elaborate and include several actors, each with specific and different objectives within the same group improvisation.

The improvisations in this chapter each suggest different means of making the actor sensitive to the objective of a character so that it can be translated into an actual role. When confronting any role, the actor must understand *why* he or she is in a scene from the content of the play itself. For the sake of clarity let us call the following our **W** check list. This check list should be applied to simple improvisations as well as to fully scripted plays. The questions the actor should ask may be enumerated as follows:

1. *Who* am I? (occupation, age, temperament, family history, social status, etc.)
2. *Where* am I? (location, size of area, climate, familiarity of locale)
3. *What* do I want in this scene or play?
4. *Why* do I want it?
5. *What* is preventing me from getting it? (Are there barriers in the way?)
6. *What* am I willing to do to get what I want? (How badly do I really want it?)
7. *Who* do I want it from? (What is my relation to others?)
8. *When* do I want it? (How urgent is it that I get what I want?)

Improvisation for Larger Groups

The following are improvisations intended for a large group of actors, perhaps somewhere between ten and twelve. The first step is to establish the basic locale and action; then determine what each actor would need to do in order to operate within that action and that locale.

Improvisation 1. A large number of people are at a major American airport (select one) when the public-address-system announcer states that all incoming and outgoing flights have been cancelled until further notice. Each character reacts accordingly. One of the actors assumes the role of the public relations person at the airport.

Every actor in the improvisation will need to answer a number of questions before proceeding. Here are just a few:

- Do I work at the airport?
- Am I at the airport to meet someone?
- If so, *why* am I at the airport to meet someone?
- Am I scheduled for an outgoing flight?
- If so, how urgent is it that I get to where I am going on time?
- How frequently do I fly?
- Do I enjoy flying?
- Am I at the airport for a reason other than meeting someone or leaving?
- Am I alone or with someone?
- What do I do while I am waiting?

These are just a few of the questions the actor must be able to answer, in addition to such a fundamental question as "Who am I?" Certainly you can think of many other questions for the airport improvisation suggested above.

Here are some other group improvisations that will test imagination and creativity. Do not be concerned if the improvisation does not have a "neat" ending; doing it is the important thing.

Group Improvisation 2.   A group of people are in the waiting room of a doctor's office. A nurse and health officer enter to inform the group that the office has been quarantined because the doctor has found a rare infectious disease in the previous patient.

Group Improvisation 3.   A group of people are waiting in line to be part of the live audience for a top-rated television quiz program. A public relations person comes out to the group and tells them that the contestant who was to go on the show to try for $50,000 cannot attend that evening. The broadcasting company is looking for someone to go on the show, "Pot Luck," and try for the grand prize. Only the public relations person knows what kind of contestant they want, and he or she is not telling.

Improvisation for One Actor

The following improvisations will help the actor provide three of the critical **W**s from the check list. In these exercises, the actor is given the *what* (the action), the *where* (the location), and the *who* (the character). It is imperative that the actor also know *why*, as well as many of the other **W**s from the list.

These improvisations contain all the necessary elements for a complete dramatic situation.

For each improvisation the actor should choose one action, one character, and one location from the lists that are provided. The actor may take the description of the action quite literally and add nothing of his or her own. Or the description may be used as a basic scenario, containing only the bare bones of the action, with the actor adding his or her own creative gifts and imagination to the scene, much as the *commedia dell'arte* performer of the past improvised richly on a few traditional formulas.

Several thousand improvisations would be possible from combinations of the items in these lists. In choosing an action, the actor must realize that within the context of that action many variables are present. It should be clear that different characters will react differently to the same stimulus. In addition, the environment in which a character operates and in which the action takes place may profoundly alter not only specific details, but the texture and execution of the entire improvisation.

At first the actor may find the three elements of the improvisation too generalized. They may even seem to follow certain stereotypes. This result, however, is to be expected from this type of improvisation. Yet, after some reflection, the actor will realize that not all bankers are the same, nor does every librarian resemble every other librarian. Within the context of the limited descriptions, the actor must add those elements of individuality that begin to bring a character and a scene to life. Taking this point of view, the actor will find that the number of improvisations is infinite.

Actions

1. You are determined to get evidence against a person who you believe has murdered your brother. You enter the premises to plant a tape recorder in an appropriate place. You examine the location carefully and then test the machine. As you are installing the device, you hear someone entering the premises. You hide, and after a short time the person leaves without seeing you. After the device has been properly planted, you leave.
2. You enter the premises to keep an appointment. After waiting briefly, you detect smoke and note that a short circuit (or similar mishap) has caused a fire to break out. Unable to get any help and faced with the rapid spread of the fire, you are forced to put out the substantial blaze alone. After resting for a short time, you leave.
3. You enter the premises on a business call and find a one-year-old child alone, unhappy, and wet. The child has specific ideas about what he or she wants to do. You try to quiet the child and keep the child happy, as there is no one else in the vicinity. After a few minutes a telephone (or radiophone) call informs you that the child's parents are nearby and you are asked to take the child to them. You react to the request as you see fit.
4. You enter the premises intending to keep an appointment and sit in a chair. After starting to read a magazine or newspaper, you hear a strange sound and look up. Between you and the door is a large poisonous snake. You then react as your chosen character would under the circumstances.
5. You enter the premises to keep an appointment. You notice that the room is well stocked with fine old liqueurs and brandies. After some internal debating (the amount depends on the character you have chosen), you begin to sample the products and become progressively drunker. You finally react to your delayed appointment as dictated by your character and the number of samples tasted.
6. You enter the premises to keep an appointment with a friend you have not seen in several years. On a table you find a collection of materials, such as letters and photographs, that remind you of your old friendship. You examine the mementoes. After a while, a phone rings (telephone or radiophone). On answering it, you learn that your friend has been accidentally killed on the way to meet you. You react in character.
7. You enter the premises to keep an appointment. You look at your watch

and realize you are an hour early. You decide to wait. While waiting, you notice a pile of papers and photographs on a table. You examine them and discover that they are documents and letters purporting to prove you guilty of murder. You react, taking whatever action is suitable to the character.

8. You enter the premises in order to prepare carefully the murder of someone who is due to arrive in five minutes. After giving your attention to planning how you will commit the murder, you lose your nerve and have to leave.

9. You enter the premises in order to keep an appointment. While waiting, you decide to sample some food that has been left on the premises. After tasting it, you realize that you have been poisoned.

10. You enter the premises in order to plant a time bomb. You carefully place the bomb and discover that you cannot leave. You attempt to stop the time mechanism on the bomb but cannot. The bomb was set to explode three to five minutes after you placed it in position. React in character.

Characters: Male

1. An army colonel (*age:* mid-fifties).
2. A banker (*age:* mid-forties).
3. A hot-rod enthusiast (*age:* early twenties).
4. A butler (*age:* mid-forties).
5. A French fashion designer (*age:* mid-thirties).
6. An international playboy (*age:* your choice).
7. A medical missionary (*age:* mid-fifties).
8. A taxi driver (*age:* mid-forties).
9. A retired clerk (*age:* mid-eighties).
10. A professional pool shark (*age:* mid-twenties).
11. A European aristocrat (*age:* forty).
12. A boy (*age:* thirteen)
13. An escaped convict (*age:* thirty).
14. A ballet dancer (*age:* thirty-five).
15. A physical-culture instructor (*age:* twenty-five).
16. An arthritic white-collar worker (*age:* mid-fifties).
17. A college student (*age:* nineteen).
18. A university president (*age:* mid-fifties).
19. A robust day-laborer (*age:* mid-twenties).
20. A professional con-man (*age:* mid-forties).

Characters: Female

1. A maid (*age:* mid-forties).
2. A ballet dancer (*age:* mid-thirties).

3. A girl (*age:* twelve).
4. A nearly blind seamstress (*age:* mid-fifties).
5. A European aristocrat (*age:* mid-forties).
6. An international film star (*age:* twenty-nine).
7. A college student (*age:* nineteen).
8. A registered nurse (*age:* mid-thirties).
9. A housewife (*age:* mid-forties).
10. A librarian (*age:* mid-thirties).
11. A burlesque dancer (*age:* thirty).
12. A fashion model (*age:* mid-twenties).
13. An arthritic clerk (*age:* mid-fifties).
14. A professional wrestler (*age:* mid-thirties).
15. A waitress (*age:* mid-twenties).
16. A retired white-collar worker (*age:* mid-eighties).
17. A business executive (*age:* thirty-five).
18. A debutante (*age:* nineteen).
19. A society matron (*age:* mid-forties).
20. A cleaning woman (*age:* mid-sixties).

Locations

1. The small cabin of a ship at sea during a heavy storm.
2. A business office late at night.
3. A farmhouse.
4. A dirty shack near an old mine in the mountains.
5. A small grocery store in a New England village.
6. A decrepit thatched hut in the tropics.
7. The deserted stage of an old theatre.
8. The kitchen of a famous restaurant.
9. The living room of a palatial mansion.
10. A stable.
11. A penthouse.
12. A deserted tomb.
13. An igloo in the Arctic.

Improvisations for Two or More Characters

The following improvisations make more complicated demands on the actor than did those for one character. The actor must now take into account the elements of reaction and interplay and must also be prepared to maintain the character and intentions as actions unfold that are not completely under his or her control. These exercises are intended to make the actor know precisely the *why* of the character in the scene, as well to know the other **Ws** from the list. How does the actor wish to see his or her problem resolved?

Each of the improvisations is a springboard for a large number of different actions. Let us examine the first improvisation. "A has come in response to an ad, placed in the newspaper by B, advertising a dog for sale." On the surface there seems to be little dramatic conflict suggested. However, on closer study we find that there are several possible purposes each character might have for participating in this situation.

It is possible that:

- A wants a dog as a pet for a small child.
- A wants a good watchdog.
- A wants to make the acquaintance of the person selling the dog.
- A wants a dog to give to someone else as a gift.
- A wants a dog for medical experiments.

It is also possible that:

- B wants to get rid of the dog at any price because it is vicious.
- B loves the dog but is now impoverished and cannot afford to keep it.
- B does not love the dog and needs a good deal of money.
- B hopes to find a good home for the dog because B is leaving the country.
- B is lonely and interested in making the acquaintance of anyone who might answer the ad.

Several other possibilities should also come to mind.

As each actor in turn chooses a central purpose and settles on specific character traits, the improvisation will take on a meaningful dramatic potential. It is also worth noting that one character in the improvisation need *not* know the purpose or the *why* of the other character(s).

The possible purposes and motivations of the characters in each improvisation should be analyzed and chosen before the improvisation is played. The improvisations have deliberately been made flexible enough to permit this choice by the actors.

1. A has come in response to an ad, placed in the newspaper by B, advertising a dog for sale.
2. A and B arrive at a bargain counter at the same moment. Each wants to buy the last remaining item on sale. C, the shop manager, is behind the counter at the time.
3. A and B are walking in opposite directions along the sidewalk. In the middle of the street is a twenty-dollar bill.
4. A is answering an advertisement by B requesting an experienced tutor for a sweet child.

5. A is applying for a position in a theatre repertory company managed by B.
6. A and B are dining at the same table in a restaurant. When C, the waiter, comes with the bills, A looks in a pocket and reports that his or her wallet is missing.
7. A and B are soldiers in a wartime army. They report to C, their commanding officer, who must send one soldier on a mission which C knows will probably cause the soldier's death.
8. A and B arrive at the home of C at the same time in response to an ad which said that C wishes to buy a two-year-old Volkswagen automobile.
9. Student A is called into the office of teacher B, who announces that A's term paper is identical to another paper turned in that semester.
10. A and B are former school acquaintances. Now A is impoverished, B successful and wealthy. A calls on B in B's office to request a loan.

CHAPTER
FOUR

Stage Technique

The purpose of this chapter is to examine the fundamentals upon which the study of acting must build. It is as necessary for the actor to know the tools of the acting trade as for the painter to know the different kinds of brushes and paints and for the composer or pianist to know the notes of the scale. Sooner or later, it is imperative that an artist master the fundamentals, and all successful systems of acting require that the actor learn basic stage techniques. Moreover, a beginning actor is much more likely to be selected for roles in university, community, and other amateur productions after having studied these techniques. Directors are loath to drill actors or explain the fundamentals during rehearsal time when other important business needs to be conducted. Sound preparation in acting techniques will leave the actor free to concentrate upon other requirements of a role. Charlton Heston recalls the value of this training. He has written:

[Laurence] Olivier uses a model of the set, moving little dolls while he reads the text with the actors watching. It goes much faster than standing around for hours bumping into each other.[1]

Clearly, from that point forward Mr. Heston and his fellow actors can rely on their basic stage technique and work on their roles.

The Stage and Stage Areas[2]

The stage is divided into specific areas that are identified in theatre terminology by their relative positions. When giving directions regarding stage movement, directors use the following terms to indicate the areas to be used.

Upstage and Downstage

The area nearest the audience and footlights is called *downstage*. The area in the back of the stage, near the back wall of the stage or setting, is called *upstage*. Both the *upstage* and *downstage* areas extend across the width of the stage.

Stage Left and Stage Right

Stage areas left and right are determined by the *actor's left and right* as he faces the audience. If the actor stands directly in the center of the stage, the area to the actor's right is *stage right* and the area to the actor's left is *stage left*. The director, therefore, sitting in the auditorium and watching the stage, reverses the areas when viewing them and relates them to the actor's position on stage. The area in the middle of the stage is called *stage center*.

---

1. Charlton Heston, *The Actor's Life: Journals 1956–1976*, ed. Hollis Alpert (New York: Pocket Books, 1976), p. 109.

2. The following examinations of stage areas, movement, and body positions are directly related to the needs of the proscenium, or picture-frame, theatre. Although this is the design of the great majority of professional and educational theatres, there has been a substantial growth in recent years in the number of theatres using thrust, central, or arena staging. Under such conditions the customary stage-area and body-position designations are clearly inoperative or will need significant modification. Other rules are applicable, however, under all circumstances. The specific demands that central staging makes on the actor are discussed in Chapter 8.

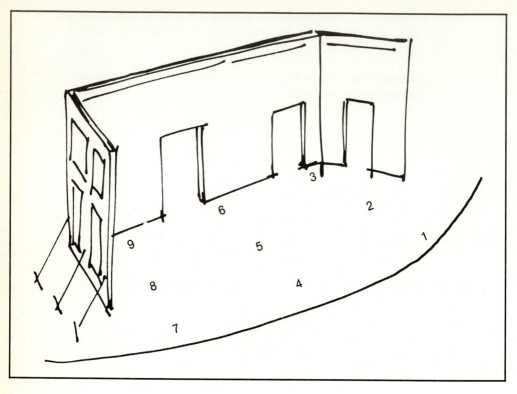

FIGURE 4.1 Stage areas.

The Stage Areas

Combining these classifications, the following basic stage areas provide the framework within which the actor must work.

1. Down left	4. Down center	7. Down right
2. Center left	5. Center	8. Center right
3. Up left	6. Up center	9. Up right

As a general rule certain areas of the stage are stronger than others. We might call it the "all-other-things-being-equal" factor. For example, the stage setting, furniture, lighting, color of the actor's costume, and so on will have a tendency to alter the relative strength of playing areas. However, as a general rule we should note that:

1. Down center is the "strongest" area, or the area that commands most attention.

2. Down left and down right are stronger than the up left and up right positions.

Assuming that the actor holds to the same relative position in each area, it should be clear that the downstage areas are more emphatic and generally maintain a higher degree of audience attention than do the upstage areas.

Stage Positions and the Actor

There are five basic body positions that may be assumed *in relation to the audience*. There is also a great variety in the combinations of body positions and stage areas. We are concerned here only with the normal standing position.

1. Full front—The actor is facing the audience with both feet facing downstage and head also facing the audience. *This is the strongest and most "open" of all body positions.*
2. Full back—The actor faces the back wall of the stage, both feet facing upstage so that the audience sees only the actor's back.
3. Profile position—The actor is in a position exactly between full front and full back so that the audience sees the side of the body. This position may be further divided:
   (a) Profile left—The actor is in profile position facing stage left.
   (b) Profile right—The actor is in profile position facing stage right.
4. One-quarter position—The actor stands halfway between the full front and the profile position. This position may be further divided:
   (a) One-quarter position left—The actor is in the one-quarter position facing the down left area.
   (b) One-quarter position right—The actor is in the one-quarter position facing the down right area.
5. Three-quarter position—The actor is in a position halfway between the full back and the profile position. Again, this position may be subdivided:
   (a) Three-quarter position left—The actor is in the three-quarter position facing the up left area.
   (b) Three-quarter position right—The actor is in the three-quarter position facing the up right area.

The terms for stage areas and body positions are obviously rather mechanical; they are intended to help the actor understand the most basic elements of working on a proscenium stage. These should become automatic, without the actor having consciously to think about them. Their real

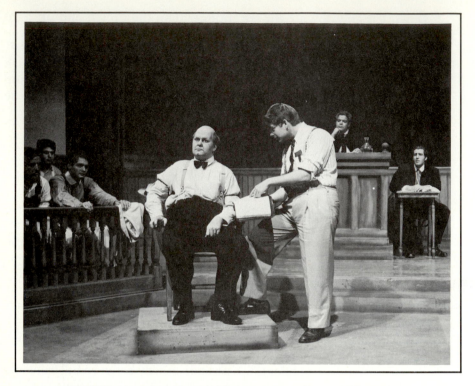

FIGURE 4.2 *Inherit the Wind* by Lawrence and Lee. California State University, Long Beach, directed by Stanley Kahan.

purpose is that they can help bring the actor a true theatrical sense of his or her working environment.

How to Stand and Move

It is clear that the type of character to be played will determine the kind of posture and walk the actor will assume. We should not expect a woman of seventy-five to walk and stand like a girl of eighteen. Nevertheless, there are certain basic rules about movement and posture that will serve to introduce this often neglected aspect of acting.

The body should be relaxed without slouching (see Figure 4.3), unless slouching is a necessary ingredient of the character, and should generally suggest attentiveness to what is happening elsewhere on stage. The weight should fall on the balls of the feet. The actor who slouches and moves about by putting the initial weight on his or her heels when walking is hardly likely to present a pleasing picture for the audience.

A general principle to remember is that the same grace and balance

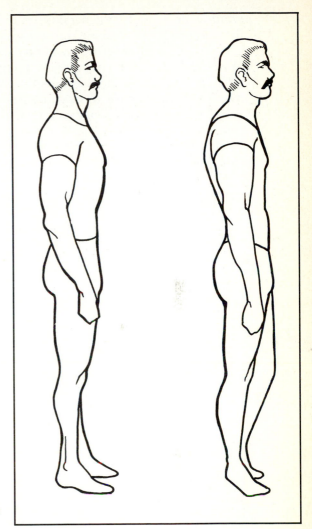

FIGURE 4.3 Good and bad stage posture.

maintained while standing on stage should be a part of the stage walk. When the actor makes a movement on stage *the first step is taken with the upstage foot*.

Since the actor in motion is normally the actor being watched by an audience, starting the movement in an "open" manner is important.

Approaches

When an actor moves from one stage area to another it is usually for the purpose of coming closer to another actor, a piece of furniture or property, or a window or door. Two general types of approaches are possible: crossing in a straight line or making the approach in a curve.

The straight cross is most often used when approaching another actor or object *parallel* with your starting point. This should invariably place the actor in a profile position. Figure 4.4 shows correct and incorrect ways of making a straight cross to various stage areas.

It is possible to avoid such problems by the use of the curved stage cross (see Figure 4.5). This will permit the actor to approach another actor or object *without being forced to make an awkward adjustment in order to compensate for a difficult body position.*

The curved approach serves to keep the actor open to the audience during the movement and generally suggests a softer quality in the movement. This type of movement is especially desirable in costume plays and often helps to give the play a gentle and formal style.

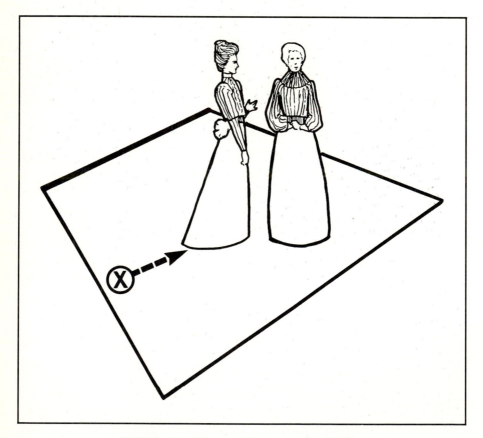

FIGURE 4.4a The straight cross used correctly.

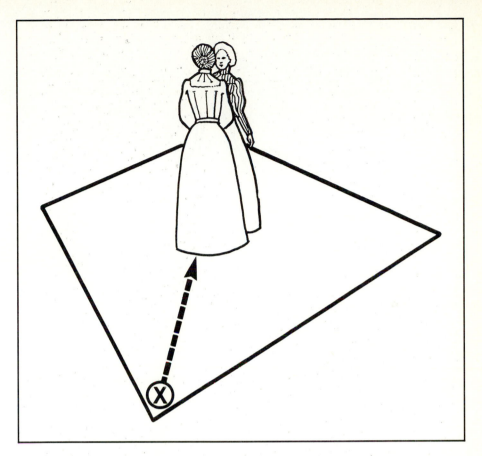

FIGURE 4.4b The straight cross used incorrectly. The approaching actress is upstaging herself.

How to Sit

It may seem, on first consideration, that sitting should present no specific problems. Yet rules exist for sitting as they do for standing and walking. These simple rules may be outlined as follows:

1. When changing from the standing to the sitting position, the actor should try to avoid turning and looking at the chair. If at all possible the actor should be in a position to sit down with seemingly little effort. Feeling with the back of the leg for the chair edge may be helpful.
2. Men should generally sit with their feet on the same plane. It is best to avoid pulling up the trouser legs when sitting.
3. Women should generally sit with one foot in front of the other or one foot slightly under the chair and one slightly extended.

FIGURE 4.4c **The straight cross used incorrectly. The actress being approached is forced to turn upstage.**

4. When sitting in a chair that is in profile, one should open up the body to a one-quarter position if a number of lines are to be read while remaining seated.

5. In rising, the back foot should push the body up to a standing position. *The first step is taken with the back foot.* (Try taking the first step with the front foot after rising and note how awkward it is.) If possible the rear foot, which pushes the body up to the standing position, should be the upstage foot.

The actor works with other actors. In order to achieve maximum effectiveness in a scene and to permit the greatest interaction with fellow actors, it is necessary to realize that stage and body positions are relative to those of other actors on stage. In addition, the element of basic stage courtesy is

FIGURE 4.5 The curved cross.

often neglected by beginning actors. This is usually not the result of bad manners but comes about because of a misunderstanding of some of the accepted stage conventions that should be conformed to by two or more actors in a scene. There are two common errors into which beginning actors fall; these should be understood before we proceed further.

Upstaging a Fellow Actor

Upstaging can be most disturbing because it tends to place one actor in an extremely dominant position while relegating the other to an unnecessarily subordinate position. There may be times when a director may deliberately want such an imbalance between two actors, but the actor should never deliberately take such a position. Upstaging usually occurs when two actors

FIGURE 4.5b   The curved cross.

are sharing a scene and speaking to each other. At this time they are on the same plane so that the audience may watch the actions and reactions of both. If one actor, however, moves *upstage* a few steps, the other is forced to turn away from the audience to look upstage. At the same time the upstage actor is able to open naturally to the audience. In Figure 4.6 Actor *A* is in a much stronger position than Actor *B*, who, in order to retain the suggestion of naturalness in the conversation, is forced to turn upstage toward *A*. Remember that the more ''open'' an actor is, the stronger is his or her stage position.

It has already been suggested that, in a scene in which Actor *A* must control the attention of the audience, upstaging may be necessary. All too often, however, upstaging is caused by a misunderstanding of basic technique.

Upstaging Oneself

Not infrequently the actor may take a position which actually upstages him- or herself. In such a situation the positions indicated above are reversed: instead of standing upstage of a fellow performer, the actor stands downstage

FIGURE 4.6 Upstaging.

of another, causing the same relative imbalance as indicated in Figure 4.6, although the position of the "guilty party" is obviously reversed. No one could suggest that the actor is selfish in assuming this position, but the actor will look most uncomfortable if he or she has a number of lines to speak.

The Shared Position

The most usual position assumed by two actors during a brief scene may be classified as a "shared position." This position may take many forms.

FIGURE 4.7 *Our Town* **by Thornton Wilder. University of British Columbia, directed by Charles Siegel.**

Essentially both actors are in the same relative body position and therefore are able to participate in a scene (from the physical standpoint) with equal emphasis.

Each of the following positions is considered shared because equal emphasis falls on each actor (See Figure 4.8).

1. Shared one-quarter position—the most common position, generally used for conversation.
2. Shared position in profile—also rather common, but indicating a situation of greater intensity, even conflict.
3. Shared full front—much less common; likely to be found in musical comedy and in period plays of a *presentational* nature.
4. Shared three-quarter position—somewhat rare; may be used to suggest an element of secrecy. This position is usually held only briefly.
5. Shared full back—again a position not often used, although it serves to offer some pictorial variety. It is difficult to communicate orally in this position unless the head is played in profile. In addition the audience is unable to follow facial reactions. Nonetheless this position may be used

FIGURE 4.8a Shared one-quarter position.

briefly to give the stage a suggestion of added dimension, and it can then easily blend into the shared three-quarter or shared profile positions.

The Given Position

The given position is not unlike ''upstaging,'' although here the position is assumed deliberately. The given position should be used when one actor is clearly the dominant character in the scene—that is, when one character has a great amount of narration or expositional material to deliver and the other character is generally passive. As shown in Figure 4.9, one actor will take a dominant, or ''focused,'' position, usually the one-quarter position, or open up to almost the full front. The other actor may take a three-quarter back position, or stay in profile. When there are three or more characters on stage, they may give the scene to a ''focused'' individual simply by turning toward that actor. This type of adjustment makes it relatively simple to adjust the focus and give a scene to the properly dominant character.

It is essential to remember, then, that *these positions are not static.* They

FIGURE 4.8b **Shared profile position.**

can be easily changed as a scene shifts in intensity and emphasis. Most directors will tell actors when to share a scene and when to give or take it. The actor should know the basic body positions and be able to adjust as the situation requires. The mastery of such techniques will give the actor greater confidence in his or her own powers as well as the respect of fellow workers.

Using Movement

Up to this point we have examined the basic stage positions and the playing of scenes with other actors. It may have been noted that the patterns for movement and stage positions are somewhat mechanical and tend to suggest set pieces rather than living actors. The actor should understand that

FIGURE 4.8c Shared full front position.

within the context of these fundamental rules he or she must be creative and interesting. The actual movement patterns, physical reactions, and exact relations to other actors will be determined by a number of factors. Let us look at those factors that affect how and why actors move on stage.

Movement as a Factor of Character.   Movement patterns will be affected by a character's age, social status, and education, as well as by any physical impairments he or she may have. A gangster's movement from one part of the stage to another should be quite different from that of a European nobleman; an aged charwoman obviously would not move as quickly or in the same manner as a society matron. Such factors of character will also affect smaller movements and positions assumed in relation to other characters.

Movement as a Part of the Plot.   Movement patterns will be affected by the specific situations of the play, the relation of one character to another, and the content or the action of any given moment. An actor would make a very different full stage cross in Act I in order casually to mix a cocktail, than a full stage cross in Act III to prevent someone from taking poison.

FIGURE 4.8d   Shared three-quarter position.

Movement and Locale.   Movement patterns will be affected by the general locale and specific setting of a play. If the scene is set in a character's home, movements should be quite different from the character's movements in strange surroundings. Movement in a cold climate will differ from movement in an extremely hot and humid locale. A skilled actor is often able to suggest the nature of the setting by movement and elements of ''business.'' The conscientious actor does not rely entirely on the designers to indicate the locale to the audience.

Movement and Furniture Properties.   Movement patterns will be affected by the stage pieces in the playing area. Movement around these pieces should be planned carefully so that it seems natural. Set pieces may also have an additional specific use: furniture may be gripped, leaned upon, or played around in scenes that otherwise require little movement.

Movement as an Indication of State of Mind.   Movement patterns will be affected by a character's state of mind—health, anxiety, happiness, ner-

FIGURE 4.8e Shared full back position.

vousness, or resoluteness. Movement can be an excellent device for suggesting these mental states to an audience even before specific lines indicate the fact.

Movement to Sustain Mood. Movement patterns will be affected by the general mood of a scene or play. Scenes requiring a particularly somber effect call for slow and deliberate movement, whereas a scene of sustained joy and hilarity will require greater vigor and energy. The projection of such moods demands a cooperative approach by all the actors.

Movement to Maintain the Style and Period of the Play. Movement patterns will be affected by the basic style of the play. Each style will impose a definite design, to which the actor must adjust his or her movement. In order to maintain consistency, movement in a presentational production will differ from movement in one that is fundamentally representational. Comedy, tragedy, and melodrama will each require a different emphasis. The historical period of the play will also influence movement. The tempo of life, social conditions, class consciousness, and particularly costumes all contribute to particular historical attitudes and mores which are signifi-

FIGURE 4.9 **The given position.**

cantly different from the way we experience life today. Human beings in the past did not move in the same manner as we move today.

Such details of movement must be understood by actors working in plays of this kind. Style is an intricate problem, one that will be examined in somewhat greater detail in a later chapter. It is sufficient to say here that the actor's viewpoint must be not only that of an individual performer but also that of someone who is part of an entire production. It is the function of the director to provide the cohesive element necessary to unite the contributions of the individual actors.

Specialized Stage Problems

Acting was defined by Shakespeare, we may remember, as "holding . . . the mirror up to nature." We have seen, however, that one cannot take this suggestion *too* literally. Much that we must do on stage is guided by certain fundamental rules dealing with being seen, being heard, and focusing attention.

FIGURE 4.10 *Blues for Mr. Charley*
by James Baldwin. University of
Minnesota, directed by Elton Wolfe.

We now come to a number of problems that require highly specialized
techniques. Such techniques *suggest to the audience* realistic action but actually are the adjustments and alterations of reality we must make for stage
purposes. One of the most common of such techniques is called
"covering." Covering occurs when the audience is permitted to see only
part of the actual business and is required to supply the remainder of the action with its own imagination. A useful formula to indicate the relation of
covering to the completion of important but difficult stage business might
be:

COVERING + SUGGESTION + REACTION = COMPLETED ACTION.

Let us look into this technique of covering in an examination of the special
problems that follow.

Eating

Eating on stage is usually a matter of camouflage and substitution. For some unexplained reason playwrights delight in writing plays in which eating and drinking are important pieces of business. In *The Petrified Forest* by Robert E. Sherwood, the central character is seated at a table down stage center where he must consume an entire meal including soup, coffee, and a bottle of beer! Throughout this scene, which lasts almost half the act, he is speaking constantly, describing his past and philosophizing about the fate of man. He also happens to be quite hungry.

He rarely is silent, yet during this time he must make the audience believe that he has eaten a good deal of the food put before him. Much of the eating and drinking in such a scene would be faked, although it must also be made believable for the audience.

There are three major reasons why the business of eating and drinking should be covered and substitutions made for the food and drink indicated in the script: (1) The mouth should remain relatively clear for proper articulation. Speaking with the mouth full is unpleasant for both actor and audience. (2) A combination of stage enunciation, the necessity for responding to specific cues, and hard and stringy foods can produce choking and severe difficulties in swallowing. (3) The eating and drinking of large quantities of stage food and beverages are often unpleasant for the actor, especially during successive performances.

The foods actually used on stage are rarely the foods indicated in the script but are usually quite palatable. Hard foods are almost always avoided; the softer foods, such as eggs, bananas, bread, and rice make good substitutes. Cold tea, ginger ale, cider, and water with vegetable color are excellent substitutes for whiskey, wine, champagne, and so on.

The actor should eat very little of the food itself. A good deal of time should be devoted to the cutting and arranging of the food with utensils. He should put only a small portion of food in his mouth at any one time but can indicate through the pantomiming of chewing and swallowing that a greater amount of food is being consumed. Because coffee and tea are usually served in opaque cups, it is very difficult for an audience to tell how much liquid is actually in the cup. Usually the cup should be poured only half full; even then little of the liquid should be drunk. When a glass is used, the actor's hand can cover part of the glass. Here also little of the liquid should actually be drunk, unless the plot absolutely demands otherwise.

The most important thing to remember is that eating and drinking, as important stage business, should be as carefully planned as any speaking cue. Nothing is more embarrassing than being forced to speak while in the process of swallowing a morsel of food or a drink.

In Edward Albee's *Who's Afraid of Virginia Woolf*, the four characters are engaged in a drinking bout that lasts almost the entire play. Somehow they must consume enormous amounts of alcohol, retain some semblance of consciousness, and still be brilliantly articulate over a wide range of subjects. Timing in this play is critical, and the continual drinking must be carefully planned.

Kissing and Love Scenes

Love scenes may sometimes prove embarrassing for the beginning actor. This is a perfectly natural reaction. To compensate, it is best to begin playing love scenes early in the rehearsal period, certainly by the time the actors become free of the script. At first there need be no more than a superficial embrace, but this will serve to make the more detailed and elaborate em-

FIGURE 4.11 **The standing embrace: (*left*) correct and (*right*) incorrect—unless awkardness by the pair is intended.**

braces easier. Audiences enjoy these scenes if they are handled with taste, but if the embrace and kiss are excessive and overdone, unless specifically required by the script, an audience will be as uncomfortable as they would be watching such a sequence handled with obvious timidity.

The standing embrace and kiss is the most difficult type of all, as it usually is performed in a very standard way, with only little variation. The most common fault to be discerned in inexperienced actors during such a sequence is in posture and body relationship.

Very often the actors' positions tend to suggest a triangle, with their heads together and feet far apart, and the man and woman *leaning* toward each other. This stance suggests timidity on the part of the actors, and, unless this is the specific relationship required in the text of the play, the embrace can become amusing rather than affectionate. Therefore this kind of embrace should normally be avoided.

The man and woman should come close together, the man putting his downstage arm around the woman's waist and the other on her arm. His downstage foot should be extended slightly with the weight on this foot to help support the woman. The woman should have her downstage arm around the neck of the man or even on his shoulder, perhaps smoothing his coat. The upstage arm should usually be above the man's shoulder. In most cases their heads should tilt, an element of covering being provided by having the man's head downstage of the woman's during the actual kiss. The traditional dancing position frequently serves as a good starting point for the embrace and kiss.

Much greater variety in kissing can be developed when the couple is seated. The kiss may vary from a passionate embrace to a gentle caress. When seated, the person on the downstage part of the sofa should provide the covering. The script will usually suggest to the actors just what type of embrace is required.

Stabbing

Accidents have occurred during stage stabbings and will continue to occur even when the greatest care is taken to blunt the weapons. Involved sequences in which sword or knife fights are an important part of the play need to be planned very carefully, often requiring the use of a stage-combat choreographer. In such plays as *Romeo and Juliet, Cyrano de Bergerac, West Side Story, Hamlet,* and *Othello,* perfectly timed movement and rhythm are carefully planned on paper, taking into account the historical period of the play, the number of combatants, theatre size, costumes, and design. In many plays, however, the actor and director do not have the services of a choreographer trained in stage combat and must work within accepted techniques of handling weapons. We can begin by looking at stage stabbing, which may only involve a few individuals rather than a large battle or

FIGURE 4.12 *Marat/Sade* by Peter Weiss. California State University, Long
Beach, directed by Michael Lyman.

combat scene. The basis of successful stabbing on stage is *covering*. This
makes stabbing from upstage the easiest and least dangerous method. Stabbing from downstage requires a definite technique. The *downstage* hand
should hold the dagger and the person being stabbed should be a step or
two upstage of the person with the dagger. The arm should swing around
and the body should turn toward the person to be stabbed. The actor doing
the stabbing should complete the slight turn so that he or she is covering the
victim. The arm should start the supposed blow with great force but hold
back the dagger at the last minute and *pass* it in front of the body. The victim
should simulate the impact of the blow, usually by clutching the ''wound''
and turning his or her body in toward the supposed injury. The victim also
must react. In withdrawing the dagger, some visible effort should be suggested, or else it will be clear that the stabbing was faked.

The murder of Julius Caesar in Shakespeare's tragedy is a specific and
important example of a scene that requires great ingenuity in the development of such details. Caesar receives innumerable wounds, all from dif-

ferent angles; all of them must be covered and made to seem realistic. In such a case the actors must find means of concealing the blows, while maintaining the element of variety. Killing on stage requires imagination!

It is useful to restate the important principle involved here:

COVERING + SUGGESTION + REACTION = COMPLETED ACTION.

Shooting

When a gun is fired on stage, the first rule to remember is never to point the gun at the audience. Guns should be fired upstage and never pointed directly at another actor. This point cannot be stressed too strongly. Guns loaded with blanks can still cause injury by discharging the wad. The gun should be aimed and fired in a position a few inches *upstage* of the intended victim. Audiences will not be aware of this bit of "stealing."

The actor who is shot can, of course, die in a variety of ways. Normally the actor grabs the part of the body that has been struck, staggers, and executes a safe "stage fall." The stage fall in a simulated shooting must be planned properly if it is not to look comic, and should suggest, where required, a semblance of reality.

Falling

A fall on stage can occur for a number of reasons. It may be due to violent action, such as a stabbing, shooting, or poisoning, or it may be the result of fainting, tripping, or other natural causes. Certain primary rules apply to all such cases. If the body has received a blow or wound, the actor should reach for the injury just before the actual fall begins. If the actor is close to a piece of furniture, this may be used to help break the fall. The fall should not be instantaneous and rigid, unless the effect intended is one of comedy. The *relaxed* body should sink (1) to one knee, (2) to the hip, (3) to the shoulder, and then (4) to the final position.

Even if a blow or wound has not been inflicted, falls induced by poison, by a heart attack, or by faintness should suggest to the actor some means of indicating the part of the body afflicted. Care must be taken, however, not to overplay such a scene. A good death scene on stage can be a moving moment, but if played to excess, with overdone grimaces and a prolonged fall, it can suggest only inept amateurism. It is no wonder that such moments are often chosen for parody, satire, and farce.

There are also some basic principles involved in completing the fall: (1) The feet should not bounce at the end of the fall (except for a highly comic effect). (2) The feet should not point downstage. Usually the body should approximate the one-quarter body position with the *head* toward the downstage area. (Again, an intended comic effect might reverse this rule.) (3) The arms should not be extended from the body either above the head or at right angles from the body.

Fights

The staging of a good fight sequence is necessarily a cooperative venture, in which covering and faking are essential. The action should usually take place so quickly that audiences will find it impossible to distinguish a well-planned stage fight from the real thing.

Of course, in film, special stunt men double for the leading actors, and the speed of the action and carefully planned camera angles permit a kind of pseudorealism which is simply not easily accomplished in the theatre. Nevertheless, if carefully planned onstage, a fight can look so realistic that audiences may react in a manner that will cross any barrier of aesthetic distance.

The most difficult aspect of the stage fight is the striking of blows. There are three separate elements that should be considered in making the punch, slap, or other type of blow realistic: (1) the blow, (2) the reaction, and (3) the sound. These occur at almost the same moment but may be examined in sequence.

The primary factor in suggesting a real fight and real blows is *proper covering*. If the audience is permitted to see only *part* of the action they will supply the additional elements that have only been suggested and in consequence will imagine they are witnessing an actual fight.

The actor striking *the blow* should be downstage, covering the person to be struck. The arm should be brought back, with the fist clenched, and then brought forward quickly. If the blow is to land on the chin, the fist should move past the face quickly. If it is to be a body blow, the fist should stop just short of the body as it is about to strike. The actor being struck will *react* to the blow immediately. The head will quickly snap back as the fist moves past the chin, or the actor will double up as a body blow is struck.

When someone is struck, the first reaction is to try to ward off the blow with his or her hands. In a stage fight the hands may also suggest this phase of the action, but in addition they should provide *the sound* by being slapped together quickly either in front of the face or near the body area being struck. If this is done correctly, the audience will not see it. What they will perceive is: (1) a fist moving quickly toward an actor partially covered by the aggressor, (2) a reaction as the "blow" lands, and (3) the sound of a blow as the fist approaches that portion of the body being struck.

The audience will combine in their minds the action which they actually see and that which was only suggested; thus the impression of a realistic fight will be created. This technique, of course, saves a good deal of wear and tear on actors. The same procedure may be used if a particularly hard slap is indicated. Otherwise a normal slap need not be entirely covered; the fingers, rather than the entire hand, should execute the slap. In those cases where a prolonged fight is required, body positions should change rapidly and many blows may be struck. The basic principles still apply here, the most important being the proper covering of the action. With this in mind an actor can employ an infinite variety of movement, blows, and reactions.

Listening

Certainly the actor's proper reading of lines requires intense preparation and concentration. The same may also be said for the development of movement, gestures, and essential business in the creation of a consistent character. Another of the essential elements of good acting, however, is often overlooked by beginning actors, yet it gets to the very heart of good acting. This is proper listening when other actors on stage are speaking. It might almost be called reacting rather than acting, except that so simple a distinction would be highly misleading. Many otherwise successful performances have been ruined when an actor who had been speaking lines with intelligence and vitality became wooden and lifeless while others were speaking.

The actor cannot perform in a vacuum, oblivious of the work of his or her colleagues. Only the closest kind of rapport between actors can bring forward decent or memorable performances. The most experienced of twentieth-century actors, Laurence Olivier, speaks from a lifetime of experience when he tells us

> Actors must understand each other, know each other, help each other, absolutely love each other: must, absolutely must.[3]

Proper listening and reacting will vary according to the situation, but it is important that the actor convey the idea that he or she hears what is being said and is *thinking* of his or her relationship to that situation. The actor should not stand woodenly on stage simply waiting for a cue and thinking of his or her next line. It is instructive for all actors today to remember that one of the most persuasive attributes of the truly great actors of the past and present was their ability to listen and react in a manner thoroughly consistent with their roles. Critics and playgoers of their times constantly referred to this admirable quality.

Of Richard Burbage it was said that:

---

3. Laurence Olivier, in *Great Acting*, ed. Hal Burton (New York: Bonanza Books, 1967), p. 29.

His auditors [were] never more delighted than when he spoke, nor more sorry than when he held his peace; yet even then he was an excellent actor still, never falling in his part when he had done speaking, but with his looks and gestures maintaining it still unto the height.[4]

Much the same quality was admired in David Garrick:

His voice [is] natural in its cadence and beautiful in its elocution. . . . When three or four are on the stage with him, he is attentive to whatever is spoken, and never drops his character when he has finished a speech.[5]

The noted American actress Julia Marlowe gave us an incisive description of Edwin Booth, made all the more meaningful because it was written after the first time she had seen him act. It is interesting to note the element that made the profoundest impression on her.

I recall, when a young girl, the first time I saw Edwin Booth. He and Lawrence Barrett were appearing in *Othello*. Barrett impersonated Othello, and Booth, Iago. As I had never seen Booth, I did not know when he appeared on the scene. Suddenly I discovered a figure at the back of the stage intently watching the Moor. You could see plainly that he contemplated some demoniac act. His eye and manner at once caught the attention of the house long before he had said a word. The look on his face was crafty and devil-like. The one incident proved to me that there was very much more in acting than the polished delivery of lines.[6]

The great English actor Henry Irving has left us his impression of this important facet of good acting. He said simply: "One of the greatest tests of an actor is his capacity for listening."[7]

And we should not forget Henry Fonda's comment in Chapter 1 that no matter how many years an actor may play a role, he must avoid "the pitfall you get into in most long runs . . . you stop listening."[8]

There is obviously a close relationship between listening and William Gillette's concept of "the illusion of the first time." This illusion will be destroyed if the actor is unable to communicate the belief that he or she is hearing and reacting to the lines for the first time. Such listening and reacting also serve to sharpen the reading of the actor's own speeches, because they help the actor to see the total perspective of the scene.

---

4. Richard Flecknoe, *The Art of Richard Burbage* (1664), quoted by E. K. Chambers in *The Elizabethan Stage* (Oxford: Clarendon Press, 1923), vol. 4, p. 370.

5. Quoted in Percy H. Fitzgerald, *Life of David Garrick* (London: Tinsley Brothers, 1868).

6. Julia Marlowe, "The Eloquence of Silence," *Green Book* 9, no. 3 (March 1913): 393–401.

7. Henry Irving, "The Art of Acting" (1893), reprinted in *Actors on Acting*, 2nd ed., eds. Toby Cole and Helen Krich Chinoy (New York: Crown Publishers, Inc., 1954), p. 333.

8. Henry Fonda in Lillian Ross and Helen Ross, *The Player: A Profile of an Art* (New York: Simon and Schuster, 1962), p. 89.

The good actor *listens to what is said on stage—reacts—then speaks the lines.* In other words, the good actor acts all the time he or she is on the stage.

EXERCISES

The following exercises should help develop a practical working knowledge of the fundamentals discussed in the chapter. You should be able to devise many more and practice these exercises until movement and body positions become almost an automatic part of your stage behavior.

Stage areas   Maintaining the full front position:

1. Move from D. L. to U. R.
2. Move from U. R. to D. C.
3. Move from U. C. to D. R.
4. Move from U. L. to D. C.
5. Move from D. R. to U. C.
6. Move from D. L. to U. L.
7. Move from Stage Center to U. R.
8. Move from Stage Center to D.R.

How many of the above stage crosses would you make in a straight line and how many in a curve? Why?

Stage areas and body positions   Simple crosses:

body position	area		body position	area
Profile left	D. R.	cross to	Full back	U. L.
Full front	D. C.	cross to	One-quarter right	U. L.
Three-quarter left	U. R.	cross to	One-quarter left	D. L.
One-quarter right	D. L.	cross to	Three-quarter left	U. L.
Full back	U. C.	cross to	One-quarter right	D. R.

Try making some of these crosses in a straight line and some with a curved line. Is there any difference? Are certain crosses better than others when made in a curved line?

Crosses that may cause some difficulty:

body position	area		body position	area
Profile left	D. L.	cross to	Profile right	U. R.
Full back	D. C.	cross to	Full front	U. L.
Three-quarter left	U. L.	cross to	Three-quarter right	D. R.
Full back	U. C.	cross to	One-quarter left	D. R.
Three-quarter right	U. L.	cross to	One-quarter right	D. R.

Working with another actor

1. Share a scene equally so that you are both open to the audience.
2. Make the scene above more intense pictorially but still share the scene equally.
3. One actor has a long speech. The other will listen. What adjustment will you make now?

4. The other actor will now be emphasized for part of the scene. Adjust again.
5. A secret is being confided. Share the scene. Would the one-quarter shared position be better than the three-quarter shared position?
6. "Give" the scene to one actor.
7. "Take" the scene.

Working with two other actors   Let three actors designated A, B, and C take stage center in a full front position. Then follow the indicated sequence.

1. A and B give the scene to C.
2. C and A give the scene to B.
3. C and B give the scene to A.
4. C focuses on A and B, who are sharing a scene.
5. A focuses on B and C, who are sharing a scene.

Scenes

1. *California Suite*, by Neil Simon
   From Act II, Scene 1

   Scene: For one man, one woman
   Characters: DIANA NICHOLS, a British actress
   SIDNEY NICHOLS, her husband, in his early 40s
   Setting: A suite of rooms in the Beverly Hills Hotel, California.
   Time: The evening of the Academy Awards banquet. The present.
   Situation: *California Suite* is composed of four short plays about couples who stay in Rooms 203 and 204 of a luxurious hotel in Beverly Hills. Diana Nichols has been nominated for an Academy Award and has come from England for the Academy Award ceremonies. She is preparing for the evening very carefully, dressed in a floor-length chiffon gown and fastening her earrings as we first see her. Her husband Sidney is sitting in the living room consuming a large gin and tonic. Diana is not only very apprehensive about the forthcoming award ceremonies, but she is also concerned about the strange clump of fabric that is sitting on her left shoulder. She calls to Sidney from the bedroom as she surveys herself in the mirror.

DIANA: Finished, Sidney. I'm dressed. I'm going to have a look. (*She examines herself in the mirror*) Sidney? Disaster! Total disaster . . . The *Titanic* in chiffon! Oh, Christ, what has the dressmaker wrought?
SIDNEY: (*Looks at his watch again*) Where the hell is the car?
DIANA: There's either not enough chiffon or too much of me . . . I'm listing to the left, Sidney. God, I hope it's the floor. Sidney, come in and look—and try to be gentle.
SIDNEY: (*Gets up, crossing toward the bedroom*) It's after five—we should have left ten minutes ago. (*He stops in the doorway and looks in at her*)
DIANA: Well?
SIDNEY: How much was it?
DIANA: Nothing. Joe Levine paid for it.
SIDNEY: Then I love it.
DIANA: You hate it. Damn it, I wish you didn't have such good taste. (*Keeps examining herself in the mirror*) What have they done to me, Sidney? I have a definite hump on my left shoulder. I mean, it's got to be seven hundred dollars if it's a penny, and I look like Richard the Third . . . Do you notice the hump, Sidney?
SIDNEY: Isn't that your regular hump?
DIANA: Don't joke with me. I'm going on national television.
SIDNEY: There are no humps. I see no humps at this particular time. (*He takes a sip of his drink*)

DIANA: It's all *bulky* on the left side. Don't you see how it bunches up?

SIDNEY: Have you taken out all the tissue paper?

DIANA: I should have worn something simple . . . My black pants suit. Why the hell didn't I wear my black pants suit?

SIDNEY: Because *I'm* wearing it.

DIANA: We shouldn't have come. I never know how to dress in this bloody country. It's so easy to dress in England. You just put on warm clothing. Why did we come, Sidney?

SIDNEY: Because it's all free, darling.

DIANA: Glenda Jackson never comes, and she's nominated every goddamned year. We could have stayed in London and waited for a phone call. Michael Caine could have accepted for me. He would be bright and witty—and no one would have seen my hump.

SIDNEY: Use it, sweetheart. People will pity you for your deformity and you're sure to win.

DIANA: Maybe if you put your arm on my shoulder . . . (*She places his arm around her*) Keep your arm on my shoulder at all times. If I win, we'll go up together, your arm around me, and they'll think we're still mad for each other after twelve years.

SIDNEY: Oh, I thought we were. I keep forgetting.

DIANA: (*Looks at him*) How many gin and tonics have you had?

SIDNEY: Three gins, one tonic.

DIANA: Well, catch up on your tonics. We don't want to be disgusting tonight, do we? (*She fluffs up her hair*) What's wrong with my hair? It looks like I've combed it with a towel.

SIDNEY: When you played Elizabeth you looked like a wart hog and you never complained once.

DIANA: That's acting, this is living. Living, I want to be beautiful . . . My hair is the strangest color. I asked for a simple rinse and that queen gave me crayons.

SIDNEY: Shall I walk with my arm on your head as well?

DIANA: That's not funny, Sidney. That's bizarre. You have the most bizarre sense of humor.

SIDNEY: Bizarre people often do.

DIANA: Oh, Christ, I hate getting dressed like this. Why am I always so much more comfortable as someone else? I would have been perfectly happy going as Hedda Gabler.

SIDNEY: Try Quasimodo.

DIANA: Try shutting up. What time is it?

SIDNEY: Late. We are definitely late.

DIANA: Just check me out. Do I have too much jewelry on?

SIDNEY: Jingle it—I can't tell if I don't hear it.

DIANA: Will you please be nice to me and pay me one bloody compliment? I've been getting dressed for this horseshit affair since six o'clock this morning.

SIDNEY: You look lovely. And if that doesn't do, please accept radiant.

DIANA: Why don't we watch it on television? We could stay in bed, have champagne, make love and switch the dial if Faye Dunaway wins. (*The phone rings. He goes toward it*)

SIDNEY: You can do what you want, love, but I wouldn't miss this circus for the world. (*Picks up the phone*) Hello? . . . Yes, it is . . . Right. We'll be down in two minutes. Thank you. (*He hangs up*)

DIANA: Why do they have these things so early? No woman can look good at five o'clock in the afternoon, except possibly Tatum O'Neal.

SIDNEY: We are being reminded that nominees *must* be there at five thirty for the press.

DIANA: The press! I can't *wait* to see how they explain my hump in the newspapers.

SIDNEY: Oh, Diana . . .

DIANA: What?

SIDNEY: I was about to say you're making a mountain out of a molehill, but I didn't think it would amuse you.

DIANA: Let me have a cigarette. (*She feels her stomach*) Oh, Christ, I'm going to be acidic tonight. Be sure and bring a roll of Tums.

SIDNEY: And sit there in front of America with a chalky-white mouth? Have a double gin instead; it'll drown all those butterflies. (*He gives her a cigarette, lights it, then goes to make her a drink*)

DIANA: This whole thing is so bizarre. Eight years with the National Theatre, two Pinter plays, two Becketts, nine Shakespeare, three Shaws, and I finally get nominated for a nauseating little comedy.

SIDNEY: That's why they call it Hollywood. (*The phone rings. He hands her the gin. He picks up the phone*)

DIANA: I'm not here. I don't care if it's the Queen Mother, I'm not here.

SIDNEY: Hello? . . . Oh, yes, how are you? . . . Well, she's a bit nervous, I think . . . Do you really think she will? . . . Well, let's hope so . . . And thank you for the flowers, the wine, the suite and everything else you send up by the hour . . . One moment, Joe. (*He puts hand over the phone. To* DIANA) Joe Levine. He wants to wish you luck.

DIANA: Tell him I'm in the can.

SIDNEY: The man paid for this trip, he paid for this suite, and he gave you the best part you've had in five years—I am not going to tell him you are in the can.

DIANA: Then I'll tell him. (*She takes the receiver*) Joe, darling, I told Sidney to tell you I was in the can . . . I didn't want to speak to you, that's why . . . Because I feel so responsible . . . I don't want to let you down tonight . . . I know how much the picture means to you, and I want so much to win this for you, Joe . . . There was no picture without you . . . Well, goddamn it, it's true. After four studios turned it down, you deserve some special perserverance award . . . You're a chubby little man and I adore you . . . If I win tonight, darling, it's not going to be an Oscar—it's going to be a Joe Levine . . . You're an angel. (*She hangs up*)

SIDNEY: That was very sweet.

DIANA: Did you like it? That's going to be my speech.

SIDNEY: Your acceptance speech?

DIANA: All except the part that I was in the can. Naturally we both know I don't have a chance in hell, but you've got to prepare *something*. I can't just stand up there sobbing with a humped back . . . Can I have another drink, darling? And stop worrying. I won't get *pissed* until *after* I lose. (*She takes his drink out of his hand. He starts making himself another one*)

SIDNEY: You have as good a chance as anyone.

DIANA: I don't have the sentiment on my side. You've got to have a sentimental reason for them to vote for you. Any decent actress can give a good performance, but a *dying husband* would have insured everything . . . You wouldn't like to get something fatal for me, would you, angel?

SIDNEY: You should have told me sooner. I could have come over on the *Hindenburg*.

DIANA: We *are* terrible, Sidney, aren't we? God will punish us.

SIDNEY: I think He already has. Drink up. (*He drinks*)

DIANA: (*Drinks*) Do you know what I might do next year, Sidney?

SIDNEY: I pray: anything but Ibsen.

DIANA: I might quit. I might get out. Give up acting. I'm not having any more fun. It used to be such fun . . . Do you know what Larry Olivier once said to me?

SIDNEY: Can you tell me in the car?

DIANA: Larry said, "Acting is the finest and most noble thing you can do with your life, unless, of course, you're lucky enough to be happy." . . . Isn't that incredible, Sid?

SIDNEY: It's absolutely awe-inspiring . . . unless of course, you're *unlucky* enough to be married to an actress. (*He starts for the door*)

DIANA: I'm sorry, Sid. Was that an insensitive thing for me to say? It has nothing to do with us. I've always been unhappy. I think that's why I'm such a damned good actress . . . But that's about *all* I am.

SIDNEY: Will you finish your drink? I don't want to miss the sound-editing awards.

DIANA: I envy you, Sidney. You have nothing *but* talent. You cook better than I do, you write better than I do, God knows, you dress better than I do . . .

SIDNEY: Better than *I.* "Do" is superfluous.

DIANA: And you speak better than I do. Jesus, I'm glad you came. I would hate to go through this alone tonight.

SIDNEY: I don't think they allow nominees to come alone. They give you Burt Reynolds or someone.

DIANA: You've never liked any of this, have you? The openings, the parties, any of it.

SIDNEY: I *love* the openings. I *adore* the parties. I lead a very gay life. I mean, let's be honest, angel, how many antique dealers in London get to go to the Academy Awards?

DIANA: And I think you hate that dusty little shop. You're never there when I call . . . Where do you spend your afternoons, Sidney?

SIDNEY: In London? We don't have afternoons. (*Looks out the window*) I should have waited for you in front of the hotel. I could have gotten a nice tan.

DIANA: You shouldn't have given it up, Sidney.

SIDNEY: Acting?

DIANA: Christ, you were good. You had more promise than any of us.

SIDNEY: Really? I can't think what it was I promised.

DIANA: You were so gentle on the stage. So unselfish, so giving. You had a sweet, gentle quality.

SIDNEY: Yes. I would have made a wonderful Ophelia.

DIANA: Well, as a matter of fact, you would.

SIDNEY: Pity I couldn't have stayed sixteen forever. What a future I had. Juliet, Roxanne—there were no end to the roles . . .

DIANA: You could go back, Sidney. You could if you wanted, you know.

SIDNEY: Married to you? Oh, there'd be problems. It would be awful for both of us to be up for the same parts . . . No, no. I'm perfectly happy selling my eighteenth-century door knockers.

DIANA: (*A pause*) What do you do with your afternoons, Sidney?

SIDNEY: I just told you, darling. I look for knockers . . . Now can we go and get this bloody thing over with?

DIANA: First kiss me and wish me luck.

SIDNEY: (*Kisses her*) There's your kiss. Now, turn around so I can rub your hump for luck.

DIANA: Don't be a shit, Sidney. I'm scared to death.

SIDNEY: (*Smiles at her; then warmly and affectionately*) I wish you everything. I wish you luck, I wish you love, I wish you happiness. You're a gifted and remarkable woman. You've put up with me and my shenanigans for twelve harrowing years, and I don't know why. But I'm grateful . . . You've had half a husband and three-quarters of a career. You deserve the full amount of everything . . . May the Academy of Arts and Sciences Board of Electees see the beauty, the talent and the courage that I have seen for a quarter of a lifetime . . . I hope you win the bloody Oscar . . . Fifty years from now I'll be able to sell it for a fortune. (*He kisses her again*)

DIANA: I love you, Sidney.

SIDNEY: Then mention me in your speech. Come on. (*He pulls her out as she grabs her purse*)

DIANA: Ladies and gentlemen of the Academy, I thank you for this award . . . I have a lump in my throat and a hump on my dress.

2. *The Fourposter,* by Jan de Hartog
   From Act II, Scene 2

    Scene: For one man, one woman
Characters: HE (Michael)
          SHE (Agnes)
    Setting: The bedroom of Michael and Agnes, dominated by a fourposter bed.
     Time: Four o'clock in the morning. The early part of this century.
 Situation: The play traces the life of a married couple from their wedding night to the day they leave their home, thirty-five years later. It is now four o'clock in the morning, and they are awaiting their eighteen-year-old son, who has not yet returned from a dance. The father, Michael, is rather disturbed because he has found a half-filled bourbon bottle in his

son's drawer. The scene begins as Michael has stepped out of the bedroom thinking that he has heard his son enter. Both Michael and Agnes are in their night clothes, she in a nightgown and he in a long nightshirt and cap. Does this costuming suggest any possibilities for movement to heighten the comic potential of the scene?

HE: Is that you, Robert? (*No answer, so he comes back.*) No.
SHE: (*sits at dressing table, opens powder box*) Why don't you go back to bed?
HE: Because I'm worried.
SHE: (*picking up hand mirror and puff and powdering her face*) Why, that's non-sense!
HE: And so are you.
SHE: What on earth gives you that idea?
HE: That you are powdering your face at four o'clock in the morning.
SHE: (*puts down mirror, puff. Realizes that there is no use in pretending any longer, goes to the bottle and picks it up from bed table*) What drawer was it?
HE: The one where he keeps all his junk.
SHE: I can't believe it. It can't be true.
HE: Well, there you are.
SHE: How did you find it?
HE: I was sitting downstairs waiting. I got more and more worried so I decided to go up to his room and see whether perhaps he had climbed in through the window, and then I happened to glance into an open drawer, and there it was.
SHE: But it isn't possible. A child can't be drinking on the sly without his mother knowing it.
HE: We'll have to face it, my dear. He is no longer a child. When I looked into that drawer and found his old teddy bears, his steam engine, and then that bottle, I—I can't tell you what I felt.
SHE: Suppose—of course it isn't—but suppose—it is true, whatever shall we do?
HE: I don't know—see a doctor.
SHE: Nonsense. It's perfectly natural childish curiosity. A boy has to try everything once.
HE: If that's going to be your attitude, he'll end by trying murder once. By the way, what were you going to say about Lizzie?
SHE: (*smiles*) She is in love.
HE: What?
SHE: She's secretly engaged.
HE: To whom?
SHE: To the boy next door.
HE: To that—ape? To that pie face?
SHE: I think it's quite serious.
HE: The child is only . . . nonsense!
SHE: She is not a child anymore. She's . . . well, the same thing Robert is, I suppose. I wouldn't be surprised if one of these days the boy came to see you to ask for her hand.
HE: If he does, I'll shoot him.
SHE: But, darling . . .

HE: But she's only sixteen! Agnes, this is a nightmare!

SHE: But, sweetheart . . .

HE: She can't be in love, and certainly not with *that!*

SHE: Why not?

HE: After spending her whole life with me, she can't fall in love with something hatched out of an egg.

SHE: Are you suggesting that the only person the child will be allowed to fall in love with is a younger edition of yourself?

HE: Of course not. Don't be indecent. What I mean is that at least we should have given them taste! They should have inherited our taste!

SHE: Well, he seems to have inherited a taste for bourbon.

HE: I don't understand how you can joke about it. This happens to be the worst night of my life.

SHE: I'm not joking, darling. I just don't think that there's much point in us sitting up all night worrying ourselves sick about something we obviously can't do anything about until the morning. Come, go back to bed.

HE: You go to bed . . . I'll wait up for him.

SHE: Shall I make you a cup of tea?

HE: Tea! Do you know that we haven't had a single crisis in our life yet for which your ultimate solution wasn't a cup of tea?

SHE: I'm sorry. I was only trying to be sensible about it.

HE: I know you are. I apologize if I've said things that I didn't mean. (*Picks up the bourbon bottle and uncorks it with his left hand.*) I think what we both need is a swig of this. Have we got any glasses up here?

SHE: Only tooth-glasses. (HE *takes a swig, then with a horrified expression thrusts the bottle and cork into her hands and runs to the bathroom.*) Michael! (SHE *smells the bottle, grimaces.*)

HE: (*rushing out of bathroom with a nauseated look on his face*) What is that?

SHE: Cod liver oil!

HE: Oh! (*Runs back into bathroom.*)

SHE: (*takes handkerchief from pocket, wipes bottle*) How on earth did it get into this bottle?

HE: God knows! (*Re-enters to just outside bathroom door.* HE *carries a glass of water.*) I think that little monster must have been trying to set a trap for me! (*Runs back into bathroom.*)

SHE: (*holding bottle up, puzzling over contents*) Michael, wait a minute! (SHE *is interrupted by the sound of gargling.*) I know! Well, this is the limit!

HE: (*re-enters, wiping mouth with towel*) What?

SHE: Do you remember, three years ago, that he had to take a spoonful of cod liver oil every night and that he didn't want to take it in my presence? Of course I measured the bottle every morning, but he poured it into this!

HE: Agnes, do you mean to say that stuff I swallowed is three years old?

SHE: The little monkey! Oh, now I am going to wait till he gets home!

HE: I think perhaps we'd better call the doctor. This stuff must be putrid by now.

SHE: You'll have to speak to him, Michael. This is one time that you'll have to speak to him. I . . . (*Hears something.*) Michael, there he is! (*Rises, goes to door.* HE *rushes to door, stops, returns to bench and picks up riding crop. Starts out.* SHE *stops him.*) No, Michael, not that! Don't go that far!

HE: Three-year-old cod liver oil!

3. *Entertaining Mr. Sloane,* by Joe Orton
   From Act I

Scene:	For one man, one woman
Characters:	MR. SLOANE, a good-looking young man
	KATH, landlady; early middle-age
Setting:	A frumpy room-to-let in an English suburb.
Time:	Evening. The mid-1960s.
Situation:	This play was the winner of the London critics' award for the best play of 1964. It is the amusing, black comedy of a young man and a middle-aged landlady who is overly eager to please. This sequence is from the beginning of the comedy; Mr. Sloane has come looking for a suitable room for himself in a house in a suburb of London.

KATH: This is my lounge.

SLOANE: Would I be able to use this room? It is included?

KATH: Oh, yes. (*Pause.*) You mustn't image it's always like this. You ought to have rung up or something. And then I'd've been prepared.

SLOANE: The bedroom was perfect.

KATH: I never showed you the toilet.

SLOANE: I'm sure it will be satisfactory. *He walks round the room examining the furniture. Stops by the window.*)

KATH: I should change them curtains. Those are our winter ones. The summer ones are more of a chintz. (*Laughs.*) The walls need re-doing. The Dadda has trouble with his eyes. I can't ask him to do any work involving ladders. It stands to reason. (*Pause.*)

SLOANE: I can't give you a decision right away.

KATH: I don't want you to. (*Pause.*) What do you think? I'd be happy to have you. (*Silence*)

SLOANE: Are you married?

KATH: (*Pause.*) I was. I had a boy . . . killed in very sad circumstances. It broke my heart at the time. I got over it though. You do, don't you? (*Pause.*)

SLOANE: A son?

KATH: Yes.

SLOANE: You don't look old enough. (*Pause.*)

KATH: I don't let myself go like some of them you may have noticed. I'm just over . . . As a matter of fact I'm forty-one. (*Pause.*)

SLOANE: (*Briskly.*) I'll take the room.

KATH: Will you?

SLOANE: I'll bring my things over tonight. It'll be a change from my previous.

KATH: Was it bad?

SLOANE: Bad?

KATH: As bad as that?

SLOANE: You've no idea.

KATH: I don't suppose I have. I've led a sheltered life.

SLOANE: Have you been a widow long?

KATH: Yes a long time. My husband was a mere boy. (*With a half-laugh.*) That sounds awful doesn't it?

SLOANE: Not at all.

KATH: I married out of school. I surprised everyone by the suddenness of it. (*Pause.*) Does that sound as if I had to get married?

SLOANE: I'm broadminded.

KATH: I should've known better. You won't breathe a word?

SLOANE: You can trust me.

KATH: My brother would be upset if he knew I told you. (*Pause.*) Nobody knows around here. The people in the nursing home imagined I *was* somebody. I didn't disillusion them.

SLOANE: You were never married then?

KATH: No.

SLOANE: What about—I hope you don't think I'm prying?

KATH: I wouldn't for a minute. What about—?

SLOANE: . . . the father?

KATH: (*Pause.*) We always planned to marry. But there were difficulties. I was very young and he was even younger. I don't believe we would have been allowed.

SLOANE: What happened to the baby?

KATH: Adopted.

SLOANE: By whom?

KATH: That I could not say. My brother arranged it.

SLOANE: What about the kid's father?

KATH: He couldn't do anything.

SLOANE: Why not?

KATH: His family objected. They were very nice but he had a duty you see. (*Pause.*) As I say, if it'd been left to him I'd be his widow today. (*Pause.*) I had a last letter. I'll show you some time. (*Silence.*) D'you like flock or foam rubber in your pillow?

SLOANE: Foam rubber.

KATH: You need a bit of luxury, don't you? I bought the Dadda one but he can't stand them.

SLOANE: I can.

KATH: You'll live with us then as one of the family?

SLOANE: I never had no family of my own.

KATH: Didn't you?

SLOANE: No, I was brought up in an orphanage.

KATH: You have the air of lost wealth.

SLOANE: That's remarkable. My parents, I believe, *were* extremely wealthy people.

KATH: Did Dr. Barnardo give you a bad time?

SLOANE: No. It was the lack of privacy I found most trying. (*Pause.*) And the lack of real love.

KATH: Did you never know your mamma?

SLOANE: Yes.

KATH: When did they die?

SLOANE: I was eight. (*Pause.*) They passed away together.

KATH: How shocking.

SLOANE: I've an idea that they had a suicide pact. Couldn't prove it of course.

KATH: Of course not. (*Pause.*) With a nice lad like you to take care of you'd think they'd've postponed it. (*Pause.*) Criminals, were they?

SLOANE: From what I remember they were respected. You know, H.P. debts. Bridge. A little light gardening. The usual activities of a cultured community. (*Silence.*) I respect their memory.

KATH: Do you? How nice.

SLOANE: Every year I pay a visit to their grave. I take sandwiches. Make a day of it. (*Pause.*) The graveyard is situated in pleasant surroundings so it's no hardship. (*Pause.*) Tomb an'all.

KATH: Marble? (*Pause.*) Is there an inscription?

SLOANE: Perhaps you'd come with me this trip?

KATH: We'll see.

SLOANE: I go in the autumn. I clean the leaves off the monument. As a tribute.

KATH: Any relations?

SLOANE: None.

KATH: Poor boy. Alone in the world. Like me.

SLOANE: You're not alone.

KATH: I am. (*Pause.*) Almost alone. (*Pause.*) If I'd been allowed to keep my boy I'd not be. (*Pause.*) You're almost the same age as he would be. You've got the same refinement.

SLOANE: (*Slowly.*) I need . . . understanding.

KATH: You do don't you. Here let me take your coat. (*She helps him off with his coat.*) You've got a delicate skin. (*She touches his neck. His cheek. He shudders a little. Pause. She kisses his cheek.*) Just a motherly kiss. A real mother's kiss. (*Silence. She lifts his arms and folds them about her.*) You'll find me very sentimental. I upset easy. (*His arms are holding her.*) When I hear of . . . tragedies happening to perfect strangers. There are so many ruined lives. (*She puts her head on his shoulder.*) You must treat me gently when I'm in one of my moods. (*Silence.*)

SLOANE: (*Clearing his throat.*) How much are you charging? I mean—I've got to know. (*He drops his arms. She moves away.*)

KATH: We'll come to some arrangement. A cup of tea?

SLOANE: Yes I don't mind.

KATH: I'll get you one.

SLOANE: Can I have a bath?

KATH: Now?

SLOANE: Later would do.

KATH: You must do as you think fit.

4. *The Petrified Forest*, by Robert E. Sherwood
   From Act I

   Scene: For one man, one woman
   Characters: ALAN SQUIER, an unsuccessful writer
   GABBY, a young woman
   Setting: A wayside cafe in Arizona.
   Time: The 1930s.
   Situation: Alan Squier, an unsuccessful writer, has been hitchkiking his way across the country to California. Now penniless, he has made his way to a small cafe in the Arizona desert only a few miles from the Petrified

Forest. Gabby, the young daughter of the owner of the cafe has developed a hard shell as compensation against the dreary environment, but she is essentially a sensible girl. Squier senses this as he sits at a table chatting with Gabby and devouring the Bar-B-Q "special." The scene provides an extensive exercise for the actor playing Squier to develop facility in handling a prolonged eating sequence intermingled with a good deal of dialogue. An additional problem is posed in the choice of seated positions which will seem logical for a prolonged discussion yet keep each actor open to the audience.

GABBY: Like the soup?

SQUIER: (*from the heart*) It was glorious!

GABBY: Want some coffee?

SQUIER: Will it mix with the beer?

GABBY: Oh, sure. Coffee will mix with anything. (*She goes to the counter to get his coffee.*)

SQUIER: That's a charming old gentleman. Your grandfather?

GABBY: Yes.

SQUIER: He told me he'd been missed by Billy the Kid.

GABBY: He tells everybody that. Poor Gramp. You get terribly sick of him after a while. (*She has brought down the coffee.*) Did I hear him say you're a writer?

SQUIER: (*humbly*) Yes.

GABBY: I haven't met many writers—except Sidney Wenzell. Ever heard of him?

SQUIER: That's not Mark Twain, is it?

GABBY: No! Sidney Wenzell—he's with Warner Brothers. He stopped here once, when he was driving out to the Coast. He said I ought to go to Hollywood, and to be sure and look him up. But—what the hell! They never mean it.

SQUIER: No! They never mean a thing. (*She has picked up her book and started to go.*) Please don't go. (*She pauses and turns.*)

GABBY: Something else you want? We got pie and layer cake.

SQUIER: No. I—I'd like to talk to you. Please sit down.

GABBY: All right. (*She sits down, across from him, at the center table.* SQUIER *eats rapidly, mechanically, during the subsequent dialogue, stowing the food away as he talks and listens.*)

SQUIER: I suppose you want to go into the movies?

GABBY: (*scornfully*) God, *no!*

SQUIER: But—I thought every beautiful girl had her heart set on Hollywood.

GABBY: That's just it. It's too common. I want to go to Bourges. (*She fails to soften the "g."*)

SQUIER: Where?

GABBY: Bourges—in France. You'd never guess it, but that's where I came from.

SQUIER: You're not French?

GABBY: Partly. I was born in Bourges—but I left it almost before I was able to walk, so all I know about it is from the picture postcards my mother sends me. They got a cathedral there.

SQUIER: Your mother still lives there?

GABBY: Yes. Dad brought us back here after the war. Mother stuck it out in this desert for a couple of years, and then she packed up and went back to Bourges. We've never seen her since. Some people seem to think it was cruel of her to leave me. But what could she do? She didn't have any money to bring me up. She just couldn't *live* here—and you can't blame her for that. Do you think she was cruel?

SQUIER: Not if you don't, Miss Maple.

GABBY: Well—I don't. She's tried lots of times to get me over there to see her— but Dad won't allow it. She got a divorce and married a Frenchman that's got a bookstore. Mother was always a great reader, so I guess it's nice for her. She's got three more kids. Just think of that! I've got a half-brother and half-sisters that can't speak a word of English. I'd sure like to see them.

SQUIER: Can you speak French?

GABBY: Only what you learn in high school—like *table* for "table." (*She takes a photograph from the book.*) Look—there's my mother's picture. That was just before she married Dad. She had her picture taken smelling a rose.

SQUIER: She's lovely! And I can see the resemblance.

GABBY: It's hard to imagine her being married to Dad, isn't it? But I guess he looked all right in his American uniform. Mother used to send me a book every year for my birthday, but they were all in French and I couldn't read them. So last year I wrote and asked if she'd mind sending me one in English, and she sent me this one. It's the Poems of François Villon. Ever read it?

SQUIER: Yes.

GABBY: It's wonderful poetry. She wrote in it: "à ma chère petite Gabrielle." That means "To my dear little Gabrielle." She gave me that name. It's about the only French thing I've got.

SQUIER: Gabrielle. It's a beautiful name.

GABBY: Wouldn't you know it would get changed into "Gabby" by these ignorant bastards around here? I guess you think I use terrible language.

SQUIER: Oh, no! It—it's picturesque.

GABBY: Well—it suits this kind of country.

SQUIER: You share your mother's opinion of the desert? (*She nods.*) But you can find solace in the Poems of François Villon.

GABBY: Yes. They get the stink of the gasoline and the hamburger out of my system.

SQUIER: Would you like to read me one of those poems, Gabrielle?

GABBY: You mean now?

SQUIER: Yes. While I'm finishing "Today's Special."

GABBY: O. K. I'll read you the one I like best. He wrote it about a friend of his who was getting married. (*She reads, with marked but inexpert emphasis*):

>"At daybreak, when the falcon claps his wings
>>No whit for grief, but noble heart held high
>With loud glad noise he stirs himself and springs,
>>And takes his meat and toward his lure draws nigh;
>>Such good I wish you! Yea, and heartily
>I'm fired with hope of true love's meed to get;
>>Knowing Love writes it in his book; for why,
>This is the end for which we twain are met."

Did you ever see a falcon?

SQUIER: Yes.

GABBY: What does it look like?

SQUIER: Not very pleasant. Like a hawk. Go on, Gabrielle.

GABBY: (*resuming reading*)

> "Mine own heart's lady with no gainsayings
> > You shall be always till I die;
> And in my right against all bitter things
> > Sweet laurel with fresh rose its force shall try;
> > Seeing reason wills not that I cast love by
> Nor here with reason shall I chide and fret
>
> [*She closes the book and recites:*]
>
> > Nor cease to serve, but serve more constantly;
> This is the end for which we twain are met."

(*She looks at him, and he at her. Then he resumes his attack on the hamburger.*) You know—that's wonderful stuff. But that's the way the French people are: They can understand everything—like life, and love—and death—and they can enjoy it, or laugh at it, depending on how they feel.

SQUIER: And that's why you want to go to France—for understanding.

GABBY: I *will* go there! When Gramp dies, we can sell this place. Dad's going to take his share and move to Los Angeles, so that he can join a really big Legion post and get to be a political power. But I'm going to spend my part of the money on a trip to Bourges, where there's something beautiful to look at, and wine, and dancing in the streets.

SQUIER: If I were you—I'd stay here, Gabrielle, and avoid disappointment.

GABBY: What makes you think I'd be disappointed?

SQUIER: I've been to France.

GABBY: You were there in the war?

SQUIER: No, I missed that. But I lived there for eight years, through seventeen changes of government.

GABBY: What were you doing—writing books?

SQUIER: No—planning to write books. You know what a gigolo is?

GABBY: Were *you* one of those? (*He nods.*) You danced with women for money?

SQUIER: Oh lord, no! I never was a good enough dancer for that. I—I married.

GABBY: Oh.

SQUIER: Please don't think too ill of me. I once actually wrote a book.

GABBY: What was it—fiction?

SQUIER: In a sense. It was a novel about the bleak, glacier-stripped hills of my native New England. I was twenty-two when I wrote it, and it was very, very stark. It sold slightly over six hundred copies. It cost the publisher quite a lot of money, and it also cost him his wife. You see, she divorced him and married me. She had faith in me, and she had the chance to display it, because her husband was very generous in the financial settlement. I suppose he had faith in me, too. She saw in me a major artist, profound, but inarticulate. She believed that all I needed was background, and she gave it to me—with southern exposure and a fine view of the Mediterranean. That was considered the thing to do in the period that followed Scott Fitzgerald. For eight years I reclined there, on the Riviera, on my background—and I waited for the major artist to step forth and say something of enduring importance. He preferred to remain inarticulate.

5. *An Enemy of the People*, by Henrik Ibsen, adapted by Arthur Miller
   From Act I, Scene 2

    Scene: For two men, two women
Characters: DR. THOMAS STOCKMANN, a medical officer
          CATHERINE STOCKMANN, his wife
          PETRA STOCKMANN, his daughter, a schoolteacher
          PETER STOCKMANN, his brother and mayor of the community
    Setting: The home of Dr. Stockmann. A small town in southern Norway.
      Time: The late nineteenth century.
Situation: The citizens of the community are very proud of the Baths or Spa, which they believe to be not only healthful but a source of income from the tourists who are coming to their small town in ever-increasing numbers. Dr. Stockmann, the health officer of the town, has found that despite the fame and money the bath waters are bringing to the community, they are actually polluted by sewage. His brother, Peter, is the mayor of the town, and, in order to protect its interests, he has forbidden Stockmann to make the news public. Dr. Stockmann refuses to obey, moved by an idealistic fervor to reveal the truth.

        This excerpt is from the twentieth-century adaptation by American playwright Arthur Miller, who has given the play and its language a distinctly modern idiomatic flavor.

PETER: Now look, I am going to lay this out once and for all. You're always barking about authority. If a man gives you an order, he's persecuting you. Nothing is important enough to respect, once you decide to revolt against your superiors. All right, then, I give up. I'm not going to try to change you any more. I told you the stakes you are playing for here, and now I'm going to give you an order and I warn you, you'd better obey it if you value your career.

STOCKMANN: What kind of an order?

PETER: You are going to deny these rumors officially.

STOCKMANN: How?

PETER: You simply say that you went into the examination of the water more thoroughly and you find that you overestimated the danger.

STOCKMANN: I see!

PETER: And that you have complete confidence that whatever improvements are needed, the management will certainly take care of them.

STOCKMANN: My convictions come from the conditions of the water. My convictions will change when the water changes, and for no other reason.

PETER: What are you talking about convictions? You're an official, you keep your convictions to yourself!

STOCKMANN: To myself?!

PETER: As an official, I said. God knows as a private person that is something else, but as a subordinate employee of the Institute, you have no right to express any convictions or personal opinions about anything connected with policy!

STOCKMANN: Now you listen to me! I am a doctor and a scientist!!

PETER: What's this got to do with science?

STOCKMANN: And I have the right to express my opinion on anything in the world!

PETER: Not about the Institute—that I forbid.

STOCKMANN: You forbid!

PETER: I forbid you as your superior, and when I give orders you obey.

STOCKMANN: (*turning away from* PETER) Peter, if you weren't my brother . . .

PETRA: (*throws* L. *door open, flies in,* CATHERINE *tries to restrain her,* PETRA *crosses to* L. *of* PETER) Father! You aren't going to stand for this!

CATHERINE: (*following* PETRA) Petra, Petra . . .

PETER: What have you two been doing, eavesdropping?

CATHERINE: You were talking so loud we couldn't help . . .

PETRA: (*interrupting*) Yes, I was eavesdropping.

PETER: (*crossing below* STOCKMANN *to his* R.) That makes me very happy.

STOCKMANN: (*moving* L.) You said something to me about forbidding—

PETER: You forced me to.

STOCKMANN: So, you want me to spit in my own face officially, is that it?

PETER: Why must you always be so colorful?

STOCKMANN: And if I don't obey?

PETER: Then we will publish our own statement, to calm the public.

STOCKMANN: Good enough! And I will write against you. I will stick to what I said, and I will prove that I am right and that you are wrong, and what will you do then?

PETER: Then I simply won't be able to prevent your dismissal.

STOCKMANN: (*steps back*) What! ⎫
PETRA: (*steps to* C.) Father! ⎬ (*Together*)
⎭

PETER: Dismissed from the Institute is what I said. If you want to make war on Kirsten Springs, you have no right to be on the Board of Directors.

STOCKMANN: You'd dare to do that?

PETER: Oh, no, you're the daring man.

PETRA: (*crossing to* PETER, *below* STOCKMANN, *who crosses* D. C., *head in hands*) Uncle, this is a rotten way to treat a man like Father.

CATHERINE: (*crossing below* STOCKMANN, *to* PETRA) Will you be quiet, Petra.

PETER: So young and you've got opinions already—but that's natural. (*to* CATHERINE) Catherine, dear, you're probably the only sane person in this house. Knock some sense into his head, will you? Make him realize what he's driving his whole family into.

STOCKMANN: (*crossing below to* PETER, *puts family behind him*) My family concerns nobody but myself.

PETER: His family and his own town!

STOCKMANN: I'm going to show you who loves his town. The people are going to get the full stink of this corruption, Peter, and then we will see who loves his town.

PETER: You love your town when you blindly, spitefully, stubbornly go ahead trying to cut off our most important industry? I think this has gone beyond opinions and convictions, Thomas. A man who can throw that kind of insinuation around is nothing but a traitor to society!

STOCKMANN: (*striving to control self*) How dare you to . . . ?

CATHERINE: (*running in front of* STOCKMANN; PETRA *pulls* STOCKMANN *back*) Tom!

PETRA: (*grabbing* STOCKMANN'S *arm*) Be careful, Father!

PETER: (*taking hat, starting out* U. R., *with dignity*) I won't expose myself to violence. You have been warned. Consider what you owe yourself and your family. Good day! (*He exits* U. R., *leaving front door open.*)

STOCKMANN: (*pacing* D. R., *then back to* D. L.) He's insulted! *He's* insulted!

CATHERINE: (*crossing* U. C., D. R., *then* L.) It's shameful, Thomas.

PETRA: (*crossing* U. L. C., *to stove, then* R. *to look after* PETER, *back to* C. *at* R. *of* CATHERINE) Oh, I would love to give him a piece of my mind.

STOCKMANN: (*still pacing*) It was my own fault—I should have shown my teeth right from the beginning. He called me a traitor to society. Me! Damn it all, that is not going to stick.

CATHERINE: Please, think; he's got all the power on his side.

STOCKMANN: Yes, but I have the truth on mine.

CATHERINE: Without power, what good is the truth? (*All turn and look at her.*)

STOCKMANN: (*crosses to* CATHERINE) That's ridiculous, Catherine. I have the liberal press with me and the majority, the solid majority. If that isn't power, what is?

CATHERINE: But for Heaven's sake, Tom, you aren't going to . . . ?

STOCKMANN: What am I not going to do—?

CATHERINE: You aren't going to fight it out in public with your brother!

STOCKMANN: What the hell else do you want me to do?

CATHERINE: But it won't do you any earthly good—if they won't do it, they won't. All you'll get out of it is a notice that you're fired.

STOCKMANN: I am going to do my duty, Catherine. Me, the man he calls a traitor to society!

CATHERINE: And how about your duty to your family—the people you're supposed to provide for?

PETRA: Don't always think of us first, Mother.

CATHERINE: You can talk—if worst comes to worst, you can manage for yourself, but what about the boys, Tom, and you and me?

STOCKMANN: What about you? You want me to be the miserable animal who'd crawl up the boots of that damn gang? Will you be happy if I can't face *myself* the rest of my life?

CATHERINE: Tom, Tom, there's so much injustice in the world—you've simply got to learn to live with it. If you go on this way, God help us, we'll have no money again. Is it so long since the North that you have forgotten what it was to live like we lived? Haven't we had enough of that for one lifetime? What will happen to them? We've got nothing if you are fired . . . !

6. *Revue Sketches*
   "Applicant," by Harold Pinter

Scene:	For one man, one woman
Characters:	LAMB, a young man
	MISS PIFFS, an interviewer
Setting:	An office.
Time:	The present.
Situation:	This scene is a self-contained unit which needs no background. The use of sound effects will be useful in playing the scene, particularly as they

help Lamb react to the strange "interview." He is young, intelligent, and eager. Miss Piffs is a model of modern bureaucratic efficiency. The scene begins as Miss Piffs enters the office where Lamb has been anxiously waiting.

PIFFS: Ah, good morning.

LAMB: Oh, good morning, miss.

PIFFS: Are you Mr. Lamb?

LAMB: That's right.

PIFFS: (*Studying a sheet of paper*) Yes. You're applying for this vacant post, aren't you?

LAMB: I am actually, yes.

PIFFS: Are you a physicist?

LAMB: Oh yes, indeed. It's my whole life.

PIFFS: (*Languidly*) Good. Now our procedure is, that before we discuss the applicant's qualifications we like to subject him to a little test to determine his psychological suitability. You've no objection?

LAMB: Oh, good heavens, no.

PIFFS: Jolly good.

(MISS PIFFS *has taken some objects out of a drawer and goes to* LAMB. *She places a chair for him.*)

PIFFS: Please sit down. (*He sits.*) Can I fit these to your palms?

LAMB: (*Affably*) What are they?

PIFFS: Electrodes.

LAMB: Oh yes, of course. Funny little things. (*She attaches them to his palms.*)

PIFFS: Now the earphones. (*She attaches earphones to his head.*)

LAMB: I say, how amusing.

PIFFS: Now I plug in. (*She plugs in to the wall.*)

LAMB: (*A trifle nervously*) Plug in, do you? Oh yes, of course. Yes, you'd have to, wouldn't you? (MISS PIFFS *perches on a high stool and looks down on* LAMB.) This help to determine my . . . my suitability does it?

PIFFS: Unquestionably. Now relax. Just relax. Don't think about a thing.

LAMB: No.

PIFFS: Relax completely. Rela-a-a-x. Quite relaxed? (LAMB *nods.* MISS PIFFS *presses a button on the side of her stool. A piercing high pitched buzz-hum is heard.* LAMB *jolts rigid. His hands go to his earphones. He is propelled from the chair. He tries to crawl under the chair.* MISS PIFFS *watches, impassive. The noise stops.* LAMB *peeps out from under the chair, crawls out, stands, twitches, emits a short chuckle and collapses in the chair.*)

PIFFS: Would you say you were an excitable person?

LAMB: Not—not unduly, no. Of course, I—

PIFFS: Would you say you were a moody person?

LAMB: Moody? No, I wouldn't say I was moody—well, sometimes occasionally I—

PIFFS: Do you ever get fits of depression?

LAMB: Well, I wouldn't call them depression exactly—

PIFFS: Do you often do things you regret in the morning?

LAMB: Regret? Things I regret? Well, it depends what you mean by often, really—I mean when you say often—

PIFFS: Are you often puzzled by women?

LAMB: Women?

PIFFS: Men.

LAMB: Men? Well, I was just going to answer the question about women—

PIFFS: Do you often feel puzzled?

LAMB: Puzzled?

PIFFS: By women.

LAMB: Women?

PIFFS: Men.

LAMB: Oh, now just a minute, I . . . Look, do you want separate answers or a joint answer?

PIFFS: After your day's work do you ever feel tired? Edgy? Fretty? Irritable? At a loose end? Morose? Frustrated? Morbid? Unable to concentrate? Unable to sleep? Unable to eat? Unable to remain seated? Unable to remain upright? Lustful? Indolent? On heat? Randy? Full of desire? Full of energy? Full of dread? Drained? of energy? of dread? of desire? (*Pause*)

LAMB: (*thinking*) Well, it's difficult to say really . . .

PIFFS: Are you a good mixer?

LAMB: Well, you've touched on quite an interesting point there—

PIFFS: Do you suffer from eczema, listlessness, or falling coat?

LAMB: Er . . .

PIFFS: Are you virgo intacta?

LAMB: I beg your pardon?

PIFFS: Are you virgo intacta?

LAMB: Oh; I say, that's rather embarrassing. I mean—in front of a lady—

PIFFS: Are you virgo intacta?

LAMB: Yes, I am, actually. I'll make no secret of it.

PIFFS: Have you always been virgo intacta?

LAMB: Oh yes, always. Always.

PIFFS: From the word go?

LAMB: Go? Oh yes, from the word go.

PIFFS: Do women frighten you? (*She presses a button on the other side of her stool. The stage is plunged into redness, which flashes on and off in time with her questions.*)

PIFFS: (*Building*) Their clothes? Their shoes? Their voices? Their laughter? Their stares? Their way of walking? Their way of sitting? Their way of smiling? Their way of talking? Their mouths? Their hands? Their feet? Their shins? Their thighs? Their knees? Their eyes? Their (*Drumbeat*). Their (*Drumbeat*). Their (*Cymbal bang*). Their (*Trombone chord*). Their (*Bass note*).

LAMB: (*In a high voice*) Well it depends on what you mean really—(*The light still flashes. She presses the other button and the piercing buzz-hum is heard again.* LAMB's *hands go to his earphones. He is propelled from the chair, falls, rolls, crawls, totters and collapses.*) (*Silence.*) (*He lies face upwards.* MISS PIFFS *looks at him then walks to* LAMB *and bends over him.*)

PIFFS: Thank you very much, Mr. Lamb. We'll let you know.

CHAPTER
FIVE

Vocal Technique for the Stage

In our examination of the fundamentals of stage movement, we have seen that firmly established rules govern many basic situations of the theatre. Within the framework of these rules the actor learns to be creative and imaginative. In the same manner, vocal technique must also be learned and used properly in order to achieve maximum effectiveness on stage.

When moving on stage the actor does not move, stand, or sit the way he or she does in everyday life. So too, when using the voice certain modifications are necessary, due to the heightened sense of life which is necessary in the theatre before an audience.

This chapter will look at some of the most important considerations of vocal technique for the stage. A detailed study of the voice is not our purpose at this time; such an examination more properly belongs in a book surveying all the elements of voice training. (For making a thorough study of voice training, the reader may consult any of the excellent texts on the subject listed at the end of this chapter.) Here we will be concerned specifically with two factors of speech in the theatre:

The Voice for Stage Purposes.   Achieving maximum effectiveness of the voice as an instrument for communicating the character to an audience; and

Getting the Most from the Dialogue.   Interpreting the dialogue so as to make it as expressive and meaningful as possible. Learning to use the voice effectively *on stage* should be the goal of every actor, and it is the purpose of this chapter to help in achieving this end.

Although we often overlook voice training in our concentration on stage movement, character analysis, emotional representation, and other facets of the actor's work, the importance of a well-trained voice cannot be too strongly emphasized. Voice, body, and thought *all* contribute toward the realization of an effective characterization.

FIGURE 5.1 *My Fair Lady* by **Lerner and Lowe. Brigham Young University.**

One Voice or Many?

A question that continually reasserts itself during the actor's development concerns versatility and flexibility of the voice. Is it better to have a voice that can project a wide variety of characters of different temperaments and ages or one that is consistent and easily identifiable with the personality of the actor? We recognize immediately that this question is related to the distinctions separating personality and character acting. We have seen that both types of acting are valid and in fact practiced with equal success by various actors. But let us not forget that the voice of uniform quality that conforms to consistent patterns of expression and phrasing will usually consign the actor to a succession of similar roles, a practice often termed "type casting." The good personality actor possesses a voice that is diversified in quality and phrasing and so variable that it may project many emotional states, moods, and temperaments.

The beginning actor would do well to consider that it is useful to make the voice capable not only of communicating the subtleties of mood, temperament, and emotion, but of suggesting various characters as well. Flexibility of voice rather than a striking vocal attractiveness should be the actor's goal. There are many beautiful voices in the theatre that immediately attract us by their quality or distinctiveness. Let us agree that the attractive voice can be a desirable asset in the theatre, *but when we begin to listen to the voice rather than to what it is saying we are not necessarily hearing good acting.* The same frequently holds true for a voice that is unusual or possessed of a peculiar quality. The actor should aim for a well-modulated voice, capable of a variety of uses, serving many characters in varying situations.

Very often we are surprised to discover an unsuspected potential in an actor's voice that has been long buried in a succession of similar roles. Many years ago the noted director Arthur Hopkins was searching for an actor to play the role of a hardened killer in his production of *The Petrified Forest.* He was in the lobby of a theatre one day, out of sight of the stage, when he heard a dry, keen voice that suggested to him exactly the quality he wanted for the role of Duke Mantee. Thus the director was evaluating a potential performer on vocal quality alone, even before he knew who the actor was. Hopkins was surprised to learn that the voice belonged to an actor who had long played a series of light-comedy and stereotyped juvenile roles in which he strolled about countless drawing rooms with a tennis racket in one hand and a drink in the other. Hopkins followed his instinct and cast the actor in the role of the vicious gangster. The actor repeated his role in a film version of the play and eventually established a reputation as one of the finest "badmen" in films. Hopkins' hunch helped to establish the successful second phase of the career of Humphrey Bogart. It is interesting to note that although again he was typecast in a series of roles as the "heavy," it was Bogart's amusing performance in *The African Queen* as a weather-beaten, drunken captain of a small boat in Equatorial Africa that won for this distinguished actor his only Academy Award.

Stark Young has pointed out the importance of a flexible stage voice:

> In a comedy of manners like the *School for Scandal* the voice should be clear, finished, the lips expert, the tongue striking well on the teeth; the tone would go up and down but always be sure of its place in the throat, be crisp, shining, in hand, like the satin and gold of the furniture and costumes, the rapier at the wrist, the lace over it, the worldliness and the wit. In Chekhov it would have the last naturalness, every closeness to feeling and impulse that the moment reveals. In Shakespeare a range of elaborate music, suited to the style, clearness, with warmth of poetic emotion. In D'Annunzio's drama the voice would have to be rich and sensuous, metallic, shading infinitely, the voice of a degenerate god. And so on through the styles and moods of all drama.[1]

Factors of a Good Stage Voice

Good acting requires the effective use of the vocal mechanism to express the intellectual and emotional content of the dialogue. When the actor has succeeded in doing this we may say that he or she is using the voice properly. The following questions may help the actor gauge his or her effectiveness in meeting the demands of voice for the theatre.

Does the Voice Call Attention to Itself?   Do we listen to the voice rather than the matter it should be communicating? Listening to recordings of actors who were prominent in the early part of this century, such as E. H. Sothern, Rose Coghlan, Julia Marlowe, and others, one is struck by the emphasis on intonation and other discarded elocutionary tricks. Speeches took on the aspect of an operatic aria, designed to display the vocal resources of the actor rather than to communicate meaning. In the present day we have departed from this formal style of reading and choose to have the voice serve the dialogue rather than the actor. The voice should be completely appropriate to the requirements of the role.

Is the Voice Difficult to Hear?   The voice should be heard easily by all members of the audience and projected with adequate volume and clarity in every situation. Volume may have to be increased or decreased by the demands of the action, but at no time should it fall below a level that is audible in every part of the auditorium.

Can the Actor Be Understood?   Good articulation plays an important role in projection and in making dialogue meaningful. Slovenly articulation is

---

1. Stark Young, *Theatre Practice* (New York: Charles Scribner's Sons, 1926), pp. 159–60.

never desirable, either in realistic or in presentational productions. Indeed, many of the great plays from the past require an extremely high degree of competence in stage diction and clarity of expression.

Is the Voice Monotonous? Variety in pitch, rate, and loudness is essential if the voice is to prove interesting. It is best if the actor does not use variety simply for the sake of avoiding monotony but permits the substance of the lines to indicate where variety will be most expressive of the meaning. Usually a comprehension of the character will induce such variety, but even well-produced and carefully articulated speech may fall short of effectiveness on the stage. As we may remember when we discussed the physical aspect of acting, the actor should assimilate the techniques of voice for the stage into his or her work so that little thought is devoted to the technique itself. This requires a thorough knowledge of the proper use of voice and articulation. Often rehearsals produce excessive fatigue, especially during a trial-and-error period when many different qualities and inflectional patterns are tried. Understanding the potentials of the voice will make this period less difficult and not only provide the means of achieving the proper vocal characterization but also lessen the strain that often accompanies an attempt to alter the normal voice.

Vocal Production

Because our speaking mechanism consists of organs primarily designed for other purposes, we refer to speech as an *overlaid function*. Speech is secondary to other vital functions that the speech organs perform. The speech process consists of four parts: (1) breathing, (2) phonation, or the initial creation of sound, (3) resonation, or the amplifying of the sound, and (4) articulation, or the shaping of intelligible syllables.

The primary function of breathing is to sustain life, not to provide the power needed for vocalization. Although we tend to think that the larynx was designed specifically for the initiation of sound, it is in fact a type of valve designed to keep unwanted foreign matter from our lungs. Our tongue and teeth were designed for eating rather than articulation. When we undergo moments of great stress we often find that the organs are unable to perform their secondary functions.

Breathing

The lungs provide the power for the vocal mechanism. It is through the control of breathing that we may increase or decrease volume, regulate phrasing, and provide the necessary support for vocal tone. To better understand the function of breathing and vocal production, it might be helpful to compare the total mechanism with a wind instrument such as a clarinet. (See Figure 5.2).

In the clarinet, sound is produced when the reed is set in vibration by air blown into the tube. Comparing the diagram of the vocal mechanism with that of the clarinet, we may note that the vocal mechanism produces sound by means of an air stream passing through the larynx, with the vocal folds performing much the same function as the reed in the wind instrument. The resonating areas in the throat and head serve to reinforce the sound in the same manner as the tube of the wind instrument.

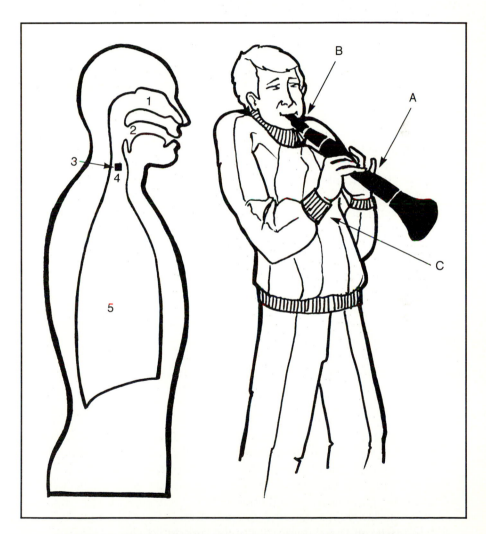

FIGURE 5.2 **Vocal production.** *Resonators:* **(1) nose, (2) mouth, (3) larynx, and (A) tube of clarinet.** *Vibrator:* **(4) vocal cords, and (B) reed. Source of air pressure: (5) lungs, and (C) lungs.**

Unless one is afflicted with a disease of the respiratory system, inhalation poses no difficulty. Although in some cases the supply of air *inhaled* may be insufficient for sustained speech in the theatre, the difficulty more often lies in establishing good habits for controlled *exhalation*. As in our analogy with the wind instrument, we know that if we can exhale air in proper quantities and in a controlled manner, we may produce a loud, clear, and sustained tone. The question, in relation to the actor's needs, is this: *How can I get more air into my lungs and control its expiration?*

Many beginning actors are surprised to learn that they are breathing improperly for stage purposes. Proper breathing involves the muscles of the thorax, the diaphragm, and the abdominal area.

The correct sequence of inhalation is as follows: (1) The muscles of the thorax elevate the ribs. (2) The diaphragm moves downward, expanding the area of the thorax. (3) The resulting differential of air pressures causes air to rush into the lungs. (4) The lungs fill the enlarged area of the thoracic cavity. (See Figure 5.3).

Exhalation reverses this process. The muscles of the abdomen push the diaphragm up into the thoracic cavity, decreasing its size and forcing air from the lungs. It is not uncommon to expel a greater amount of air than is necessary during vocalization, causing shortness of breath or gasping and limiting the ability to phrase properly when reading dialogue. The steady stream of air needed for proper volume and sustained phrasing in acting can be achieved only if the muscles of the abdomen contract gradually to provide air continually rather than all at once.

One of the more common causes of a weak voice and poor tone quality is "chest breathing." Chest breathing hinders the effective use of the voice on the speaker's platform or on the stage. This type of breathing utilizes only the upper chest for inhalation. The shoulders tense into a strained position and the collar bones rise during each inhalation. The consequences are an unsteady voice, lack of volume, and a jerkiness in exhalation during vocalization.

The following exercises should help the actor to determine whether the manner of breathing is hindering vocal effectiveness. The exercises will also provide ways to develop good breathing habits and make volume control more useful for stage purposes.

1. Lie down and place your hands on the abdominal area. Breathe as usual. Note whether the abdomen rises and falls during inhalation and exhalation. If the abdomen does not rise during inhalation, it is likely that breathing habits are poor. Relax and continue until you feel the abdomen rise and fall with each breath. Try this exercise first in a prone position and then in a standing position. Inhale slowly and make an effort to push out the abdominal muscles as you inhale.
2. In a standing, relaxed position inhale as deeply as possible. Hold the abdominal muscles as firm as possible. Count out loud in a clear, firm,

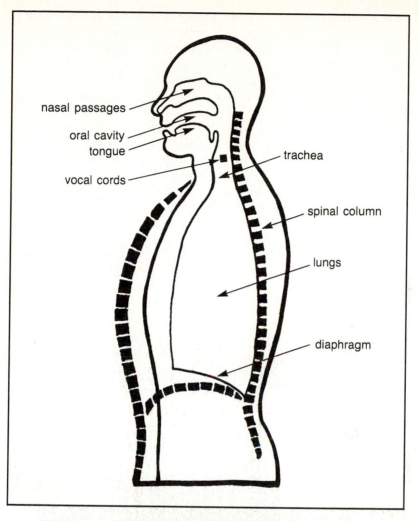

nasal passages

oral cavity
tongue

vocal cords

trachea

spinal column

lungs

diaphragm

FIGURE 5.3 The speech organs. Dotted line shows effect of deep inhalation within the thoracic cavity.

voice. Make a definite effort not to contract or to release the abdominal muscles immediately. You should be able to count to twenty without too much difficulty. Continue this exercise until you can count to thirty. Now try to inhale in the upper chest area only. As you exhale, count out loud in a clear, firm voice. How does your count compare to your count when you used the abdominal area?

3. In a standing position inhale as deeply as possible, and then emit a stream of air with a hissing sound. Continue this exercise until you can continue this hissing sound without a break for thirty seconds.

4. In a standing position inhale as deeply as possible. In one breath repeat the following phrase. Make each repetition louder than the preceding one: *Cowards die many times before their death, the valiant never taste of death but once.*

Vocal Tone

Phonation, or the production of the vocal tone, is initiated by the vocal folds, which are located in the larynx, and amplified by the resonating chambers in the head and neck. The larynx consists of masses of cartilage and muscle which support and operate the vocal folds. These thick folds, which are variously called the vocal cords, vocal bands, or vocal lips, produce the vocal tone when their outer edges are set in vibration by the air stream exhaled from the lungs.

Tautness and constriction may be the most serious impediments to using the voice with maximal effectiveness. Constriction in the throat and laryngeal area may be brought on by nervousness, fatigue, or emotional stress and can become a serious problem, for it will affect both phonation and the resonation of vocal tone. Frequently the result is harshness and stridency. Projecting extensive dialogue from a constricted throat during successive performances may give rise to longer-lasting consequences: the voice may eventually become hoarse and laryngitis may result.

Lynn Redgrave recalls problems with her voice during her years of training. She said:

> It used to go up from nerves a lot; it was fairly thin and didn't have much body to it . . . What I hadn't realized was how badly I had used it for a long time: I started to lose it even when I wasn't pushing it very hard . . . If you're using it wrong, it can be thrown out so early; a bit of nerves, you tighten and that's it.[2]

In more serious cases permanent damage may be done to the vocal folds.

The vocal tone initiated by the vibrating of the vocal folds is quite meager, and if it were not for the amplification of the sound by several resonating chambers, human speech would be almost inaudible. The major resonators are the pharynx, the mouth, and the nasal passages. Differences in the size and shape of these resonators from one person to another account for the distinctive quality of each person's voice. Any factor that influences the functioning of these resonating chambers will produce a marked change in vocal quality. The change in tone brought about by slight modifications of nasal resonance is known to every victim of hay fever and the common head cold.

---

2. Lynn Redgrave, quoted in Joanmarie Kalter, *Actors on Acting* (New York: Sterling Publishing Co., Inc., 1979), p. 84.

The nasal passages have little function in resonation; the pharynx and mouth are more important. Like phonation, resonation is also hampered by tenseness and constriction. An "open" throat and mouth are essential for achieving proper resonance. Any partial closure of the resonating chambers may seriously hamper the production of good vocal tone. One such problem frequently encountered is a tendency to arch the back of the tongue during phonation. This simple habit narrows the oral opening, resulting in a considerable loss of volume and fullness of the tone.

Because acting may impose greater emotional stress and tension than a person's normal activities, projecting good vocal tone is often a serious problem. The importance of *relaxation* as the proper means of eliminating these difficulties cannot be stressed too strongly. Relaxation helps to produce good vocal quality, with fullness of tone and freedom from hoarseness, stridency, and strain. The following exercises are designed to help develop relaxation for the production of good vocal tone:

1. In order to clarify the difference between tension and relaxation, follow this procedure. (a) Stand at attention. Tense every muscle. Pull in the chin and the abdomen, keeping the back straight. Hold this position for ten seconds. Note how uncomfortable it is to retain this position. (b) Begin to relax *slowly*. Let the head and shoulders droop, the arms and hands hang loosely. Try to eliminate every semblance of tension. Try to feel the tension leave through the fingers. Wiggle them if it helps. Note the difference between the tensed and relaxed positions. (c) Sit down and tense yourself as you did in the standing position. After maintaining the tension for ten seconds, slowly relax. Again note the difference between the tensed and relaxed positions.

2. Work on Exercise 1 until you have little difficulty in making the transition from tension to relaxation. Try to make the change from an extremely tensed to an extremely relaxed position as rapidly as possible. Continue to do this so that you may be able to make an immediate and complete change.

3. Tense your neck and throat until they become rigid. If possible make the cords stand out in the neck. Relax the throat by yawning several times. Read the following passages, first with a tense neck and throat and then after you have yawned and relaxed the throat. Compare your readings. After comparing the two readings, work for as full and rich a vocal tone as possible.

GHOST: I am thy father's spirit,
   Doomed for a certain term to walk the night
   And for the day confined to fast in fires
   Till the foul crimes done in my days of nature
   Are burnt and purged away.

William Shakespeare, *Hamlet*

ANTONY: This was the noblest Roman of them all.
     All the conspirators, save only he,
     Did that they did in envy of great Caesar;
     He only, in a general honest thought
     And common good to all, made one of them.
     His life was gentle, and the elements
     So mixed in him that Nature might stand up
     And say to all the world, "This was a man."

William Shakespeare,
Julius Caesar

Out upon the angry wind! how from sighing, it began to bluster round the merry forge, banging at the wicket, and grumbling in the chimney, as if it bullied the jolly bellows from doing anything to order.

Charles Dickens,
Martin Chuzzlewit

4. Observe the back of your tongue and your soft palate in a mirror. Inhale as if to begin a yawn, and note the height of the soft palate and the lowered position of the tongue. Practice until you are able to develop this "open throat" position without inhaling prior to the yawn.
5. Practice the open-throat position until you feel it to be relaxed. Remember that the tongue should be depressed and the soft palate raised. With the throat open, read the following short passages:

Oh, how I long for good oral tone.

Tomorrow, and tomorrow, and tomorrow,
Creeps in this petty pace from day to day,
To the last syllable of recorded time.

William Shakespeare,
Macbeth

O you that are so strong and cold,
O blower, are you young or old?
Are you a beast of field and tree,
Or just a stronger child than me?
    O wind, a-blowing all day long,
    O wind, that sings so loud a song!

Robert Louis Stevenson

The voice of the west wind is wooing my footsteps,
The clouds scamper onward to show me the way:
The grasses are mocking the high, swaying treetops;
I'm off at their bidding—
    Away!

Author Unknown

Distinctness

Audiences have great difficulty in understanding speech that is poorly enunciated and slovenly. The stage situation focuses attention upon carelessness in speech which is generally overlooked in normal conversation.

Any number of factors can create improper articulation—among them substitution of improper speech sounds, incorrect use of the articulators, and foreign-language influences. Such functional speech problems, however, constitute only a small fraction of the difficulties that beset the actor when reading. *The most common articulation fault results from carelessness.* Poor enunciation may usually be traced to lazy or slovenly movement of the lips and tongue. The carry-over of habits from everyday conversation and the added tensions of stage activities simply amplify the problem.

Good articulation does not mean an overly precise or exaggerated pronunciation of every word. Exaggeration of this kind will only draw attention to itself and may be as detrimental as careless articulation. In striving to overcome poor enunciation, some actors overarticulate to the extent that their speech is obviously forced and false. Excessively precise articulation of syllables in unstressed positions may serve only to highlight the actor's problem. One young actor with careless speech learned this lesson when he was cast in the role of a gangster. Acutely aware of his diction problem, he attempted to correct it by consciously and carefully overarticulating every word he spoke on stage. The result was speech that had the tempo and rhythm of a hardened hoodlum but suggested that the character had spent a few months at an English finishing school for gentlemen. The audience's reaction to his performance may be imagined. Distinct speech on stage calls for the proper and clear articulation of sounds in the context of *correct pronunciation* and *stress*.

Distinctness may be improved by simply opening the mouth more than is habitual in nonstage speech and increasing the activity of the articulators, without adding any undue stress to the words themselves. No matter how well the actor has mastered control of volume, projection is seriously limited when speech is not crisp and clear.

An excellent exercise to help make the actor aware of the importance of the articulators involves the use of a pencil and some dialogue from any well-written play.

Read at usual stage projection level a passage such as those found at the end of this chapter. After finishing, take a pencil and place it lengthwise between the front teeth. Clamp down on the pencil with the teeth and re-read the monologue for a period of two minutes. You will notice that proper articulation is difficult because of the impediment between the teeth. You will need to work harder than usual to make the passage meaningful. It is also very likely that the muscles around the jaw will hurt when you are doing this exercise. This sensation indicates that muscles that have not been used extensively are getting a good workout.

Remove the pencil and read the speech a third time. You should be aware immediately that this reading is more distinct than the first attempt. You have been forced to use the articulators more than is customary, and it has produced surprisingly crisp speech. Eventually the old habits will return, but continued practice with the pencil should help to eliminate the habits causing indistinctiveness in speech.

Projection

Projection seems to have become an increasing problem during the past several years. A number of factors have contributed to this difficulty, especially the frequency with which we watch television drama, and the increasing "naturalism" of the motion picture. The close-up techniques of these media, which produce an effect of intimacy, make projection above a conversational level inappropriate. New actors whose early exposure to acting technique has come primarily from these media may find particular difficulty with stage projection.

Undoubtedly the introspective nature of many contemporary plays has also served to amplify the problem. Also, the trend toward a quieter and less exuberant style of theatre produces in many young actors a natural reticence about really "letting go" on stage. Often the tensions of stage performance interfere with good speech habits and hence limit the ability of the actor to project the dialogue so that it is *heard and understood by every member of the audience.*

Projection is not synonymous with adequate volume level. Proper projection of dialogue includes effective use of the entire speech mechanism. The following three factors are directly related to good projection on stage:

1. *Controlled exhalation for adequate volume level.* This does not mean shouting or yelling, but the use of good breathing habits to produce a reasonably loud, firm voice.
2. *Proper phonation and resonation* so that the voice is not pinched and small. The throat should be relaxed and open.
3. *Crisp articulation* so that dialogue is spoken distinctly.

A breakdown in any of these three closely related elements will result in faulty projection, and with it failure to communicate to part of the audience.

Getting the Most from the Dialogue

Making the voice an instrument of the actor's intention requires both sensitivity and understanding. The sensitivity will grow as the actor's perception of the role increases. Although dialogue must never be read in accordance with inflexible and mechanical rules, knowledge of the basic factors of vocal expressiveness is essential.

Rate

The term "rate" refers to the *number of words spoken during a given period of time*. The rate of speech, therefore, will be affected both by the actual speed of speech and by the number and length of the pauses inserted. The average rate of speech varies considerably from one actor to another, and indeed during any given play it will differ for the same individual from one scene to the next. Usually the rate of stage speech is about 130 to 150 words per minute, but there will be occasions when a faster or slower rate is required. One point worth remembering is that *stage speech requires a much slower rate than that which is used in everyday conversation*. If one were to use the normal rate of everyday speech on stage, it might well be unintelligible. Certain considerations help to determine the appropriate rate of speech:

1. *The role.* The rate of speech used on stage often suggests certain character traits or temperament. A young, excitable, or dynamic individual might well use a faster rate than one who is aged, reflective, or of a quiet disposition.
2. *The type of play.* The tempo of a play may well determine the rate to be used by the entire cast. A comedy or farce, for example, will usually require a faster tempo than a melodrama or tragedy.
3. *The purpose of the dialogue.* The actual content of the dialogue often will suggest to the actor when rate should be increased or decreased. Material of a trivial or inconsequential nature will require a relatively faster rate. When the content is important or when important exposition is to be communicated, a decrease in rate will often help to make the dialogue more meaningful.

In plays that require a particularly rapid tempo, often it is wise to decrease the rate of the more important words or ideas. Significant phrases may be made relatively important by prolonging selected words or inserting pauses in the most meaningful places. It is well to remember that no matter what rate is dictated by the character or tempo of the play, *variety of rate* is essential to avoid monotony during the playing of any protracted scene. The best rule to follow when determining the rate to use is this: *Proper rate will vary with the demands of the action and the character.*

It may be of value now to turn back to the exercise monologues in Chapter 1 and at the end of this chapter in order to re-evaluate them in terms of proper rate. Some monologues will undoubtedly require a faster rate than others. It will be helpful also to experiment in order to determine how the intent of the character's meaning may be changed by the simple device of altering the rate in different parts of the monologue.

Pitch

Pitch refers to the position of the spoken sound on the musical scale. Voices are classified on both the basis of quality and pitch range. Thus, the tenor voice has a higher pitch range than that of the bass; the soprano voice is higher than the contralto. Pitch is also a major factor in the actor's technique of expression. There are normally three recurrent pitch difficulties that inhibit the actor's effectiveness:

1. *Pitch may be too high or too low.* The habitual pitch of the actor may be above or below the *optimum* or ideal pitch, limiting the actor in the range of pitch changes which are possible in one direction.
2. *There may be a lack of variety in pitch.* When there is failure to make pitch changes during speech, the result is *monopitch*, sometimes mistakenly called *monotone*. Such speech is dull, uninteresting, and unlikely to retain audience attention for long.
3. *The voice may fall into a pitch pattern.* There may be a number of pitch changes while speaking, but such changes may be repetitious and used without any regard for the exact nature of the material.

The actor will have occasion to depict a great range of emotions in various plays. Many of our basic emotional responses are normally associated with certain pitch levels, and it is imperative that the actor be able to call upon a pitch range adequate to project these emotions. Pitch levels have the following associational values for the listener:

Low pitch is generally associated with deep-keyed emotional states, such as religious awe and sorrow, and is also suggestive of sincerity.

High pitch is often associated with a heightened emotional state such as fear and terror, uncontrollable anger or rage, great excitement, and even hysteria.

As we have just noted in our discussion of rate, variety is important if the actor is to maintain the interest of the audience. Pitch, too, must be varied, not only to avoid monotony but to aid in the communication of meaning. The voice may be varied in pitch by the use of *step* and *inflection*. It is well to make a distinction between these two terms, because they are easily confused.

Step is a pitch change from word to word in a phrase or sentence. Pitch changes of this type are frequently used as a means of emphasizing a key word or idea. In a *step* pitch change, then, there is no change within a word but there is a change in pitch as the speaker moves from one word to another.

Inflection refers to pitch change or slide *within* one word or sound, in either an upward or downward direction. The word ''really'' serves as a simple example to illustrate how a change in inflection produces a change in meaning. If the word is read with an upward inflection (reálly) a question is clearly implied; read with a downward inflection (reàlly) it may connote boredom or an affirmative statement of understanding. A change in inflectional pitch often conveys a completely different meaning for the same word.

Changing pitch by step or inflection is a fundamental technique in stage speech and must be mastered by all competent actors. Variety in pitch will grow from the needs of the characterization and the drama. *Mechanical pitch changes made simply to avoid monotony in speech must not be used.*

Getting Meaning from the Line

In analyzing dialogue and attempting to extract meaning, the actor should be careful not to put too much value on the first reading given to any line. There is rarely only one right way to read a line.

Dialogue in any competently written play cannot be divorced from the play without suffering a fundamental loss of meaning. Because dialogue is written to advance action and illustrate character, to set mood or establish locale, a line may have several meanings suggestive of each of these factors. During the preliminary examination and early rehearsals we often tend to give dialogue a somewhat mechanical and stereotyped interpretation. As we proceed through the rehearsal period, we discover new and subtle relationships among several portions of the dialogue. As our understanding of the character of the play and the purpose of each line of dialogue increases, we add nuances that make for an interpretation quite different from that which we gave to the dialogue during our first reading.

The actor should try to avoid imparting meaning simply by mechanical means during the early rehearsal period. Too often such readings become permanently fixed in the playing of the role. A mechanical and studied reading becomes all too evident to the audience, who will reject such a performance as lifeless and dull. The meaning and emotional color of a line or phrase will grow as perception of the character and the character's motivations grow. As an understanding of the play and character develops, the actor should be able to make the dialogue meaningful by the use of shading, organization, and emphasis.

Shading

The simplest word or vocal response may have a number of contrasting meanings. Seizing on the more obvious meaning may prevent a deeper understanding of its value in the scene or the play. This point can be easily illustrated by choosing as an example the simple exclamation "Oh." Let us assume that it is spoken in the following brief sequence of dialogue:

JANE: Tom fell down and injured his leg.
MARY: Oh.

How is one to interpret the exclamation "Oh"? The meaning "What a terrible thing to happen to Tom" may be absolutely correct. Further consideration, however, may suggest many different ways of replying to the statement about the unfortunate and clumsy young man. The short dialogue should be examined again to see how many of the following *nine* meanings it can be given.

   Try to read the word "Oh" in a manner that will suggest each of the following possible reactions:

	An Attitude	*That Intends to Convey the Meaning:*
1.	Indifference	"It makes no difference to me. I couldn't care less!"
2.	Comprehension	"So he did go through with his plan to climb the tree after all."
3.	Noncomprehension	"I don't follow you. Who's Tom?"
4.	Inattention	"I'm sorry, what did you say? I was thinking of something else."
5.	Disbelief	"It couldn't possibly be Tom."
6.	Disgust	"He did it again, the young fool."
7.	Pity	"What a shame, he's such a nice young man."
8.	Shock	"But Tom is due to play halfback tomorrow in the football game."
9.	Pleasure	"Good, I never liked him anyway. Serves him right."

It is clear that the response in itself has no inherent meaning until we relate it to the context of the play. Other words or exclamations easily provide the same type of exercise. They are helpful in sharpening our perception of the values that we might wish to attach to any word or short phrase. This list might include: "Really!" "So!" "Yes!" "No!" "Of course!" "You!" As an exercise, these words should be read with an attempt to give at least five different meanings to each.

Organization and Emphasis

We easily recognize that simple words and phrases may suggest various meanings and emotional colors. The extended phrase or complete sentence may call for more complex techniques. The way to decide on the organization and emphasis of words is to understand the *ideas* they convey. Mental laziness is often the cause of our failure to perceive the correct relationship between words and the ideas they are intended to convey.

Many individuals are unable to transmit the real meaning of what they intend to say. Confusion, misinterpretations, and misunderstandings frequently arise from our inability to state clearly what we mean. We develop a type of "mental laziness" which gives rise to a half-idea, a half-conception, a half-truth. This occurs not only in the theatre but in everyday life as well.

The following sentence serves as an illustration of how disaster will occur when we misplace a pause and fail to scrutinize the value of the *organization* of ideas in reading.

Victory unlikely for army to fail again.

Read the sentence with the pause after "victory" and we have:

Victory—unlikely for army to fail again.

Insert the pause after "unlikely" and the phrase reads:

Victory unlikely—for army to fail again.

Emphasis is the meaningful stress we give to any word in a phrase or sentence. Just as we may stress certain syllables in a word and leave others unstressed, so too we may stress key words in a phrase and give to others a subsidiary emphasis. Words may be emphasized by (*a*) force, (*b*) pause (before or after), (*c*) prolongation of the word, and (*d*) inflection. A phrase such as "John won the race today" may seem a simple statement of fact, but the shifting of emphasis from one key word to another may completely alter the significance of the sentence. All of the four devices for emphasis may be used in this phrase to connote the intended meaning.

1. "*John* won the race today." The phrase indicates clearly that John won against all competition. The others (our friends, perhaps?) lost.
2. "John won the *race* today." John may have lost in some other competition but he did win the race. Perhaps he failed his math exam.
3. "John *won* the race today." Despite the doubt raised in some quarters, John really did win. Those sore losers!
4. "John won the race *today*." John may not have won yesterday, but he was certainly victorious today. It's about time, too!

Clearly the implications are quite dissimilar, differentiated by the shift of emphasis from one key word to another. The importance of organization and emphasis may be illustrated by choosing any number of phrases or sentences taken at random from the dialogue of a play and searching for the key words.

The following straightforward sentence will serve to illustrate how it is possible, by means of organization and emphasis, to suggest numerous and almost unexpected meanings from one line of dialogue.

I want to go to the party with Jim Saturday night.

Try reading the sentence without any emotional overtones, attempting only to communicate a simple piece of information. How did you read it? What does it really mean? Might not any of the following implications be correct?

Read the line to mean:

1. I want to go not on Friday but on Saturday.
2. I want to go in the evening, not in the afternoon.
3. I don't want to go to the movies; I prefer the party.
4. I don't want to go with Harry, but with Jim.
5. I don't want to meet Jim there; I want him to take me.
6. Only one of us can go to the party, and I have decided to go.
7. What you may have heard is wrong; I really do want to go.
8. I don't want to go to the small party, but to the big formal.

Each of these meanings may be suggested directly by emphasis and organization *without* any emotional coloring. If we were to give to these various meanings the character's emotional viewpoint, the number of readings that might be given to the line would increase greatly. The character might be very happy and still intend to impart any of the eight suggested meanings relative to state of mind.

Now read the line with each of the meanings already suggested and any others you care to add, but include the following *emotional colorings: sadness, gaiety, anger, love, timidity, indifference.*

We now have forty-eight combinations that may correctly convey the meaning of the line. Many more are certainly possible. If we were to ask, "which meaning is correct?" the answer, of course, would be that we don't know. We do not have enough information about the character, the action, or the mood of the play. Such information comes as we delve into the play, analyze the character, and rehearse with our fellow actors. What we do know, however, is that it is possible to give even the simplest line of dialogue a multiplicity of meanings, deriving primarily from our comprehension of its purpose in the play. At any rate, let us hope the speaker gets to the party.

Vocal technique, then, is only a means to an end. When we understand and utilize its great potential, however, we take a great step forward on the road to the successful fulfillment of the actor's goal—a believable and *meaningful* portrayal of character.

SUGGESTIONS FOR FURTHER READING

Akin, Johnnye. *And So We Speak: Voice and Articulation.* New York: Prentice-Hall, Inc., 1958.

Berry, Cecily. *Voice and the Actor.* New York: Macmillan Co., 1974.

Blunt, Jerry. *Stage Dialects.* San Francisco: Chandler Publishing Co., 1967.

Brigance, William N., and Henderson, Florence. *A Drill Manual for Improvising Speech.* New York: J. B. Lippincott Co., 1939.

Eisenson, Jon. *Voice and Diction.* 3rd ed. New York: Macmillan Co., 1974.

Hahn, Elise et al. *Basic Voice Training for Speech.* New York: McGraw-Hill, 1957.

Kenyon, John S., and Knott, Thomas A. *A Pronouncing Dictionary of American English.* Springfield, Mass.: Merriam, 1944.

Lessac, Arthur. *The Use and Training of the Human Voice.* 2nd ed. New York: Drama Book Specialists, 1967.

Linklatter, Kristin. *Freeing the Natural Voice.* New York: Drama Book Specialists, 1976.

Machlin, Evangeline. *Speech for the Stage.* New York: Theatre Arts Books, 1970.

Turner, J. Clifford, *Voice and Speech for the Theatre.* 3rd ed. Revised by Malcolm Morrison. New York: Drama Book Specialists, 1977.

Vocal Exercises

As important as it is to develop the physical mechanism in order to make it flexible and able to project the greatest possible range of physical expressiveness, so too must the actor make the voice adequate to the demands placed on it in any given role. The purpose of the following selections is to provide practical exercises that will help develop a wide range of vocal expressiveness. The first group of exercises contains articulation problems frequently found in certain types of plays. The second group makes demands on a greater range of vocal resources, including variety, phrasing, emphasis, and dramatic pointing. Although many of the selections are not from dramatic literature, all of them require the fullest competence in stage speech, if the actor is to realize their dramatic potential.

Articulation

Each of the following selections contains pitfalls for the actor with sloppy speech. Most of them are patter songs from the operettas of Gilbert and Sullivan. These passages require not only precise articulation but facility in delivery and careful pointing. Merely getting through the selection without error should not be the goal of the actor here: *scintillating and seemingly effortless delivery* is necessary for the successful presentation of these exercises.

> Oh! my name is John Wellington Wells,
> I'm a dealer in magic and spells,
>> In blessings and curses
>> And ever-filled purses,
> In prophecies, witches, and knells.
>
> If you want a proud foe to "make tracks"—
> If you'd melt a rich uncle in wax—
>> You've but to look in
>> On our resident Djinn,
> Number seventy, Simmery Axe!
>
> We've a first-class assortment of magic;
>> And for raising a posthumous shade
> With effects that are comic or tragic,
>> There's no cheaper house in the trade.
> Love-philtre—we've quantities of it;
>> And for knowledge if any one burns,
> We keep an extremely small prophet, a prophet
>> Who brings us unbounded returns:

For he can prophesy
With a wink *of* his eye,
Peep with security
Into futurity,
Sum up your history,
Clear up a mystery,
Humour proclivity
For a nativity—for a nativity;
With mirrors so magical,
Tetrapods tragical,
Bogies spectacular,
Answers oracular,
Facts astronomical,
Solemn or comical,
And, if you want it, he
Makes a reduction on taking a quantity!

Oh! If any one anything lacks,
He'll find it all ready in stacks,
    If he'll only look in
    On the resident Djinn,
Number seventy, Simmery Axe!

He can raise you hosts
    Of ghosts,
  And that without reflectors;
And creepy things
    With wings,
  And gaunt and grisly spectres.
He can fill you crowds
    Of shrouds,
  And horrify you vastly;
He can rack your brains
    With chains,
  And gibberings grim and ghastly!

    Then, if you plan it, he
    Changes organity,
    With an urbanity,
    Full of Satanity,
    Vexes humanity
    With an inanity
    Fatal to vanity—
Driving your foes to the verge of insanity!

    Barring tautology,
    In demonology,
    'Lectro-biology,

Mystic nosology,
Spirit philology,
High-class astrology,
Such is his knowledge, he
Isn't the man to require an apology!

Oh! my name is John Wellington Wells,
I'm a dealer in magic and spells,
In blessings and curses
And ever-filled purses,
In prophecies, witches, and knells.
If any one anything lacks,
He'll find it all ready in stacks,
If he'll only look in
On the resident Djinn,
Number seventy, Simmery Axe!

"The Sorcerer's Song,"
W. S. Gilbert, *The Sorcerer*

I am the very model of a modern Major-General,
I've information vegetable, animal, and mineral,
I know the kings of England, and I quote the fights historical,
From Marathon to Waterloo, in order categorical;
I'm very well acquainted too with matters mathematical,
I understand equations, both the simple and quadratical,
About binomial theorem I'm teeming with a lot o' news—
With many cheerful facts about the square of the hypotenuse.
I'm very good at integral and differential calculus,
I know the scientific names of beings animalculous;
In short, in matters vegetable, animal, and mineral,
I am the very model of a modern Major-General.

I know our mythic history, King Arthur's and Sir Caradoc's,
I answer hard acrostics, I've a pretty taste for paradox,
I quote in elegiacs all the crimes of Heliogabalus,
In conics I can floor peculiarities parabolous.
I can tell undoubted Raphaels from Gerard Dows and Zoffanies,
I know the croaking chorus from the *Frogs* of Aristophanes,
Then I can hum a fugue of which I've heard the music's din afore,
And whistle all the airs from that infernal nonsense *Pinafore*.
Then I can write a washing bill in Babylonic cuneiform,
And tell you every detail of Caractacus's uniform;
In short, in matters vegetable, animal, and mineral,
I am the very model of a modern Major-General.

In fact, when I know what is meant by "mamelon" and "ravelin,"
When I can tell at sight a chassepôt rifle from a javelin,
When such affairs as sorties and surprises I'm more wary at,
And when I know precisely what is meant by "commissariat,"

When I have learnt what progress has been made in modern gunnery,
When I know more of tactics than a novice in a nunnery:
In short, when I've a smattering of elemental strategy,
You'll say a better Major-General has never *sat* a gee—
For my military knowledge, though I'm plucky and adventury,
Has only been brought down to the beginning of the century;
But still in matters vegetable, animal, and mineral,
I am the very model of a modern Major-General.

> "The Major-General's
> Song," W. S. Gilbert, *The
> Pirates of Penzance*

When you're lying awake with a dismal headache, and repose is tabooed by
    anxiety,
I conceive you may use any language you choose to indulge in without
    impropriety;
For your brain is on fire—the bedclothes conspire of usual slumber to plunder
    you:
First your counterpane goes and uncovers your toes, and your sheet slips de-
    murely from under you;
Then the blanketing tickles—you feel like mixed pickles, so terribly sharp is the
    pricking,
And you're hot and you're cross, and you tumble and toss till there's nothing
    'twixt you and the ticking;
Then your bedclothes all creep to the floor in a heap, and you pick 'em all up in
    a tangle,
Next your pillow resigns and politely declines to remain at its usual angle.
Well, you get some repose in the form of a doze, with hot eyeballs and head
    ever aching,
But your slumbering teems with such horrible dreams that you'd very much
    better be waking;
For you dream you are crossing the Channel, and tossing about in a steamer
    from Harwich—
Which is something between a large bathing machine and a very small second-
    class carriage—
And you're giving a treat (penny ice and cold meat) to a party of friends and
    relations—
They're a ravenous horde—and they all came on board at Sloan Square and
    South Kensington Stations.
And bound on that journey you find your attorney (who started that morning
    from Devon);
He's a bit undersized, and you don't feel surprised when he tells you he's only
    eleven.
Well, you're driving like mad with this singular lad (by the by, the ship's now a
    four-wheeler),
And you're playing round games, and he calls you bad names when you tell
    him that "ties pay the dealer";
But this you can't stand, so you throw up your hand, and you find you're as
    cold as an icicle,

In your shirt and your socks (the black silk with gold clocks), crossing Salisbury
  Plain on a bicycle:
And he and the crew are on bicycles too—which they've somehow or other in-
  vested in—
And he's telling the tars all the particu*lars* of a company he's interested in—
It's a scheme of devices, to get at low prices all goods from cough mixtures to
  cables
(Which tickled the sailors), by treating retailers as though they were all *vege*ta-
  bles—
You get a good spadesman to plant a small tradesman (first take off his boots
  with a boot-tree),
And his legs will take root, and his fingers will shoot, and they'll blossom and
  bud like a fruit-tree—
From the greengrocer tree you get grapes and green pea, cauliflower, pine-
  apple, and cranberries,
While the pastrycook plant cherry brandy will grant, apple puffs, and three-
  corners, and Banburys—
The shares are a penny, and ever so many are taken by Rothschild and Baring,
And just as a few are allotted to you, you awake with a shudder despairing—
You're a regular wreck, with a crick in your neck; and no wonder you snore for
  your head's on the floor, and you're needles and pins from your soles to
  your shins; and your flesh is a-creep, and your left leg's asleep; and you've
  cramps in your toes, and a fly on your nose, and some fluff in your lung,
  and a feverish tongue, and a thirst that's intense, and a general sense that
  you haven't been sleeping in clover;
But the darkness has passed, and it's daylight at last, and the night has been
  long—ditto, ditto, my song—and thank Goodness they're both of them
  over!

> "The Lord Chancellor's
> Nightmare," W. S.
> Gilbert, *Iolanthe*

A *short* direction
To avoid dejection,
By variations
In occupations,
And prolongation
Of relaxation,
And combinations
Of recreations,
And disputation
On the state of the nation
In adaptation
To your station,
By invitations
To friends and relations,
By evitation
Of amputation,
By permutation
In conversation,

And deep reflection
You'll avoid dejection.

Learn well your grammar,
And never stammer,
Write well and neatly,
And sing most sweetly,
Be enterprising,
Love early rising,
Go walk of six miles,
Have ready quick smiles,
With lightsome laughter,
Soft flowing after.
Drink tea, not coffee;
Never eat toffy.
Eat bread with butter.
Once more, don't stutter.
Don't waste your money,
Abstain from honey.
Shut doors behind you,
(Don't slam them, mind you.)
Drink beer, not porter.
Don't enter the water
Till to swim you are able.
Sit close to the table.
Take care of a candle.
Shut a door by the handle,
Don't push with your shoulder
Until you are older.
Lose not a button.
Refuse cold mutton.

"Rules and Regulations,"
Lewis Carroll

In enterprise of martial kind,
    When there was any fighting,
He led his regiment from behind—
    He found it less exciting.
But when away his regiment ran,
    His place was at the fore, O—
        That celebrated,
        Cultivated,
        Underrated
            Nobleman,
    The Duke of Plaza-Toro!

In the first and foremost flight, ha, ha!
You always found that knight, ha, ha!
        That celebrated,

   Cultivated,
   Underrated
    Nobleman,
 The Duke of Plaza-Toro!

When, to evade Destruction's hand,
  To hide they all proceeded,
No soldier in that gallant band
  Hid half as well as he did.
He lay concealed throughout the war,
  And so preserved his gore, O!
  That unaffected,
  Undetected,
  Well-connected
   Warrior,
 The Duke of Plaza-Toro!

In every doughty deed, ha, ha!
He always took the lead, ha, ha!
  That unaffected,
  Undetected,
  Well-connected
   Warrior,
 The Duke of Plaza-Toro!

When told that they would all be shot
  Unless they left the service,
That hero hesitated not,
  So marvellous his nerve is.
He sent his resignation in,
  The first of all his corps, O!
   That very knowing,
   Overflowing,
   Easy-going
    Paladin,
 The Duke of Plaza-Toro!

To men of grosser clay, ha, ha!
He always showed the way, ha, ha!
   That very knowing,
   Overflowing,
   Easy-going
    Paladin,
 The Duke of Plaza-Toro!

        "The Duke of
        Plaza-Toro," W. S.
        Gilbert, *The Gondoliers*

Into the street the Piper stept,
  Smiling first a little smile,

As if he knew what magic slept
　　In his quiet pipe the while;
Then, like a musical adept,
To blow the pipe his lips he wrinkled,
And green and blue his sharp eyes twinkled,
Like a candle-flame where salt is sprinkled;
And ere three shrill notes the pipe uttered,
You heard as if an army muttered;
And the muttering grew to a grumbling;
And the grumbling grew to a mighty rumbling;
And out of the houses the rats came tumbling.
Great rats, small rats, lean rats, brawny rats,
Brown rats, black rats, gray rats, tawny rats,
Grave old plodders, gay young friskers,
　　Fathers, mothers, uncles, cousins,
Cocking tails and pricking whiskers,
　　Families by tens and dozens,
Brothers, sisters, husbands, wives—
Followed the Piper for their lives.
From street to street he piped advancing,
And step for step they followed dancing,
Until they came to the river Weser,
　　Wherein all plunged and perished!
—Save one who, stout as Julius Caesar,
Swam across and lived to carry
　　(As he, the manuscript he cherished)
To Rat-land home his commentary:
Which was, "At the first shrill notes of the pipe,
I heard a sound as of scraping tripe,
And putting apples, wondrous ripe,
Into a cider-press's gripe:
And a moving away of pickle-tub-boards,
And a leaving ajar of conserve-cupboards,
And a drawing the corks of train-oil-flasks,
And a breaking the hoops of butter-casks:
And it seemed as if a voice
　　(Sweeter far than by harp or by psaltery
Is breathed) called out, 'Oh rats, rejoice!
　　The world is grown to one vast drysaltery!
So munch on, crunch on, take your nuncheon,
Breakfast, supper, dinner, luncheon!'
And just as a bulky sugar-puncheon,
All ready staved, like a great sun shone
Glorious scarce an inch before me,
Just as methought it said, 'Come, bore me!'
—I found the Weser rolling o'er me."

"The Piper Pipes,"
Robert Browning, *The Pied
Piper of Hamelin*

Vocal Variety

Many of the following selections test the actor's ability to work with material of a highly descriptive nature. All of the vocal resources of emphasis, phrasing, pause, and dramatic pointing should be called into play. Actual monologues from plays have not been widely used here because characterization is not a basic concern in this section; the actor's attention should be devoted primarily to the development of vocal flexibility. Extensive work in making these isolated examples of prose and poetry exciting and dramatically effective will serve to extend the range of the actor's vocal expressiveness. Such exercises provide a means of preparing the actor to cope with the full vocal demands of a play.

> That is the issue that will continue in this country when these poor tongues of Judge Douglas and myself shall be silent. It is the eternal struggle between these two principles—right and wrong—throughout the world. They are the two principles that have stood face to face from the beginning of time; and will ever continue to struggle. The one is the common right of humanity, and the other the divine right of kings. It is the same principle in whatever shape it develops itself. It is the same spirit that says, "You toil and work and earn bread, and I'll eat it." No matter in what shape it comes, whether from the mouth of a king who seeks to bestride the people of his own nation and live by the fruit of their labor, or from one race of men as an apology for enslaving another race, it is the same tyrannical principle.
>
> "On the Enslavement of Men," Abraham Lincoln, *Debate with Stephen Douglas, Alton, Illinois, October 15, 1858*

> It is said an Eastern monarch once charged his wise men to invent him a sentence to be ever in view, and which should be true and appropriate in all times and situations. They presented him the words: "And this, too, shall pass away." How much it expresses! How chastening in the hour of pride! How consoling in the depths of affliction! . . . And yet, let us hope, it is not quite true. Let us hope, rather, that by the best cultivation of the physical world beneath and around us, and the best intellectual and moral world within us, we shall secure an individual, social, and political prosperity and happiness, whose course shall be onward and upward, and which, while the earth endures, shall not pass away.
>
> "A True Sentence?" Abraham Lincoln, *Address, September 30, 1859*

> When I had made an end of these labors, it was four o'clock—still dark as midnight. As the bell sounded the hour, there came a knocking at the street door. I went down to open it with a light heart,—for what had I *now* to fear? There entered three men, who introduced themselves, with perfect suavity, as officers of the police. A shriek had been heard by a neighbor during the night; suspicion of foul play had been aroused; information had been lodged at the police office, and they (the officers) had been deputed to search the premises.

I smiled,—for *what* had I to fear? I bade the gentlemen welcome. The shriek, I said, was my own in a dream. The old man, I mentioned, was absent in the country. I took my visitors all over the house. I bade them search—search *well.* I led them, at length, to *his* chamber. I showed them his treasures, secure, undisturbed. In the enthusiasm of my confidence, I brought chairs into the room, and desired them *here* to rest from their fatigues, while I myself, in the wild audacity of my perfect triumph, placed my own seat upon the very spot beneath which reposed the corpse of the victim.

The officers were satisfied. My *manner* had convinced them. I was singularly at ease. They sat, and while I answered cheerily, they chatted of familiar things. But, ere long, I felt myself getting pale and wished them gone. My head ached, and I fancied a ringing in my ears: but still they sat and still chatted. The ringing became more distinct:—it continued and became more distinct: I talked more freely to get rid of the feeling: but it continued and gained definitiveness—until, at length, I found that the noise was *not* within my ears.

No doubt I now grew *very* pale;—but I talked more fluently, and with a heightened voice. Yet the sound increased—and what could I do? It was *a low, dull, quick sound—much such a sound as a watch makes when enveloped in cotton.* I gasped for breath—and yet the officers heard it not. I talked more quickly— more vehemently; but the noise steadily increased. I arose and argued about trifles, in a high key and with violent gesticulations, but the noise steadily increased. Why *would* they not be gone? I paced the floor to and fro with heavy strides, as if excited to fury by the observation of the men—but the noise steadily increased. Oh God! what *could* I do? I foamed—I raved—I swore! I swung the chair upon which I had been sitting, and grated it upon the boards, but the noise rose over all and continually increased. It grew louder—louder—*louder!* And still the men chatted pleasantly, and smiled. Was it possible they heard not? Almighty God!—no, no! They heard!—they suspected!—they *knew!*— they were making a mockery of my horror!—this I thought, and this I think. But anything was better than this agony! Anything was more tolerable than this derision! I could bear those hypocritical smiles no longer! I felt that I must scream or die!—and now—again!—hark! louder! louder! louder! *louder!*—

"Villains!" I shrieked, "dissemble no more! I admit the deed!—tear up the planks!—here, here!—it is the beating of his hideous heart!"

"The Beating Heart,"
Edgar Allan Poe, *The Tell-Tale Heart*

Why, man, he doth bestride the narrow world
Like a Colossus, and we petty men
Walk under his huge legs and peep about
To find ourselves dishonourable graves.
Men at some time are masters of their fates:
The fault, dear Brutus, is not in our stars,
But in ourselves, that we are underlings.
Brutus and Caesar: what should be in that Caesar?
Why should that name be sounded more than yours?
Write them together, yours is as fair a name;

Sound them, it doth become the mouth as well;
Weigh them, it is as heavy; conjure with 'em,
Brutus will start a spirit as soon as Caesar.
Now, in the names of all the gods at once,
Upon what meat doth this our Caesar feed,
That he is grown so great? Age, thou are shamed!
Rome, thou hast lost the breed of noble bloods!
When went there by an age, since the great flood,
But it was famed with more than with one man?
When could they say till now, that talk'd of Rome,
That her wide walls encompass'd but one man?
Now is it Rome indeed and room enough,
When there is in it but one only man.
O, you and I have heard our fathers say,
There was a Brutus once that would have brook'd
The eternal devil to keep his state in Rome
As easily as a king.

> "Cassius's Speech,"
> William Shakespeare,
> *Julius Caesar*

But whatever may be our fate, be assured that this Declaration will stand. It may cost treasure and it may cost blood; but it will stand, and it will richly compensate for both. Through the thick gloom of the present, I see the brightness of the future as the sun in heaven. We shall make this a glorious, an immortal day. When we are in our graves, our children will honor it. They will celebrate it with thanksgiving, with festivity, with bonfires, and illuminations. On its annual return, they will shed tears, copious, gushing tears, not of subjection and slavery, not of agony and distress, but of exultation, of gratitude, and of joy.

Sir, before God, I believe the hour is come. My judgment approves this measure, and my whole heart is in it. All that I have, and all that I am, and all that I hope in this life, I am now ready here to stake upon it; and I leave off as I began, that, live or die, survive or perish, I am for the Declaration. It is my living sentiment, and by the blessing of God it shall be my dying sentiment—Independence now, and INDEPENDENCE FOREVER!

> "On the Declaration of
> Independence," Daniel
> Webster, *Supposed Speech
> of John Adams*

It was the best of times, it was the worst of times, it was the age of wisdom, it was the age of foolishness, it was the epoch of belief, it was the epoch of incredulity, it was the season of Light, it was the season of Darkness, it was the spring of hope, it was the winter of despair, we had everything before us, we had nothing before us, we were all going direct to Heaven, we were all going direct the other way—in short, the period was so far like the present period, that some of its noisiest authorities insisted on its being received, for good or for evil, in the superlative degree of comparison only.

There were a king with a large jaw and a queen with a plain face, on the throne of England; there were a king with a large jaw and a queen with a fair face, on the throne of France. In both countries it was clearer than crystal to the lords of the State preserves of loaves and fishes, that things in general were settled for ever.

> "The Best of Times,"
> Charles Dickens, *A Tale of Two Cities*

Out upon the angry wind! how from sighing, it began to bluster round the merry forge, banging at the wicket, and grumbling in the chimney, as if it bullied the jolly bellows from doing anything to order. And what an impotent swaggerer it was, too, for all its poise; for if it had any influence on that hoarse companion, it was but to make him roar his cheerful song the louder, and by consequence to make the fire burn the brighter, and the sparks to dance more gayly yet; at length, they whizzed so madly round and round, that it was too much for such a surly wind to bear; so off it flew with a howl, giving the old sign before the alehouse door such a cuff as it went, that the Blue Dragon was more rampant than usual ever afterwards, and, indeed, before Christmas, reared clear out of his crazy frame.

It was small tyranny for a respectable wind to go wreaking its vengeance on such poor creatures as the fallen leaves, but this wind happening to come up with a great heap of them just after venting its humor on the insulted Dragon, did so disperse and scatter them that they fled away, pell-mell, some here, some there, rolling over each other, whirling round and round upon their thin edges, taking frantic flights into the air, and playing all manner of extraordinary gambols in the extremity of their distress. Nor was this enough for its malicious fury: for not content with driving them abroad, it charged small parties of them and hunted them into the wheel-wright's saw-pit, and below the planks and timbers in the yard, and scattering the sawdust in the air, it looked for them underneath, and when it did meet with any, whew, how it drove them on and followed at their heels!

The scared leaves only flew the faster for all this, and a giddy chase it was; for they got into unfrequented places, where there was no outlet, and where their pursuer kept them eddying round and round at his pleasure; and they crept under the eaves of the houses and clung tightly to the sides of hayricks, like bats; and tore in at open chamber windows, and cowered close to hedges; and, in short, went anywhere for safety. But the oddest feat they achieved was, to take advantage of the sudden opening of Mr. Pecksniff's front door, to dash wildly into his passage; whither the wind following close upon them, and finding the back door open, incontinently blew out the lighted candle held by Miss Pecksniff, and slammed the front door against Mr. Pecksniff who was at that moment entering, with such violence, that in the twinkling of an eye he lay on his back at the bottom of the steps. Being by this time weary of such trifling performances, the boisterous rover hurried away, rejoicing, roaring over moor and meadow, hill and flat, until it got out to sea, where it met with other winds similarly disposed, and made a night of it.

> "The Wind,"
> Charles Dickens,
> *Martin Chuzzlewit*

The Pequod's whale being decapitated and the body stripped, the head was hoisted against the ship's side—about half way out of the sea, so that it might yet in great part be buoyed up by its native element. And there with the strained craft steeply leaning over it, by reason of the enormous downward drag from the lower mast-head, and every yard-arm on that side projecting like a crane over the waves; there, that blood-dripping head hung to the Pequod's waist like the giant Holofernes's from the girdle of Judith.

When this last task was accomplished it was noon, and the seamen went below to their dinner. Silence reigned over the before tumultuous but now deserted deck. An intense copper calm, like a universal yellow lotus, was more and more unfolding its noiseless measureless leaves upon the sea.

A short space elapsed, and up into this noiselessness came Ahab alone from his cabin. Taking a few turns on the quarter-deck, he paused to gaze over the side, then slowly getting into the main-chains he took Stubb's long spade—still remaining there after the whale's decapitation—and striking it into the lower part of the half-suspended mass, placed its other end crutch-wise under one arm, and so stood leaning over with eyes attentively fixed on this head.

It was a black and hooded head; and hanging there in the midst of so intense a calm, it seemed the Sphynx's in the desert. "Speak, thou vast and venerable head," muttered Ahab, "which, though ungarnished with a beard, yet here and there lookest hoary with mosses; speak, mighty head, and tell us the secret thing that is in thee. Of all divers, thou hast dived the deepest. That head upon which the upper sun now gleams, has moved amid this world's foundations. Where unrecorded names and navies rust, and untold hopes and anchors rot; where in her murderous hold this frigate earth is ballasted with bones of millions of the drowned; there, in that awful water-land, there was thy most familiar home. Thou hast been where bell or diver never went; hast slept by many a sailor's side, where sleepless mothers would give their lives to lay them down. Thou saw'st the locked lovers when leaping from their flaming ship; heart to heart they sank beneath the exulting wave; true to each other, when heaven seemed false to them. Thou saw'st the murdered mate when tossed by pirates from the midnight deck; for hours he fell into the deeper midnight of the insatiate maw; and his murderers still sailed on unharmed—while swift lightnings shivered the neighboring ship that would have borne a righteous husband to outstretched, longing arms. O head! thou has seen enough to split the planets and make an infidel of Abraham, and not one syllable is thine!"

> "The Dead Whale,"
> Herman Melville, *Moby Dick*

When the eyes of Prince Prospero fell upon this spectral image (which with a slow and solemn movement, as if more fully to sustain its role, stalked to and fro among the waltzers) he was seen to be convulsed in the first moment with a strong shudder either of terror or distaste; but in the next his brow reddened with rage.

"Who dares?" he demanded hoarsely of the courtiers who stood near him—"who dares insult us with this blasphemous mockery? Seize him and unmask him, that we may know whom we have to hang at sunrise from the battlements!''

It was the eastern or blue chamber in which stood the Prince Prospero as he uttered these words. They rang throughout the seven rooms loudly and clearly—for the prince was a bold and robust man, and the music had become hushed at the waving of his hand.

It was in the blue room where stood the prince, with a group of pale courtiers by his side. At first, as he spoke, there was a slight rushing movement of this group in the direction of the intruder, who at the moment was also near at hand, and now, with deliberate and stately step, made closer approach to the speaker. But, from a certain nameless awe with which the mad assumptions of the mummer had inspired the whole party, there were found none who put forth hand to seize him; so that unimpeded he passed within a yard of the prince's person; and while the vast assembly, as if with one impulse, shrank from the centres of the rooms to the walls, he made his way uninterruptedly, but with the same solemn and measured step which had distinguished him from the first, through the blue chamber to the purple—through the purple to the green—through the green to the orange—through this again to the white—and even thence to the violet, ere a decided movement had been made to arrest him. It was then, however, that the Prince Prospero, maddening with rage and shame of his own momentary cowardice, rushed hurriedly through the six chambers, while none followed him on account of a deadly terror that had seized upon all. He bore aloft a drawn dagger, and had approached in rapid impetuosity, to within three or four feet of the retreating figure, when the latter, having attained the extremity of the velvet apartment, turned suddenly and confronted his pursuer. There was a sharp cry—and the dagger dropped gleaming upon the sable carpet, upon which, instantly afterwards, fell prostrate in death the Prince Prospero. Then, summoning the wild courage of despair, a throng of the revellers at once threw themselves into the black apartment, and, seizing the mummer, whose tall figure stood erect and motionless within the shadow of the ebony clock, gasped in unutterable horror at finding the grave cerements and corpse-like mask which they handled with so violent a rudeness, untenanted by any tangible form.

And now was acknowledged the presence of the Red Death. He had come like a thief in the night. And one by one dropped the revellers in the blood-bedewed halls of their revel, and died each in the despairing posture of his fall. And the life of the ebony clock went out with that of the last of the gay. And the flames of the tripods expired. And Darkness and Decay and the Red Death held illimitable dominion over all.

"The Uninvited Guest,"
Edgar Allan Poe, *The Masque of the Red Death*

He was, in fact, an odd mixture of small shrewdness and simple credulity. His appetite for the marvelous, and his powers of digesting it, were equally extraordinary; and both had been increased by his residence in this spell-bound region. No tale was too gross or monstrous for his capacious swallow. It was often his delight, after school was dismissed in the afternoon, to stretch himself on the rich bed of clover, bordering the little brook that whimpered by the schoolhouse, and there con over old Mather's direful tales, until the gathering dusk of the evening made the printed page a mere mist before his eyes. Then, as he wended his way by swamp, and stream and awful woodland, to the farmhouse where he happened to be quartered, every sound of nature at that witching hour, fluttered his excited imagination: the voice of the whippoor-will, that harbinger of storm; the dreary hooting of the screech-owl, or the sudden rustling in the thicket of birds frightened from their roost. The fireflies, too, which sparkled most vividly in the darkest places now and then startled him, as one of uncommon brightness would stream across his path, and if, by chance, a huge blockhead of a beetle came winging his blundering flight against him, the poor varlet was ready to give up the ghost, with the idea that he was struck with a witch's token. His only resource on such occasions, either to drown thought or drive away evil spirits, was to sing psalm tunes;—and the good people of Sleepy Hollow, as they sat by their doors of an evening, were often filled with awe, at hearing his nasal melody, "in linked sweetness long drawn out," floating from the distant hill or along the dusky road.

"Ichabod Crane,"
Washington Irving, *The Legend of Sleepy Hollow*

Everybody said he looked like a haunted man. The extent of my present claim for everybody is, that they were so far right. He did.

Who could have seen his hollow cheek; his sunken brilliant eye; his black-attired figure, indefinably grim, although well-knit and well-proportioned; his grizzled hair hanging, like tangled sea-weed, about his face,—as if he had been, through his whole life, a lonely mark for the chafing and beating of the great deep of humanity,—but might have said he looked like a haunted man?

Who could have observed his manner, taciturn, thoughtful, gloomy, shadowed by habitual reserve, retiring always and jocund never, with a distraught air of reverting to a bygone place and time, or of listening to some old echoes in his mind, but might have said it was the manner of a haunted man?

Who could have heard his voice, slow-speaking, deep, and grave, with a natural fulness and melody in it which he seemed to set himself against and stop, but might have said it was the voice of a haunted man?

Who that had seen him in his inner chamber, part library and part laboratory,—for he was, as the world knew, far and wide, a learned man in chemistry, and a teacher on whose lips and hands a crowd of aspiring ears and eyes hung daily,—who that had seen him there, upon a winter night, alone, surrounded by his drugs and instruments and books; the shadow of his shaded lamp a monstrous beetle on the wall, motionless among a crowd of spectral shapes raised there by the flickering of the fire upon the quaint objects around him; some of these phantoms (the reflection of glass vessels that held liquids), trembling at heart like things that knew his power to uncombine them, and to give back their component parts to fire and vapour;—who that had seen him then, his work done, and he pondering in his chair before the rusted grate and red flame, moving his thin mouth as if in speech, but silent as the dead, would not have said that the man seemed haunted and the chamber too?

"A Haunted Man,"
Charles Dickens, *The*
Haunted Man and the
Ghost's Bargain

A little while ago, I stood by the grave of the old Napoleon—a magnificent tomb of gilt and gold, fit almost for a dead deity—and gazed upon the sarcophagus of black Egyptian marble, where rest at last the ashes of that restless man. I leaned over the balustrade and thought about the career of the greatest soldier of the modern world.

I saw him walking upon the banks of the Seine, contemplating suicide. I saw him at Toulon—I saw him putting down the mob in the streets of Paris—I saw him at the head of the army of Italy—I saw him crossing the bridge of Lodi with the tri-color in his hand—I saw him in Egypt in the shadow of the Pyramids—I saw him conquer the Alps and mingle the eagles of France with the eagles of the crags. I saw him at Marengo—at Ulm and Austerlitz. I saw him in Russia, where the infantry of the snow and the cavalry of the wild blast scattered his legions like winter's withered leaves. I saw him at Leipsic in defeat and disaster—driven by a million bayonets back upon Paris—clutched like a wild beast—banished to Elba. I saw him escape and retake an empire by the force of his genius. I saw him upon the frightful field of Waterloo, where Chance and Fate combined to wreck the fortunes of their former king. And I saw him at St. Helena, with his hands crossed behind him, gazing out upon the sad and solemn sea.

I thought of the orphans and widows he had made—of the tears that had been shed for his glory, and of the only woman who ever loved him, pushed from his heart by the cold hand of ambition. And I said I would rather have been a French peasant and worn wooden shoes. I would rather have lived in a hut with a vine growing over the door, and the grapes growing purple in the kisses of the autumn sun. I would rather have been that poor peasant with my loving wife by my side, knitting as the day died out of the sky—with my children upon my knees and their arms about me. I would rather have been that man and gone down to the tongueless silence of the dreamless dust than to have been that imperial impersonation of force and murder, known as Napoleon the Great.

"At the Tomb of
Napoleon," Robert G.
Ingersoll, *Selected Lectures*

Scenes

1. *Blithe Spirit,* by Noel Coward
    From Act II, Scene I

Scene:	For one man, two women
Characters:	CHARLES CONDOMINE
	RUTH CONDOMINE, his second wife
	THE GHOST OF ELVIRA CONDOMINE, his first wife
Setting:	The living room of Charles Condomine's house in Kent, England.
Time:	A summer morning. The present.
Situation:	Gathering material for a book, author Charles Condomine invited a spiritualist, Madame Arcati, to hold a seance. Unfortunately, she brought back the spirit of Charles' first wife, Elvira. However, Elvira is visible only to Charles. As a result, his present wife, Ruth, believes that Charles is either losing his mind or else deliberately insulting her. All his

FIGURE 5.4 *Blithe Spirit* **by Noel Coward. California State University, Long Beach, directed by W. David Sievers.**

explanations have been of no avail. Just as Elvira makes one of her appearances, Ruth is trying to determine whether or not Charles is still seeing things. "You're not hearing or seeing anything in the least unusual?" she asks. "Not a thing," replies Charles.

[ELVIRA *comes in from the garden, carrying an armful of roses. The roses are as grey as the rest of her.*]

ELVIRA: You've absolutely ruined that border by the sundial—it looks like a mixed salad.

CHARLES: O my God!

RUTH: What's the matter now?

CHARLES: She's here again!

RUTH: What do you mean? Who's here again?

CHARLES: Elvira.

RUTH: Pull yourself together and don't be absurd.

ELVIRA: It's all those nasturtiums—they're so vulgar.

CHARLES: I like nasturtiums.

RUTH: You like what?

ELVIRA: (*putting her grey roses into a vase*) They're all right in moderation but in mass like that they look beastly.

CHARLES: Help me, Ruth—you've got to help me—

RUTH: (*rises*) What did you mean about nasturtiums?

CHARLES: Never mind about that now—I tell you she's here again.

ELVIRA: You have been having a nice scene, haven't you? I could hear you right down the garden.

CHARLES: Please mind your own business.

RUTH: If your behaving like a lunatic isn't my business nothing is.

ELVIRA: I expect it was about me, wasn't it? I know I ought to feel sorry but I'm not—I'm delighted.

CHARLES: How can you be so inconsiderate?

RUTH: (*shrilly*) Inconsiderate—I like that, I must say—

CHARLES: Ruth—darling—please . . .

RUTH: I've done everything I can to help—I've controlled myself admirably—I should like to say here and now that I don't believe a word about your damned hallucinations—you're up to something, Charles—there's been a certain furtiveness in your manner for weeks— Why don't you be honest and tell me what it is?

CHARLES: You're wrong—you're dead wrong—I haven't been in the least furtive—I—

RUTH: You're trying to upset me—for some obscure reason you're trying to goad me into doing something that I might regret—I won't stand for it any more— You're making me utterly miserable—(*She bursts into tears and collapses on sofa.*)

CHARLES: Ruth—please—(*sits on sofa beside* RUTH)

RUTH: Don't come near me—

ELVIRA: Let her have a nice cry—it'll do her good.

CHARLES: You're utterly heartless!

RUTH: Heartless!

CHARLES: (*wildly*) I was not talking to you—I was talking to Elvira.

RUTH: Go on talking to her then, talk to her until you're blue in the face but don't talk to me—

CHARLES: Help me, Elvira—

ELVIRA: How?

CHARLES: Make her see you or something.

ELVIRA: I'm afraid I couldn't manage that—it's technically the most difficult business—frightfully complicated, you know—it takes years of study—

CHARLES: You are here, aren't you? You're not an illusion?

ELVIRA: I may be an illusion but I'm most definitely here.

CHARLES: How did you get here?

ELVIRA: I told you last night—I don't exactly know—

CHARLES: Well, you must make me a promise that in future you only come and talk to me when I'm alone—

ELVIRA: (*pouting*) How unkind you are—making me feel unwanted—I've never been treated so rudely—

CHARLES: I don't mean to be rude, but you must see—

ELVIRA: It's all your own fault for having married a woman who is incapable of seeing beyond the nose on her face—if she had a grain of real sympathy or affection for you she'd believe what you tell her.

CHARLES: How could you expect anybody to believe this?

ELVIRA: You'd be surprised how gullible people are—we often laugh about it on the other side.

[RUTH, *who has stopped crying and been staring at* CHARLES *in horror, suddenly gets up.*]

RUTH: (*gently*) Charles—

CHARLES: (*surprised at her tone*) Yes, dear—

RUTH: I'm awfully sorry I was cross—

CHARLES: But, my dear—

RUTH: I understand everything now, I do really—

CHARLES: You do?

RUTH: (*patting his arm reassuringly*) Of course I do.

ELVIRA: Look out—she's up to something—

CHARLES: Will you please be quiet?

RUTH: Of course, darling—we'll be quiet, won't we? We'll be as quiet as little mice.

CHARLES: Ruth dear, listen—

RUTH: I want you to come upstairs with me and go to bed—

ELVIRA: The way that woman harps on bed is nothing short of erotic.

CHARLES: I'll deal with you later—

RUTH: Whenever you like, darling. Come along.

CHARLES: Ruth dear—I'd really rather not go to bed in the middle of the morning—

ELVIRA: How you've changed, darling!

CHARLES: Don't be disgusting.

RUTH: (*sweetly*) I'm sorry, dear—I didn't mean to be.

CHARLES: What are you up to?

RUTH: I'm not up to anything—I just want you to go quietly to bed and wait there until Doctor Bradman comes—

CHARLES: No, Ruth—you're wrong—

RUTH: (*firmly*) Come, dear—

ELVIRA: She'll have you in a strait jacket before you know where you are.

CHARLES: (*frantically*) Help me—you must help me—

ELVIRA: (*enjoying herself*) My dear, I would with pleasure, but I can't think how—

CHARLES: I can—listen, Ruth—

RUTH: Yes, dear?

CHARLES: If I promise to go to bed will you let me stay here for five minutes longer?

RUTH: I really think it would be better—

CHARLES: Bear with me—however mad it may seem—bear with me for just five minutes longer—

RUTH: (*letting go of him*) Very well—what is it?

CHARLES: Sit down then.

RUTH: (*sitting down*) All right—there.

CHARLES: Now listen—listen carefully—

ELVIRA: Have a cigarette, it will soothe your nerves.

CHARLES: I don't want a cigarette.

RUTH: (*indulgently*) Then you shan't have one, darling.

CHARLES: Ruth, I want to explain to you clearly and without emotion that beyond any shadow of doubt the ghost or shade or whatever you like to call it of my first wife Elvira is in this room now.

RUTH: Yes, dear.

CHARLES: I know you don't believe it and are trying valiantly to humour me but I intend to prove it to you.

RUTH: Why not lie down and have a nice rest and you can prove anything you want to later on?

CHARLES: She may not be here later on.

ELVIRA: Don't worry—she will!

CHARLES: O God!

RUTH: Hush, dear.

CHARLES: (*to* ELVIRA) Promise you'll do what I ask?

ELVIRA: That all depends what it is.

CHARLES: Ruth—you see that bowl of flowers on the piano?

RUTH: Yes, dear—I did it myself this morning.

ELVIRA: Very untidily if I may say so.

CHARLES: You may not.

RUTH: Very well—I never will again—I promise.

CHARLES: Elvira will now carry that bowl of flowers to the mantelpiece and back again. You will, Elvira, won't you—just to please me?

ELVIRA: I don't really see why I should—you've been quite insufferable to me ever since I materialized.

CHARLES: Please.

ELVIRA: All right, I will just this once—not that I approve of all these Herman The Great carryings on. (*She goes over to the piano.*)

CHARLES Now, Ruth—watch carefully.

RUTH: (*patiently*) Very well, dear.

CHARLES: Go on, Elvira—bring it to the mantelpiece and back again.

[ELVIRA *does so, taking obvious pleasure in doing it in a very roundabout way. At one moment she brings it up to within an inch of* RUTH's *face.* RUTH *shrinks back with a scream and then jumps to her feet.*]

RUTH: (*furiously*) How dare you, Charles! You ought to be ashamed of yourself!

CHARLES: What on earth for?

RUTH: (*hysterically*) It's a trick—I know perfectly well it's a trick—you've been working up to this—it's all part of some horrible plan—

CHARLES: It isn't—I swear it isn't—Elvira—do something else for God's sake—

ELVIRA: Certainly—anything to oblige.

RUTH: (*becoming really frightened*) You want to get rid of me—you're trying to drive me out of my mind—

CHARLES: Don't be so silly.

RUTH: You're cruel and sadistic and I'll never forgive you—(ELVIRA *lifts up a light chair and waltzes solemnly round the room with it, then she puts it down with a bang. Making a dive for the door*) I'm not going to put up with this any more.

CHARLES: (*holding her*) You must believe it—you must—

RUTH: Let me go immediately—

CHARLES: That was Elvira—I swear it was—

RUTH: (*struggling*) Let me go—

CHARLES: Ruth—please—

[RUTH *breaks away from him and runs towards the windows.* ELVIRA *gets there just before her and shuts them in her face.* RUTH *starts back, appalled.*]

RUTH: (*looking at* CHARLES *with eyes of horror*) Charles—this is madness—sheer madness! It's some sort of auto-suggestion, isn't it—some form of hypnotism, swear to me it's only that? Swear to me it's only that.

ELVIRA: (*taking an expensive vase from the mantelpiece and crashing it into the grate*) Hypnotism my foot!

[RUTH *gives a scream and goes into violent hysterics as the curtain falls.*]

2. *Private Lives*, by Noel Coward
   From Act I

   Scene: For one man, one woman
   Characters: ELYOT, a sophisticated man of the world
   SIBYL, his second wife
   Setting: The terrace of a hotel in France.
   Time: Evening. Between the two World Wars.
   Situation: Sibyl and Elyot are on their honeymoon. However, Elyot's first wife, Amanda, has also remarried, and by a strange coincidence is also on her honeymoon in the same hotel; as a matter of fact, in the adjoining suite. Elyot has just seen her and tries desperately to get Sibyl to leave immediately. Elyot is on the terrace with an expression of horror on his face as Sibyl comes brightly onto the terrace.

   SIBYL: Cocktail, please. (ELYOT *doesn't answer.*) Elli, what's the matter?
   ELYOT: I feel very odd.
   SIBYL: Odd, what do you mean? Ill?

FIGURE 5.5 *Private Lives* by Noel
Coward. Auburn University, directed
by Cleveland Harrison.

ELYOT: Yes, ill.

SIBYL: *(alarmed)* What sort of ill?

ELYOT: We must leave at once.

SIBYL: Leave!

ELYOT: Yes, dear. Leave immediately.

SIBYL: Elli!

ELYOT: I have a strange foreboding.

SIBYL: You must be mad.

ELYOT: Listen, darling. I want you be very sweet, and patient, and understanding, and not be upset, or ask any questions, or anything. I have an absolute conviction that our whole future happiness depends upon our leaving here instantly.

SIBYL: Why?

ELYOT: I can't tell you why.

SIBYL: But we've only just come.

ELYOT: I know that, but it can't be helped.

SIBYL: What's happened, what has happened?

ELYOT: Nothing has happened.

SIBYL: You've gone out of your mind.

ELYOT: I haven't gone out of my mind, but I shall if we stay here another hour.

SIBYL: You're not drunk, are you?

ELYOT: Of course I'm not drunk. What time have I had to get drunk?

SIBYL: Come down and have some dinner, darling, and then you'll feel ever so much better.

ELYOT: It's no use trying to humour me. I'm serious.

SIBYL: But darling, please be reasonable. We've only just arrived; everything's unpacked. It's our first night together. We can't go away now.

ELYOT: We can have our first night together in Paris.

SIBYL: We shouldn't get there until the small hours.

ELYOT: (*with great effort at calmness*) Now please, Sibyl, I know it sounds crazy to you, and utterly lacking in reason and sense, but I've got second sight over certain things. I'm almost psychic. I've got the most extraordinary sensation of impending disaster. If we stay here something appalling will happen. I know it.

SIBYL: (*firmly*) Hysterical nonsense.

ELYOT: It isn't hysterical nonsense. Presentiments are far from being nonsense. Look at the woman who cancelled her passage on the *Titanic*. All because of a presentiment.

SIBYL: I don't see what that has to do with it.

ELYOT: It has everything to do with it. She obeyed her instincts, that's what she did, and saved her life. All I ask is to be allowed to obey my instincts.

SIBYL: Do you mean that there's going to be an earthquake or something?

ELYOT: Very possibly, very possibly indeed, or perhaps a violent explosion.

SIBYL: They don't have earthquakes in France.

ELYOT: On the contrary, only the other day they felt a distinct shock at Toulon.

SIBYL: Yes, but that's in the South where it's hot.

ELYOT: Don't quibble, Sibyl.

SIBYL: And as for explosions, there's nothing here that can explode.

ELYOT: Oho, isn't there.

SIBYL: Yes, but Elli—

ELYOT: Darling, be sweet. Bear with me. I beseech you to bear with me.

SIBYL: I don't understand. It's horrid of you to do this.

ELYOT: I'm not doing anything. I'm only asking you, imploring you to come away from this place.

SIBYL: But I love it here.

ELYOT: There are thousands of other places far nicer.

SIBYL: It's a pity we didn't go to one of them.

ELYOT: Now, listen, Sibyl—

SIBYL: Yes, but why are you behaving like this, why, why, why?

ELYOT: Don't ask why. Just give in to me. I swear I'll never ask you to give in to me over anything again.

SIBYL: (*with complete decision*) I won't think of going to-night. It's utterly ridiculous. I've done quite enough travelling for one day, and I'm tired.

ELYOT: You're as obstinate as a mule.

SIBYL: I like that, I must say.

ELYOT: (*hotly*) You've got your nasty little feet dug into the ground, and you don't intend to budge an inch, do you?

SIBYL: (*with spirit*) No, I do not.

ELYOT: If there's one thing in the world that infuriates me, it's sheer wanton stubbornness. I should like to cut off your head with a meat axe.

SIBYL: How dare you talk to me like that, on our honeymoon night.

ELYOT: Damn our honeymoon night. Damn it, damn it, damn it!

SIBYL: (*bursting into tears*) Oh, Elli, Elli—

ELYOT: Stop crying. Will you or will you not come away with me to Paris?

SIBYL: I've never been so miserable in my life. You're hateful and beastly. Mother was perfectly right. She said you had shifty eyes.

ELYOT: Well, she can't talk. Hers are so close together, you couldn't put a needle between them.

SIBYL: You don't love me a little bit. I wish I were dead.

ELYOT: Will you or will you not come to Paris?

SIBYL: No, no I won't.

ELYOT: Oh, my God! (*He stamps indoors.*)

SIBYL: (*following him, wailing*) Oh, Elli, Elli, Elli—

3.   *The Importance of Being Earnest,* by Oscar Wilde
     From Act I

      Scene: For one man, one woman
Characters: JACK WORTHING (also known as Ernest)
                GWENDOLEN FAIRFAX
    Setting: The morning room of Algernon Moncrieff's flat in Half-moon Street, London.
       Time: An afternoon in the 1890s.
  Situation: In an interview given to a journalist just before *Earnest* opened, Wilde reportedly said that his new play was "exquisitely trivial, a delicate bubble of fancy," and that it had its "philosophy." Wilde offered this definition of the play's philosophy: "We should treat all the trivial things of life seriously, and all the serious things of life with sincere and studied triviality."

               Jack is in love with Gwendolen in as passionately trivial a manner as possible. He takes the opportunity to propose marriage to her while her mother is out of the room. Gwendolen does not know that her suitor's real name is Jack; she believes it to be Ernest, the name Jack assumes while carrying on his bachelor escapades. His name is "Ernest in town and Jack in the country." He is proposing to Gwendolen in town.

               See also the other scene from *The Importance of Being Earnest* (p. 253), which occurs later in the play.

JACK: Charming day it has been, Miss Fairfax.

GWENDOLEN: Pray don't talk to me about the weather, Mr. Worthing. Whenever people talk to me about the weather, I always feel quite certain that they mean something else. And that makes me so nervous.

JACK: I do mean something else.

GWENDOLEN: I thought so. In fact, I am never wrong.

JACK: And I would like to be allowed to take advantage of Lady Bracknell's temporary absence . . .

GWENDOLEN: I would certainly advise you to do so. Mamma has a way of coming back suddenly into a room that I have often had to speak to her about.

FIGURE 5.6 *The Importance of Being Earnest* by Oscar Wilde. California State University, Long Beach, directed by W. David Sievers.

JACK: (*nervously*) Miss Fairfax, ever since I met you I have admired you more than any girl . . . I have ever met since . . . I met you.

GWENDOLEN: Yes, I am quite aware of the fact. And I often wish that in public, at any rate, you had been more demonstrative. For me you have always had an irresistible fascination. Even before I met you I was far from indifferent to you. (JACK *looks at her in amazement.*) We live, as I hope you know, Mr. Worthing, in an age of ideals. The fact is constantly mentioned in the more expensive monthly magazines, and has reached the provincial pulpits I am told: and my ideal has always been to love some one of the name of Ernest. There is something in that name that inspires absolute confidence. The moment Algernon first mentioned to me that he had a friend called Ernest, I knew I was destined to love you.

JACK: You really love me, Gwendolen?

GWENDOLEN: Passionately!

JACK: Darling! You don't know how happy you've made me.

GWENDOLEN: My own Ernest!

JACK: But you don't really mean to say that you couldn't love me if my name wasn't Ernest?

GWENDOLEN: But your name is Ernest.

JACK: Yes, I know it is. But supposing it was something else? Do you mean to say you couldn't love me then?

GWENDOLEN: (*glibly*) Ah! that is clearly a metaphysical speculation, and like most metaphysical speculations has very little reference at all to the actual facts of real life, as we know them.

JACK: Personally, darling, to speak quite candidly, I don't much care about the name of Ernest . . . I don't think that name suits me at all.

GWENDOLEN: It suits you perfectly. It is a divine name. It has a music of its own. It produces vibrations.

JACK: Well, really, Gwendolen, I must say that I think there are lots of other much nicer names. I think, Jack, for instance, a charming name.

GWENDOLEN: Jack? . . . No, there is very little music in the name Jack, if any at all, indeed. It does not thrill. It produces absolutely no vibrations . . . I have known several Jacks, and they all, without exception, were more than usually plain. Besides, Jack is a notorious domesticity for John! And I pity any woman who is married to a man called John. She would probably never be allowed to know the entrancing pleasure of a single moment's solitude. The only really safe name is Ernest.

JACK: Gwendolen, I must get christened at once—I mean we must get married at once. There is no time to be lost.

GWENDOLEN: Married, Mr. Worthing?

JACK: (*astounded*) Well . . . surely. You know that I love you, and you led me to believe, Miss Fairfax, that you were not absolutely indifferent to me.

GWENDOLEN: I adore you. But you haven't proposed to me yet. Nothing has been said at all about marriage. The subject has not even been touched on.

JACK: Well . . . may I propose to you now?

GWENDOLEN: I think it would be an admirable opportunity. And to spare you any possible disappointment, Mr. Worthing, I think it only fair to tell you quite frankly beforehand that I am fully determined to accept you.

JACK: Gwendolen!

GWENDOLEN: Yes, Mr. Worthing, what have you got to say to me?

JACK: You know what I have got to say to you.

GWENDOLEN: Yes, but you don't say it.

JACK: Gwendolen, will you marry me? (*goes on his knees*)

GWENDOLEN: Of course I will, darling. How long you have been about it! I am afraid you have had very little experience in how to propose.

JACK: My own one, I have never loved anyone in the world but you.

GWENDOLEN: Yes, but men often propose for practice. I know my brother Gerald does. All my girl-friends tell me so. What wonderfully blue eyes you have, Ernest! They are quite, quite blue. I hope you will always look at me just like that, especially when there are other people present.

4. *Pygmalion*, by G. Bernard Shaw
From Act IV

Scene: For one man, one woman
Characters: HENRY HIGGINS, bachelor, a teacher of phonetics; early middle age
ELIZA DOOLITTLE, a Cockney flower girl
Setting: Higgins's drawing room and laboratory in Wimpole Street, London.

> *Time:* 1912. Midnight.
> *Situation:* Higgins has wagered with a friend that he could take any reasonably intelligent girl, even one with the speech and manners of the lower class, and with sufficient grooming and training in speech and etiquette, pass her off as a duchess. Liza Doolittle, first seen selling flowers outside the Covent Garden flower and vegetable market, has become the object of the bet. Eliza and Higgins have just returned from an elite social gathering where she has succeeded in winning the bet for him. He is now content to leave things as they are, but Eliza realizes that she has made a transition into a new life. Frustrated and irritated at Higgins's ordering her as if she were a servant, she responds accordingly.
>
> *My Fair Lady*, the famous musical version of this play, had remarkable success both in the theatre and as a film and is continually revived all over the world.

HIGGINS: (*in despairing wrath outside*) What the devil have I done with my slippers? (*He appears at the door*).

LIZA: (*snatching up the slippers, and hurling them at him one after the other with all her force*) There are your slippers. And there. Take your slippers; and may you never have a day's luck with them!

HIGGINS: (*astounded*) What on earth—!(*He comes to her*). Whats the matter? Get up. (*He pulls her up*). Anything wrong?

LIZA: (*breathless*) Nothing wrong—with you. Ive won your bet for you, havnt I? Thats enough for you. *I* dont matter, I suppose.

HIGGINS: You won my bet! You! Presumptuous insect! *I* won it. What did you throw those slippers at me for?

LIZA: Because I wanted to smash your face. I'd like to kill you, you selfish brute. Why didnt you leave me where you picked me out of—in the gutter? You thank God it's all over, and that now you can throw me back again there, do you? (*She crisps her fingers frantically*).

HIGGINS: (*looking at her in cool wonder*). The creature is nervous, after all.

LIZA: (*gives a suffocated scream of fury, and instinctively darts her nails at his face*)!!

HIGGINS: (*catching her wrists*) Ah! would you? Claws in, you cat. How dare you shew your temper to me? Sit down and be quiet. (*He throws her roughly into the easy-chair*).

LIZA: (*crushed by superior strength and weight*) Whats to become of me? Whats to become of me?

HIGGINS: How the devil do I know whats to become of you? What does it matter what becomes of you?

LIZA: You dont care. I know you dont care. You wouldnt care if I was dead. I'm nothing to you—not so much as them slippers.

HIGGINS: (*thundering*) Those slippers.

LIZA: (*with bitter submission*) Those slippers. I didnt think it made any difference now.

(*A pause. Eliza hopeless and crushed. Higgins a little uneasy.*)

HIGGINS: (*in his loftiest manner*) Why have you begun going on like this? May I ask whether you complain of your treatment here?

LIZA: No.

HIGGINS: Has anybody behaved badly to you? Colonel Pickering? Mrs. Pearce? Any of the servants?

LIZA: No.

HIGGINS: I presume you dont pretend that *I* have treated you badly.

LIZA: No.

HIGGINS: I am glad to hear it. (*He moderates his tone.*) Perhaps youre tired after the strain of the day. Will you have a glass of champagne? (*He moves towards the door*).

LIZA: No. (*Recollecting her manners*) Thank you.

HIGGINS: (*good-humored again*) This has been coming on you for some days. I suppose it was natural for you to be anxious about the garden party. But thats all over now. (*He pats her kindly on the shoulder. She writhes*). Theres nothing more to worry about.

LIZA: No. Nothing more for you to worry about. (*She suddenly rises and gets away from him by going to the piano bench, where she sits and hides her face*). Oh God! I wish I was dead.

HIGGINS: (*staring after her in sincere surprise*) Why? in heaven's name, why? (*Reasonably, going to her*) Listen to me, Eliza. All this irritation is purely subjective.

LIZA: I dont understand. I'm too ignorant.

HIGGINS: It's only imagination. Low spirits and nothing else. Nobody's hurting you. Nothing's wrong. You go to bed like a good girl and sleep it off. Have a little cry and say your prayers: that will make you comfortable.

LIZA: I heard your prayers. "Thank God it's all over!"

HIGGINS: (*impatiently*) Well, dont you thank God it's all over? Now you are free and can do what you like.

LIZA: (*pulling herself together in desperation*) What am I fit for? What have you left me fit for? Where am I to go? What am I to do? Whats to become of me?

HIGGINS: (*enlightened, but not at all impressed*) Oh, thats whats worrying you, is it? (*He thrusts his hands into his pockets, and walks about in his usual manner, rattling the contents of his pockets, as if condescending to a trivial subject out of pure kindness*). I shouldnt bother about it if I were you. I should imagine you wont have much difficulty in settling yourself somewhere or other, though I hadnt quite realized that you were going away. (*She looks quickly at him: he does not look at her, but examines the dessert stand on the piano and decides that he will eat an apple*). You might marry, you know. (*He bites a large piece out of the apple, and munches it noisily*). You see, Eliza, all men are not confirmed old bachelors like me and the Colonel. Most men are the marrying sort (poor devils!); and youre not bad-looking: it's quite a pleasure to look at you sometimes—not now, of course, because youre crying and looking as ugly as the very devil; but when youre all right and quite yourself, youre what I should call attractive. That is, to the people in the marrying line, you understand. You go to bed and have a good nice rest; and then get up and look at yourself in the glass; and you wont feel so cheap.

(*Eliza again looks at him, speechless, and does not stir.*)

(*The look is quite lost on him: he eats his apple with a dreamy expression of happiness, as it is quite a good one.*)

HIGGINS: (*a genial afterthought occurring to him*) I daresay my mother could find some chap or other who would do very well.

LIZA: We were above that at the corner of Tottenham Court Road.

HIGGINS: (*waking up*) What do you mean?

LIZA: I sold flowers. I didnt sell myself. Now youve made a lady of me I'm not fit to sell anything else. I wish youd left me where you found me.

HIGGINS: (*slinging the core of the apple decisively into the grate*) Tosh, Eliza. Dont you insult human relations by dragging all this cant about buying and selling into it. You neednt marry the fellow if you dont like him.

LIZA: What else am I to do?

HIGGINS: Oh, lots of things. What about your old idea of a florist's shop? Pickering could set you up in one: hes lots of money. (*Chuckling*) He'll have to pay for all those togs you have been wearing today; and that, with the hire of the jewellery, will make a big hole in two hundred pounds. Why, six months ago you would have thought it the millennium to have a flower shop of your own. Come! youll be all right. I must clear off to bed: I'm devilish sleepy. By the way, I came down for something: I forget what it was.

LIZA: Your slippers.

HIGGINS: Oh yes, of course. You shied them at me.

(*He picks them up, and is going out when she rises and speaks to him*).

LIZA: Before you go, sir—

HIGGINS: (*dropping the slippers in his surprise at her calling him Sir*) Eh?

LIZA: Do my clothes belong to me or to Colonel Pickering?

HIGGINS: (*coming back into the room as if her question were the very climax of unreason*) What the devil use would they be to Pickering?

LIZA: He might want them for the next girl you pick up to experiment on.

HIGGINS: (*shocked and hurt*) Is that the way you feel towards us?

LIZA: I dont want to hear anything more about that. All I want to know is whether anything belongs to me. My own clothes were burnt.

HIGGINS: But what does it matter? Why need you start bothering about that in the middle of the night?

LIZA: I want to know what I may take away with me. I dont want to be accused of stealing.

HIGGINS: (*now deeply wounded*) Stealing! You shouldnt have said that, Eliza. That shews a want of feeling.

LIZA: I'm sorry. I'm only a common ignorant girl; and in my station I have to be careful. There cant be any feelings between the like of you and the like of me. Please will you tell me what belongs to me and what doesn't?

HIGGINS: (*very sulky*) You may take the whole damned houseful if you like. Except the jewels. Theyre hired. Will that satisfy you? (*He turns on his heel and is about to go in extreme dudgeon.*)

LIZA: (*drinking in his emotion like nectar, and nagging him to provoke a further supply*) Stop, please. (*She takes off her jewels.*) Will you take these to your room and keep them safe? I dont want to run the risk of their being missing.

HIGGINS: (*furious*) Hand them over. (*She puts them into his hands.*) If these belonged to me instead of to the jeweler, I'd ram them down your ungrateful throat. (*He perfunctorily thrusts them into his pockets, unconsciously decorating himself with the protruding ends of the chains.*)

LIZA: (*taking a ring off*) This ring isnt the jeweler's: it's the one you bought me in Brighton. I dont want it now. (*Higgins dashes the ring violently into the fireplace, and turns on her so threateningly that she crouches over the piano with her hands over her face, and exclaims)* Dont you hit me.

HIGGINS: Hit you! You infamous creature, how dare you accuse me of such a thing? It is you who have hit me. You have wounded me to the heart.

LIZA: *(thrilling with hidden joy)* I'm glad. Ive got a little of my own back, anyhow.

HIGGINS: *(with dignity, in his finest professional style)* You have caused me to lose my temper: a thing that has hardly ever happened to me before. I prefer to say nothing more tonight. I am going to bed.

LIZA: *(pertly)* Youd better leave a note for Mrs. Pearce about the coffee; for she wont be told by me.

HIGGINS: *(Formally)* Damn Mrs. Pearce; and damn the coffee; and damn you; and damn my own folly in having lavished hard-earned knowledge and the treasure of my regard and intimacy on a heartless guttersnipe. *(He goes out with impressive decorum, and spoils it by slamming the door savagely.)*

(Eliza smiles for the first time; expresses her feelings by a wild pantomine in which an imitation of Higgins's exit is confused with her own triumph; and finally goes down on her knees on the hearthrug to look for the ring. When she finds it she considers for a moment what to do with it. Finally she flings it down on the dessert stand and goes upstairs in a tearing rage.)

5.   *Antigone*, by Jean Anouilh (translated by Lewis Galantiere)

   Scene: For one man, one woman
Characters: ANTIGONE, a young woman
   HAEMON, her fiancé
   Setting: The steps of the castle in Thebes.
   Time: Yesterday, Today, or Tomorrow.
Situation: This is a modern-dress adaptation of the famous Greek tragedy by Sophocles. Antigone, the daughter of Oedipus, has defied the orders of Creon and has buried the body of her brother, who was a rebel against the state. She must reconcile in her own mind the conflicting duties between the laws of man on one side and moral law and decency on the other. The burial of her brother has not been discovered, and Haemon, Creon's son, does not know of her action, although she understands that the punishment for her act is death. She realizes that she and Haemon may never see each other again.

ANTIGONE: *(Rising)* Haemon, Haemon! Forgive me for quarreling with you last night. *(She crosses quickly to* HAEMON *and they embrace.)* Forgive me for everything. It was all my fault. I beg you to forgive me.

HAEMON: You know that I've forgiven you. You had hardly slammed the door, your perfume still hung in the room, when I had already forgiven you. *(He holds her in his arms and smiles at her. Then draws slightly back)* You stole that perfume. From whom?

ANTIGONE: Ismene.

HAEMON: And the rouge? and the face powder? and the frock? Whom did you steal them from?

ANTIGONE: Ismene.

HAEMON: And in whose honor did you get yourself up so elegantly?

ANTIGONE: I'll tell you everything. (*She draws him closer.*) Oh darling, what a fool I was! To waste a whole evening! A whole, beautiful evening!

HAEMON: We'll have other evenings, my sweet.

ANTIGONE: Perhaps we won't.

HAEMON: And other quarrels, too. A happy love is full of quarrels, you know.

ANTIGONE: A happy love, yes. Haemon, listen to me.

HAEMON: Yes?

ANTIGONE: Don't laugh at me this morning. Be serious.

HAEMON: I am serious.

ANTIGONE: And hold me tight. Tighter than you have ever held me. I want all your strength to flow into me.

HAEMON: There! With all my strength. (*A pause*)

ANTIGONE: (*Breathless*) That's good. (*They stand for a moment, silent and motionless.*) Haemon! I wanted to tell you. You know—the little boy we were going to have when we were married?

HAEMON: Yes?

ANTIGONE: I'd have protected him against everything in the world.

HAEMON: Yes, dearest.

ANTIGONE: Oh, you don't know how I should have held him in my arms and given him my strength. He wouldn't have been afraid of anything, I swear he wouldn't. Not of the falling night, nor of the terrible noonday sun, nor of all the shadows or all the walls in the world. Our little boy, Haemon! His mother wouldn't have been very imposing; her hair wouldn't always have been brushed; but she would have been strong where he was concerned, so much stronger than all those real mothers with their real bosoms and their aprons round their middle. You believe that, don't you, Haemon?

HAEMON: (*Soothingly*) Yes, yes, my darling.

ANTIGONE: And you believe me when I say that you would have had a real wife?

HAEMON: Darling, you are my real wife.

ANTIGONE: (*Pressing against him and crying out*) Haemon, you loved me! You did love me that night, didn't you? You're sure of it!

HAEMON: (*Rocking her gently*) What night, my sweet?

ANTIGONE: And you are very sure, aren't you, that that night at the dance, when you came to the corner where I was sitting, there was no mistake? It was me you were looking for? It wasn't another girl? And you're sure that never, not in your most secret heart of hearts, have you said to yourself that it was Ismene you ought to have asked to marry you?

HAEMON: (*Reproachfully*) Antigone, you are idiotic. You might give me credit for knowing my own mind. It's you I love, and no one else.

ANTIGONE: But you love me as a woman—as a woman wants to be loved, don't you? Your arms round me aren't lying, are they? Your hands, so warm against my back—they're not lying? This warmth that's in me; this confidence, this sense that I am safe, secure, that flows through me as I stand here with my cheek in the hollow of your shoulder: they are not lies, are they?

HAEMON: Antigone, darling. I love you exactly as you love me. With all of myself. (*They kiss.*)

ANTIGONE: I'm sallow, and I'm scrawny. Ismene is pink and golden. She's like a fruit.

HAEMON: Look here, Antigone—

ANTIGONE: Ah, dearest, I am ashamed of myself. But this morning, this special morning, I must know. Tell me the truth! I beg you tell me the truth! When you think about me, when it strikes you suddenly that I am going to belong to you—do you have the feeling that—that a great empty space is being hollowed out inside you, that there is something inside you that is just—dying?

HAEMON: Yes, I do. I do. (*A pause*)

ANTIGONE: That's the way I feel. And another thing. I wanted you to know that I should have been very proud to be your wife—the woman whose shoulder you would put your hand on as you sat down to table, absent-mindedly, as upon a thing that belonged to you. (*After a moment, draws away from him. Her tone changes.*) There! Now I have two things more to tell you. And when I have told them to you, you must go away instantly, without asking any questions. However strange they may seem to you. However much they hurt you. Swear that you will!

HAEMON: (*Beginning to be troubled*) What are these things that you are going to tell me?

ANTIGONE: Swear, first, that you will go away without one word. Without so much as looking at me. (*She looks at him, wretchedness in her face.*) You hear me, Haemon. Swear it please. This is the last mad wish that you will ever have to grant me. (*A pause*)

HAEMON: I swear it, since you insist. But I must tell you that I don't like this at all.

ANTIGONE: Please, Haemon. It's very serious. You must listen to me and do as I ask. First, about last night, when I came to your house. You asked me a moment ago why I wore Ismene's dress and rouge. It was because I was stupid. I wasn't very sure that you loved me as a woman; and I did it—because I wanted you to want me. I was trying to be more like other girls.

HAEMON: Was *that* the reason? My poor—

ANTIGONE: Yes. And you laughed at me. And we quarreled: and my awful temper got the better of me and I flung out of the house . . . the real reason was that I wanted you to take me: I wanted to be your wife before—

HAEMON: Oh, my darling—

ANTIGONE: (*Shuts him off*) You swore you wouldn't ask any questions. You swore, Haemon. (*Turns her face away and goes on in a hard voice*) As a matter of fact, I'll tell you why. I wanted to be your wife last night because I love you that way very—very strongly. And also because—Oh, my darling, my darling, forgive me; I'm going to cause you quite a lot of pain. (*She draws away from him.*) I wanted it also because I shall never, never be able to marry you, never! (HAEMON *is stupefied and mute; then he moves a step toward her.*) Haemon! You took a solemn oath! You swore! Leave me quickly! Tomorrow the whole thing will be clear to you. Even before tomorrow: this afternoon. If you please, Haemon, go now. It is the only thing left that you can do for me if you still love me. (*A pause as* HAEMON *stares at her. Then he turns and goes out through the arch.* ANTIGONE *stands motionless, then moves to chair at end of table and lets herself gently down on it. In a mild voice, as of calm after storm*) Well, it's over for Haemon, Antigone.

6. *The Crucible*, by Arthur Miller
    From Act II, Scene 2

Scene:	For one man, one woman
Characters:	JOHN PROCTOR
	ABIGAIL WILLIAMS
Setting:	A wood outside Salem, Massachusetts.
Time:	An evening in the spring of 1692.
Situation:	The town of Salem has entered the period of the infamous witch trials. One of the accusers is Abigail Williams, a young woman who has served in John Proctor's house as a servant during the illness of his wife. She has accused a number of Salem citizens of practicing witchcraft. John knows that Abigail's charges are false and that she is far from being the innocent girl the court believes her to be. He hopes that she can be made to change her testimony.
	Although Proctor was quiet during the initial development of the trials, an accusation brought against his wife forced him to face the problem. When Abigail was in the Proctor household, she and Proctor were intimate. Proctor believes that Abigail's accusation is an attempt to eliminate his wife Elizabeth as a rival. Abigail still desires Proctor, but he wishes only to be free of her so that he may be reconciled with his wife.

[PROCTOR *appears with lantern. He enters glancing behind him, then halts, holding the lantern raised.* ABIGAIL *appears with a wrap over her nightgown, her hair down. A moment of questioning silence*]

PROCTOR: (*searching*) I must speak with you, Abigail. (*She does not move, staring at him.*) Will you sit?

ABIGAIL: How do you come?

PROCTOR: Friendly.

ABIGAIL: (*glancing about*) I don't like the woods at night. Pray you, stand closer. (*He comes closer to her, but keeps separated in spirit.*) I knew it must be you. When I heard the pebbles on the window, before I opened up my eyes I knew. I thought you would come a good time sooner.

PROCTOR: I had thought to come many times.

ABIGAIL: Why didn't you? I am so alone in the world now.

PROCTOR: (*as a fact. Not bitterly*) Are you? I've heard that people come a hundred mile to see your face these days.

ABIGAIL: Aye, my face. Can you see my face?

PROCTOR: (*holds the lantern to her face*) Then you're troubled?

ABIGAIL: Have you come to mock me?

PROCTOR: (*sets lantern and sits down*) No, no, but I hear only that you go to the tavern every night, and play shovelboard with the Deputy Governor, and they give you cider.

ABIGAIL: (*as though that did not count*) I have once or twice played the shovelboard. But I have no joy in it.

PROCTOR: (*He is probing her.*) This is a surprise, Abby. I'd thought to find you gayer than this. I'm told a troop of boys go step for step with you wherever you walk these days.

ABIGAIL: Aye, they do. But I have only lewd looks from the boys.

PROCTOR: And you like that not?

ABIGAIL: I cannot bear lewd looks no more, John. My spirit's changed entirely. I ought to be given Godly looks when I suffer for them as I do.

PROCTOR: Oh? How do you suffer, Abby?

ABIGAIL: (*pulls up dress*) Why, look at my leg. I'm holes all over from their damned needles and pins. (*touching her stomach*) The jab your wife gave me's not healed yet, y'know.

PROCTOR: (*seeing her madness now*) Oh, it isn't.

ABIGAIL: I think sometimes she pricks it open again while I sleep.

PROCTOR: Ah?

ABIGAIL: And George Jacobs . . . (*sliding up her sleeve*) He comes again and again and raps me with his stick—the same spot every night all this week. Look at the lump I have.

PROCTOR: Abby—George Jacobs is in the jail all this month.

ABIGAIL: Thank God he is, and bless the day he hangs and lets me sleep in peace again! Oh, John, the world's so full of hypocrites. (*astonished, outraged*) They pray in jail! I'm told they all pray in jail!

PROCTOR: They may not pray?

ABIGAIL: And torture me in my bed while sacred words are comin' from their mouths? Oh, it will need God himself to cleanse this town properly!

PROCTOR: Abby—you mean to cry out still others?

ABIGAIL: If I live, if I am not murdered, I surely will, until the last hypocrite is dead.

PROCTOR: Then there is no one good?

ABIGAIL: (*softly*) Aye, there is one. *You* are good.

PROCTOR: Am I? How am I good?

ABIGAIL: Why, you taught me goodness, therefore you are good. It were a fire you walked me through, and all my ignorance was burned away. It were a fire, John, we lay in fire. And from that night no woman dare call me wicked anymore but I knew my answer. I used to weep for my sins when the wind lifted up my skirts; and blushed for shame because some old Rebecca called me loose. And then you burned my ignorance away. As bare as some December tree I saw them all—walking like saints to church, running to feed the sick, and hypocrites in their hearts! And God gave me strength to call them liars, and God made men listen to me, and by God I will scrub the world clean for the love of Him! Oh, John, I will make you such a wife when the world is white again! (*She kisses his hand in high emotion.*) You will be amazed to see me every day, a light of heaven in your house, a . . . (*He rises and backs away, frightened, amazed.*) Why are you cold?

PROCTOR: (*in a business-like way, but with uneasiness, as though before an unearthly thing*) My wife goes to trial in the morning, Abigail.

ABIGAIL: (*distantly*) Your wife?

PROCTOR: Surely you knew of it?

ABIGAIL: (*coming awake to that*) I do remember it now. (*as a duty*) How—how—is she well?

PROCTOR: As well as she may be, thirty-six days in that place.

ABIGAIL: You said you came friendly.

PROCTOR: She will not be condemned, Abby.

ABIGAIL: (*her holy feelings outraged. But she is questioning.*) You brought me from my bed to speak of her?

PROCTOR: I come to tell you, Abby, what I will do tomorrow in the court. I would not take you by surprise, but give you all good time to think on what to do to save yourself.

ABIGAIL: (*incredibly, and with beginning fear*) Save myself!

PROCTOR: If you do not free my wife tomorrow, I am set and bound to ruin you, Abby.

ABIGAIL: (*her voice small—astonished*) How—ruin me?

PROCTOR: I have rocky proof in documents that you knew that poppet* were none of my wife's; and that you yourself bade Mary Warren stab that needle into it.

ABIGAIL: (*A wildness stirs in her; a child is standing here who is unutterably frustrated, denied her wish; but she is still grasping for her wits.*) I bade Mary Warren . . . ?

PROCTOR: You know what you do, you are not so mad!

ABIGAIL: (*She calls upwards.*) Oh, hypocrites! Have you won him, too? (*directly to him*) John, why do you let them send you?

PROCTOR: I warn you, Abby.

ABIGAIL: They send you! They steal your honesty and . . .

PROCTOR: I have found my honesty.

ABIGAIL: No, this is your wife pleading, your sniveling, envious wife! This is Rebecca's voice, Martha Corey's voice. You were no hypocrite!

PROCTOR: (*He grasps her arm and holds her.*) I will prove you for the fraud you are!

ABIGAIL: And if they ask you why Abigail would ever do so murderous a deed, what will you tell them?

PROCTOR: (*It is hard even to say it.*) I will tell them why.

ABIGAIL: What will you tell? You will confess to fornication? In the court?

PROCTOR: If you will have it so, so I will tell it! (*She utters a disbelieving laugh.*) I say I will! (*She laughs louder, now with more assurance he will never do it. He shakes her roughly.*) If you can still hear, hear this! Can you hear! (*She is trembling, staring up at him as though he were out of his mind.*) You will tell the court you are blind to spirits; you cannot see them anymore, and you will never cry witchery again, or I will make you famous for the whore you are!

ABIGAIL: (*She grabs him.*) Never in this world! I know you, John—you are this moment singing secret Hallelujahs that your wife will hang!

PROCTOR: (*throws her down*) You mad, you murderous bitch!

ABIGAIL: (*rises*) Oh, how hard it is when pretense falls! But it falls, it falls! (*She wraps herself up as though to go.*) You have done your duty by her. I hope it is your last hypocrisy. I pray you will come again with sweeter news for me. I

---

*A cloth doll.

know you will—now that your duty's done. Good night, John. (*She is backing away, raising her hand in farewell.*) Fear naught. I will save you tomorrow. From yourself I will save you. (*She is gone.*)
[PROCTOR *is left alone, amazed in terror. He takes up his lantern and slowly exits as the curtain falls.*]

7. *Saint Joan*, by George Bernard Shaw
    From Scene 2

    Scene: For one man, one woman
    Characters: JOAN
        CHARLES, THE DAUPHIN
    Setting: The throne room of the Dauphin of France at Chinon, in Touraine.
    Time: Late afternoon. March, 1429.
    Situation: Joan, the maid, has come to the court of the Dauphin to persuade him to give her arms so that she may lead the disconsolate French armies to victory against the English. Shaw has developed an interesting portrait of Joan, creating a character imbued with common sense, determination, and idealism. Charles is twenty-six years old, physically weak and of an ungainly appearance, but with a good sense of humor. Despite his age he has not matured sufficiently to exercise real control over his court. At the opening of this scene, the court has left, and Joan is alone with Charles for the first time. A product of Shaw's irreverent wit, this scene contains as much humor as any excerpt in this section.

JOAN: (*to the* DAUPHIN) Who be old Gruff-and-Grum?
CHARLES: He is the Duke de la Trémouille.
JOAN: What be his job?
CHARLES: He pretends to command the army. And whenever I find a friend I can care for, he kills him.
JOAN: Why dost let him?
CHARLES: (*petulantly moving to the throne side of the room to escape from her magnetic field*) How can I prevent him? He bullies me. They all bully me.
JOAN: Art afraid?
CHARLES: Yes: I am afraid. It's no use preaching to me about it. It's all very well for these big men with their armor that is too heavy for me, and their swords that I can hardly lift, and their muscle and their shouting and their bad tempers. They like fighting: most of them are making fools of themselves all the time they are not fighting; but I am quiet and sensible; and I dont want to kill people: I only want to be left alone to enjoy myself in my own way. I never asked to be a king: it was pushed on me. So if you are going to say "Son of St. Louis: gird on the sword of your ancestors, and lead us to victory" you may spare your breath to cool your porridge; for I cannot do it. I am not built that way; and there is an end of it.
JOAN: (*trenchant and masterful*) Blethers! We are like that to begin with. I shall put courage into thee.
CHARLES: But I dont want to have courage put into me. I want to sleep in a comfortable bed, and not live in continual terror of being killed or

wounded. Put courage into the others, and let them have their bellyful of fighting; but let me alone.

JOAN: It's no use, Charlie: thou must face what God puts on thee. If thou fail to make thyself king, thoult be a beggar: what else art fit for? Come! Let me see thee sitting on the throne. I have looked forward to that.

CHARLES: What is the good of sitting on the throne when the other fellows give all the orders? However! (*He sits enthroned, a piteous figure.*) here is the king for you! Look your fill at the poor devil.

JOAN: Thourt not king yet, lad: thourt but Dauphin. Be not led away by them around thee. Dressing up dont fill empty noddle. I know the people: the real people that make thy bread for thee; and I tell thee they count no man king of France until the holy oil has been poured on his hair, and himself consecrated and crowned in Rheims Cathedral. And thou needs new clothes, Charlie. Why does not Queen look after thee properly?

CHARLES: We're too poor. She wants all the money we can spare to put on her own back. Besides, I like to see her beautifully dressed; and I dont care what I wear myself: I should look ugly anyhow.

JOAN: There is some good in thee, Charlie; but it is not yet a king's good.

CHARLES: We shall see. I am not such a fool as I look. I have my eyes open; and I can tell you that one good treaty is worth ten good fights. These fighting fellows lose all on the treaties that they gain on the fights. If we can only have a treaty, the English are sure to have the worst of it, because they are better at fighting than at thinking.

JOAN: If the English win, it is they that will make the treaty: and then God help poor France! Thou must fight; Charlie, whether thou will or no. I will go first to hearten thee. We must take our courage in both hands: aye, and pray for it with both hands too.

CHARLES: (*descending from his throne and again crossing the room to escape from her dominating urgency*) Oh do stop talking about God and praying. I cant bear people who are always praying. Isnt it bad enough to have to do it at the proper times?

JOAN: (*pitying him*) Thou poor child, thou has never prayed in thy life. I must teach thee from the beginning.

CHARLES: I am not a child: I am a grown man and a father; and I will not be taught any more.

JOAN: Aye, you have a little son. He that will be Louis the Eleventh when you die. Would you not fight for him?

CHARLES: No: a horrid boy. He hates me. He hates everybody, selfish little beast! I dont want to be bothered with children. I dont want to be a father; and I dont want to be a son: especially a son of St. Louis. I dont want to be any of these fine things you all have your heads full of: I want to be just what I am. Why cant you mind your own business, and let me mind mine?

JOAN: (*again contemptuous*) Minding your own business is like minding your own body: it's the shortest way to make yourself sick. What is my business? Helping mother at home. What is thine? Petting lapdogs and sucking sugarsticks: I call that muck. I tell thee it is God's business we are here to do: not our own. I have a message to thee from God; and thou must listen to it, though thy heart break with the terror of it.

CHARLES: I dont want a message; but can you tell me any secrets? Can you do any cures? Can you turn lead into gold, or anything of that sort?

JOAN: I can turn thee into a king, in Rheims Cathedral; and that is a miracle that will take some doing, it seems.

CHARLES: If we go to Rheims, and have a coronation, Anne will want new dresses. We cant afford them. I am all right as I am.

JOAN: As you are! And what is that? Less than my father's poorest shepherd. Thourt not lawful owner of thy own land of France till thou be consecrated.

CHARLES: But I shall not be lawful owner of my own land anyhow. Will the consecration pay off my mortgages? I have pledged my last acre to the Archbishop and that fat bully. I owe money even to Bluebeard.

JOAN: (*earnestly*) Charlie: I come from the land, and have gotten my strength working on the land; and I tell thee that the land is thine to rule righteously and keep God's peace in, and not to pledge at the pawnshop as a drunken woman pledges her children's clothes. And I come from God to tell thee to kneel in the cathedral and solemnly give thy kingdom to Him for ever and ever, and become the greatest king in the world as His steward and His bailiff, His soldier and His servant. The very clay of France will become holy; her soldiers will be the soldiers of God: the rebel dukes will be rebels against God: the English will fall on their knees and beg thee let them return to their lawful homes in peace. Wilt be a poor little Judas, and betray me and Him that sent me?

CHARLES: (*tempted at last*) Oh, if I only dare!

JOAN: I shall dare, dare, and dare again, in God's name! Art for or against me?

CHARLES: (*excited*) I'll risk it, I warn you I shant be able to keep it up; but I'll risk it. You shall see. (*running to the main door and shouting*) Hallo! Come back, everybody. (*to* JOAN, *as he runs back to the arch opposite*) Mind you stand by and dont let me be bullied. (*through the arch*) Come along, will you: the whole Court. (*He sits down in the royal chair as they all hurry in to their former places, chattering and wondering.*) Now I'm in for it; but no matter: here goes! (*to the* PAGE) Call for silence, you little beast, will you?

CHAPTER
SIX

Preparing a Role

No matter how well the actor has assimilated the fundamentals of stage movement and speech, it is not until actually preparing and undertaking a role that the actor discovers how effectively he or she is able to use these techniques. Actors differ in the emphasis they give certain features of character preparation, and their sequence of study will often vary, but certain elements are invariably utilized by all competent actors.

Basic Steps in Developing a Role

Analyzing the Play

Obviously the first step in preparing a role is to read the play. This first reading tells something of the personality of the character to be undertaken and may suggest stage movement and pieces of business that will bring the play to life from the printed page. Even this first reading should put the actor's imagination to work.

The early readings are important. Some actors read through a play hastily, underlining their speeches with a red pencil and never going beyond this superficial examination of the play. Many difficulties encountered later during the rehearsal period could easily have been avoided by a more responsible study of the play during this preliminary stage. Much of the meaning of the play is lost if the actor fails to study it as an integrated whole but skims through it, examining only his or her own lines.

At the first reading of the play one should follow the plot, enjoy the humor or suspense, and let the conflict of the play sustain interest until reaching the climax and final resolution of the story. A play is held together by the action, and it is the story that helps to sustain interest in the characters. After this first reading the actor should read the play again, with greater care, this time examining its organization, its style and mood, and the relation of all the characters to one another and to the play itself. It may be useful to do some preliminary thinking about the following questions during this and subsequent readings:

1. What is the theme of the play? What is the author trying to say?
2. Does the play have a distinctive style?
3. Is the sequence of events clear?
4. Why do the characters react as they do to the various situations developed in the play?
5. What is the function of the character who is to be portrayed by the reader?
6. What is that character's relationship to the other characters in the play?

These and other questions should be discussed with the director and cast members during the early rehearsals. This exchange of ideas will serve to put the character in proper perspective as the actor relates the part (in the literal sense) to the whole. Katharine Cornell has told us that "To understand one's own character thoroughly one must see it in relation not only to itself but to the other characters in the play."[1] Helen Hayes holds much the same point of view. Her first conception of a drama is "entirely objective." She is concerned with the structure of the play, and she examines all the parts in order to understand "what they look like, what they are thinking of, what their relationship is to one another, the quality of their personalities."[2] Not until she understands the play "in the language of the theatre" does she begin a detailed examination of her role in terms of its creative challenge.

---

1. Morton Eustis, *Players at Work: Acting According to the Actors* (New York: Theatre Arts Books, 1937), p. 65.
2. Ibid., p. 15.

It is well that few actors in the theatre today follow the example of one popular eighteenth-century actress who had secured a noteworthy reputation as Lady Macbeth. Unfortunately she was so wrapped up in her own performance that she paid little attention to her relation to the play as a whole. When asked one day how her characterization of Lady Macbeth fit into the total fabric of Shakespeare's tragedy, she answered, "I don't know." It seems she had read only those scenes in which she appeared and therefore had only a vague idea as to how the play ended. Just as acting styles have changed during the past hundred years, so too has the actor's responsibility to the play. Extensive rehearsals and attention to detail are important because they help to achieve an integrated production instead of the haphazard productions of the past.

Analyzing the Character

The next step in the preparation of a role requires a thorough examination of the character. This involves a careful scrutiny of the script—a scrutiny to which the actor brings his or her accumulation of experience and observation. This accumulation should continue to be used through the rehearsal period and actual performances. It is used as long as the actor is receptive to new ideas and impressions and does not close off the great potential of the imagination.

As the actor studies the play it is important to begin to form a solid impression about his or her character. A few simple problems need to be solved in order to provide a preliminary approach to the character. Nazimova, the noted Russian actress, felt it imperative to "study the woman. I look at her under a magnifying glass and say to myself: 'Is she right? Is she logical? Is she true to herself? Can *I* act that woman?'" As an actress she wanted to know "what she is thinking, what her inner response is, her feeling . . . once you know what she *is*, what she does becomes easy to interpret."[3]

Nazimova has left us some valuable advice. Her most significant comment on the preparation of the role is: *"once you know what she is, what she does becomes easy to interpret."* Clearly, the first step in developing a role is to understand it as thoroughly as possible. It is at this point that the actor may begin to use all available technical and emotional resources to build a believable characterization. "Half the actor's battle is won," says Helen Hayes, "once a clear picture of the character is firmly engraved in the senses."[4]

Once a general picture of the character is formed, the actor begins to build from specific details and ask specific questions about the character.

3. Ibid., p. 53.
4. Ibid., p. 18.

Sidney Poitier works in this manner, and insists that ''I must understand what are the driving forces in the man. In order to understand that, you must find out what are his political, social, economic, religious milieus''[5] in order to understand how they contribute to the full personality of the character. This type of work is essential for all actors. The following analysis chart may be useful in helping to analyze the character.

1. *Social Factors*
   a. Class status: upper, middle, lower
   b. Occupation: What kind of work, attitude toward the job, income, hours at work
   c. Education: Level of education, schools attended, probable grades, best subjects, worst subjects, etc.
   d. Home: Single, married, divorced, orphan, living with family, living alone, kind of home, etc.
   e. Religion
   f. Community: rural, suburban, city, inner city, place in the community
   g. Race, nationality, ethnic background
   h. Political preferences, activities, interests, etc.
2. *Personal Factors*
   a. Hobbies, amusements, kinds of reading, etc.
   b. Sex life, moral views and attitudes
   c. Ambitions
   d. Attitude to life: Resigned, rebellious, defeatist, etc.
   e. Mental health: complexes, neuroses, obsessions, superstitions, etc.
   f. Personality: introverted, extroverted
   g. Dress habits: neat, sloppy, casual, well-groomed, traditional, non-conformist, etc.
   h. Talents and creativity

One means of helping to realize the character is to establish a general impression about his or her physical and vocal personality. How does the character move and walk on stage: quickly or slowly, with harsh or gentle movements, erect or stooped bearing? Is the character soft-spoken or does he or she speak in a loud voice, rapidly or slowly, in short bursts or in smooth and even phrasing? What kind of pitch, inflectional patterns, and articulation will make the character more meaningful?

A good starting point for determining these working elements is the script itself. Careful examination of the play will reveal a wealth of detailed information about the character. Five important keys to understanding may be derived from the script:

---

5. Sidney Poitier, quoted in Lewis Funke and John E. Booth, *Actors Talk About Acting* (New York: Random House, 1961), p. 378.

1. The playwright's description and comments.
2. The character's manner of speech. How the character sees himself or herself.
3. What others in the play say about the character.
4. Suggested business inserted by the playwright.
5. Distinctive changes in attitude on the part of the character throughout the play.

These considerations and ideas about the role should not be maintained too rigidly. They should serve as a basis for developing a characterization through the rehearsal period, but the actor must be prepared to make adjustments and continue to probe into the subtleties of the characterization. It will be useful here to remind ourselves of the questions the actor should ask in any scene or improvisation, which we called the **W** check list, in Chapter 3.

1. *Who* am I?
2. *Where* am I?
3. *What* do I want?
4. *Why* do I want it?
5. *What* is preventing me from getting it?
6. *What* am I willing to do to get what I want?
7. *Who* do I want it from?
8. *When* do I need it?

Often, during this early period, such questions as "How does my character walk, move, speak, and so on?" should be resolved only in general terms. Specific solutions will be realized through the use of observation and imagination.

Observation

As Sherlock Holmes often reminded his constant and rather muddle-headed companion, Dr. Watson, to see is not enough. One must learn to use the power of observation. Individuals are differentiated by habits of movement, gesture, posture, and speech patterns. The actor who is sensitive to these differentiations in people will often find much that may be meaningfully transferred to the stage. This process should go on not only as the actor works on a specific role but during everyday activities. It is not necessary to become a walking diary of all that occurs during a day, but sensitive awareness of the environment and those who inhabit it will help solve many difficulties arising out of challenging characterizations. Walter Matthau goes so far as to suggest that it is like being a sponge, in that an observant actor "soaks up everything." Matthau indicates that he enjoys wandering into a cafeteria anonymously and just watching people. "I can look around as much as I like, not that you ever imitate people as such. But you get the feel and smell and the taste of how they behave. . . . Then, when I'm onstage, I use it."[6]

Probably the most famous impersonation in the history of acting was Charlie Chaplin's immortal tramp. So closely associated is this actor with this role that often we have difficulty in separating the two. We need simply mention the name Charlie Chaplin, and an image of a tramp with baggy pants, oversized shoes, and bowler hat immediately springs to mind. The manner in which this great character was created illustrates how observation may be translated into the creative impulse. In this case it was a chance meeting with a hobo on a street in San Francisco that fanned the spark of Chaplin's imagination. We all meet interesting people every day, but are we aware of the potential such meetings hold for the actor? Let Chaplin describe the meeting in his own words and we may see how his keen observation worked to refine the character of the tramp which he brought to the screen.

> We went into a barroom, he got a drink, and we sat right down then and there to have a bite of lunch. The food and the drink warmed him and brought to the surface the irresponsible joy of life possessed by the nomad and the ne'er-do-well. He told me the story of his life, of long jaunts through the beautiful country, of longer rides on convenient freights, or misfortunes which attend the unfortunate who are found stealing a ride on a "side-door pullman," and of the simplicity of the farmers who lived only a short distance from the city. It was a delight to hear him talk, to gather from it the revelations of his character, to watch his gestures, and his trick of facial expression. *All these elements were carefully watched by me, and noted for future reference.* He was rather surprised when we parted, at my profuse thanks. He had given me a good deal more than I had given him, but he didn't know it. He had obtained a little food and drink and a chance talk from me. From him, I had a brand new idea for a picture.[7]

Obviously it is not always possible to find one model from which to build a characterization. In many ways Chaplin was lucky, but it is important to remember that he was ready and able to assimilate qualities of the hobo's gestures, facial expression, and attitude toward life into the projected role.

Observation may be useful also in helping to provide a clue to the handling of particularly difficult scenes or problems. One of the legends of the theatre tells of David Garrick while he was working on his role of King

---

6. Walter Matthau in Lillian Ross and Helen Ross, *The Player: A Profile of an Art* (New York: Simon and Schuster, 1962), p. 422.

7. Charlie Chaplin, "How I Made My Success," *Theatre*, September 1915, pp. 120 ff. (italics added).

Lear and examining the best means of simulating madness. A neighbor, unhappily, provided him with the key. One day the neighbor was holding his two-year-old daughter in his arms as he leaned out of his upper-story window. The child slipped from his grasp and was killed instantly on the stone street below. The unfortunate man lost his mind from shock. Garrick often stopped by his neighbor's home and would see him hold an imaginary child in his arms and then seem to drop it from the same window, breaking off into horrible screams and sobs of anguish. From his observation of the distraught father Garrick was able to build his shattering portrayal of the maddened King Lear, one of the most memorable characterizations in the English theatre.

On such incidents are great roles built. Such occurrences are certainly rare and not likely to be part of our everyday experience. Yet even the most seemingly unimportant observation may be of value to the actor. The smallest gesture, a unique reaction to an incident, a twist of the head, the gait or stoop of an acquaintance may serve to bring individuality to a characterization.

Laurence Olivier in 1980, after acting for fifty years in the theatre and film, took time during the shooting of the latest version of *The Jazz Singer* to wander through the East Side of New York watching elderly Jewish men, in order to help him prepare his role as the cantor in the film. He never stopped watching, learning, remembering.

Alertness to events in our everyday life is surprisingly useful. Careful scrutiny of interesting people in a bus, on the street, or in any meeting place has provided more than one alert actor with the means of building a successful portrait. The important thing to remember is that we must be receptive to the events that take place around us and be ready to make use of them when the need arises in our role.

Imagination

There will be circumstances in which even the most careful observation or experience will fail to provide the clue needed to develop a character or to play an especially difficult sequence. Observation is essential, but sometimes we may find that no file of experience can serve our needs. We may also legitimately argue that there are many emotional situations in the course of a play for which our stock of experience and observation will be unable to provide valid information.

Ingrid Bergman amusingly pointed out that when you are playing a murderer, "you don't go out and murder somebody." The imagination may supply the means of coping with these difficulties. However, we must be careful not to equate imagination simply with sheer invention. Rather, imagination requires creative inspiration and originality firmly based on experience and observation. "Imagination, industry, and intelligence," said

Ellen Terry, ''are all indispensable to the actress, but of these three the greatest is . . . imagination.''[8]

Imagination provides the creative spark that makes meaningful and exciting the most difficult characters and scenes. One of the best examples of the use of imagination involved a particularly difficult scene for the actor Jacob Ben-Ami in Tolstoy's *Redemption*. The character Fedya, on the verge of suicide, is required to place a gun to his temple; but at the fatal moment he must lose his nerve, so that, shattered in spirit, he becomes a broken, ruined shadow of a man for the remainder of the play. Ben-Ami, of course, had never been in a similar situation, nor had he observed anything resembling such an incident. Simply trying to imagine the situation might have been useful, but this too would leave him short of the effect he wished to achieve. His solution was actually quite simple, and the reaction of the audience to his playing of the scene was clear evidence of his success.

Ben-Ami reasoned that a fundamental element in Fedya's loss of courage was his terror of the bullet searing through his brain and the physical pain that would accompany it. Having no accurate experience to serve as a guide, the actor remembered the shock he experienced in the morning stepping into an ice-cold shower. It was this sensation Ben-Ami utilized as he prepared to pull the trigger and was seized by his terrifying hesitation. The actor's imagination had provided the solution that made a highly difficult scene believable.[9]

One distinguished actor has suggested, quite seriously, that when playing a love scene, he often contemplated a delicious plate of spaghetti and meatballs. Perhaps he didn't like his costar.

When used properly, imagination opens up an entire world of creative potential. It makes feasible the acting of difficult scenes and emotional climaxes which might otherwise be difficult, if not impossible. Imagination may be used as simply as the projection of rage at an adversary by the device of imagining the anger we have felt as we slap furiously at a bothersome mosquito, or it may be used to build a complete character.

Two fine actresses also describe this use of imagination quite clearly and practically. When Anne Bancroft first looked at the script of *The Miracle Worker*, she asked herself

> What is the whole thing about? It's about a woman who if she does not teach this child, both she and the child will perish. Of course, I have nothing like that in my own life, so I have to take something else in my life about which I have to say 'If I don't do a certain thing, I will perish.'[10]

---

8. Ellen Terry, *Ellen Terry's Memoirs* (New York: G. P. Putnam's Sons, 1932), p. 34.
9. This story is known to many actors and directors. Burgess Meredith has spoken of it in his discussion of acting. A detailed retelling of the incident is to be found in Robert Lewis's *Method—or Madness* (New York: Samuel French, Inc., 1958), pp. 12–13.
10. Anne Bancroft, quoted in Funke and Booth, op. cit., p. 450.

In *The Chapman Report*, Jane Fonda was asked to play a frigid woman and a widow. She did it, she recalled, not by being "like that woman. Instead, I call on what every woman has felt at some time in her life—doubts about herself. This feeling is enough to give me 'insight' into the way that woman feels."[11]

Imagination may not always provide us with the right solution to our difficulties, but it is virtually boundless in its potential. In the trial-and-error process of the early stages of preparing a role, it is better to take a wrong turn than not to make a bold attempt to utilize the actor's creativity.

Learning Lines

The learning of lines is often the most unpleasant task connected with the actor's work in a production. It is recognized as a basic responsibility in the preparation of the role, although little creativeness is involved. Burgess Meredith has called it "turmoil and headsweat," and many actors agree with him. There is no one right way to learn lines. Some actors have the facility to learn lines quickly; others find it laborious and time consuming.

Three approaches to the learning of lines may be suggested. It is possible, however, that some combination of the three will be most helpful in the memorization of dialogue.

1. *Lines may be learned by constant repetition through silent reading.* This approach is the type most commonly used and involves the age-old drudgery of reading and rereading until the dialogue is firmly fixed in the memory. The dialogue may be studied line by line, or phrase by phrase, until constant exposure firmly establishes the lines and cues in the memory. This approach will be most successful for the actor having good visual memory.
2. *Lines may be learned by examining their emotional and intellectual context.* Rather than memorizing the lines mechanically, some actors find it useful to work for the meaning of the line, striving to find vivid elements or some association of ideas that serve to establish the sense of the line in the memory. This approach has the value of developing comprehension of the role while it frees the actor from the script.
3. *Lines may be learned by relating them to the movement in the play.* We find this device utilized after rehearsals are well under way and the actor is able to *associate* dialogue with movement and principal pieces of business. Often the dialogue is so closely related to the physical characteristics of the production that such association is simple. Long

---

11. Jane Fonda, quoted in Ross and Ross, op. cit., pp. 99–100.

speeches with little movement are clearly the most difficult to memorize in this way. If the movement has already been blocked out, recapitulating the planned movement in private may be helpful in the study of lines.

Most directors prefer that the actor not memorize lines until the play has been blocked out. This prevailing philosophy underscores the belief that the learning of lines should grow out of the meaning and emphasis of the production. If lines need to be learned before rehearsals begin, or if the rehearsal period is somewhat limited (as in summer stock), the first two methods will usually prove necessary.

The following description of how one actor approaches the learning of lines is not intended to be dogmatic, but it does illustrate a prevalent practice which many actors find successful. Paul Muni's outline of his approach to the learning of lines indicated use of the first two methods, with somewhat greater emphasis on the first.

> This method has been most helpful to me. I have found it best to parrot my lines, to memorize them directly, so that I can speak them without analysis or thought for their meaning. Often I will read a speech over and over, at home, until the phrases come to me automatically and rhythmically.
>
> While parroting my lines, some of the thought behind them is bound to penetrate subconsciously, so that my interpretation is partially set, but not so rigidly that I cannot change it. Once the lines come to me automatically, I discard them completely and think of the thoughts they express . . . until I am confident that the lines are mine and that I need no longer think of them.[12]

Unless a director insists to the contrary, it is wise to learn the lines and cues as soon as possible after blocking rehearsals have started. "Getting rid of the book" is an important step forward, for it permits the actor to concentrate on developing the role without the impediment of the script.

Developing Business

Stage business may be defined as any action, other than the basic movement of the play, that accompanies a situation or a line of dialogue. It may help to tell the story and to impart variety to the production. The insertion of business necessary to propel the story forward is invariably the concern of the director, who will find suggestions for this type of business explicitly

---

12. Paul Muni, "The Actor Plays His Part," in *We Make the Movies,* ed. Nancy Naumberg (New York: W. W. Norton Co., 1937), pp. 131–42.

indicated in the script or may develop it in relation to the plan of production.

Because business also serves to give an added dimension to the character, the actor must take a major responsibility for developing pieces of business to enhance and enrich the role. Business that grows directly out of the indicated action of the play presents little difficulty in execution once stage technique is mastered. Business that the actor develops personally as an integral part of the character may prove somewhat more difficult to create, in that it places greater demands on the actor's imagination and creativity. Despite such difficulties, the value of inserting business designed to enhance the character must be clearly recognized.

Business utilized for character embellishment is usually carefully detailed and often quite distinctive from the business that simply advances the plot. Pantomimic action should be used by the actor as a mean of expanding and clarifying the character. The development of even the smallest piece of business may turn a lifeless, cardboard figure into a distinctive personality. The most common pieces of business involve the lighting of cigarettes, the moving of small pieces of furniture, the arrangement of articles of clothing, and the handling of small properties, such as a pencil and pad, a cigarette lighter, a glass, a cup, a book, and the like. Such properties are useful in helping to project particular personality traits. With or without properties, selected pieces of pantomimic action add variety to a performance and may tell us something important about the character. One character may consistently drop cigarette ashes on his coat, another may be addicted to doodling with pad and pencil, another may have the habit of scratching an ear, rubbing his chin, taking off eyeglasses for continual cleaning, and so on.

Clues that may be useful in developing business are often found in the dialogue, either in what the character says or in what others say about him. Sometimes it will grow out of the physical appearance of the character. In his performance as Henry Drummond in *Inherit the Wind*, Paul Muni made skillful use of his colorful suspenders to project a character who was at the same time thoughtful, vigorous, and dynamic. The excellent description by one character of Mrs. Millamant as she is about to make an entrance in Congreve's *The Way of the World:* ''Here she comes, i' faith, full sail, with her fan spread and her streamers out, . . .'' should provide any intelligent actress wtih several ideas for business to enliven her portrait of this character.

Business may develop constantly throughout the rehearsal period. Some ideas will undoubtedly occur with the first analysis of the character. When rehearsals with actual properties begin, still more business will become obvious and may be integrated into the pattern of the characterization. It is important to remember that the growth of the character, through patience, imagination, and experimentation, continues during each stage of the preparation of the role.

Avoidance of Clichés

A cliché is a conventionalized and stereotyped projection of an emotion or character. It is obvious that few situations and characters in plays are identical; yet the actor is often tempted to fall back on stock tricks and devices because of the failure to develop a role carefully and with perseverance. Such devices may include imitating another performer or using pieces of business that the actor may have found successful in previous plays.

Even more damaging to creativity is the belief by some actors that all emotional situations can be portrayed by one or another standardized external device. The following descriptions illustrating this type of thinking may seem amusing, but they have been seriously advanced even in recent years as one means of "acting emotional states." We read in one text that to project *contempt* the actor should do as follows: The corner of the mouth twitches up, which exposes a glint on the pointed dog-tooth; the nostril on that side of the face curls, and the eyes narrow. To enact *grief* we are told that the actor should bring the lips together tightly, attempting to control their quivering. The eyes must be veiled slightly by the eyelids, and the brow should be contracted so that the wrinkles lift in the center.[13]

The question of using external means is not the issue here, for such means are certainly valid and useful for many actors. However, total reliance on such a stock set of reactions and responses is detrimental to creative work. Reliance on stereotyped reactions creates a one-dimensional performance which is unlikely to produce satisfaction for either the audience or the actor. How simple it would be if all villains and heroes could be played in the same manner! Unfortunately we see too many stock performances of this kind caused either by haste or by poor judgment.

The lessons of history and our own observation tell us how erroneous stereotyping may be. Nero stands out clearly as the embodiment of evil and cruelty. When he is enacted on the stage, the actor may be tempted to use all the stock devices to develop a character of consummate evil. Yet it was this man who exclaimed as he signed the routine death sentence of a convicted criminal, "Would to God I had never learned to write!" Clearly there was more to the man than a superficial appraisal would indicate. When Charlton Heston played Michelangelo in *The Agony and the Ecstasy*, he read several biographies, novels, and collections of letters about the subject before beginning to prepare even a preliminary judgment about his role.

All stock responses are not to be condemned out of hand. On the contrary, they will occasionally be useful in helping the beginning actor over a particularly difficult hurdle. The continual use, however, of a series of cut-and-dried responses for the purpose of playing certain characters and situations is dangerous, and, if extended over a number of plays, it is likely to

---

13. This approach is explained in detail in C. C. Mather, A. H. Spaulding, and M. H. Skillen, *Behind the Footlights* (New York: Silver Burdett Co., 1935).

limit seriously the development of the actor's resources. There is no substitute for thought and hard work. Good acting requires a good deal of both.

Finding One's Own Approach

"Nothing is more fleeting than any traditional method of impersonation." Henry Irving's remark implies that the actor of the present must not be tied too closely to the past. It is also a plea for *individuality* in the theatre, a point it would be well for all actors to consider.

There is no question that tradition is an important cohesive element in theatre work, binding the present with the best work of the past. However, there is frequently a tendency to rely too heavily on the accepted styles and interpretations of successful performers rather than to utilize the well-springs of one's own creative force. Imitation is surely a distinctive type of flattery, and the study of the methods of fine actors, such as Alec Guinness, Laurence Olivier, or Hal Holbrook is useful for the beginning actor. Many successful actors who began their professional careers at an early age, watching backstage and learning from the work of more seasoned performers, openly admit the value of such experience. But they were able to blend these experiences with their own personality and temperament and, instead of becoming carbon copies of their elders, added something refreshing of their own. On the other hand, many young actors who modeled themselves after the distinctive styles and personalities of their favorite actors were more adept at imitating their idols' idiosyncrasies than they were at understanding the creative nature of their work.

Reliance on the past is helpful at the outset, but must not be permitted to limit the actor's own style and approach. Laurence Olivier's *Richard III* is a case in point. In the film version of the play, Olivier read the lines in a choppy but rhythmic cadence which was reportedly suggested by the style used by Henry Irving half a century before. We may be sure that Olivier's performance was no drab imitation of Irving's but one tempered with his own personality and experience. Olivier was not afraid to use the best of the past; indeed, the past had provided a clue, but the actor had held his own mirror up to nature.

It is so easy to fall into the trap of imitation that the actor should be on guard against it at all times. *Hamlet* probably provides the actor with more traditional methods of interpretation than any other play. It would be difficult not to rely on some of the hints offered by other actors who have successfully played the role. Yet the finest American Hamlet of this century, John Barrymore, took no such easy path in his interpretation. His director, Arthur Hopkins, described his approach in unmistakable terms:

FIGURE 6.1 Albert Finney as Hamlet, National Theatre.

We began with our own conception, and developed it in all parts of the play. I doubt if Hamlet had ever been given a clearer course to sail. . . . We made ourselves completely servants of the play, untempted by any beckoning to leave our personal and peculiar imprint on it.[14]

The same responsibility to individuality applies to every aspect of the creation of a role. It is up to the actor to decide: "How much technique should I use? Should I feel my role? What do I know about my character? What can I put meaningfully onstage? What sort of business, movement, and voice can I use for a specific character?" The truly creative actor will impress upon each role the stamp of his or her own personality and insight. The major consideration is that the actor approach the role without preconceived notions that might limit the actor's own creative potential. If the actor does this honestly, he or she will be able to maintain individuality as an actor and, hopefully, as an artist.

---

14. Gene Fowler, *Good Night, Sweet Prince* (New York: Viking Press, 1944), p. 208.

EXERCISES

1. (a) Each evening try to remember every new person you have met or observed that day.
   (b) Learn to discern at least one distinctive characteristic about each one.
   (c) Make a distinction between the person's manner of speech and his or her movement, whenever possible.
2. Choose an incident that happened the day before you attempt this exercise. Relate the incident in all its details to the group, attempting to recreate your attitude during the incident, and suggest the attitudes of other people connected with the incident by acting out their participation.
3. Write a detailed analysis of one of the following sets of characters from the scenes included in Chapters 3 through 8: Edmund and Jamie from *Long Day's Journey into Night* (Chapter 6); Amanda and Laura from *The Glass Menagerie* (Chapter 7); Howard and Willie from *Death of a Salesman* (Chapter 7); Elyot and Victor from *Private Lives* (Chapter 8); Regina and Alexandra from *The Little Foxes* (Chapter 6). Try to suggest the environmental influences that may have shaped their personalities, and compare them as individuals. This exercise will require a careful study of the play and its characters and the use of imagination.
4. In order to develop proficiency in the handling of small pieces of business, do the following exercises in pantomime before the class. Have the class evaluate the realism you create. Your observation and imagination will also be called into play in these exercises.
   (a) Sew a button on a coat.
   (b) Mix a cocktail, using various ingredients including ice.
   (c) Try on a new suit (or dress) in a clothing store. Examine it in a full-length mirror.
   (d) Put icing and decorations on a cake.
   (e) Examine a number of books in a library until you find the information you want.
   (f) Try to open a door, discover that none of your keys fits, and proceed to pick the lock.
   (g) Scramble some eggs and serve them to a guest.
   (h) Pack a cardboard box carefully with fragile items, and then tie and label the box.

AMBIGUOUS DIALOGUE

The following exercises deal with purposely ambiguous text. They offer the actor an opportunity to utilize acting skills using brief and complete units. The actor must deal with all the aspects of text work except that it is not necessary to seek for comments by the playwright or look for character qualities in the text. The characters and situations are to be created entirely by the actors, working with the ambiguous dialogue which provides almost complete freedom for the actor.

In each of the following dialogues there are two characters: A and B. They are engaged in an action that is complete in an even number of speeches from 20 to 26. There are implied objectives and obstacles in each. No references to location, gender, relationship, activity, objects, etc., are given. The scene partners must create the missing information, but it can be from their own experiential level. Then they must rehearse to make the dialogue honest and believable.

These exercises are an effective intermediate step into text study, or they may be used as a supplement to text work.

The focus can be on:

Dealing with lines/words/language.
Reconciling language with character intention and objective.
Making transitions/adjustments to obstacles.
Use of concentration and imagination.

The actor must answer the following questions about the characters in the performance of these very brief "scenes."

Who are they?
Where are they?
What are they doing?
What does each want?
Why does each want what they want?
What stands in the way of each?
What does each do to get what they want?

Some basic ground rules might include the following. The actor must stay with the written words in the order in which they appear. The actor, however, may create physical business or pauses or change the punctuation. Suggestions to the actor as to how different characterizations and situations may arise out of the ambiguous dialogue follow example seven. Try to make these dialogues as creative as possible.

Ambiguous Dialogue One

A: Come on in here.
B: Just a minute I'm busy.
A: It will only take a second.
B: I'm right in the middle of something.
A: I only want you to see something . . . just a second.
B: I can't right this minute, tell me about it.
A: I can't tell you about it, if I could tell you about it I wouldn't want you to
    come and look at it.
B: Do I really have to see it?
A: In a minute it won't make any difference, come on.
B: Okay. (*Enters the space.*) Yeah?
A: Well?
B: What? What am I supposed to see?
A: You know.
B: I wouldn't ask if I knew, would I?
A: It's so easy.
B: But there's a whole lot of stuff to look at.
A: This.
B: This?

A: Yeah. Well?

B: This is what you called me in for?

A: Yeah. Isn't it great?

B: You made me drop what I was doing to look at this?

A: I love it.

B: I can't believe it, I can't believe it.

A: It's great. I love it.

B: I can't believe it.

Ambiguous Dialogue Two

A: Yoohoo, yoohoo . . . hey, somebody . . .

B: What? What's up?

A: I need some help with this.

B: Just a minute.

A: Please hurry, it's slipping.

B: Okay, now what?

A: Hold this.

B: I can't see what you're talking about.

A: Well get out of the light.

B: This?

A: Right. Just hold it tightly, until I . . .

B: Yuck, something's dripping on me.

A: It won't hurt you, just don't let go of that.

B: It's all slimy, yuck.

A: Don't wiggle so much.

B: Watch out with that thing, you might hurt me.

A: I won't hurt you, I've done this a lot of times before.

B: There's always a first time.

A: Just pay attention to what you're supposed to be doing.

B: I am. This is boring. When can I let go and get out of here?

A: Very, very shortly . . . now in fact.

B: Good, I'm glad that's over, oh this slimy stuff stinks.

A: Well go and wash it off.

B: I certainly will.

A: Thanks for the help.

B: Yuck!

Ambiguous Dialogue Three

A: Do you come here often?

B: First time this year.

A: Me too.

B: I try to make it at least three times a year.

A: Yeah. Some people come a lot more.

B: I have a friend who does. Once a month.

A: Once a month! How does he find time?

B: He says that you have to make the time.
A: I guess so. I'm sure you'd get more out of once a month.
B: Lots more. It sure shows on him.
A: Look at that, did you ever see anything like it?
B: Never, it's amazing isn't it how they can do that.
A: And it looks so easy, so very easy.
B: I've always wondered. If I took the time and really committed myself, would I be able to do that?
A: I think you would. I think it's just what you said, a matter of commitment. They made an early committment to what they believed in and look now at the result.
B: Yeah.
A: What do you think?
B: I think you may be right.
A: Darn right I'm right.
B: Well let's move on, ready?
A: Yeah.
B: Next!

Ambiguous Dialogue Four

A: Did you get the other one?
B: I got it.
A: Bring it here. Set it down.
B: I'll start with this.
A: Okay, I'll finish here.
B: Hand me those.
A: What?
B: Those. There.
A: Oh, yeah. You want this too?
B: Huh? Yeah.
A: Where do we keep these things?
B: Under there, right.
A: Now, how can I help.
B: Hold this. Put it in there.
A: That looks good.
B: It's going to be terrific.
A: Is that all?
B: Yeah, take it easy.
A: If you need me . . .
B: Right!

Ambiguous Dialogue Five

A: Oh! Rats!
B: What the devil are you doing?
A: What the devil are you doing?

B: What I'm supposed to be doing.
A: So, what are we going to do about it?
B: What we're supposed to do about it.
A: If we've both got . . .
B: I don't think . . . I don't.
A: You don't?
B: No. Forget it.
A: Now what do we do? You sure you don't have any?
B: If it was my fault, I'll do what I'm supposed to.
A: Well, . . . let's see. I guess we'd better get out the old . . .
B: Okay, here.
A: This had better be good. I don't want to go out because of the way I'm dressed.
B: Oh boy, am I going to be . . .
A: Don't worry about it, I'm not out to hurt anybody.
B: Hey, this is my whole life we're talking about.
A: Calm down, for Pete's sake. I'll get in touch with you later.
B: Don't forget.

Ambiguous Dialogue Six

A: Okay now, just lean back like this . . . and then let all of your body weight go forward, while throwing your arm out . . .
B: Ahhh . . . here goes . . . ahhh oooh!
A: Wait, hold it, I think it's caught.
B: You're telling me.
A: Just a sec . . .
B: Ah . . . good grief . . . what do you think I am? . . .
A: You were having fun until now.
B: Do you like this happening to you?
A: It's all part of being . . .
B: Don't give me that stuff.
A: Hey, you're the one who wanted to come.
B: I didn't think that it would be like . . . this . . . it smells.
A: Here goes.
B: Eeeeeeeyyyyoooooooooooow!!!!
A: Okay?
B: My arm!!!
A: Come on, let's get started . . .
B: So, how do I do this?
A: Just lean back a little . . .
B: Like this . . . ?

Ambiguous Dialogue Seven

A: Hey! (*pause*) Hey, you out there?
B: What do you want?
A: Come'ere.

B: What?
A: I want you to see something.
B: What for?
A: Just come in here.
B: I'm busy.
A: I want to show you something important.
B: Is it really important?
A: I have to show you.
B: Why don't you just tell me about it?
A: You have to see this.
B: If I don't have a choice in the matter.
A: You coming?
B: Yeah. Okay.
A: Well?
B: What am I supposed to do about it?
A: Isn't it great?
B: What?
A: Have you seen anything like this before?
B: I can't believe it.
A: So?
B: I can't believe you called me in to see that.
A: Well, what do you think now?
B: I'm thirsty.
A: I really like it.
B: That's it for this one, out of here!

The scene could be about:

A sister who is doing her nails on the dining room table at home. Her brother is making a house of cards on a table in his bedroom.

or:

Two plumbers are working on different projects in the same house but in different rooms. The first one is in the kitchen working hard, but the second one is balancing his wrenches on the table.

or:

Father is in the living room reading the daily paper and his daughter is in her bedroom blowing a big bubble gum bubble.

or:

One old man is in the kitchen icing a cake and another old man is watering his roses in the garden.

Note the similarity of Ambiguous Dialogue One and Ambiguous Dialogue Seven. Note the subtleties, however, which make for different relationships and possibly different situations.

Scenes

---

1. *The Diary of Anne Frank,* by Frances Goodrich and Albert Hackett
   From Act II, Scene 2

   Scene: For one man, one woman
   Characters: ANNE FRANK, a girl of fourteen
                 PETER VAN DAAN, a boy of eighteen
   Setting: Peter's room in the attic of a storage annex in Amsterdam, Holland (a
                 hiding place for the Frank and Van Daan families).
   Time: Holland during World War II. Early 1940s.
   Situation: The play is based on the actual diary of young Anne Frank, which she
                 kept during the early 1940s. The play relates the plight of two Jewish
                 families, the Franks and the Van Daans, who are hiding from the Nazis
                 during World War II. In all, eight people (including Dr. Dussel, a den-
                 tist) have been living secretly in the attic since Anne was thirteen. In
                 fact, they managed to hide from 1942 to 1944, when they were dis-
                 covered and sent to concentration camps. All died except Otto Frank,

FIGURE 6.2 *The Diary of Anne Frank* by Goodrich and Hackett. **California State University, Long Beach, directed by W. David Sievers.**

Anne's father, who returned to Amsterdam after the war and was given Anne's diary, which had escaped the eye of the Nazis. The building where they hid is now a permanent shrine to Anne's memory and to those who suffer political and religious persecution everywhere.

In this scene from the play, the families have been hiding for some time and their close confinement has led to irritability and personality clashes. The two youngsters find comradeship with each other and also feel the first blush of love.

ANNE: Aren't they awful? Aren't they impossible? Treating us as if we're still in the nursery. (*She sits on the cot.* PETER *gets a bottle of pop and two glasses.*)

PETER: Don't let it bother you. It doesn't bother me.

ANNE: I suppose you can't really blame them . . . they think back to what *they* were like at our age. They don't realize how much advanced we are . . . when I think what wonderful discussions we've had! . . . Oh, I forgot. I was going to bring you some more pictures.

PETER: Oh, these are fine, thanks.

ANNE: Don't you want some more? Miep just brought me some new ones.

PETER: Maybe later. (*He gives her a glass of pop and, taking some for himself, sits down facing her.*)

ANNE: (*Looking up at one of the photographs*) I remember when I got that . . . I won it. I bet Jopie that I could eat five ice cream cones. We'd all been playing ping-pong . . . we used to have heavenly times . . . we'd finish up with ice cream at the Delphi, or the Oasis, where Jews were allowed . . . there'd always be a lot of boys . . . we'd laugh and joke . . . I'd like to go back to it for a few days or a week. But after that I know I'd be bored to death. I think more seriously about life now. I want to be a journalist . . . or something. I love to write. What do you want to do?

PETER: I thought I might go off some place . . . work on a farm or something . . . some job that doesn't take much brains.

ANNE: You shouldn't talk that way. You've got the most awful inferiority complex.

PETER: I know I'm not smart.

ANNE: That isn't true. You're much better than I am in dozens of things . . . arithmetic and algebra and . . . well, you're a million times better than I am in algebra. (*With sudden directness*) You like Margot, don't you? Right from the start you liked her, liked her much better than me.

PETER: (*Uncomfortably*) Oh, I don't know.

ANNE: It's all right. Everyone feels that way. Margot's so good. She's sweet and bright and beautiful and I'm not.

PETER: I wouldn't say that.

ANNE: Oh, no, I'm not. I know that. I know quite well that I'm not a beauty. I never have been and never shall be.

PETER: I don't agree at all. I think you're pretty.

ANNE: That's not true!

PETER: And another thing. You've changed . . . from at first, I mean.

ANNE: I have?

PETER: I used to think you were awful noisy.

ANNE: And what do you think now, Peter? How have I changed?

PETER: Well . . . er . . . you're . . . quieter.

ANNE: I'm glad you don't just hate me.

PETER: I never said that.

ANNE: I bet when you get out of here you'll never think of me again.

PETER: That's crazy.

ANNE: When you get back with all of your friends, you're going to say . . . now what did I ever see in that Mrs. Quack Quack?

PETER: I haven't got any friends.

ANNE: Oh, Peter, of course you have. Everyone has friends.

PETER: Not me, I don't want any. I get along all right without them.

ANNE: Does that mean you can get along without me? I think of myself as your friend.

PETER: No. If they were all like you, it'd be different. (*He takes the glasses and the bottle and puts them away. There is a second's silence and then Anne speaks, hesitantly, shyly.*)

ANNE: Peter, did you ever kiss a girl?

PETER: Yes. Once.

ANNE: (*To cover her feelings*) That picture's crooked. (*Peter goes over, straightening the photograph*) Was she pretty?

PETER: Huh?

ANNE: The girl that you kissed.

PETER: I don't know. I was blindfolded. It was at a party. One of those kissing games.

ANNE: (*Relieved*) Oh, I don't suppose that really counts, does it?

PETER: It didn't with me.

ANNE: I've been kissed twice. Once a man I'd never seen before kissed me on the cheek when he picked me up off the ice and I was crying. And the other was Mr. Kopphuis, a friend of Father's who kissed my hand. You wouldn't say those counted, would you?

PETER: I wouldn't say so.

ANNE: I know almost for certain that Margot would never kiss anyone unless she was engaged to them. And I'm sure too that Mother never touched a man before Pim. But I don't know . . . things are so different now . . . what do you think? Do you think a girl shouldn't kiss anyone except if she's engaged or something? It's so hard to try to think what to do, when here we are with the whole world falling around our ears and you think . . . well . . . you don't know what's going to happen tomorrow and . . . what do you think?

PETER: I suppose it'd depend on the girl. Some girls, anything they do's wrong. But others . . . well . . . it wouldn't necessarily be wrong with them. I've always thought that when two people—(*The carillon starts to ring nine o'clock*)

ANNE: Nine o'clock. I have to go.

PETER: That's right.

ANNE: (*Without moving*) Good night. (*There is a second's pause. Then* PETER *gets up and moves towards the door.*)

PETER: You won't let them stop you coming?

ANNE: No. (*She rises and starts for the door.*) Sometime I might bring my diary.

There are so many things in it that I want to talk over with you. There's a lot about you.

PETER: What kind of things?

ANNE: I wouldn't want you to see some of it. I thought you were a nothing, just the way you thought about me.

PETER: Did you change your mind, the way I changed my mind about you?

ANNE: Well . . . you'll see . . . (*For a second* ANNE *stands looking up at* PETER, *longing for him to kiss her. As he makes no move, she turns away. Then suddenly* PETER *grabs her awkwardly in his arms, kissing her on the cheek.* ANNE *walks out, dazed.*)

2. *Butterflies are Free*, by Leonard Gershe
   From Act I, Scene 1

Scene: For one man, one woman

Characters: DON BAKER, twenty years old, lean and good looking. He is blind.
JILL TANNER, nineteen. His neighbor in the adjoining apartment.

Setting: Don Baker's apartment on the top floor of an apartment building on the Lower East Side of Manhattan.

Time: A warm morning in June. The present.

Situation: Don has been trying to develop an independent life for himself despite his blindness and a somewhat over-protective mother. His neighbor in the adjoining apartment has been playing the TV at a loud volume, and Don has pounded on the walls asking that the sound be lowered. A conversation between Don and Jill begins with the wall serving as a minor barrier. Jill asks if she can have a cup of coffee and then enters Don's apartment through his unlocked door. Don is in the kitchen lighting the burner under the coffee pot as Jill makes her way into his apartment. She is unaware of the fact that he is blind.

JILL: Hi! I'm Jill Tanner.

DON: (*Turning toward her and extending his hand*) Don Baker. (JILL *shakes his hand*)

JILL: I hope you don't mind me inviting myself in. (*Turning her back to him*) Would you do the zipper on my blouse? I can't reach back there. (*There is just a flash of awkwardness as* DON *reaches out for the zipper and zips it up*) Your living room is bigger than mine. How long have you been here?

DON: A month. This isn't the living room. This is the apartment. That's all there is except I have a big bathroom.

JILL: I've got three rooms if you count the kitchen. I just moved in two days ago, but I didn't sign a lease or anything—just by the month. God, you're neat. Everything is so tidy.

DON: It's easy when you haven't got anything.

JILL: (*Looking around*) I haven't got anything, but it manages to wind up all over the place. I'm afraid I'm a slob. I've heard that boys are neater than girls. (*Looking up*) I like your skylight. I don't have that. (*Moves to the bed*) What's this?

DON: What?

JILL: This thing on stilts.

DON: Oh, my bed.

JILL: (*Climbing the ladder*) Your bed? Wow! This is WILD!

DON: Do you like it?

JILL: (*Climbing on the bed*) This is the greatest bed I've ever seen in my life. . . . and I've seen a lot of beds. Did you build it?

DON: No, the guy who lived here before me built it. He was a hippie. He liked to sleep high.

JILL: Suppose you fall out? You could break something.

DON: You could break something falling out of any bed. (*He pours the coffee into the cup, goes to the coffee table and sets it down*) Cream or sugar?

JILL: No, just black.

DON: I could have had your apartment, but I took this one because of the bed.

JILL: I don't blame you. (*Moving to the sofa*) You know, I buy flowers and dumb things like dishtowels and paper napkins, but I keep forgetting to buy coffee. (JILL *settles on the sofa with her feet beneath her. She picks up the coffee and sips it*)

DON: Is it hot enough?

JILL: Great. This'll save my life. I'll pay you back some day.

DON: You don't have to.

JILL: Do you need any dishtowels or paper napkins?

DON: No.

JILL: I've got lots of light bulbs, too—everything but coffee. May I ask you a personal question?

DON: Sure.

JILL: Why don't you want your mother to come here?

DON: How did you know that?

JILL: If you can hear me, I can hear you. I think the sound must go right under that door. What's that door for, anyway?

DON: Your apartment and mine were once one apartment. When they converted it into two, they just locked that door instead of sealing it up. I guess in case they want to make it one again.

JILL: You didn't answer my question.

DON: I forgot what you asked.

JILL: Why don't you want your mother here?

DON: It's a long story. No, it's a short story—it's just been going on a long time. She didn't want me to leave home. She thinks I can't make it on my own. Finally, we agreed to letting me try it for two months. She's to keep away from me for two months. I've got a month to go.

JILL: Why did you tell her you had a party last night?

DON: Boy, you don't miss anything in there, do you?

JILL: Not much.

DON: I always tell her I've had a party . . . or went to one. She wouldn't understand why I'd rather be here alone than keeping her and the cook company. She'll hate this place. She hates it now without even seeing it. She'll walk in and the first thing she'll say is, "I could absolutely cry!"

JILL: Does she cry a lot?

DON: No—she just threatens to.

JILL: If she really wants to cry, send her in to look at my place. At least you're neat. You're old enough to live alone, aren't you? I'm nineteen. How old are you?

DON: As far as my mother's concerned, I'm still eleven—going on ten.

JILL: We must have the same mother. Mine would love me to stay a child all my life—or at least all *her* life. So *she* won't age. She loves it when people say we look like sisters. If they don't say it, she tells them. Have you got a job?

DON: Not yet . . . but I play the guitar, and I've got a few prospects.

JILL: I heard you last night.

DON: Sorry.

JILL: No, it was good. First I thought it was a record till you kept playing one song over and over.

DON: I can't read music, so I have to learn by ear. I'm trying to put together an act.

JILL: Then what?

DON: Then I'll try to cash in on some of those prospects. I know one thing—I ain't a-goin' back to Scarsdale.

JILL: What is Scarsdale?

DON: You don't know Scarsdale?

JILL: I don't know much about the East. I'm from Los Angeles.

DON: Scarsdale's just outside of New York—about twenty miles.

JILL: Is that where you live?

DON: No, I live here. It's where I used to live.

JILL: Scars-dale. It sounds like a sanitarium where they do plastic surgery. Is there any more coffee?

DON: (*Putting his cigarette out in the ashtray*) Plenty.

JILL: I can get it.

DON: (*Rises and holds out his hand for the cup*) I'm up. (JILL *hands him the cup. He goes to the kitchen to pour her more coffee*) What did you say your name is?

JILL: Jill Tanner. Technically, I guess I'm Mrs. Benson. I was married once . . . when I was sixteen.

DON: Sixteen! Did you have your parents' permission?

JILL: My mother's. I told her I was pregnant, but I wasn't. She cried her eyes out. She hated the thought of becoming a grandmother. I'll bet I know what you're thinking.

DON: What? (DON *returns, sets the cup on the table, and resumes his seat*)

JILL: You're thinking I don't look like a *divorcée*.

DON: No, I wasn't thinking that. What does a divorcée look like?

JILL: Oh, you know. They're usually around thirty-five with tight-fitting dresses and high-heel patent leather shoes and big boobs. I look more like the kid in a custody fight.

DON: How long were you married?

JILL: God, it seemed like weeks! Actually, it was six days. (*She lights a cigarette*) It wasn't Jack's fault. It wasn't anybody's fault. It was just one of those terrible mistakes you make before you can stop yourself, even though you know it's a mistake while you're doing it.

DON: What was he like?

JILL: Jack? Oh . . . (*Uncomfortably*) I really can't talk about him.

DON: Then don't. I'm sorry.

JILL: No, I will talk about him. Once in a while it's good for you to do something you don't want to do. It cleanses the insides. He was terribly sweet and groovy-looking, but kind of adolescent, you know what I mean? Girls mature faster than boys. Boys are neater, but girls mature faster. When we met it was like fireworks and rockets. I don't know if I'm saying it right, but it was a marvelous kind of passion that made every day like the Fourth of July. Anyway, the next thing I knew we were standing in front of a justice of the peace getting married.

DON: How long had you known him?

JILL: Two or three weeks, but I mean there we were getting *married!* I hadn't even finished high school and I had two exams the next day and they were on my mind, too. I heard the justice of the peace saying, "Do you, *Jack*, take Jill to be your lawfully wedded wife?" Can you imagine going through life as Jack and Jill? And then I heard "Till death do you part," and suddenly it wasn't a wedding ceremony. It was a funeral service.

DON: (*Lighting a cigarette*) Jesus!

JILL: You know, that wedding ceremony is very morbid when you think about it. I hate anything morbid and there I was being buried alive . . . under Jack Benson. I wanted to run screaming out into the night!

DON: Did you?

JILL: I couldn't. It was ten o'clock in the morning. I mean you can't go screaming out into ten o'clock in the morning—so I passed out. If only I'd fainted before I said "I do."

DON: As long as you were married, why didn't you try to make it work?

JILL: I did try—believe me. (*She picks up an ashtray and holds it in her hand*) I tried for six days, but I knew it was no good.

DON: Were you in love with him? (DON *flicks an ash from his cigarette onto the table where the ashtray had been before* JILL *moved it.* JILL *reacts to this fleetingly, and shrugs it off*)

JILL: In my way.

DON: What's your way?

JILL: I don't know . . . Well, I think just because you love someone, that doesn't necessarily mean that you want to spend the rest of your life with him. But Jack loved me. I mean he really, really loved me, and I hurt him and that's what I can't stand. I just never want to hurt anybody. I mean marriage is a commitment, isn't it? I just can't be committed or involved. Can you understand?

DON: I understand, but I don't agree. (DON *flicks his ashes onto the table*)

JILL: Then you don't understand really. (JILL *looks at him, oddly*) What is this? Maybe I've got it wrong. Maybe boys mature faster and girls are neater.

DON: What do you mean?

JILL: Or maybe you know something I don't know—like ashes are good for the table? Is that why you keep dropping them there?

DON: Did you move the ashtray?

JILL: (*Holding up the ashtray beside her*) It's right here. Are you blind?

DON: Yes.

JILL: What do you mean *yes*?

DON: I mean yes. I'm blind.

JILL: You're putting me on.

DON: No, I'm blind. I've always been blind.

JILL: Really blind? Not just near-sighted?

DON: The works. I can't see a thing. (JILL *leans over and runs her hands across* DON'S *eyes. When he doesn't blink, she realizes he is indeed blind*)

JILL: God! I hope I didn't say anything . . .

DON: Now, don't get self-conscious about it. I'm not.

JILL: Why didn't you tell me?

DON: I just did.

JILL: I mean when I came in.

DON: You didn't ask me.

3. *The Little Foxes*, by Lillian Hellman
   From Act III

Scene:	For two women
Characters:	REGINA GIDDENS, an avaricious and shrewd woman
	ALEXANDRA, her attractive daughter
	(The one line by ADDIE may be cut)
Setting:	The Giddens's living room. A small town in the deep South.
Time:	The turn of the present century.
Situation:	Regina's husband, Horace, has just died of a heart attack, not without a little prodding from Regina. She is anxious to get hold of his securities, which will permit her to leave her provincial surroundings and, if invested properly, to live in the populous and socially attractive North. Regina's daughter, Alexandra, is well aware of her mother's intentions and has become increasingly suspicious of the circumstances that led to the death of her father.

REGINA: (*Sits quietly for a second, stretches, turns to look at* ALEXANDRA) What do you want to talk to me about, Alexandra?

ALEXANDRA: (*Slowly*) I've changed my mind. I don't want to talk. There's nothing to talk about now.

REGINA: You're acting very strange. Not like yourself. You've had a bad shock today. I know that. And you loved Papa, but you must have expected this to come some day. You knew how sick he was.

ALEXANDRA: I knew. We all knew.

REGINA: It will be good for you to get away from here. Good for me, too. Time heals most wounds, Alexandra. You're young, you shall have all the things I wanted. I'll make the world for you the way I wanted it to be for me. (*Uncomfortably*) Don't sit there staring. You've been around Birdie so much you're getting just like her.

ALEXANDRA: (*Nods*) Funny. That's what Aunt Birdie said today.

REGINA: (*Nods*) Be good for you to get away from all this. (ADDIE *enters.*)

ADDIE: Cal is back, Miss Regina. He says Dr. Sloan will be coming in a few minutes.

REGINA: We'll go in a few weeks. A few weeks! That means two or three Saturdays, two or three Sundays. (*Sighs*) Well, I'm very tired. I shall go to bed.

I don't want any supper. Put the lights out and lock up. (ADDIE *moves to the piano lamp, turns it out*) You go to your room, Alexandra. Addie will bring you something hot. You look very tired. (*Rises. To* ADDIE) Call me when Dr. Sloan gets here. I don't want to see anybody else. I don't want any condolence calls tonight. The whole town will be over.

ALEXANDRA: Mama, I'm not coming with you. I'm not going to Chicago.

REGINA: (*Turns to her*) You're very upset, Alexandra.

ALEXANDRA: (*Quietly*) I mean what I say. With all my heart.

REGINA: We'll talk about it tomorrow. The morning will make a difference.

ALEXANDRA: It won't make any difference. And there isn't anything to talk about. I am going away from you. Because I want to. Because I know Papa would want me to.

REGINA: (*Puzzled, careful, polite*) You *know* your papa wanted you to go away from me?

ALEXANDRA: Yes.

REGINA: (*Softly*) And if I say no?

ALEXANDRA: (*Looks at her*) Say it Mama, say it. And see what happens.

REGINA: (*Softly, after a pause*) And if I make you stay?

ALEXANDRA: That would be foolish. It wouldn't work in the end.

REGINA: You're very serious about it, aren't you? (*Crosses to stairs*) Well, you'll change your mind in a few days.

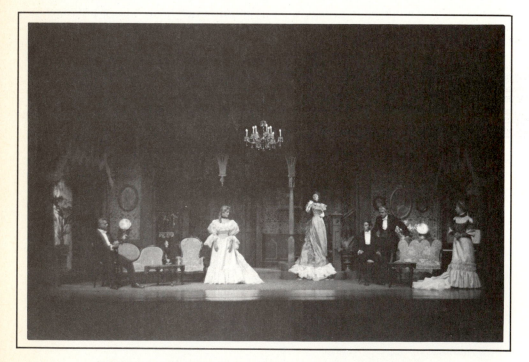

FIGURE 6.3 *The Little Foxes* **by Lillian Hellman. California State University, Long Beach, directed by Stanley Kahan.**

ALEXANDRA: You only change your mind when you want to. And I won't want to.

REGINA: (*Going up the steps*) Alexandra, I've come to the end of my rope. Somewhere there has to be what I want, too. Life goes too fast. Do what you want; think what you want; go where you want. I'd like to keep you with me, but I won't make you stay. Too many people used to make me do too many things. No, I won't make you stay.

ALEXANDRA: You couldn't, Mama, because I want to leave here. As I've never wanted anything in my life before. Because now I understand what Papa was trying to tell me. (*Pause*) All in one day: Addie said there were people who ate the earth and other people who stood around and watched them do it. And just now Uncle Ben said the same thing. Really, he said the same thing. (*Tensely*) Well, tell him for me, Mama, I'm not going to stand around and watch you do it. Tell him I'll be fighting as hard as he'll be fighting (*Rises*) some place where people don't just stand around and watch.

REGINA: Well, you have spirit, after all. I used to think you were all sugar water. We don't have to be bad friends. I don't want us to be bad friends, Alexandra. (*Starts, stops, turns to* ALEXANDRA) Would you like to come and talk to me, Alexandra? Would you—would you like to sleep in my room tonight?

ALEXANDRA: (*Takes a step toward her*) Are you afraid, Mama? (REGINA *does not answer. She moves slowly out of sight . . .*)

4. *Death of a Salesman*, by Arthur Miller
   From Act I

   Scene: For three men, one woman
   Characters: WILLY LOMAN
   LINDA LOMAN, his wife
   BIFF LOMAN, his older son
   HAPPY LOMAN, his younger son
   Setting: The kitchen and bedroom of a small, middle-class frame house in Brooklyn. It is surrounded by the towering walls of apartment houses.
   Time: A spring evening in the late 1940s.
   Situation: Willy Loman, a salesman, is old and exhausted. His wife Linda has just finished berating Biff for his lack of consideration for his father and his refusal to stay at home. As the scene opens, Biff is contrite. When Willy enters, however, another angry conflict ensues. Yet between Willy and Biff there is a strong bond of affection.

   See the other scene from *Death of a Salesman* (p. 222), which occurs later in the play.

BIFF: (*kissing her*) All right, pal, all right. It's all settled now. I've been remiss. I know that, Mom. But now I'll stay, and I swear to you, I'll apply myself. (*kneeling in front of her, in a fever of self-reproach*) It's just—you see, Mom, I don't fit in business. Not that I won't try. I'll try, and I'll make good.

HAPPY: Sure you will. The trouble with you in business was you never tried to please people.

BIFF: I know, I—

HAPPY: Like when you worked for Harrison's. Bob Harrison said you were tops, and then you go and do some damn fool thing like whistling whole songs in the elevator like a comedian.

BIFF: (*against* HAPPY) So what? I like to whistle sometimes.

HAPPY: You don't raise a guy to a responsible job who whistles in the elevator!

LINDA: Well, don't argue about it now.

HAPPY: Like when you'd go off and swim in the middle of the day instead of taking the line around.

BIFF: (*his resentment rising*) Well, don't you run off? You take off sometimes, don't you? On a nice summer day?

HAPPY: Yeah, but I cover myself!

LINDA: Boys!

HAPPY: If I'm going to take a fade the boss can call any number where I'm supposed to be and they'll swear to him that I just left. I'll tell you something that I hate to say, Biff, but in the business world some of them think you're crazy.

FIGURE 6.4 *Death of a Salesman* by Arthur Miller. California State University, Long Beach, directed by W. David Sievers.

BIFF: (*angered*) Screw the business world!

HAPPY: All right, screw it! Great, but cover yourself!

LINDA: Hap, Hap!

BIFF: I don't care what they think! They've laughed at Dad for years, and you know why? Because we don't belong in this nuthouse of a city! We should be mixing cement on some open plain, or—or carpenters. A carpenter is allowed to whistle! (WILLY *walks in from the entrance of the house, at left.*)

WILLY: Even your grandfather was better than a carpenter. (*pause. They watch him.*) You never grew up. Bernard does not whistle in the elevator, I assure you.

BIFF: (*as though to laugh* WILLY *out of it*) Yeah, but you do, Pop.

WILLY: I never in my life whistled in an elevator! And who in the business world thinks I'm crazy?

BIFF: I didn't mean it like that, Pop. Now don't make a whole thing out of it, will ya?

WILLY: Go back to the West! Be a carpenter, a cowboy, enjoy yourself!

LINDA: Willy, he was just saying—

WILLY: I heard what he said!

HAPPY: (*trying to quiet* WILLY) Hey, Pop, come on now . . .

WILLY: (*continuing over* HAPPY'S *line*) They laugh at me, heh? Go to Filene's, go to the Hub, go to Slattery's, Boston. Call out the name Willy Loman and see what happens! Big shot!

BIFF: All right, Pop.

WILLY: Big!

BIFF: All right!

WILLY: Why do you always insult me?

BIFF: I didn't say a word. (*to* LINDA) Did I say a word?

LINDA: He didn't say anything, Willy.

WILLY: (*going to the doorway of the living room*) All right, good night, good night.

LINDA: Willy, dear, he just decided . . .

WILLY: (*to* BIFF) If you get tired hanging around tomorrow, paint the ceiling I put up in the living room.

BIFF: I'm leaving early tomorrow.

HAPPY: He's going to see Bill Oliver, Pop.

WILLY: (*interestedly*) Oliver? For what?

BIFF: (*with reserve, but trying, trying*) He always said he'd stake me. I'd like to go into business, so maybe I can take him up on it.

LINDA: Isn't that wonderful?

WILLY: Don't interrupt. What's wonderful about it? There's fifty men in the City of New York who'd stake him. (*to* BIFF) Sporting goods?

BIFF: I guess so. I know something about it and—

WILLY: He knows something about it! You know sporting goods better than Spalding, for God's sake! How much is he giving you?

BIFF: I don't know, I didn't even see him yet, but—

WILLY: Then what're you talkin' about?

BIFF: (*getting angry*) Well, all I said was I'm gonna see him, that's all!

WILLY: (*turning away*) Ah, you're counting your chickens again.

BIFF: (*starting for the stairs*) Oh, Jesus, I'm going to sleep!

WILLY: (*calling after him*) Don't curse in this house!

BIFF: (*turning*) Since when did you get so clean?

HAPPY: (*trying to stop them*) Wait a . . .

WILLY: Don't use that language to me! I won't have it!

HAPPY: (*grabbing* BIFF, *shouts*) Wait a minute! I got an idea. I got a feasible idea. Come here, Biff, let's talk this over now, let's talk some sense here. When I was down in Florida last time, I thought of a great idea to sell sporting goods. It just came back to me. You and I, Biff—we have a line, the Loman Line. We train a couple of weeks, and put on a couple of exhibitions, see?

WILLY: That's an idea!

HAPPY: Wait! We form two basketball teams, see? Two water-polo teams. We play each other. It's a million dollars' worth of publicity. Two brothers, see? The Loman Brothers. Displays in the Royal Palms—all the hotels. And banners over the ring and the basketball court: "Loman Brothers." Baby, we could sell sporting goods!

WILLY: That is a one-million-dollar idea!

LINDA: Marvelous!

BIFF: I'm in great shape as far as that's concerned.

HAPPY: And the beauty of it is, Biff, it wouldn't be like a business. We'd be out playin' ball again . . .

BIFF: (*filled with enthusiasm*) Yeah, that's . . .

WILLY: Million-dollar . . .

HAPPY: And you wouldn't get fed up with it, Biff. It'd be the family again. There'd be the old honor, and comradeship, and if you wanted to go off for a swim or somethin'—well, you'd do it! Without some smart cooky gettin' up ahead of you!

WILLY: Lick the world! You guys together could absolutely lick the civilized world.

BIFF: I'll see Oliver tomorrow. Hap, if we could work that out . . .

LINDA: Maybe things are beginning to—

WILLY: (*wildly enthusiastic, to* LINDA) Stop interrupting! (*to* BIFF) But don't wear sport jacket and slacks when you see Oliver.

BIFF: No, I'll—

WILLY: A business suit, and talk as little as possible, and don't crack any jokes.

BIFF: He did like me. Always liked me.

LINDA: He loved you!

WILLY: (*to* LINDA) Will you stop! (*to* BIFF) Walk in very serious. You are not applying for a boy's job. Money is to pass. Be quiet, fine, and serious. Everybody likes a kidder, but nobody lends him money.

HAPPY: I'll try to get some myself, Biff. I'm sure I can.

WILLY: I see great things for you kids, I think your troubles are over. But remember, start big and you'll end big. Ask for fifteen. How much you gonna ask for?

BIFF: Gee, I don't know—

WILLY: And don't say "Gee." "Gee" is a boy's word. A man walking in for fifteen thousand dollars does not say "Gee!"

BIFF: Ten, I think, would be top though.

WILLY: Don't be so modest. You always started too low. Walk in with a big laugh. Don't look worried. Start off with a couple of your good stories to lighten things up. It's not what you say, it's how you say it—because personality always wins the day.

LINDA: Oliver always thought the highest of him—

WILLY: Will you let me talk?

BIFF: Don't yell at her, Pop, will ya?

WILLY: (*angrily*) I was talking, wasn't I?

BIFF: I don't like you yelling at her all the time, and I'm tellin' you, that's all.

WILLY: What're you, takin' over this house?

LINDA: Willy—

WILLY: (*turning on her*) Don't take his side all the time, god-dammit!

BIFF: (*furiously*) Stop yelling at her!

WILLY: (*suddenly pulling on his cheek, beaten down, guilt ridden*) Give my best to Bill Oliver—he may remember me. (*He exits through the living-room doorway.*)

LINDA: (*her voice subdued*) What'd you have to start that for? (BIFF *turns away.*) You see how sweet he was as soon as you talked hopefully? (*She goes over to* BIFF.) Come up and say good night to him. Don't let him go to bed that way.

HAPPY: Come on, Biff, let's buck him up.

LINDA: Please, dear. Just say good night. It takes so little to make him happy. Come. (*She goes through the living-room doorway, calling upstairs from within the living room.*) Your pajamas are hanging in the bathroom, Willy!

HAPPY: (*looking toward where* LINDA *went out*) What a woman! They broke the mold when they made her. You know that, Biff?

BIFF: He's off salary. My God, working on commission!

HAPPY: Well, let's face it: he's no hot-shot selling man. Except that sometimes, you have to admit, he's a sweet personality.

BIFF: (*deciding*) Lend me ten bucks, will ya? I want to buy some new ties.

HAPPY: I'll take you to a place I know. Beautiful stuff. Wear one of my striped shirts tomorrow.

BIFF: She got gray. Mom got awful old. Gee, I'm gonna go in to Oliver tomorrow and knock him for a—

HAPPY: Come on up. Tell that to Dad. Let's give him a whirl. Come on.

BIFF: (*steamed up*) You know, with ten thousand bucks, boy!

HAPPY: (*as they go into the living room*) That's the talk, Biff, that's the first time I've heard the old confidence out of you! (*from within the living room, fading off*) You're gonna live with me, kid, and any babe you want just say the word . . . (*The last lines are hardly heard. They are mounting the stairs to their parents' bedroom.*)

LINDA: (*entering her bedroom and addressing* WILLY, *who is in the bathroom. She is straightening the bed for him.*) Can you do anything about the shower? It drips.

WILLY: (*from the bathroom*) All of a sudden everything falls to pieces! Goddam plumbing, oughta be sued, those people. I hardly finished putting it in and the thing . . . (*His words rumble off.*)

LINDA: I'm just wondering if Oliver will remember him. You think he might?

WILLY: (*coming out of the bathroom in his pajamas*) Remember him? What's the matter with you, you crazy? If he'd've stayed with Oliver he'd be on top by now! Wait'll Oliver gets a look at him. You don't know the average caliber any more. The average young man today—(*He is getting into bed.*)—is got a caliber of zero. Greatest thing in the world for him was to bum around. (BIFF *and* HAPPY *enter the bedroom. Slight pause*)

WILLY: (*stops short, looking at* BIFF) Glad to hear it, boy.

HAPPY: We wanted to say good night to you, sport.

WILLY: (*to* BIFF) Yeah. Knock him dead, boy. What'd you want to tell me?

BIFF: Just take it easy, Pop. Good night. (*He turns to go.*)

WILLY: (*unable to resist*) And if anything falls off the desk while you're talking to him—like a package or something—don't you pick it up. They have office boys for that.

LINDA: I'll make a big breakfast—

WILLY: Will you let me finish? (*to* BIFF) Tell him you were in the business in the West. Not farm work.

BIFF: All right, Dad.

LINDA: I think everything—

WILLY: (*going right through her speech*) And don't undersell yourself. No less than fifteen thousand dollars.

BIFF: (*unable to bear him*) Okay. Good night, Mom. (*He starts moving.*)

WILLY: Because you got a greatness in you, Biff, remember that. You got all kinds a greatness. . . . (*He lies back, exhausted.* BIFF *walks out.*)

LINDA: (*calling after* BIFF) Sleep well, darling!

HAPPY: I'm gonna get married, Mom. I wanted to tell you.

LINDA: Go to sleep, dear.

HAPPY: (*going*) I just wanted to tell you.

WILLY: Keep up the good work. (HAPPY *exits.*) God . . . remember that Ebbets Field game? The championship of the city?

LINDA: Just rest. Should I sing to you?

WILLY: Yeah. Sing to me. (LINDA *hums a soft lullaby.*) When that team came out—he was the tallest, remember?

LINDA: Oh, yes. And in gold. (BIFF *enters the darkened kitchen, takes a cigarette, and leaves the house. He comes downstage into a golden pool of light. He smokes, staring at the night.*)

WILLY: Like a young god. Hercules—something like that. And the sun, the sun all around him. Remember how he waved to me? Right up from the field, with the representatives of three colleges standing by? And the buyers I brought, and the cheers when he came out—Loman, Loman, Loman! God Almighty, he'll be great yet. A star like that, magnificent, can never really fade away!

5. *Long Day's Journey into Night,* by Eugene O'Neill
   From Act II, Scene 1

    Scene: For two men
Characters: EDMUND TYRONE, twenty-three
           JAMIE TYRONE, his brother, thirty-three
             Sons of the actor James Tyrone
    Setting: The living room of James Tyrone's summer home in an eastern seacoast town.

Time: Early afternoon. August 1912.

Situation: The Tyrone family is closely based on O'Neill's own family, and Edmund is, in fact, the young Eugene O'Neill. His father, James Tyrone (O'Neill, Sr.), is a famous but aged actor who gave up a great career as a classical actor to appear in popular but trashy plays. James' wife, Mary, a once-beautiful girl educated in a convent, is now a hopeless drug addict. Jamie is a self-destructive alcoholic who has been leading his brother deeper into the many excesses Jamie himself has enjoyed. Edmund is suffering from tuberculosis, although he prefers to believe at the moment it may be a "summer cold." They are all awaiting the diagnosis from Doctor Hardy as to Edmund's real condition.

Edmund has just had a drink from the whiskey bottle on the table, and now he hastily puts his glass down as Jamie comes into the room.

EDMUND: I wasn't sure it was you coming.

JAMIE: I made the Old Man look at his watch. I was halfway up the walk when Cathleen burst into song. Our wild Irish lark! She ought to be a train announcer.

EDMUND: That's what drove me to drink. Why don't you sneak one while you've got a chance?

JAMIE: I was thinking of that little thing. (*He goes quickly to the window at right.*) The Old Man was talking to old Captain Turner. Yes, he's still at it. (*He comes back and takes a drink.*) And now to cover up from his eagle eye. (*He memorizes the level in the bottle after every drink. He measures two drinks of water and pours them in the whisky bottle and shakes it up.*) There. That fixes it. (*He pours water in the glass and sets it on the table by Edmund.*) And here's the water you've been drinking.

EDMUND: Fine! You don't think it will fool him, do you?

JAMIE: Maybe not, but he can't prove it. (*Putting on his collar and tie.*) I hope he doesn't forget lunch listening to himself talk. I'm hungry. (*He sits across the table from Edmund—irritably.*) That's what I hate about working down in front. He puts on an act for every damned fool that comes along.

EDMUND: (*Gloomily.*) You're in luck to be hungry. The way I feel I don't care if I ever eat again.

JAMIE: (*Gives him a glance of concern.*) Listen, Kid. You know me. I've never lectured you, but Doctor Hardy was right when he told you to cut out the redeye.

EDMUND: Oh, I'm going to after he hands me the bad news this afternoon. A few before then won't make any difference.

JAMIE: (*Hesitates—then slowly.*) I'm glad you've got your mind prepared for bad news. It won't be such a jolt. (*He catches Edmund staring at him.*) I mean, it's a cinch you're really sick, and it would be wrong dope to kid yourself.

EDMUND: (*Disturbed.*) I'm not. I know how rotten I feel, and the fever and chills I get at night are no joke. I think Doctor Hardy's last guess was right. It must be the damned malaria come back on me.

JAMIE: Maybe, but don't be too sure.

EDMUND: Why? What do you think it is?

JAMIE: Hell, how would I know? I'm no Doc. (*Abruptly.*) Where's Mama?

EDMUND: Upstairs.

JAMIE: (*Looks at him sharply.*) When did she go up?

EDMUND: Oh, about the time I came down to the hedge, I guess. She said she was going to take a nap.

JAMIE: You didn't tell me—

EDMUND: (*Defensively.*) Why should I? What about it? She was tired out. She didn't get much sleep last night.

JAMIE: I know she didn't. (*A pause. The brothers avoid looking at each other.*)

EDMUND: That damned foghorn kept me awake, too. (*Another pause.*)

JAMIE: She's been upstairs all morning, eh? You haven't seen her?

EDMUND: No. I've been reading here. I wanted to give her a chance to sleep.

JAMIE: Is she coming down to lunch?

EDMUND: Of course.

JAMIE: (*Dryly.*) No of course about it. She might not want any lunch. Or she might start having most of her meals alone upstairs. That's happened, hasn't it?

EDMUND: (*With frightened resentment.*) Cut it out, Jamie! Can't you think any-thing but—? (*Persuasively.*) You're all wrong to suspect anything. Cathleen saw her not long ago. Mama didn't tell her she wouldn't be down to lunch.

JAMIE: Then she wasn't taking a nap?

EDMUND: Not right then, but she was lying down, Cathleen said.

JAMIE: In the spare room?

EDMUND: Yes. For Pete's sake, what of it?

JAMIE: (*Bursts out.*) You damned fool! Why did you leave her alone so long? Why didn't you stick around?

EDMUND: Because she accused me—and you and Papa—of spying on her all the time and not trusting her. She made me feel ashamed. I know how rot-ten it must be for her. And she promised on her sacred word of honor—

JAMIE: (*With a bitter weariness.*) You ought to know that doesn't mean anything.

EDMUND: It does this time!

JAMIE: That's what we thought the other times. (*He leans over the table to give his brother's arm an affectionate grasp.*) Listen, Kid, I know you think I'm a cynical bastard, but remember I've seen a lot more of this game than you have. You never knew what was really wrong until you were in prep school. Papa and I kept it from you. But I was wise ten years or more before we had to tell you. I know the game backwards and I've been thinking all morning of the way she acted last night when she thought we were asleep. I haven't been able to think of anything else. And now you tell me she got you to leave her alone upstairs all morning.

EDMUND: She didn't! You're crazy!

JAMIE: (*Placatingly.*) All right, Kid. Don't start a battle with me. I hope as much as you do I'm crazy. I've been as happy as hell because I'd really begun to believe that this time—(*He stops—looking through the front parlor toward the hall—lowering his voice, hurriedly.*) She's coming downstairs. You win on that. I guess I'm a damned suspicious louse. (*They grow tense with a hopeful, fearful expectancy. Jamie mutters.*) Damn! I wish I'd grabbed another drink.

EDMUND: Me, too. (*He coughs nervously and this brings on a real fit of coughing. Jamie glances at him with worried pity.*)

CHAPTER
SEVEN

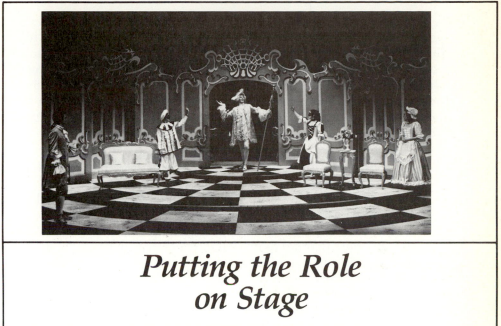

Putting the Role on Stage

Thomas Alva Edison was reputed to have told a young reporter that his inventions were the result of 10 per cent inspiration plus 90 per cent perspiration. It is not likely that such a formula radically distorts the proportions used by the successful actor in building a role. All the preparation the actor undergoes, both in developing as an actor and in working on a specific role, is pointed to the moment when, on opening night, the house lights dim, the curtain rises, and the actor steps out before an audience. Before that moment arrives, the actor should have carefully evolved the characterization, worked out in detail all the business, learned the lines and movement of the play, and prepared carefully to present a character through hard work, tenacity, and imagination. There remain at this point a few vital considerations that must be taken into account before the actor faces the audience for the first time.

Rehearsal Guidelines

Paul Newman has observed that when he begins to rehearse he usually gets everything wrong. However, after rehearsals start, he finds that slowly but surely he gets rid of the "wrong things bit by bit" until he begins to feel secure and move more comfortably within the part. Knowing *how* to rehearse and how to get the maximum from the rehearsal process is important for all actors. The following suggestions constitute a minimum standard for the actor during rehearsals, from the standpoint of both attitude and procedure.

1. *Promptness.* The actor should be on time or early for every rehearsal call.
2. *Warming-up.* The actor must take responsibility as an individual to be *ready* to rehearse. You must be prepared mentally and physically for creative work during the rehearsal period.
3. *Homework.* The actor must realize that work must be done also outside rehearsal hours in order to make the rehearsal as meaningful as possible.
   a. *Study your script.* Analyze your character. Understand the problems of your character in relation to other characters, or special problems that you have specifically in relation to the role.
   b. *Review your work.* There should be a daily review of what happened during previous rehearsals. Review the blocking and other pertinent notes you have made during the rehearsal periods.
   c. Learn your lines and movement (blocking) as soon as possible—absolutely no later than the time when the director has called for them.
4. *Actor's Rights.* Respect the rights and privileges of your coworkers, including every member of the cast, the director, and the production staff. Work with discipline and energy. Concentrate. Distractions waste time and affect the work of fellow actors and the director. This lack of concentration during rehearsals will eventually show when the play is performed before an audience.

The Three V's of Good Acting

As the time approaches for the final dress rehearsal and the first performance, the good actor takes stock in order to determine whether his or her approach is fundamentally correct and whether the actor is going to realize the full potential of the role. One means of simplifying this period of self-scrutiny is to codify the most important elements into what we shall call the three V's of good acting. They must be a part of every performance, and when utilized properly they make for exciting and memorable theatre.

Vitality

Of all the factors generally considered essential to any good performance, vitality is the one most difficult to define precisely in terms of the theatre. Some actors refer to this quality as vivacity or intensity; some equate it with the energy expended during the performance; and others suggest that it is an intangible spark possessed by all good actors.

Two actors may approach a role in fundamentally the same manner, rehearse as intensively, and execute it in the same technical terms, yet one performance may be exciting and memorable and the other lifeless and dull. Vitality is probably the most meaningful word that may be found to describe the factor that makes the difference. Vitality has been defined in the dictionary as "vital power, *the ability to sustain life*" (the words italicized here are especially appropriate), and it would be difficult to find a better analysis of what the actor must do with a role before an audience. For the actor, vitality must mean the infusing of the character with the intensity we expect to find in any living thing.

Sometimes a particular stimulus may serve to make a performance exciting and vital. There is a well-known proverb in the theatre that a bad dress rehearsal means a good show. Unhappily, this is usually wishful thinking on the part of cast and director, serving to boost low morale, but we should not overlook an element of truth in the statement. Often a magic transformation takes place when the lights dim, the curtain rises, and the actor steps out before a live audience. Opening night often provides the catalyst to make an otherwise lackluster production intense and alive. For this reason also, many actors give their best performances on opening night. It is said that they are "up" for the performance. The creative juices and adrenalin are flowing.

The actor will usually feel more energy being used when performing before an opening-night audience than he or she had used during any of the rehearsals. The intelligent actor will channel this energy into the vitalization of the role. If one is conscientious, a high degree of energy should be expended during the rehearsal period as well. This will ease the number of adjustments necessary for the first performance.

This expenditure of energy places severe demands on all actors. A healthy body is a prime requisite for every performance, but frequently the beginning actor miscalculates the extent of these demands. The dissipation of the actor's energies in extraneous and unnecessary activities prior to performance may be unwise. The actor alone is the best judge of how to expend energy offstage and still bring to the role a full measure of vitality. Lynn Fontanne's comment that she slept fifteen hours after the opening of Eugene O'Neill's *Strange Interlude* is testimony to the toll of energy imposed on all conscientious actors.

A word of warning is in order here. Vitality must not be confused with loudness, exaggeration, or overemphasis. Such devices are far from the true meaning of vitality. One may think of vitality as the insatiable urge to communicate to an audience all that one has within oneself. If the actor has properly prepared the role and is then truly eager to share his or her concept of the role with the audience, the actor will have taken a solid step forward toward achieving the mysterious force in the theatre known as fire, spark, intensity, or *vitality.*

Variety

A common failing of beginning actors is repetitiousness. Variety in vocal expressiveness and business and in the handling of the body and movement is necessary in every role.

Shakespeare knew that audiences find it difficult to endure a long play that consists only of tragic events, no matter how brilliantly the play may be written and performed. It was primarily for this reason that he invested his great tragedies with many of his finest comic creations: the Nurse in *Romeo and Juliet,* Polonius and the gravediggers in *Hamlet,* the Porter in *Macbeth,* the Fool in *King Lear,* and so on. The tragic portions of the play are more clearly highlighted because of the moments of relief that the comic elements provide. (It is true that the Greeks utilized little comic relief in their tragedies, but the plays were comparatively short, and music and dance imparted the necessary variety.)

Another illustration may be even clearer. We all have dishes that appeal particularly to our palate. We may even look forward eagerly to the next opportunity to indulge our taste. A constant diet of this food, however, would cloy our appetite until we would probably react by pushing away in disgust the very food that had once so appealed to us.

Variety in acting is as necessary as in diet. Constant repetition of a style of phrasing and a piece of business or movement, or the unvaried pacing of dialogue, soon calls attention to itself. The brilliant piece of business and the deft reading of a line stand out because they are unique. Repeat the same piece of business, rely on the same inflections and pat reactions, and the performance becomes monotonous and dull. The actor would do well to understand that *variety* is one of the most important considerations in bringing *balance* to a performance.

Validity

Although validity may simply be called truth or honesty, it most neatly sums up all the diverse responsibilities that the actor faces. Validity requires that the actor work honestly and believe in what he or she is doing with the role. Essentially these two ideas are one. Bruce Dern calls this element "reality, honesty, truth. You're saying real things to each other."[1]

As the actor appraises his or her work, honesty must be the touchstone for measuring accomplishment. The actor who resorts to tricks and old habits designed solely to achieve approval from the audience is guilty of bad acting. A beginning actor may be tempted to utilize a piece of business which he or she considers excellent even though it is not consistent with the character the actor is playing. When asked the reason for choosing that particular piece of business, the actor may seem shocked that someone would question such a clever idea. Sometimes the actor may resort to a trick as a feat of exhibitionism; sometimes the move is simply a miscalculation. No matter what the cause, any business, inflection, or movement that does not truly grow out of the characterization must be eliminated.

A young university actor, for example, cast in the role of a European nobleman of great charm and cultivation, had many opportunities to insert little pieces of business to help project the character's old-world sophistication. The young man sustained his role quite well until he came to the climactic moment. After a duel in which he had been wounded, he staggered across the stage and reached for a cup of wine on a nearby table. The young man seized the wine, gulped it down so rapidly that it was seen to run down his chin, and then wiped his face roughly on the sleeve of his uniform. It was an intense scene and an interesting piece of business calculated to excite the pity of the audience, but in that moment the illusion the actor had striven so hard to achieve during the entire performance was completely shattered. The action might have suited any number of other characters but could not have been part of the personality the actor had worked so hard to formulate. He had evidently hoped that he was projecting suffering, but instead he had permitted a jarring note to intrude itself upon the validity of his characterization. The scene certainly had vitality and it provided variety, but it lacked the third essential V, *validity*, to make it really good acting.

Katharine Cornell has commented directly on this point:

> In your mind, worked out with all the imagination and skill you possess, is the thing you want to do. When the performance comes, you must be intent only on that—on the sincerest, best thing that is in you. . . . Nothing else counts, certainly not whether the audience will like it. To try to please the front of the house is nothing short of ruinous.[2]

A spirit of responsibility to the role and to the production will help to eliminate any falseness from the actor's presentation. Self-awareness of a job done honestly and with integrity is more than enough justification for

1. Bruce Dern, quoted in Joanmarie Kalter, *Actors on Acting* (New York: Sterling Publishing Co., Inc., 1979), p. 185.
2. Quoted in Helen Ormsbee, *Backstage With Actors* (New York: Thomas Y. Crowell Co., 1938), p. 237.

acting and will allow the actor to bring a spirit of truth to the role. Many famous actors have urged this point on their contemporaries and students. Raymond Massey has stated it bluntly: "Good actors, like good plays, are made of flesh and blood, not bundles of tricks."[3]

Concentration

The actor at work is constantly hampered by a number of distractions: the whispering of crew members backstage preparing for their next cue, coughs from the audience, and the stumbling of late-comers trying to find their seats. If the actor is affected by such distractions, his or her performance will suffer; it is necessary to accept them as a normal accompaniment to stage performance.

Concentration—or, rather, attention to the work at hand—is the most obvious means of dealing with such distractions. But no simple formula for concentration can be evolved that will be meaningful for all people. Everyone has known students who claim that they are able to study without difficulty with the radio, television, or stereo on at high volume and other students who are distracted by the slightest disturbance.

Simply trying to eliminate a distraction by an effort to ignore it is not likely to solve the actor's problem. Concentration for stage work does not mean ignoring undesirable disturbances but rather focusing attention in a different direction. We all have had the experience of laughing at an inopportune moment at some inconsequential remark or action and then trying to force ourselves to stop. The more we try to stop laughing by concentrating on the laughter itself, the more difficult it becomes, and we may continue to giggle for a long time. The best way to eliminate the laughter is to concentrate not on it but on some unrelated idea or object. This principle may be applied by the actor: it is possible to learn to eliminate unwarranted disturbances by attention to the role and to objects and actors on stage.

Attention to the Role.   The actor may concentrate entirely upon the performance, upon the execution of business, the reading of lines, and the maintenance of the character. This is usually helpful for the beginning actor with limited stage experience. The first few ventures on stage will be a novel experience, and it may prove extremely useful to concentrate attention on all the planned details of performance until the actor attains more assurance of his or her powers as an interpreter.

Attention to Objects and Actors.   Distractions may be ignored by concentrating on the other actors, their dialogues, business, and movement, or on

---

3. Raymond Massey, "Acting," in *The Theatre Handbook and Digest of Plays,* ed. Bernard Sobel (New York: Crown Publishers, Inc., 1948), p. 27.

some of the significant stage properties. At first such concentration may be difficult to achieve. It may be helpful to focus attention on an object on stage. Fingering a prop, rubbing the hand on the back of a chair or sofa, or feeling a table top may be perfectly consistent with the character and may prove to be a good starting point for concentration on the performance.

Whichever means the actor employs, it is imperative to concentrate at all times while on stage. When the actor's attention is diverted, the continuity of the perormance is lost and may never be regained. Missing a beat in the pulse of the play may prove fatal.

How Much Emotion?

Most beginning actors, and even many quite experienced ones, ponder the question of how much emotion they should actually feel during a performance. A history of the controversy over this question has already been sketched in Chapter 2, and it may be helpful to refer to it again at this time. However, this review may seem rather academic and not directly related to the actor's own needs. It is all very well, one may say, to know that there is disagreement on this point, but what approach should *I* take in my work? Unfortunately no pat answer can be given, but it may be useful to anticipate some of the dangers of excess in either direction.

Excessive Emotionalism

Uncontrolled or uncoordinated emotion may be most harmful to a production. Two obvious dangers confront the actor who relies on the inspiration of the moment to bring forth the emotional fervor of a scene. Undoubtedly startling and thrilling effects may be produced during a performance when the actor is so inspired, but there is no guarantee of being able to rely on this "emotional seizure" night after night. In his study of Mrs. Leslie Carter (1862–1937), a famous actress who utilized this approach, Garff Wilson commented:

> Whenever she was able to throw herself into a state of semi-hysteria, she stirred and titillated her audiences; when the mood escaped her she failed to make an impression. Thus it followed that her early performances in any role were generally her best; the longer she played a part the more mechanical it became because, with each repetition she was less able to lose herself in the appropriate emotions.[4]

---

4. Garff B. Wilson, "Emotionalism in Acting," *Quarterly Journal of Speech* 42 (February 1955): 55.

The second danger stemming from reliance on spur-of-the-moment emotionalism is the risk of destroying the coordinated work of the other actors in the production. It may be very well to startle and excite an audience by one's fervor, but if the other actors are startled also at a sudden, unrehearsed outburst of passion, the production can only suffer. When Mrs. Carter was taken by emotional fervor, she would "weep, vociferate, shriek, rant, become hoarse with passion, and finally . . . flop and beat the floor."[5] You need only ask if you would wish to perform on stage with an actress given to such unpredictable outbursts.

Lack of Emotionalism

The other side of the coin also poses some difficulties. Complete reliance upon technical devices and artifice may produce a stilted and unexciting performance. Few responsible actors do not at least attempt to understand the nature of the emotion the character is supposed to feel. Even if they do not feel it themselves, they must still be able to make the audience believe that the character is feeling it. Some actors, however, remain so aloof from any penetration into the emotional context of a scene that the audience fails to believe any particle of the performance.

Reliance on technique alone has produced many fine performances, but it is usually a technique that is thoroughly refined. The best technique is one that deceives the viewer into thinking it does not exist. Too often the use of technique simply as a demonstration of the actor's adeptness implies, "Look how clever I am." The wheels are seen going around in the actor's head, and the audience is impressed at how well this person "acts" at acting. Such an impression, however, is a condemnation of any performance. Another result of using technique without imagination is the conventional, stereotyped playing of all emotional scenes in the same key, which, as we have already noted, should be avoided. The important thing to remember is that it is not really important whether or not the actor feels the emotion but whether or not the audience *thinks* the actor does, in the guise of the character.

The James-Lange Theory

Before we leave this question of emotionalism in acting, it is important to note a psychological theory that has special implications for the actor. We tend to believe that our emotions trigger our physical responses, or that *passion is a cue for action*. In other words, we become frightened and we run; we become unhappy and we cry; we are happy and we laugh. The *James-Lange*

---

5. William Winter, *The Wallet of Time* (New York: Moffat, Yard, 1913), vol. 2, p. 327.

theory[6] would reverse this sequence to imply that we are happy *because* we laugh, we are unhappy *because* we cry, and so on. We may see a wild beast and, because experience has trained us to avoid an encounter, we turn and run. Our fright does not come, according to the theory, before we run but is developed and exaggerated by our flight. The physiological reaction thus *follows* the physical action. James explained that, although this sequence might not be applicable in every case, he believed that emotion did follow "upon the bodily expression, in the coarser emotions."

There is now no general agreement in regard to this theory, although it was strongly supported many years ago. The actor should not miss its implications, however. In relation to acting, the theory suggests that if the actor can simulate laughter, he or she will feel happy; if the actor can tremble, he or she may become excited, and so on.

If this theory is correct, the actor does not need to wait to be "carried away" by inspiration in order to vitalize a performance; if the motor activity associated with an emotion can be reproduced correctly, the emotion itself will come. The imaginative, well-rehearsed actor will then be assured of having some emotional reaction during every performance. It may in part explain why the actor who feels "down" before a performance may still be able to work himself or herself into the role once the performance has started. Reliance on the James-Lange theory may be termed as working from the outside in, as opposed to the Stanislavski system, which strongly advocates working from the inside out.

The question as to which approach is more useful for the actor's needs can be answered only by the individual. We have attempted to suggest some of the pitfalls that exist in the utilization of either extreme. A happy balance between emotion and technique, often termed the "warm heart and cool head" method, may be the most desirable compromise. Only experience will tell the actor which balance of values is most suitable for his or her personality and temperament.

Judging One's Own Work

One of the most difficult acting responsibilities is to evaluate one's own performance objectively. It is true that such judgment is one of the primary duties of the director, but the director can serve only as a guide for the actor. Although it is often useful to seek the advice of others, the actor who wishes to judge the quality of his or her own acting should view each performance as dispassionately as possible, applying to it the following set of standards. Honest and considered answers to these questions will provide the most useful framework for judging a performance.

---

6. This theory was propounded separately by C. H. Lange in 1885 and by William James (in *Principles of Psychology*) in 1890.

The Total Concept

Action	1.	Have I thoroughly analyzed the entire play, understanding the sequence of the action and the relation of each part to the other?
Theme	2.	Do I understand what the playwright is trying to say in the play?
Organization	3.	Can I relate my role to the total fabric of the play?
Style	4.	Is my style of playing consistent with that used by the entire cast?

The Role Itself

Speech	1.	Have I chosen the voice, manner of speech, and phrasing that best serve my character?
Business	2.	Does the business I have chosen truly illuminate the character?
Movement	3.	Is my manner of movement and posture consistent with the needs of the role?
Motivation	4.	Do I understand my character, and what he or she *wants* in the play, and *why*?

The Actor's Responsibilities

Imagination	1.	Have I made full use of my imagination in formulating the characterization?
Clichés	2.	Am I satisfied with superficial tricks and clichés, or have I taken the time to delve into all the subtleties of the role?
Three V's:		
variety	3.	Do I play the role with sufficient diversity to maintain the interest of the audience during an entire performance?
vitality	4.	Will I make every effort to communicate my character to the audience with all the energy necessary?
validity	5.	Is my characterization an honest portrait, consistent with my integrity as an actor?
Individuality	6.	Does this characterization grow out of my own creative initiative?

All of these questions are important, and any unsatisfactory answer should be the stimulus for more work and investigation.

One more question remains to be answered. It is not only a summation of all the questions the actor should ask but must be considered every day from the first rehearsal to the final performance.

Responsibility	7.	At this time, is this the best job I am capable of doing?

If the answer to this last question is in the affirmative, the actor should await with great anticipation that moment when the stage manager announces: "Curtain going up."

Scenes

1. *No Time for Sergeants,* by Ira Levin and Mac Hyman
   From Act I

   Scene: For two men
   Characters: WILL STOCKDALE, an Army private
   AN ARMY PSYCHIATRIST
   Setting: The office of a psychiatrist, a major in the United States Army.
   Time: Some of it is happening now and some of it happened a while back.
   Situation: For anyone who has served in the armed forces, this scene should need
   no introduction. It is another comic view of a blundering recruit's upset
   of Army routine. Will's behavior at boot camp has hardly endeared him
   to the noncommissioned officers. Hoping to have him transferred,
   Will's sergeant sends him to the Army psychiatrist with an order to
   answer the psychiatrist's questions properly. When told that the
   psychiatrist might ask him what he dreams about, Will worries about
   how he should answer the question. But he solves this problem and the
   others that follow during his interview. The naiveté and common sense
   of Will's responses provide much of the humor of the play.
   (The satirical handling of the Army psychiatrist is not unlike the
   treatment accorded another psychiatrist in *Teahouse of the August Moon.*
   See the scene from *Teahouse* on p. 215, immediately after this scene.)

(PSYCHIATRIST, *a major, signs and stamps a paper before him, then takes form from*
WILL, *seated next to desk.* PSYCHIATRIST *looks at form, looks at* WILL. *A moment of*
silence.)
WILL: I never have no dreams at all.
PSYCHIATRIST: (*a pause. He looks carefully at* WILL, *looks at form.*) Where you from,
Stockdale?
WILL: Georgia.
PSYCHIATRIST: That's . . . not much of a state, is it?
WILL: Well . . . I don't live all over the state. I just live in this one little place
in it.
PSYCHIATRIST: That's where "Tobacco Road" is, Georgia.
WILL: Not around my section. (*pause*) Maybe you're from a different part than
me?
PSYCHIATRIST: I've never been there. What's more I don't think I would ever
want to go there. What's your reaction to that?
WILL: Well, I don't know.
PSYCHIATRIST: I think I would sooner live in the rottenest pigsty in Alabama or
Tennessee than in the fanciest mansion in all of Georgia. What about that?
WILL: Well, sir, I think where you want to live is your business.
PSYCHIATRIST: (*pause, staring*) You don't mind if someone says something bad
about Georgia?

WILL: I ain't heared nobody say nothin' bad about Georgia.

PSYCHIATRIST: What do you think I've been saying?

WILL: Well, to tell you the truth, I ain't been able to get too much sense out of it. Don't you know?

PSYCHIATRIST: Watch your step, young man. (*pause*) We psychiatrists call this attitude of yours "resistance."

WILL: You do?

PSYCHIATRIST: You sense that this interview is a threat to your security. You feel yourself in danger.

WILL: Well, kind of I do. If'n I don't get classified Sergeant King won't give me the wrist watch. (PSYCHIATRIST *stares at* WILL *uncomprehendingly.*) He *won't!* He said I only gets it if I'm classified inside a week.

PSYCHIATRIST: (*turns forlornly to papers on desk. A bit subdued*) You get along all right with your mother?

WILL: No, sir, I can't hardly say that I do—

PSYCHIATRIST: (*cutting in*) She's very strict? Always hovering over you?

WILL: No, sir, just the opposite—

PSYCHIATRIST: She's never there.

WILL: That's right.

PSYCHIATRIST: You resent this neglect, don't you?

WILL: No, I don't resent nothin'.

PSYCHIATRIST: (*leaning forward paternally*) There's nothing to be ashamed of, son. It's a common situation. Does she ever beat you?

WILL: No!

PSYCHIATRIST: (*silkily*) So defensive. It's not easy to talk about your mother, is it.

WILL: No, sir. She died when I was borned.

PSYCHIATRIST: (*a long, sick pause*) You . . . could have told me that sooner . . .

WILL: (*looks hang-dog.* PSYCHIATRIST *returns to papers.* WILL *glances up at him.*) Do you hate *your* Mama? (PSYCHIATRIST'S *head snaps up, glaring.*) I figgered as how you said it was so common . . .

PSYCHIATRIST: I do not hate my mother.

WILL: I should hope not! (*pause*) What, does she beat you or somethin'?

PSYCHIATRIST: (*glares again, drums his fingers briefly on table. Steeling himself, more to self than* WILL) This is a transference. You're taking all your stored up antagonisms and loosing them in my direction. Transference. It happens every day. . . .

WILL: (*excited*) It does? To the Infantry?

PSYCHIATRIST: (*aghast*) The Infantry?

WILL: You give Ben a transfer. I wish you'd give me one too. I'd sure love to go along with him.

PSYCHIATRIST: Stop! (*The pause is a long one this time. Finally* PSYCHIATRIST *points at papers.*) There are a few more topics we have to cover. We will not talk about transfers, we will not talk about my mother. We will only talk about what *I* want to talk about, do you understand?

WILL: Yes, sir.

PSYCHIATRIST: Now then—your father. (*quickly*) Living?

WILL: Yes, sir.

PSYCHIATRIST: Do you get along with him okay?

WILL: Yes, sir.

PSYCHIATRIST: Does he ever beat you?

WILL: You bet!

PSYCHIATRIST: Hard?

WILL: And how! Boy, there ain't nobody can beat like my Pa can!

PSYCHIATRIST: (*beaming*) So *this* is where the antagonism comes from! (*pause*) You hate your father, don't you?

WILL: No . . . I got an uncle I hate! Every time he comes out to the house he's always wantin' to rassle with the mule, and the mule gets all wore out, and *he* gets all wore out . . . Well, I don't really *hate* him; I just ain't exactly partial to him.

PSYCHIATRIST: (*pause*) Did I ask you about your uncle?

WILL: I thought you wanted to talk about hatin' people.

PSYCHIATRIST: (*glares, drums his fingers, retreats to form. Barely audible*) Now— girls. How do you like girls?

WILL: What girls is that, sir?

PSYCHIATRIST: Just girls. Just any girls.

WILL: Well, I don't like just any girls. There's one old girl back home that ain't got hair no longer than a hound-dog's and she's always—

PSYCHIATRIST: No! Look, when I say girls I don't mean any one specific girl. I mean girls in general; women, sex! Didn't that father of yours ever sit down and have a talk with you?

WILL: Sure he did.

PSYCHIATRIST: Well?

WILL: Well what?

PSYCHIATRIST: What did he say?

WILL: (*with a snicker*) Well, there was this one about these two travelin' salesmen that their car break down in the middle of this terrible storm—

PSYCHIATRIST: Stop!

WILL: —so they stop at this farmhouse where the farmer has fourteen daughters who was—

PSYCHIATRIST: *Stop!*

WILL: You heared it already?

PSYCHIATRIST: (*writing furiously on form*) No, I did not hear it already . . .

WILL: Well, what did you stop me for? It's a real knee-slapper. You see, the fourteen daughters is all studyin' to be trombone players and—

PSYCHIATRIST: (*shoving form at* WILL) Here. Go. Good-by. You're through. You're normal. Good-by. Go. Go.

WILL: (*takes form and stands, a bit confused by it all*) Sir, if girls is what you want to talk about, you ought to come down to the barracks some night. The younger fellows there is always tellin' spicy stories and all like that.

2.   *Teahouse of the August Moon*, by John Patrick
From Act II, Scene 3

Scene: For two men

Characters: CAPTAIN FISBY, United States Army
CAPTAIN McLEAN, an Army psychiatrist

Setting: Captain Fisby's makeshift office in the village of Tobiki, Okinawa.

Time: During the American occupation of Okinawa, following World War II.

Situation: Captain Fisby, an ineffectual Army officer, but a humane and intelligent individual, has been given the assignment of bringing law, order, and democracy to the tiny village of Tobiki. Unfortunately, his progress reports do not please his commanding officer, Colonel Purdy. Instead of teaching the Okinawan children to sing "God Bless America" in English, he has attempted to introduce some industry into the village, such as manufacturing cricket cages and getas (a type of thonged wooden sandal) and raising goats. The disconcerted colonel decides to send Captain McLean, a psychiatrist, to look into the situation. The psychiatrist soon discovers that Captain Fisby has gone quite native.

(CAPTAIN MCLEAN *enters. He is an intense, rather wild-eyed man in his middle forties. He glances about furtively, then begins to examine the papers on* FISBY'S *desk. He makes several notes in a notebook. He picks up* FISBY'S *cricket cage and is examining it intently when* FISBY *enters behind him. He halts upon seeing* MCLEAN. FISBY *is wearing his blue bathrobe, his getas, and a native straw hat.*)

FISBY: Well, who are you?

MCLEAN: (*gasps in surprise*) Oh, you startled me.

FISBY: Can I do anything for you? I'm Captain Fisby.

MCLEAN: I'm Captain McLean. There was no one here . . . so I came in.

FISBY: (*He looks at his insignia*) Oh, medical corps. What brings you to Tobiki?

MCLEAN: Well, I'm—I'm on leave. Thought I'd spend it making some—ethnological studies. (*He adds quickly*) Of the natives.

FISBY: Well, you couldn't have come to a more interesting spot. Sit down, Captain.

MCLEAN: (*sits*) Thank you. Would you have any objection to my spending a week or so making my studies, Captain?

FISBY: Not at all. Make yourself at home. I'll take that if it's in your way. (*He reaches out to relieve* MCLEAN *of the cricket cage he still holds.*)

MCLEAN: (*glances at the cage in his hand and laughs awkwardly*) Oh, yes. I was just examining it.

FISBY: (*pleased at his authority on the subject*) It's a cricket cage.

MCLEAN: (*pauses*) You . . . like crickets?

FISBY: I haven't found one yet. But at least I've got the cage. I've got two . . . if you want one.

MCLEAN: Thank you, no. Thank you very much. (*He looks at* FISBY'S *attire.*) What happened to your uniform, Captain?

FISBY: It's around. I find getas and a kimono much more comfortable in this climate.

MCLEAN: But isn't that a bathrobe?

FISBY: (*shrugs*) It passes for a kimono. Would you like to take off your shoes, Captain?

MCLEAN: Thank you . . . no. I'll keep them on if you don't mind.

FISBY: Can I offer you some tsukemono? You eat these during the day between meals. (*He extends a platter.*) Tsukemono means fragrant things.

MCLEAN: I just had a chocolate bar, thank you. (*He rises and looks out the door.*) May I ask what you're building down the road?

FISBY: (*proudly*) That's my cha ya. (*He pops a few tsukemonos into his mouth.*) It's really going to be something to write home about.

MCLEAN: Cha ya?

FISBY: Well, it just so happens, Captain, that I own a geisha girl. That might sound strange to you, but you get used to these things after a while. And if you have a geisha, you've got to have a cha ya. Sure you don't want some tsukemono?

MCLEAN: I really couldn't eat a thing. (*He glances out the door again.*) May I ask what the men are doing down there wading in that irrigation ditch?

FISBY: They're not wading, they're building a lotus pond. You can't have a cha ya without a lotus pond.

MCLEAN: (*sits opposite* FISBY) How have you felt lately, Fisby?

FISBY: McLean, I'll tell you something. I've never been happier. I feel reckless and free. And it all happened the moment I decided not to build that damn pentagon-shaped school.

MCLEAN: That what?

FISBY: The good colonel ordered me to build a pentagon-shaped schoolhouse down here. But the people wanted a teahouse. Believe it or not, someone gave me a geisha girl. So I'm giving this village what it wants. That must all sound pretty crazy to you, Mac.

MCLEAN: Well, yes and no.

FISBY: These are wonderful people with a strange sense of beauty. And hardworking . . . when there's a purpose. You should have seen them start out day before yesterday, great bundles of things they'd made piled high on their heads. Getas, cricket cages, lacquer ware—things to sell as souvenirs up north. Don't let anyone tell you these people are lazy.

MCLEAN: Oh. I see. I see.

FISBY: No, you don't. But you'll have a chance to study them.

MCLEAN: So you're building them a teahouse.

FISBY: Next thing I'm going to do for them is find out if this land here will grow anything besides sweet potatoes. I'm going to send for fertilizers and DDT and—

MCLEAN: (*leaps to his feet*) Chemicals!

FISBY: Sure, why not?

MCLEAN: Do you want to poison these people?

FISBY: No, but—

MCLEAN: Now you've touched on a subject that is very close to me. For years I've planned to retire and buy a farm—raise specialties for big restaurants. So let me tell you this. Chemicals will kill all your earthworms, and earthworms aerate your soil.

FISBY: They do?

MCLEAN: Do you know an earthworm leaves castings eight times its own weight every day?

FISBY: That much!

MCLEAN: Organic gardening is the only thing. Nature's way—compost, manure, but no chemicals.

FISBY: Hey! You know a lot about this.

MCLEAN: (*modestly*) I should. I've subscribed to all the farm journals for years.

FISBY: Say, you could help these people out while you're here—if you would.

Do you think you could take over supervision—establish a sort of experimental station for them?

McLean: Well, I—no—no—I haven't time.

Fisby: Take time. This is a chance for you to put some of your theories into practice.

McLean: (*haughtily*) They are not theories. They are proven facts.

Fisby: I'll give you a couple of men to help, and all you'd have to do is tell us how.

McLean: (*hesitates*) Is your soil acid or alkaline?

Fisby: Gosh, I don't know.

McLean: Well, that's the very *first* thing you have to find out. Do you have bees?

Fisby: I haven't seen any.

McLean: (*shakes his head sadly*) People always underestimate the importance of bees for pollinating.

Fisby: (*slaps him on the back*) Mac, you're just the man we've needed down here. You're a genius!

McLean: I'll want plenty of manure.

Fisby: You'll get it.

McLean: And I'll want to plan this program scientifically. I wish I had some of my books . . . and my seed catalogues. (*He measures from the floor.*) I've got a stack of catalogues that high.

Fisby: Why don't you make a list, and I'll get the boys over at the airstrip to fly us in seeds from the States.

McLean: (*The gardener fever possesses the doctor as he begins to make his list.*) Every spring I've made lists of seeds and never had any soil to put them in. And now . . . I could actually germinate. (*He writes*) Corn—Golden Bantam. (*then adds enthusiastically*) And Country Gentleman! Hybrid.

Fisby: Why don't I just leave you with your list while I check on the lotus pond? (McLean *doesn't hear him.*) Well, I'll be back for tea. We have tea in the pine grove and watch the sun go down. (*He goes out.*)

McLean: (*continues with his list reading aloud*) Cucumbers—Extra Early Green Prolific. (*His enthusiasm mounts.*) Radishes—Crimson Giant! (*The telephone begins to ring; he ignores it as he writes.*) Tomatoes—Ponderosa Earliana. (*The telephone rings insistently.*) Watermelon! (*He closes his eyes ecstatically.*)

3. *The Glass Menagerie*, by Tennessee Williams
   From Scene II

   Scene: For two women
   Characters: AMANDA WINGFIELD
   LAURA WINGFIELD, her daughter
   Setting: The Wingfield apartment at the rear of a building facing an alley. St. Louis, Missouri.
   Time: Afternoon. The 1930s.
   Situation: After her husband abandoned her, Amanda Wingfield reared her children, Tom and Laura. Amanda has great dreams for her children, now grown, far outstripping their potential or their wishes. Laura is an

exceedingly shy, introverted young woman. Her personality has been affected by a deformed foot which causes her to limp. She has retreated to the world of her glass menagerie, a collection of small glass animals. Amanda has been paying for typing lessons for Laura so that she might be employable as a secretary.

As the scene begins, Laura has been polishing her glass collection when she hears Amanda. She thrusts the ornaments away and sits stiffly before a typewriter diagram on the wall. Amanda slowly lets herself in.

LAURA: Hello, Mother, I was—(*She makes a nervous gesture toward the chart on the wall.* AMANDA *leans against the shut door and stares at* LAURA *with a martyred look.*)

AMANDA: Deception? Deception? (*She slowly removes her hat and gloves, continuing the sweet suffering stare. She lets the hat and gloves fall on the floor—a bit of acting.*)

LAURA: (*shakily*) How was the D.A.R. meeting? (AMANDA *slowly opens her purse and removes a dainty white handkerchief which she shakes out delicately and delicately touches to her lips and nostrils.*) Didn't you go to the D.A.R. meeting, Mother?

AMANDA: (*faintly, almost inaudibly*)—No.—No. (*then more forcibly*) I did not have the strength—to go to the D.A.R. In fact, I did not have the courage! I wanted to find a hole in the ground and hide myself in it forever! (*She crosses slowly to the wall and removes the diagram of the typewriter keyboard. She holds it in front of her for a second, staring at it sweetly and sorrowfully—then bites her lips and tears it in two pieces.*)

LAURA: (*faintly*) Why did you do that, Mother? (AMANDA *repeats the same procedure with the chart of the Gregg Alphabet.*) Why are you—

AMANDA: Why? Why? How old are you, Laura?

LAURA: Mother, you know my age.

AMANDA: I thought that you were an adult; it seems that I was mistaken. (*She crosses slowly to the sofa and sinks down and stares at* LAURA.)

LAURA: Please don't stare at me, Mother. (AMANDA *closes her eyes and lowers her head. Count ten.*)

AMANDA: What are we going to do, what is going to become of us, what is the future? (*Count ten.*)

LAURA: Has something happened, Mother? (AMANDA *draws a long breath and takes out the handkerchief again. Dabbing process*) Mother, has—something happened?

AMANDA: I'll be all right in a minute, I'm just bewildered—(*Count five.*)—by life. . . .

LAURA: Mother, I wish that you would tell me what's happened!

AMANDA: As you know, I was supposed to be inducted into my office at the D.A.R. this afternoon. But I stopped off at Rubicam's Business College to speak to your teachers about your having a cold and ask them what progress they thought you were making down there.

LAURA: Oh. . . .

AMANDA: I went to the typing instructor and introduced myself as your mother. She didn't know who you were. Wingfield, she said. We don't have any such student enrolled at the school!

I assured her she did, that you have been going to classes since early in January.

"I wonder," she said, "if you could be talking about that terribly shy little girl who dropped out of school after only a few days' attendance?"

"No," I said, "Laura, my daughter, has been going to school every day for the past six weeks!"

"Excuse me," she said. She took the attendance book out and there was your name, unmistakably printed, and all the dates you were absent until they decided you had dropped out of school.

I still said, "No, there must have been some mistake! There must have been some mix-up in the records!"

And she said, "No—I remember her perfectly now. Her hands shook so that she couldn't hit the right keys! The first time we gave a speed-test, she broke down completely—was sick at the stomach and almost had to be carried into the wash-room! After that morning she never showed up any more. We phoned the house but never got any answer"—while I was working at Famous and Barr, I suppose, demonstrating those—Oh!

I felt so weak I could barely keep on my feet!

I had to sit down while they got me a glass of water!

Fifty dollars' tuition, all of our plans—my hopes and ambitions for you—just gone up the spout, just gone up the spout like that. (LAURA *draws a long breath and gets awkwardly to her feet. She crosses to the victrola and winds it up.*) What are you doing?

LAURA: Oh! (*She releases the handle and returns to her seat.*)

AMANDA: Laura, where have you been going when you've gone out pretending that you were going to business college?

LAURA: I've just been going out walking.

AMANDA: That's not true.

LAURA: It is. I just went walking.

AMANDA: Walking? Walking? In winter? Deliberately courting pneumonia in that light coat? Where did you walk to, Laura?

LAURA: All sorts of places—mostly in the park.

AMANDA: Even after you'd started catching that cold?

LAURA: It was the lesser of two evils, Mother. I couldn't go back up. I—threw up—on the floor!

AMANDA: From half past seven till after five every day you mean to tell me you walked around in the park, because you wanted to make me think that you were still going to Rubicam's Business College?

LAURA: It wasn't as bad as it sounds. I went inside places to get warmed up.

AMANDA: Inside where?

LAURA: I went in the art museum and the birdhouses at the Zoo. I visited the penguins every day! Sometimes I did without lunch and went to the movies. Lately I've been spending most of my afternoons in the Jewel-box, that big glass house where they raise tropical flowers.

AMANDA: You did all this to deceive me, just for deception? (LAURA *looks down.*) Why?

LAURA: Mother, when you're disappointed, you get that awful suffering look on your face, like the picture of Jesus' mother in the museum!

AMANDA: Hush!

LAURA: I couldn't face it. (*Pause. A whisper of strings*)

AMANDA: (*hopelessly fingering the huge pocketbook*) So what are we going to do the rest of our lives? Stay home and watch the parades go by? Amuse ourselves with the glass menagerie, darling? Eternally play those worn-out phonograph records your father left as a painful reminder of him?

We won't have a business career—we've given that up because it gave us nervous indigestion! (*laughs wearily*) What is there left but dependency all our lives? I know so well what becomes of unmarried women who aren't prepared to occupy a position. I've seen such pitiful cases in the South—barely tolerated spinsters living upon the grudging patronage of sister's husband or brother's wife!—stuck away in some little mouse-trap of a room—encouraged by one in-law to visit another—little birdlike women without any nest—eating the crust of humility all their life!

Is that the future that we've mapped out for ourselves?

I swear it's the only alternative I can think of!

It isn't a very pleasant alternative, is it?

Of course—some girls *do marry*. (LAURA *twists her hands nervously.*) Haven't you ever liked some boy?

LAURA: Yes, I liked one once. (*rises*) I came across his picture a while ago.

AMANDA: (*with some interest*) He gave you his picture?

LAURA: No, it's in the year-book.

AMANDA: (*disappointed*) Oh—a high-school boy.

LAURA: Yes. His name was Jim. (LAURA *lifts the heavy annual from the claw-foot table.*) Here he is in *The Pirates of Penzance*.

AMANDA: (*absently*) The what?

LAURA: The operetta the senior class put on. He had a wonderful voice and we sat across the aisle from each other Mondays, Wednesdays and Fridays in the Aud. Here he is with the silver cup for debating! See his grin?

AMANDA: (*absently*) He must have had a jolly disposition.

LAURA: He used to call me—Blue Roses.

AMANDA: Why did he call you such a name as that?

LAURA: When I had that attack of pleurosis—he asked me what was the matter when I came back. I said pleurosis—he thought that I said Blue Roses! So that's what he always called me after that. Whenever he saw me, he'd holler, "Hello, Blue Roses!" I didn't care for the girl that he went out with. Emily Meisenbach. Emily was the best-dressed girl at Soldan. She never struck me, though, as being sincere . . . It says in the Personal Section—they're engaged. That's—six years ago! They must be married by now.

AMANDA: Girls that aren't cut out for business careers usually wind up married to some nice man. (*gets up with a spark of revival*) Sister, that's what you'll do! (LAURA *utters a startled, doubtful laugh. She reaches quickly for a piece of glass.*)

LAURA: But, Mother—

AMANDA: Yes? (*crossing to photograph*)

LAURA: (*in a tone of frightened apology*) I'm—crippled!

AMANDA: Nonsense! Laura, I've told you never, never to use that word. Why, you're not crippled, you just have a little defect—hardly noticeable, even! When people have some slight disadvantage like that, they cultivate other things to make up for it—develop charm—and vivacity—and—*charm!* That's all you have to do! (*She turns again to the photograph.*) One thing your father had *plenty of*—was *charm!*

4. *Death of a Salesman,* by Arthur Miller
    From Act II

      Scene: For two men
Characters: WILLY LOMAN, a salesman
             HOWARD, his boss.
    Setting: Howard's office
      Time: A morning in the late 1940s.
Situation: See the preceding scene from *Death of a Salesman* (p. 195), which occurs earlier in the play.

Arthur Miller's perceptive drama of the slow erosion and self-destruction of the little man is generally considered to be among the few great American plays of our time. Willy Loman, a travelling salesman, finds that at sixty-three he is unable to earn enough money on a straight commission basis to support his family. He escapes from reality by daydreaming and has even considered suicide.

    Hoping to change his job on the road for a position at the home office, Willy comes to Howard's office to request a transfer. Howard seems preoccupied.

WILLY: Pst! Pst!
HOWARD: Hello, Willy, come in.
WILLY: Like to have a little talk with you, Howard.
HOWARD: Sorry to keep you waiting. I'll be with you in a minute.
WILLY: What's that, Howard?
HOWARD: Didn't you ever see one of these? Wire recorder.
WILLY: Oh. Can we talk a minute?
HOWARD: Records things. Just got delivery yesterday. Been driving me crazy, the most terrific machine I ever saw in my life. I was up all night with it.
WILLY: What do you do with it?
HOWARD: I bought it for dictation, but you can do anything with it. Listen to this. I had it home last night. Listen to what I picked up. The first one is my daughter. Get this. (*He flicks the switch and "Roll out the Barrel!" is heard being whistled.*) Listen to that kid whistle.
WILLY: That is lifelike, isn't it?
HOWARD: Seven years old. Get that tone.
WILLY: Ts, ts. Like to ask a little favor of you . . . (*The whistling breaks off, and the voice of* HOWARD'S *daughter is heard.*)
HIS DAUGHTER: "Now you, Daddy."

HOWARD: She's crazy for me! (*Again the same song is whistled.*) That's me! Ha!
   (*He winks.*)

WILLY: You're very good! (*The whistling breaks off again. The machine runs silent
   for a moment.*)

HOWARD: Sh! Get this now, this is my son.

HIS SON: "The capital of Alabama is Montgomery; the capital of Arizona is
   Phoenix; the capital of Arkansas is Little Rock; the capital of California is
   Sacramento . . ." (*and on, and on*)

HOWARD: (*holding up five fingers*) Five years old, Willy.

WILLY: He'll make an announcer some day!

HIS SON: (*continuing*) "The capital . . ."

HOWARD: Get that—alphabetical order! (*The machine breaks off suddenly.*) Wait
   a minute. The maid kicked the plug out.

WILLY: It certainly is a—

HOWARD: Sh, for God's sake.

HIS SON: "It's nine o'clock, Bulova watch time. So I have to go to sleep."

WILLY: That really is—

HOWARD: Wait a minute! The next is my wife. (*They wait.*)

HOWARD'S VOICE: "Go on, say something." (*pause*) "Well, you gonna talk?"

HIS WIFE: "I can't think of anything."

HOWARD'S VOICE: "Well, talk—it's turning."

HIS WIFE: (*shyly, beaten*) "Hello." (*silence*) "Oh, Howard, I can't talk into
   this . . ."

HOWARD: (*snapping the machine off*) That was my wife.

WILLY: This is a wonderful machine. Can we—

HOWARD: I tell you, Willy, I'm gonna take my camera, and my bandsaw, and
   all my hobbies, and out they go. This is the most fascinating relaxation I
   ever found.

WILLY: I think I'll get one myself.

HOWARD: Sure, they're only a hundred and a half. You can't do without it.
   Supposing you wanna hear Jack Benny, see? But you can't be at home at
   that hour. So you tell the maid to turn the radio on when Jack Benny comes
   on, and this automatically goes on with the radio . . .

WILLY: And when you come home you . . .

HOWARD: You can come home twelve o'clock, one o'clock, any time you like,
   and you get yourself a Coke and sit yourself down, throw the switch, and
   there's Jack Benny's program in the middle of the night!

WILLY: I'm definitely going to get one. Because lots of time I'm on the road,
   and I think to myself, what I must be missing on the radio!

HOWARD: Don't you have a radio in the car?

WILLY: Well, yeah, but who ever thinks of turning it on?

HOWARD: Say, aren't you supposed to be in Boston?

WILLY: That's what I want to talk to you about, Howard. You got a minute?
   (*He draws a chair in from the wing.*)

HOWARD: What happened? What're you doing here?

WILLY: Well . . .

HOWARD: You didn't crack up again, did you?

WILLY: Oh, no. No . . .

HOWARD: Geez, you had me worried there for a minute. What's the trouble?

WILLY: Well, tell you the truth, Howard. I've come to a decision that I'd rather not travel any more.

HOWARD: Not travel! Well, what'll you do?

WILLY: Remember, Christmas time, when you had the party here? You said you'd try to think of some spot for me here in town.

HOWARD: With us?

WILLY: Well, sure.

HOWARD: Oh, yeah, yeah. I remember. Well, I couldn't think of anything for you, Willy.

WILLY: I tell ya, Howard. The kids are all grown up, y'know. I don't need much any more. If I could take home—well, sixty-five dollars a week, I could swing it.

HOWARD: Yeah, but Willy, see I—

WILLY: I tell ya why, Howard. Speaking frankly and between the two of us, y'know—I'm just a little tired.

HOWARD: Oh, I could understand that, Willy. But you're a road man, Willy, and we do a road business. We've only got a half-dozen salesmen on the floor here.

WILLY: God knows, Howard, I never asked a favor of any man. But I was with the firm when your father used to carry you in here in his arms.

HOWARD: I know that, Willy, but—

WILLY: Your father came to me the day you were born and asked me what I thought of the name of Howard, may he rest in peace.

HOWARD: I appreciate that, Willy, but there just is no spot here for you. If I had a spot I'd slam you right in, but I just don't have a single solitary spot. (*He looks for his lighter.* WILLY *has picked it up and gives it to him. Pause.*)

WILLY: (*with increasing anger*) Howard, all I need to set my table is fifty dollars a week.

HOWARD: But where am I going to put you, kid?

WILLY: Look, it isn't a question of whether I can sell merchandise, is it?

HOWARD: No, but it's a business, kid, and everybody's gotta pull his own weight.

WILLY: (*desperately*) Just let me tell you a story, Howard—

HOWARD: 'Cause you gotta admit, business is business.

WILLY: (*angrily*) Business is definitely business, but just listen for a minute. You don't understand this. When I was a boy—eighteen, nineteen—I was already on the road. And there was a question in my mind as to whether selling had a future for me. Because in those days I had a yearning to go to Alaska. See, there were three gold strikes in one month in Alaska, and I felt like going out. Just for the ride, you might say.

HOWARD: (*barely interested*) Don't say.

WILLY: Oh, yeah, my father lived many years in Alaska. He was an adventurous man. We've got quite a little streak of self-reliance in our family. I thought I'd go out with my older brother and try to locate him, and maybe settle in the North with the old man. And I was almost decided to go, when I met a salesman in the Parker House. His name was Dave Singleman. And he was eighty-four years old, and he drummed merchandise in thirty-one states. And old Dave, he'd go up to his room, y'understand, put on his green velvet slippers—I'll never forget—and pick up his phone and call the buyers, and without ever leaving his room, at the age of eighty-four, he made his living. And when I saw that, I realized that selling was the greatest career a man could want. 'Cause what could be more satisfying than to be able to go, at the age of eighty-four, into twenty or thirty different cities, and pick up a phone, and be remembered and loved and helped by so many different people? Do you know? when he died—and by the way he died the death of a salesman, in his green velvet slippers in the smoker of the New York, New Haven and Hartford, going into Boston—when he died, hundreds of salesmen and buyers were at his funeral. Things were sad on a lotta trains for months after that. (*He stands up.* HOWARD *has not looked at him.*) In those days there was personality in it, Howard. There was respect, and comradeship, and gratitude in it. Today, it's all cut and dried, and there's no chance for bringing friendship to bear—or personality. You see what I mean? They don't know me any more.

HOWARD: (*moving away, to the right*) That's just the thing, Willy.

WILLY: If I had forty dollars a week—that's all I'd need. Forty dollars, Howard.

HOWARD: Kid, I can't take blood from a stone, I—

WILLY: (*Desperation is on him now.*) Howard, the year Al Smith was nominated, your father came to me and—

HOWARD: (*starting to go off*) I've got to see some people, kid.

WILLY: (*stopping him*) I'm talking about your father! There were promises made across this desk! You mustn't tell me you've got people to see—I put thirty-four years into this firm, Howard, and now I can't pay my insurance! You can't eat the orange and throw the peel away—a man is not a piece of fruit! (*after a pause*) Now pay attention. Your father—in 1928 I had a big year. I averaged a hundred and seventy dollars a week in commissions.

HOWARD: (*impatiently*) Now, Willy, you never averaged—

WILLY: (*banging his hand on the desk*) I averaged a hundred and seventy dollars a week in the year of 1928! And your father came to me—or rather, I was in the office here—it was right over this desk—and he put his hand on my shoulder—

HOWARD: (*getting up*) You'll have to excuse me, Willy, I gotta see some people. Pull yourself together. (*going out*) I'll be back in a little while. (*On* HOWARD'S *exit, the light on his chair grows very bright and strange.*)

WILLY: Pull myself together! What the hell did I say to him? My God, I was yelling at him! How could I! (WILLY *breaks off, staring at the light, which occupies the chair, animating it. He approaches this chair, standing across the desk from it.*) Frank, Frank, don't you remember what you told me that time? How you put your hand on my shoulder, and Frank . . . (*He leans on the desk and as he speaks the dead man's name he accidentally switches on the recorder, and instantly*)

HOWARD'S SON: ". . . of New York is Albany. The capital of Ohio is Cincinnati, the capital of Rhode Island is . . ." (*The recitation continues.*)

WILLY: (*leaping away with fright, shouting*) Ha! Howard! Howard! Howard!

HOWARD: (*rushing in*) What happened?

WILLY: (*pointing at the machine, which continues nasally, childishly, with the capital cities*) Shut it off! Shut it off!

HOWARD: (*pulling the plug out*) Look, Willy . . .

WILLY: (*pressing his hands to his eyes*) I gotta get myself some coffee. I'll get some coffee . . . (WILLY *starts to walk out.* HOWARD *stops him.*)

HOWARD: (*rolling up the cord*) Willy, look . . .

WILLY: I'll go to Boston.

HOWARD: Willy, you can't go to Boston for us.

WILLY: Why can't I go?

HOWARD: I don't want you to represent us. I've been meaning to tell you for a long time now.

WILLY: Howard, are you firing me?

HOWARD: I think you need a good long rest, Willy.

WILLY: Howard—

HOWARD: And when you feel better, come back, and we'll see if we can work something out.

WILLY: But I gotta earn money, Howard. I'm in no position to—

HOWARD: Where are your sons? Why don't your sons give you a hand?

WILLY: They're working on a very big deal.

HOWARD: This is no time for false pride, Willy. You go to your boys and you tell them that you're tired. You've got two great boys, haven't you?

WILLY: Oh, no question, no question, but in the meantime . . .

HOWARD: Then that's that, heh?

WILLY: All right, I'll go to Boston tomorrow.

HOWARD: No, no.

WILLY: I can't throw myself on my sons. I'm not a cripple!

HOWARD: Look, kid, I'm busy this morning.

WILLY: (*grasping* HOWARD'S *arm*) Howard, you've got to let me go to Boston!

HOWARD: (*hard, keeping himself under control*) I've got a line of people to see this morning. Sit down, take five minutes, and pull yourself together, and then go home, will ya? I need the office, Willy. (*He starts to go, turns, remembering the recorder, starts to push off the table holding the recorder.*) Oh, yeah. Whenever you can this week, stop by and drop off the samples. You'll feel better, Willy, and then come back and we'll talk. Pull yourself together, kid, there's people outside. (HOWARD *exits, pushing the table off left.* WILLY *stares into space, exhausted.*)

5. *Barefoot in the Park*, by Neil Simon
   From Act I

Scene:	For one man, two women
Characters:	CORIE, early twenties
	PAUL, her husband, a young lawyer
	MOTHER, her mother
Setting:	A small walk-up apartment (top floor) in Manhattan.
Time:	Evening. The present.
Situation:	Corie and Paul, a young married couple, have just set up housekeeping

in a walk-up flat in New York. In fact, it is such a walk-up flat that getting to it requires stamina and mountain-climbing ability. The roof also has a tendency to leak, particularly when it snows or rains, as it does this particular evening. Paul and Corie are "moderately" happy in their new home and are trying to adjust to the awkward conditions when they find out that Corie's mother is about to pay them a visit. She soon gets a tour of the cramped room(s) Corie and Paul are living in.

   The scene begins after Corie finds that she has had no success starting a fire in order to give the room some warmth.

CORIE: What are you doing? (*She gives up attempting to light the log*)
PAUL: I'm checking to see if the windows are closed.
CORIE: They're closed. I looked.
PAUL: Then why is it windy in here?
CORIE: (*Moves toward* PAUL) I don't feel a draft.
PAUL: (*Moves away from the windows*) I didn't say draft. I said wind . . . There's a brisk northeasterly wind blowing in this room.
CORIE: You don't have to get sarcastic.
PAUL: (*Moving up into the kitchen area*) I'm not getting sarcastic, I'm getting chapped lips. (*Looking up, he glimpses the hole in the skylight*)
CORIE: How could there be wind in a closed room?
PAUL: How's this for an answer? There's a hole in the skylight. (*He points up*)
CORIE: (*Looks up, sees it, and is obviously embarrassed by it*) Gee, I didn't see that before. Did you?
PAUL: (*Moves to the ladder*) I didn't see the *apartment* before.
CORIE: (*Defensively. She crosses to the railing and gets her coat*) All right, Paul, don't get upset. I'm sure it'll be fixed. We could plug it up with something for tonight.
PAUL: (*Gets up on the ladder*) How? How? That's twenty feet high. You'd have to fly over in a plane and *drop* something in.
CORIE: (*Putting on her coat*) It's only for one night. And it's not that cold.
PAUL: In February? Do you know what it's like at three o'clock in the morning? In February? Ice-cold freezing.
CORIE: It's not going to be freezing. I called the Weather Bureau. It's going to be cloudy with a slight s—(*She catches herself and looks up*)
PAUL: What? (CORIE *turns away*) What? . . . A light what?
CORIE: Snow!
PAUL: (*Coming down the ladder*) Snow?? . . . It's going to snow tonight? . . . In here?
CORIE: They're wrong as often as they're right.
PAUL: I'm going to be shoveling snow in my own living room.
CORIE: It's a little hole.
PAUL: With that wind it could blow six-foot drifts in the bathroom. Honestly, Corie, I don't see how you can be so calm about all this.
CORIE: Well, what is it you want me to do?
PAUL: Go to pieces, like me. It's only natural.
CORIE: (*Goes to him and puts her arms around him*) I've got a better idea. I'll keep you warm . . . And there's no charge for electricity . . . (*She kisses him*)
PAUL: I can see I haven't got much of a law career ahead of me.

CORIE: Good. I hope we starve. And they find us up here dead in each other's arms.

PAUL: "Frozen skinny lovers found on Forty-eighth Street." (*They kiss*)

CORIE: Are we in love again?

PAUL: We're in love again. (*They kiss again, a long passionate embrace. The doorbell buzzes*)

CORIE: (*Breaking away*) The bed. I hope it's the bed. (*She buzzes back, and then opens the door and yells down*) Helllooooo! Bloomingdale's? (*From below, a female voice: Surprise!* CORIE *turns to* PAUL) Oh, God.

PAUL: What's wrong.

CORIE: Please, let it be a woman delivering the furniture.

PAUL: A woman?

VOICE: Corie?

CORIE: But it's my mother.

PAUL: Your mother? Now?

CORIE: (*Taking off the nightgown and slipping into her top*) She couldn't wait. Just one more day.

PAUL: Corie, you've got to get rid of her. I've got a case in court tomorrow.

CORIE: It's ugly in here without furniture, isn't it. She's just going to hate it, won't she?

VOICE: Corie? Where are you?

CORIE: (*Crosses to the door and yells down the stairs*) Up here, Mom. Top floor.

PAUL: (*Hides the attaché case in a corner to the left of the windows*) How am I going to work tonight?

CORIE: She'll think this is the way we're going to live. Like gypsies in an empty store. (*Attempting to button her top*)

PAUL: (*Throwing the nightgown and lingerie into a suitcase*) Maybe I ought to sleep in the office.

CORIE: She'll freeze to death. She'll sit there in her fur coat and freeze to death.

PAUL: (*Helps her button her top*) I don't get you, Corie. Five minutes ago this was the Garden of Eden. Now it's suddenly Cannery Row.

CORIE: She doesn't understand, Paul. She has a different set of values. She's practical. She's not young like us.

PAUL: (*Gathers up the suitcase with lingerie and takes it into the bedroom*) Well, I'm twenty-six and cold as hell.

VOICE: (*Getting nearer*) Corie?

CORIE: (*Yells down at the door*) One more flight, Mother . . . Paul, promise me one thing. Don't tell her about the rent. If she asks, tell her you're not quite sure yet.

PAUL: (*Crossing to the door with his coat collar up around his face*) Not sure what my rent is? I *have* to know what my rent is. I'm a college graduate.

CORIE: (*Stopping* PAUL) Can't you lie a little? For me? You don't have to tell her it's a hundred and twenty-five.

PAUL: All right. How much is it?

CORIE: Sixty?

PAUL: What?

CORIE: Sixty-five?

PAUL: Corie—

CORIE: Seventy-five, all right? Seventy-five dollars and sixty-three cents a month. Including gas and electricity. She'll believe that, won't she?

PAUL: *Anyone* would believe that. It's the hundred and twenty-five that's hard to swallow. (*He combs his hair*)

CORIE: She's taking a long time. I hope she's all right.

PAUL: I can't lie about the stairs. She's going to figure out it's six floors all by herself.

CORIE: Shh. Shh, she's here. (*She starts to open the door*)

PAUL: (*Grabs her*) Just promise *me* one thing. Don't let her stay too long because I've got a . . .

CORIE: (*With him*) . . . case in court in the morning . . . I know, I know . . . (*She opens the door and goes into the hall*) . . . Mother! (MOTHER *shoots by her into the room and grabs the rail to keep from falling. She is in her late forties, pretty, but has not bothered to look after herself these past few years. She could use a permanent and a whole new wardrobe*)

PAUL: (*Rushes to support her*) Hello, Mom. (MOTHER *struggles for air*)

MOTHER: Oh! . . . Oh! . . . I can't breathe.

CORIE: Take it easy, Mom. (*Holding her other arm*)

MOTHER: I can't catch my breath.

PAUL: You should have rested.

MOTHER: I did . . . But there were always more stairs.

CORIE: Paul, help her.

PAUL: Come on, Mom. Watch the step. (*He starts to lead her up the step into the room*)

MOTHER: More stairs? (*She steps up and* CORIE *and* PAUL *lead her toward* PAUL'S *suitcase, still standing near the wall*)

CORIE: You want some water?

MOTHER: Later. I can't swallow yet.

PAUL: Here, sit down. (*She sits on the suitcase*)

MOTHER: Oh, my.

CORIE: It's not *that* high, Mother.

MOTHER: I know, dear. It's not bad really . . . What is it, nine flights?

PAUL: Five. We don't count the stoop.

MOTHER: I didn't think I'd make it . . . If I'd known the people on the third floor I'd have gone to visit them . . . (PAUL *sits on the bottom step of the ladder*)

CORIE: This is a pleasant surprise, Mother.

MOTHER: Well, I really had no intention of coming up, but I had a luncheon in Westchester and I thought, since it's on my way home, I might as well drop in for a few minutes . . .

CORIE: On your way home to New Jersey?

MOTHER: Yes. I just came over the Whitestone Bridge and down the Major Deegan highway and now I'll cut across town and onto the Henry Hudson Parkway and up to the George Washington Bridge. It's no extra trouble.

PAUL: Sounds easy enough.

MOTHER: Yes . . .

CORIE: We were going to ask you over on Friday.

MOTHER: Friday. Good. I'll be here Friday . . . I'm not going to stay now, I know you both must be busy.

PAUL: Well, as a matter of fact . . .

229

CORIE: (*Stopping him*) No, we're not, are we, Paul? (*He kills her with a glance*)

MOTHER: Besides, Aunt Harriet is ringing the bell for me in ten minutes . . . Just one good look around, that's all. I'm not sure I'm coming back.

CORIE: I wish you could have come an hour later. After the furniture arrived.

MOTHER: (*Gets up, looks, and stops cold*) Don't worry. I've got a marvelous imagination.

CORIE: Well . . . ?

MOTHER: (*Stunned*) Oh, Corie . . . it's . . . beautiful.

CORIE: You hate it . . .

MOTHER: (*Moves toward windows*) No, no . . . It's a charming apartment. (*She trips over the platform*) I love it.

CORIE: (*Rushes to her*) You can't really tell like this.

MOTHER: I'm crazy about it.

CORIE: It's not your kind of apartment. I knew you wouldn't like it.

MOTHER: (*Moves down to* PAUL) I love it . . . Paul, didn't I say I loved it? (*She takes his hand*)

PAUL: She said she loved it.

MOTHER: I knew I said it.

CORIE: (*To* MOTHER) Do you really, Mother? I mean are you absolutely crazy in love with it?

MOTHER: Oh, yes. It's very cute . . . And there's so much you can do with it.

CORIE: I told you she hated it.

MOTHER: (*Moves toward the bedroom landing*) Corie, you don't give a person a chance. At least let me see the whole apartment.

PAUL: This *is* the whole apartment.

MOTHER: (*Cheerfully*) It's a nice, large room.

CORIE: There's a bedroom.

MOTHER: Where?

PAUL: One flight up.

CORIE: It's four little steps. (*She goes up the steps to the bedroom door*) See. One-two-three-four.

MOTHER: (*To* PAUL) Oh. Split-level. (*She climbs the steps*) And where's the bedroom? Through there?

CORIE: No. *In* there. That's the bedroom . . . It's really just a dressing room but I'm going to use it as a bedroom.

MOTHER: (*At the bedroom door*) That's a wonderful idea. And you can just put a bed in there.

CORIE: That's right.

MOTHER: How? (PAUL *moves to the steps*)

CORIE: It'll fit. I measured the room.

MOTHER: A double bed?

CORIE: No, an oversized single.

MOTHER: Oh, they're nice. And where will Paul sleep?

CORIE: With me.

PAUL: (*Moves up on the landing*) In an oversized single?

MOTHER: I'm sure you'll be comfortable.

CORIE: I'm positive. (PAUL *moves back down the stairs and glumly surveys the room*)

MOTHER: It's a wonderful idea. Very clever . . .

CORIE: Thank you.

MOTHER: Except you can't get to the closet.

CORIE: Yes you can.

MOTHER: Without climbing over the bed?

CORIE: No, you *have* to climb over the bed.

MOTHER: That's a good idea.

CORIE: (*Leaves the bedroom, crosses to the ladder, and climbs up*) Everything's just temporary. As they say in *McCall's*, it won't really take shape until the bride's own personality becomes more clearly defined.

MOTHER: I think it's *you* right now. (*She turns to the other door*) What's in here? . . . (*She opens the door and looks in*) The bathroom . . . (*She closes the door*) No bathtub . . . You really have quite a lot here, for one room. (*She moves down the steps*) And where's the kitchen? (*She sees the stove and refrigerator, stops in horror, and then crosses toward the kitchen*) Whoo, there it is . . . Very cozy. I suppose you'll eat out a lot the first year.

CORIE: We're never eating out. It's big enough to make spaghetti and things.

MOTHER: What "things"?

CORIE: It's a dish I make called "Things." Honestly, Mother, we won't starve.

MOTHER: I know, dear. (*Under the skylight*) It's chilly in here. Do you feel a draft?

PAUL: (*Looks up*) Uh, stand over here, Mom.

CHAPTER
EIGHT

Special Problems and Areas

We have endeavored in the preceding chapters to familiarize the actor with
the fundamentals of acting, which are applicable in most acting situations.
Nevertheless, various types of plays and productions create special problems. This chapter will examine a number of the problems that occur in specialized areas of acting.

Comedy and Farce

Let us immediately clear up a common misconception regarding the playing
of comedy as distinct from the so-called "serious" play. Comedy is not
easier to play, nor does it require less acting ability than tragedy. The
reverse is often true, for good acting in comedy requires an acute sense of

timing, the knack of punching a line properly, and the ability to project the incongruities and exaggerations that make up the comic tradition.

No single definition will fit all the varied types of comedy that the actor will encounter. It is easier to know when we are watching a comedy than to define it exactly. Nevertheless, it is clear that a comedy is usually a play that ends happily and aims primarily at amusing the audience.

The best comedy usually grows out of the foibles of the characters involved. This is the essence of the comedy of Ben Jonson, Shakespeare, and Molière. Comedy of character which is vested with scintillating dialogue and wit is usually classified as *high comedy*. When the pretensions of aristocrats or highly sophisticated characters are lampooned, we may be witnessing a *comedy of manners*, which has much in common with high comedy. If our sympathies are aroused as we watch young and virtuous lovers triumph over the obstacles of society or the ''wrongdoer,'' we may be viewing *sentimental comedy*.

Comedy and farce are related, but when we examine them closely we may recognize certain differences. Both may grow out of *character* or *incident and intrigue*. The basic distinction separating comedy and farce is related to the probability of the action. Whereas the characters and incidents of comedy may be well within the realm of reason, farce supposes that we have left the sane world and have embarked on a journey where the impossible has become theatrically feasible. Many critics would go so far as to separate the two forms rather than include farce as a branch of comedy. However, farce can be closely related even to highly literate comedy, as in the case of Oscar Wilde's farce *The Importance of Being Earnest*, which has much in common with the tradition of the English comedy of manners. It is not uncommon to find a farcical character in a play that is otherwise a comedy; the reverse is even more likely to be true. Such difficulties present problems in defining each type satisfactorily. The actor will find much in common between these forms, and for our purposes we will treat the two areas together.

A number of elements are evident in all good comedies and farces. Let us consider three of the most important: *incongruity, exaggeration,* and the *comic spirit*.

Incongruity

One of the fundamental causes of laughter is *incongruity*. The umbrella-wielding female wading into a husky man, the bullfighter running in fright from the bull, the rich matron being slapped in the face with a custard pie, the fainting of a professional wrestler at the sight of a mouse—these move us to laughter by the incongruity of the action.

In creating the role of Inspector Clouseau in *The Pink Panther* film series, Peter Sellers relied heavily on incongruity in developing his delightful character. Presumably an inspector of police is an intelligent individual, but Clouseau's mangling of the language (English or French?) adds to the mirth. He wonders why one has a "bemp" on the head, and destroys property with the same ease with which he destroys words. Incongrously, his preposterous self-assurance only grows. When jumping into bed on a rare Stradivarius violin he comments: "When you've seen one Stradivarius, you've seen them all." Destroying another fine musical instrument, he responds to the comment that "That's a rare Steinway piano" with an unconcerned shrug: "Not any more," he says.

Any incongruity of values may very well aid the comic spirit. The following sequence, typical of old minstrel humor, may indicate how this principle operates. When asked to define a miracle, one of the end men replied:

> Man, if you see a thistle in de meadow, dat ain't no miracle. If you see a bull grazing in de meadow, dat ain't a miracle, an if you see a lark singin' in dat same meadow, pretty as can be, dat still ain't no miracle. But if you see dat bull, sittin' on dat thistle singin' like a lark,—man dat's a miracle.

This story, if well told, will provide the audience with a mirth-provoking picture of the lyrical bull balancing himself on the thistle. The actor must search out any incongruities and point them up in the playing of comedy.

Exaggeration

Exaggeration of physical characteristics or personality traits is a common source of comic invention. Martha Raye and Joe E. Brown have made effective use of their large mouths for comic effect. Jimmy Durante's famous nose provided a fortune for him throughout his career. Don Rickles' excessive and exaggerated assault upon individuals of all social levels consistently moves his audiences to laughter. Foster Brooks and Dean Martin have transformed personal alcoholic excesses beyond pity to comedy. The calculated stinginess of Jack Benny was used in almost every radio and television production in which he appeared for several decades. The sight of someone being forced to put a quarter in a slot in order to start Benny's borrowed lawn mower moves us to laughter both by the *exaggeration* of his stinginess and the very *incongruity* of the action.

Much of the humor of Falstaff stems from his tremendous bulk. Cyrano de Bergerac's comment about his enormous nose "which marches on before me by a quarter of an hour" is an obvious example of exaggeration. The miserliness of Harpagon in *The Miser*, the excessive puritanism of Malvolio in *Twelfth Night*, the snobbishness of Lady Bracknell in *The Importance of Being Earnest* all move us to laughter by their excessiveness.

Within the bounds of good taste and the three V's of good acting, exaggeration may be used by the actor to highlight the comic potential of his character. In farce, particularly, restraint upon exaggeration is almost entirely removed, and excessive exaggeration is, indeed, one of the hallmarks of farcical acting.

The Comic Spirit

Good acting in comedy and farce requires that the audience know as soon as possible that they are supposed to laugh. They must have a frame of reference for the action they will see and the dialogue they will hear. This frame of reference may be termed the *comic spirit*. Watching a comedian in the movies dangling from a clothesline in a blanket five stories above the pavement is amusing; we laugh in the circus as clowns bash each other over the head with crowbars, mallets, baseball bats, and other assorted weapons (usually made of rubber). We laugh because we know that the characters are in no real danger and everything will be solved satisfactorily. Consider also the continual mayhem in the *Tom and Jerry* and *Roadrunner* cartoons. We know, because the form is a cartoon rather than the illusion of life, that nothing in it is really harmful. The mangling of arms, legs, heads, and entire bodies by every means possible is the primary source of amusement. There is never any question in our mind of real danger.

   If, however, we are going about our everyday business and see a man dangling precariously above the street or being attacked by another person with a deadly weapon, we would hardly laugh; we would likely be moved to serious action. The actor, therefore, must *project* to the audience that all is *in fun*, that the comic spirit is prevailing, that the work is a comedy. Comic acting means that the actor must not be hesitant about pointing up the incongruity and exaggeration of *both* situation and character.

Timing

One of the most delicate problems in the handling of the comic situation is timing. Timing is something that cannot truly be taught, but some discussion of its value may be useful. Often a well-timed pause will make a seemingly simple line exceedingly amusing. In *Born Yesterday*, a tough but delightful racketeer, Eddie Brock, comes into a dark room and switches on the lights, revealing the ''heroine'' and her ''teacher'' sitting on the sofa. Brock's first line, directed to the pair, is ''What's this? Night school?'' The line will receive its comic impact if the actor pauses after the first brief phrase, reading it as

   ''What's this?'' (*He looks at Paul and Billie and seems somewhat surprised.*) ''Night school?''

A word of caution is in order. If the technique is too evident, or if the actor is trying too obviously for a laugh, it is easy to kill it. Often the harder one tries to make a line funny, the less amusing it becomes. A good rule: *Do not make the technique obvious.*

An illustration of this fact is often told in theatre circles. Some years ago when Alfred Lunt and Lynne Fontanne opened in a comedy, Lunt told his wife and partner that he was certain he would get a laugh on his line "I would like a cup of tea." After two weeks of performances, he had not received a laugh on that line. He asked his wife why he wasn't getting the anticipated laugh, and her response is well worth noting. "My dear Alfred," she is reported to have told him, "you are asking for a laugh, not for a cup of tea."

Handling laughter can also cause some difficulties. An audience should rarely be prevented from laughing if it is so inclined. Jumping in with a cue as the audience begins to laugh at the preceding line is one sure way to restrict their laughter and cause difficulties in being heard. Nor should the actor wait until the laughter has completely died out. This will make the production too labored and slow the pace of the show. Most laughter begins at a low level, builds to a peak, and then fades away. The cue should be picked up *after* the peak is reached and the laughter has started to fade away. If a cue is picked up, and suddenly the laugh builds after a slow start, the actor should simply stop, wait for the downturn in the laugh, and *begin again.*

It is best to go through the rehearsal period without pauses for laughter. It is impossible to predict exactly how an audience will react to a comedy on any given night. During a run of performances in one production, it is surprising to discover how an audience's reactions will differ from night to night. Although the actor has rehearsed without stopping for anticipated laughter, during a performance it is necessary to be ready to make adjustments to the laughter which says that the purpose is being achieved and the audience is enjoying the actor's comic efforts.

Tragedy

Although both comedy and tragedy grew out of the religious rites of the ancient Greeks in honor of the god Dionysus, the entire mental and spiritual tone of tragedy differs radically from that of comedy. It is not surprising that tragedy had such early roots, for death and suffering are universal to all human beings, as well as being the most enigmatic of experiences. Questions that ask "Why must this be so?" may never be answered satisfactorily, but that does not prevent Oedipus, Antigone, Job, Hamlet, and Willy Loman from asking them; these characters have come to their own terms with the inevitable legacy of all mankind.

The Nature of Tragedy

Much has been written about the nature of tragedy, yet a precise definition upon which all critics may agree has eluded us. In recent years there has been much provocative discussion about Arthur Miller's fine play *Death of a Salesman*. Some critics acclaim it as a tragedy; others find in it fundamental departures from what they believe to be the tragic spirit.

In a tragedy the central figure, or protagonist, suffers a crushing defeat, usually ending in death. The protagonist's downfall, accompanied by suffering and violence, does not stem from any accidental source but is triggered by some flaw in his or her personality or by the enigmatic influence of fate. The tragic figure, when placed under the stress of circumstances, is inevitably destroyed.

The protagonist, essentially a good individual of stature and respectability, is like all fellow men and women in the credo "I am a person with the weaknesses common to humanity." Its universal implication makes tragedy meaningful and harrowing for all audiences. The protagonist, altered in the crucible of suffering, comes to terms with his or her problem and dies, not in despair, but in an awareness of the problem and of his or her place in the universe.

One of the qualities most frequently associated with tragedy is the intensification of dialogue to bring into focus the tragic essence of the work and to couch the ideas of the play in the most expressive language possible. For this reason many of the world's great tragedies are *poetic* dramas as well.

Acting Technique in Tragedy

The actor's responsibility and efforts in tragedy are clearly different from those imposed by comedy. As a general rule tragedy requires less "exterior" technique than comedy. Whereas comedy achieves its effects by the careful timing of visual situations and humorous lines, tragedy makes its greatest demands on the emotional and spiritual resources of the actor. Good tragic acting is often as much a sign of human sensitivity as it is of competent acting. This fact re-emphasizes the point made in Chapter 1 that the good actor is one who is conversant with human nature, who has observed and has read widely the story of the human race.

More specifically, the actor working in tragedy must fully utilize the potential of the voice to communicate the grandeur of the play's language, which, as we have already noted, is expressive of the real essence and nature of the tragic state. Failure to project properly to an audience the impact of the language will result in a less than successful performance.

The development of business must be approached in a completely different manner from that assumed in comedy. Nothing should be done to interfere with the emotional bond that exists between the audience and the play. All business inserted by the actor should be keyed to the tests of simplicity and honesty and should be less developed than in comedy. The business should normally be projected in broad strokes, keeping audience attention centered on the characters and dialogue. Any digression caused by the insertion of clever business may be perfectly acceptable in comedy but is often antagonistic to the inevitable and methodical development of good tragedy.

Although technique can never be dismissed entirely from the preparation of any role, tragedy will make the greatest demands on the actor's inner resources of imagination and understanding.

Period Plays in General

Period plays, especially the dramas of Shakespeare, are often frightening for beginning actors who like to cut their teeth on modern "realistic" plays. This attitude certainly is not to be condemned, but it would be unfortunate indeed if the actor were always to refrain from participation in some of the greatest plays ever written. One of the reasons for this hesitancy to act in plays of the past—the drama of the Greeks and Romans, Shakespeare, Molière, the Restoration, and the eighteenth century—has already been suggested: they are not "realistic" in the present-day sense of the term. Time has also erected a barrier which makes it difficult for us to understand the social conventions and restraints that work upon the plays and the characters. We often say we have difficulty in "relating" to these works.

This fact poses two specific problems for the actor who is experienced only in modern realistic plays. First, period plays generally require a higher degree of presentational acting than our contemporary drama. In simplest terms, these plays are often frankly theatrical, making no pretense at being "a slice of life." In their own time they were performed primarily in a presentational, or audience-centered, manner. The actors were constantly aware of the fact that theirs was a stage performance, and their acting was directed *to* the audience. Little attempt was made to disguise the fact that a theatrical performance was in progress. Despite this, it should be noted, the actors still attempted to sustain the *illusion* that their actions were real and consistent, and the audience undoubtedly believed the situations and the emotions of the characters. In producing these plays today there is invariably an attempt to retain something of the presentational style in the production so as to preserve the original flavor and intent of the piece. This does not imply that the actor makes no attempt to persuade the audience to believe what they are seeing and hearing. To this extent the presentational style is perfectly consistent with the creating of an illusion of life, and it may be termed *presentational-illusionistic*. The actor must be aware, however, that these plays are rarely acted in the *representational-illusionistic* style that is utilized for the modern realistic play.

The second problem, often most disturbing to the beginning actor, is posed by the fact that many of the dramas of an earlier period are written in verse rather than prose. Their authors used the verse form because poetry is a heightening of language, a means by which the author is able to express the play's meaning with greater subtlety and economy than is possible in prose. When Horatio, in *Hamlet,* describes the coming of the dawn with the beautiful sequence

> But look, the morn, in russet mantle clad,
> Walks o'er the dew of yon high eastward hill.

we may be sure that he is creating a vivid image for the audience which a long detailed description in prose *might* equal. To state simply "Look, the sun is coming up" would miss the point and convey little of the essence of the beauty of the new day.

In the preface to *The Admirable Bashville,* George Bernard Shaw, probably the finest prose dramatist of our century, explained that he had written this piece in verse because he didn't have enough time to write the play in prose. Shaw was, of course, being somewhat facetious, as was his habit on many occasions, but he had a sound purpose in mind. He pointed up the fact that verse permits greater economy than prose in the expression of images and ideas.

In verse drama it is essential that the actor be aware of the full meaning of the images he or she is attempting to communicate. If the actor does not examine and understand the means by which the playwright has given expression to the play's characters and ideas, it is likely that the audience will not understand them either.

Shakespearean Plays

The plays of Shakespeare are produced in American colleges and universities more often than those of any other playwright. His works have transcended his own age; they are meaningful for our day as well. "He was not of an age, but for all time," wrote Ben Jonson of his friend; Jonson certainly was endowed with the gift of prophecy in this instance. Yet too often the contemporary actor is unable to find a point at which to begin work on these plays. This seems to be true not only for Shakespearean plays but many other fine plays of the past separated from our day by manners, habits, and language that may be alien to us.[1]

---

1. Although in this section we shall be examining the problems specific to Shakespearean plays, we should not ascribe the implications of these remarks to those plays alone. Much of what we say here applies also to the great dramas of the Greeks and the Romans, Molière, and the Restoration period. All these plays are truly pieces for the theatre, meant to be *performed* to reveal their complete intent.

Some difficulty may also be traced to our early exposure to works of this type. If we have been bogged down in literary dissections of the so-called ''classics'' and exposed to teaching that treats these dramas as musty relics, we lose sight of their origins and purposes. Shakespeare is the most obvious case in point. If we consider him as nothing but required reading in high-school and college literature courses, we forget the most important consideration of all: Shakespeare was an actor. He wrote for actors. He was the most popular playwright of his day because people were willing to pay to be entertained by his plays. His primary intention was to have his plays performed; only secondary was his concern that they be read. Indeed, half of his plays were not published until *after* his death, and even that publication was due only to two loyal friends, who published his plays as a testimonial to their colleague. The actor must approach the plays not as relics of a bygone age but as exciting dramas with flesh-and-blood characters who have provided us with some of our most moving moments in the theatre.

It must be granted that the playing of Shakespeare presents something of a challenge. No doubt a hint from the past will be helpful for the modern actor. Although some questions are clouded by debate among modern scholars, there are enough clues to provide a fairly complete picture of the Elizabethan actor. He was evidently a highly flexible performer, capable of acting in both comedy and tragedy, trained in music and dancing, and able to do full justice to the many scenes of violent action that are so important in Shakespeare's plays: the fencing matches, battle scenes, wrestling bouts, swordplay, and so on. Because the plays were generally performed in outdoor theatres, the actor had to have a well-projected voice, capable not only of being heard but also of expressing the subtleties and nuances of Shakespeare's dialogue. The Elizabethan actor, then, was a well-rounded performer, supple in body, and expressive in the use of the voice. The same should hold true for the modern interpreter of Shakespeare.

In dealing with the plays of Shakespeare the modern actor is concerned with two working areas: *interpretation* and the determination of a *reading style.* Let us examine each of these two elements in turn so that we may formulate an approach to the development of such roles.

Interpretation

Although the work of actors of the past may afford us some help in determining how to develop these roles, we must avoid a too deliberate imitation of earlier interpretations. The wisest approach is to depend as much as possible on the texts of the plays themselves. Even if we knew exactly what Burbage's first Hamlet was like, we would want to steer away from a recapitulation of what someone else had done. After all, there is no one

FIGURE 8.1 *A Midsummer Night's Dream* by Shakespeare. Wayne State
University, directed by Robert Emmett McGill.

right way to do Hamlet. If there were, there would be little need ever to produce the play again. Finding one's own approach is the only truly creative
work in the theatre.

The clues the actor needs to be able to interpret these characters properly are to be found in the plays themselves. Shakespeare has created full-
blooded characters, and the plays are filled with illuminating little details
that the observant actor should have no difficulty in translating into an exciting characterization. Such comments about the characters are to be found
not in an introduction or in stage directions but from the lips of the
characters themselves. A few examples may illustrate the storehouse of information to be derived about Shakespeare's characters from the dialogue
of the plays. We find such descriptions as the following:

Pinch, the schoolmaster in *The Comedy of Errors,* is "a hungry lean-
faced villain, . . . a fortune teller, a needy, hollow-eyed, sharp-looking
wretch, a living dead man." Gratiano, in *The Merchant of Venice,* the talkative

friend of Bassanio, is "too wild, too rude, and bold of voice [and] speaks an infinite deal of nothing. . . ." Falstaff, in *Henry IV: Part II,* is "a fool and a jester [who needs] two and twenty yards of satin" [for a suit of clothes]. Hamlet is "the glass of fashion and the mould of form. . . . He was likely, had he been put on, to have proved most royally."

We need look no further than Iago's description of Othello for the perfect clue to the playing of this great role. Iago described the Moor as "of a free and open nature, that thinks men honest that but seem to be so. . . ." The actor taking the cue from Shakespeare should have little difficulty in making us understand why Othello was such easy prey for the evil Iago.

In addition, new facets of the character will undoubtedly continue to be uncovered as the actor works on a role. Even experienced actors who play Shakespeare for the first time are impressed by the great freedom that Shakespeare's plays provide. After Alfred Lunt's first Shakespearean role, as Petruchio in *The Taming of the Shrew,* his enthusiasm was unbounded. He was moved to write:

> You read a speech or do a scene, giving it a certain meaning. Then, all of a sudden, a wholly different implication dawns on you, and you say to yourself, 'Of course! *This* is what it really means. Why didn't I see it long ago?' And that keeps happening constantly. There is so much room to turn around in, in Shakespeare. No other dramatist old or new gives you so much . . . In that way, Shakespeare is like the Bible. The Bible has a great deal of room to turn around in, too—that is why there are so many opinions about it. With Shakespeare, I suppose the actor's greatest problem is how to fill up the space he finds himself in.[2]

A challenge indeed!

Reading Style

We have already noted that the verse play is essentially nonrealistic and utilizes imagery with telling effect in the projection of description and ideas. We have also noted that the plays of Shakespeare are not performed in the same manner as the modern realistic play. The reading of dialogue is an integral part of this consideration, for we cannot read verse in the same manner as we read dialogue suggestive of everyday conversation. The actor must not hesitate to give full sway to the rhythm and beauty of the language. The reading and the movement (which is related to the style adopted for the reading) should be full and robust. It must be remembered that the playwright has chosen poetry as the vehicle of expression because it permits an elevation of expression, a nobility, and a grandeur that ordinary prose cannot hope to achieve.

---

2. Quoted in Helen Ormsbee, *Backstage with Actors* (New York: Thomas Y. Crowell Co., 1938), p. 262.

FIGURE 8.2 *Love's Labour's Lost* by Shakespeare. California State University, Long Beach, directed by Clayton Garrison.

The young actor is often loath to give full meaning to the dynamics and tone coloring of the language. He may be afraid of being called a "ham." One question often heard in reference to this problem is: "Isn't it better to try to get the meaning across rather than project only the rhythm and structure of the poetry?" The answer, of course, is that it is best to strike a happy medium, to achieve a balance between the meaning and the rhythm of the verse. It is well to give an intelligent, carefully detailed reading of the lines, but the beauty of the sound must not be overlooked. The young actor would do well to *start by striving primarily for the meaning,* and, if he is an alert reader, *the poetry will begin to take care of itself.* Above all else, it is best to avoid the old sing-song elocutionary method so popular early in this century and rightly called "ham" when used today.

If we keep in mind the third V of good acting, validity, we will agree with the early-twentieth-century critic Percy Fitzgerald, who tried to bring truth back to the playing of Shakespeare in a period that favored a more stilted style of playing. He noted that:

> It is always understood that to present *Hamlet* properly and according to tradition, we must adopt a sort of stilted, pedantic system of elocution and bearing.

> We must recite, declaim, growl, or vociferate, and stride about. All such things
> would disappear if the players could only persuade themselves that they were
> ordinary men and women concerned in a terrible and momentous tragedy—if
> they would but put emotion and passion and warmth and nature into all they
> say and do.[3]

Sound advice, and applicable not only for the playing of Shakespeare but
for all presentational verse drama as well.

The plays of Shakespeare have appealed to actors of every generation, some of whom have built brilliant reputations through their playing of
Shakespeare's characters. Other actors have been less than successful, but
all have found Shakespeare to be the playwright who brings most to the actor ready to come to him with an open mind and spirit. Walter Huston, a
versatile and creative stage and film actor, had one notable failure during
his long career. It was the role of Othello. Yet even in failure his pithy and
frank comments provide a perfect summation for any discussion of
Shakespeare and the actor.

> But the truth is that I have become ensnared by the magic of the guy's web. It is
> quite clear to me now why so many of the world's great actors (practically all of
> them) have grown up to play Shakespeare. His work is a challenge to any ac-
> tor. His work holds a fascination for the actor such as nothing else in the
> literature of our theatre does. Having played Shakespeare, even in a produc-
> tion which flopped, was an experience by which my life is immensely en-
> riched. I'm tickled pink to have done it.[4]

Sustained Speeches

Long speeches or monologues must be approached by the actor with special
care. Although the extended monologue is often thought to be a characteristic of plays of the past, especially verse drama, it appears in many modern
plays as well. A not uncommon habit actors adopted not long ago was to approach a sustained monologue as a *tour-de-force,* so that the speech might
serve the same function as a showpiece aria in an opera. Fortunately, few
actors have this attitude today. Yet there is no question that the sustained
speech poses a special problem for all actors, regardless of their training and
experience.

The good actor not only will lavish care on the development of a role
but also will take special pains to probe into the structure and organization
of extended passages. An extended speech is often one of the highlights of a

---

3. Percy Fitzgerald, *Shakespearean Representation* (London: Elliot Stock, 1906), p. 7.
4. Walter Huston, ''In and Out of the Bag: Othello Sits Up in Bed the Morning After
and Takes Notice,'' *Stage*, March 1937, pp. 54–57.

play, in which the character most thoroughly reveals him- or herself to the audience or in which the playwright sees to it that the theme of the play is enunciated in unmistakable terms. As the actor develops an understanding of the role, it will become possible to place the monologue in its proper perspective, that is, in relation to its function in the play. This is the first step, permitting the emotional or intellectual context of the sequence to be related to the play as a whole. The key to the proper preparation of a monologue is good organization. During the preparation of the monologue, it may help the actor to consider four factors: pattern of organization, transitions, emphasis, and climax.

Pattern of organization refers to specific divisions that the playwright may insert in the speech, such as paragraphs, sentences, colons; or any arbitrary division used to set off one portion of the material from another.

Words or phrases may indicate a shifting of mood or interest. Such *transitions* may relate to time (e.g., *then, now,* or *later*) or to contrast (e.g., *but, yet, despite all,* or *also*). They may provide a distinct clue to a change in the character's mood or attitude which the actor must impart to the audience.

In examining the sequence of the material, the actor must determine whether all the dialogue is of equal value or whether one portion of the speech requires greater *emphasis.* Even in speeches of simple exposition it is likely that certain portions will need to be highlighted.

A *climax,* or build, is required in speeches of emotional fervor or those that represent a passionate outburst by a character. Careful pacing is important here so that the monologue logically and steadily builds to its peak. A re-examination of the monologues from *Death of a Salesman* and *There Shall Be No Night* (in the exercise section of Chapter 1) should reveal this kind of accelerated drive to a climax.

The following selection will serve to illustrate how careful examination can reveal ways and means of extracting the full dynamic range of an extended speech. The numbers in brackets point out where a mood shifts or a new idea interrupts a stream of thought. We include here only one possible means of preparing this particular monologue. Any actress might approach this role and monologue in a number of different ways.

We have chosen Nina's speech to Trepleff from the last act of Chekhov's *The Sea Gull.* (This was one of the first exercises in Chapter 1.) Nina has returned home after a dismal attempt to find success as an actress and an unhappy affair with the playwright Trigorin. Arriving tired and lonely in Trepleff's study, she unburdens herself to him.

NINA: [1] Why do you say you kiss the ground I walk on? I ought to be killed. [2] I'm so tired. If I could rest—rest. I'm a sea gull. No, that's not it. I'm an actress. Well, no matter. [3] He didn't believe in the theatre, all my dreams he'd laugh at, and little by little I quit believing in it myself, and lost heart. And there was the strain of love, jealousy, constant anxiety about my little

FIGURE 8.3 *The Seagull* by Anton Chekhov. University of Nebraska-Lincoln.

baby. [4] I got to be small and trashy, and played without thinking. I didn't know what to do with my hands, couldn't stand properly on the stage, couldn't control my voice. [5] You can't imagine the feeling when you are acting and know it's dull. [6] I'm a sea gull. No, that's not it. [7] Do you remember, you shot a sea gull? A man comes by chance, sees it, and out of nothing else to do, destroys it. [8] That's not it— (*Puts her hand to her forehead.*) What was I—? [9] I was talking about the stage. Now I'm not like that. I'm a real actress, I act with delight, with rapture, I'm drunk when I'm on the stage, and feel that I am beautiful. And now, ever since I've been here, I've kept walking about, kept walking and thinking, thinking and believing my soul grows stronger every day. Now I know, I understand, Kostya, that in our work—acting or writing—what matters is not fame, not glory, not what I used to dream about, it's how to endure, to bear my cross, and have faith. I have faith and it all doesn't hurt me so much, and when I think of my calling I'm not afraid of life.

This speech may first be divided into two distinct portions. The first part (including notations [1] through [8] is morbid and self-pitying; the second (notation [9] to the end) is rapturous and lyric. Yet even within this broad division we may discern little transitions which provide means of projecting subtleties and nuances that tell us much about Nina's state of mind.

Part I   *Keyed to Self-Pity and Remorse*

1. The mood of remorse is set.
2. A slight transition indicating her emotional and physical fatigue.
3. Nina tries to tell Trepleff of her affair with the playwright, Trigorin.
4. Nina honestly faces up to her failure as an actress.
5. A rapid transition in which she reveals her anguish at her own failure.
6. She wanders off for a moment, symbolically comparing herself to the carefree sea gull.
7. A subtle transition in which she relates the symbolic destruction of the sea gull to her own failure.
8. She has lost the sequence of her thoughts for a moment.

Part II   *Complete Shift of Mood*

9. Nina recovers herself, and in this last portion as a whole we may note a continued build, rising almost to exaltation, as she dismisses her unfortunate past in a burst of idealistic fervor.

Not all monologues can be handled in the same manner, but clearly this type of analysis of the material should be useful. While progressing through the rehearsal period, the actor is likely to discover new shades of meaning in such passages. With effective organization and an intelligent awareness of the great variety that may be imparted to them, the actor can make such sequences truly the high moments of a performance.

Central Staging

Although there has been an increasing interest in it in recent years, central staging is actually the oldest of all theatre forms. The outdoor theatre of the Greeks, the medieval pageant-wagons of the craft guilds, and the Elizabethan playhouses all made use of staging techniques that we recognize as a type of central staging. The increasing contemporary vogue of this theatre form requires that we examine how this style of production affects the work of the actor.

Central staging is a term descriptive of a theatre using a centrally located playing area (in relation to the audience) with spectators sitting around two or more sides of the stage area. The most common type of central staging, in which the audience completely surrounds the playing area, is known as *arena staging* or *arena theatre*. Other names often used to describe types of central staging are *flexible staging, circus staging, circle staging,* and *theatre in the round*. The playing area may be one of several shapes and sizes—a square, rectangle, circle, or oval.

The fundamental feature that distinguishes central staging from proscenium, or conventional, staging is the absence of the proscenium arch

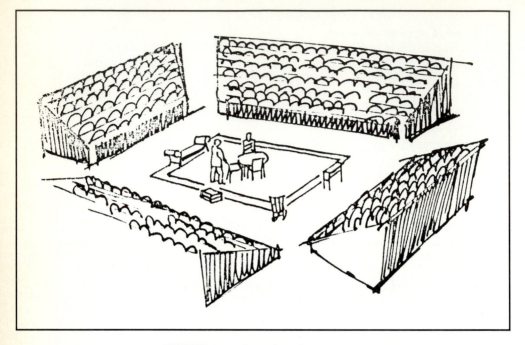

FIGURE 8.4a Central staging: Arena.

separating stage and audience. The removal of this barrier results in a greater proximity of audience to actor. Of all the qualities of central staging, *intimacy* is the one that will require the greatest adjustment on the actor's part.

Most recently great interest has been shown in *thrust* staging, in which the stage extends well beyond the proscenium arch, much in the fashion of the theatre in Shakespeare's time. Thrust staging provides a great sense of ''communion'' with the audience yet permits entrances and exits to be made from the stage area itself and not through the audience, as is required in true arena staging.

Because of the intimacy of spectator and actor and the usual elimination of all but the basic pieces of stage setting, the oft-repeated statement that this is an actor's theatre is very true. Under such circumstances the work of the actor takes on added dominance over the other aspects of a production, so there is a greater burden upon the actor than in conventional staging. The work of both the good and the bad actor is inevitably placed under the magnifying glass of close audience scrutiny.

Adjustments for the Actor

Any competent actor should have little difficulty in making the change from conventional to central staging. The fundamental preparation and development of a role are the same under all production styles. Keeping this in

FIGURE 8.4b Central staging: Three-sided or thrust.

mind, we may examine the few necessary adjustments the actor must make when working in central staging.

Subtlety.   The intimacy provided by central staging will immediately reveal to the spectators any superficiality in the actor's technique and characterization. Especially important in the small arena theatre is the problem of detailed business, which in conventional staging may need to be projected over a distance of perhaps a hundred to two hundred feet. Business must be toned down and performed with almost as much subtlety and simplicity as we would expect to find in an everyday nontheatrical situation.

Body Positions.   The rules relating to body positions and emphatic areas no longer hold true when the audience views the play from more than one direction. An open position to one portion of the audience will seem most awkward and unnatural when viewed from a different section of the house. Rules of body position for conventional staging should be disregarded.

When two actors share a scene, they should rarely face the same direction at the same time. Space between the actors should be sufficient to provide visibility for the members of the audience. Except when one actor is playing with the back to an aisle (in arena staging) actors should *not* face

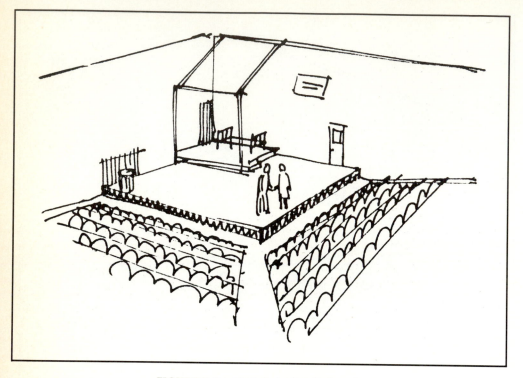

FIGURE 8.4c Central staging: L-shaped.

another actor directly. One or both actors should stand slightly sideways in an open position, facing each other in a one-quarter rather than a full-front stance. This is what has been called "twisting the pairs," meaning that part of the audience can see each of the actors over the shoulder of the other. The significant thing to remember is that normally the actors should maintain the same visual relationship as one adopts unconsciously in one's own living room. At home there is no thought of a fourth wall through which the audience is privileged to peep. The same attitude should prevail in the actor's work in a production with central staging.

Concentration. Because of the proximity of the audience (some actors describe central staging as playing in the laps of the audience), noise made by late-comers, spectators' coughing and jostling, and other distractions are greatly magnified. The actor, playing to an audience assembled just at the edge of the playing area, may find it very difficult to achieve the detachment to which he or she is accustomed in the proscenium theatre. Although the actor can never totally disregard the audience, it is essential to concentrate fully on the play so as not to permit audience distractions to affect the work.

FIGURE 8.5 Proscenium stage.

Projection. The level of projection used by the actor in central staging will depend directly upon the size and shape of the playing area and auditorium. Although the intimacy of central staging may permit the volume level to be dropped, another important principle also operates here. The actor cannot focus all speech in one direction but must be heard by the audience seated on all sides. The actor must be heard as clearly by the spectator seated directly behind as by one in front.

Volume alone is certainly not the solution. We should remember that good projection depends on a number of factors, including volume, clarity, and good articulation. In order to be heard in all parts of the house, the actor must take special care to project effectively, even if the intimacy of the auditorium requires a lowering of the volume level.

Acting in any of the numerous types of central staging provides a very useful experience, especially for actors who have been working exclusively in proscenium theatre. Because of the importance of details, participation in *any* intimate theatre production is helpful in sharpening the acting faculties of the performer. Even if an actor may prefer to work in the conventional stage situation, some exposure to central staging will prove a stimulating experience.

SUGGESTIONS FOR FURTHER READING

Boyle, Walden P. *Central and Flexible Staging.* Berkeley and Los Angeles: University of California Press, 1956.

Chisman, Isabel, and Raven-Hart, Hester E. *Manners and Movements in Costume Plays.* London: Kenyon-Deane Ltd.; Boston: Walter H. Baker, n. d.

Joseph, Bertram. *Acting Shakespeare.* New York: Theatre Arts Books, 1969.

Oxenford, Lynn. *Playing Period Plays.* Chicago: Coach House Press, 1974.

Sievers et al. *Directing for the Theatre.* 3rd ed. Dubuque, Iowa: Wm. C. Brown Co. Publishers, 1974.

Scenes

1. *The Importance of Being Earnest,* by Oscar Wilde
    From Act I

      Scene: For one man, one woman
Characters: LADY BRACKNELL, Gwendolen's mother
            JACK WORTHING
     Setting: The morning room of Algernon Moncrieff's flat in Half-moon Street, London.
       Time: An afternoon in the 1890s.
Situation: See the other scene from *The Importance of Being Earnest* (p. 151), which occurs earlier in the play.

            This scene follows almost immediately the preceding scene. Lady Bracknell has entered the room as Jack is kneeling before Gwendolen. She assumes that Jack wishes to propose to her daughter, and she dismisses Gwendolen in order to talk to him to determine if he will be a suitable husband. Gwendolen has just left the room as Lady Bracknell begins the interview.

LADY BRACKNELL: (*sitting down*) You can take a seat, Mr. Worthing. (*looks in her pocket for note-book and pencil*)

JACK: Thank you, Lady Bracknell, I prefer standing.

LADY BRACKNELL: (*pencil and note-book in hand*) I feel bound to tell you that you are not down on my list of eligible young men, although I have the same list as the dear Duchess of Bolton has. We work together, in fact. However, I am quite ready to enter your name, should your answers be what a really affectionate mother requires. Do you smoke?

JACK: Well, yes, I must admit I smoke.

LADY BRACKNELL: I am glad to hear it. A man should always have an occupation of some kind. There are far too many idle men in London as it is. How old are you?

JACK: Twenty-nine.

LADY BRACKNELL: A very good age to be married at. I have always been of opinion that a man who desires to get married should know either everything or nothing. Which do you know?

JACK: (*after some hesitation*) I know nothing, Lady Bracknell.

LADY BRACKNELL: I am pleased to hear it. I do not approve of anything that tampers with natural ignorance. Ignorance is like a delicate exotic fruit; touch it and the bloom is gone. The whole theory of modern education is radically unsound. Fortunately in England, at any rate, education produces no effect whatsoever. If it did, it would prove a serious danger to the upper classes, and probably lead to acts of violence in Grosvenor Square. What is your income?

FIGURE 8.6 *The Importance of Being Earnest* by Oscar Wilde. California State University, Long Beach, directed by W. David Sievers.

JACK: Between seven and eight thousand a year.

LADY BRACKNELL: (*makes a note in her book*) In land, or in investments?

JACK: In investments, chiefly.

LADY BRACKNELL: That is satisfactory. What between the duties expected of one during one's lifetime, and the duties exacted from one after one's death, land has ceased to be either a profit or a pleasure. It gives one position, and prevents one from keeping it up. That's all that can be said about land.

JACK: I have a country house with some land, of course, attached to it, about fifteen hundred acres, I believe; but I don't depend on that for my real income. In fact, as far as I can make out, the poachers are the only people who make anything out of it.

LADY BRACKNELL: A country house! How many bedrooms? Well, that point can be cleared up afterwards. You have a town house, I hope? A girl with a simple, unspoiled nature, like Gwendolen, could hardly be expected to reside in the country.

JACK: Well, I own a house in Belgrave Square, but it is let by the year to Lady Bloxham. Of course, I can get it back whenever I like, at six months' notice.

LADY BRACKNELL: Lady Bloxham? I don't know her.

JACK: Oh, she goes about very little. She is a lady considerably advanced in years.

LADY BRACKNELL: Ah, now-a-days that is no guarantee of respectability of character. What number in Belgrave Square?

JACK: 149.

LADY BRACKNELL: (*shaking her head*) The unfashionable side. I thought there was something. However, that could easily be altered.

JACK: Do you mean the fashion, or the side?

LADY BRACKNELL: (*sternly*) Both, if necessary, I presume. What are your politics?

JACK: Well, I am afraid I really have none. I am a Liberal Unionist.

LADY BRACKNELL: Oh, they count as Tories. They dine with us. Or come in the evening, at any rate. Now to minor matters. Are your parents living?

JACK: I have lost both my parents.

LADY BRACKNELL: To lose one parent, Mr. Worthing, may be regarded as a misfortune; to lose both looks like carelessness. Who was your father? He was evidently a man of some wealth. Was he born in what the Radical papers call the purple of commerce, or did he rise from the ranks of the aristocracy?

JACK: I am afraid I really don't know. The fact is, Lady Bracknell, I said I had lost my parents. It would be nearer the truth to say that my parents seem to have lost me . . . I don't actually know who I am by birth. I was . . . well, I was found.

LADY BRACKNELL: Found!

JACK: The late Mr. Thomas Cardew, an old gentleman of a very charitable and kindly disposition, found me, and gave me the name of Worthing, because he happened to have a first-class ticket for Worthing in his pocket at the time. Worthing is a place in Sussex. It is a seaside resort.

LADY BRACKNELL: Where did the charitable gentleman who had a first-class ticket for this seaside resort find you?

JACK: (*gravely*) In a hand-bag.

LADY BRACKNELL: A hand-bag?

JACK: (*very seriously*) Yes, Lady Bracknell. I was in a hand-bag—a somewhat large, black leather hand-bag, with handles to it—an ordinary hand-bag in fact.

LADY BRACKNELL: In what locality did this Mr. James, or Thomas, Cardew come across this ordinary hand-bag?

JACK: In the cloak-room at Victoria Station. It was given to him in mistake for his own.

LADY BRACKNELL: The cloak-room at Victoria Station?

JACK: Yes. The Brighton line.

LADY BRACKNELL: The line is immaterial. Mr. Worthing, I confess I feel somewhat bewildered by what you have just told me. To be born, or at any rate bred, in a hand-bag, whether it had handles or not, seems to me to display a contempt for the ordinary decencies of family life that remind one of the worst excesses of the French Revolution. And I presume you know what that unfortunate movement led to? As for the particular locality in which the hand-bag was found, a cloak-room at a railway station might serve to conceal a social indiscretion—has probably, indeed, been used for that purpose before now—but it could hardly be regarded as an assured basis for a recognized position in good society.

JACK: May I ask you then what you would advise me to do? I need hardly say I would do anything in the world to ensure Gwendolen's happiness.

LADY BRACKNELL: I would strongly advise you, Mr. Worthing, to try and acquire some relations as soon as possible, and to make a definite effort to produce at any rate one parent, of either sex, before the season is quite over.

JACK: Well, I don't see how I could possibly manage to do that. I can produce the hand-bag at any moment. It is in my dressing-room at home. I really think that should satisfy you, Lady Bracknell.

LADY BRACKNELL: Me, sir! What has it to do with me? You can hardly imagine that I and Lord Bracknell would dream of allowing our only daughter—a girl brought up with the utmost care—to marry into a cloakroom, and form an alliance with a parcel? Good morning, Mr. Worthing!

[LADY BRACKNELL *sweeps out in majestic indignation.*]

JACK: Good morning!

2.   *The Miser,* by Molière (translated and adapted by Stanley Kahan)
From Act I

Scene: For two men
Characters: HARPAGON, a miser
LA FLÈCHE, a valet to Harpagon's son, Cleante
Setting: Harpagon's home in Paris
Time: Mid-seventeenth century
Situation: Harpagon is such a miser that he hides his money in various exotic places, including a particularly large sum in his garden. He lives in continual fear that someone will find his money and rob him. His main passion in life is to pinch pennies and hoard all his money. In this scene, he suspects his son's valet, La Flèche, of spying on him and of finding his hidden money. The scene begins as Harpagon has angrily ordered La Flèche out of the house. The play is filled with sharp satire and delightful comic touches. Harpagon particularly is a sharply drawn comedic character.

HARPAGON: Get out of my house immediately, do you hear? Get out of here, you liar, you cheat, you gallow's meat, and don't answer back!

LA FLÈCHE: (*aside*) I have never seen anyone as nasty as this crusty old man, and if I am not mistaken, the devil has taken possession of him.

HARPAGON: What are you muttering about over there, eh?

LA FLÈCHE: Why do you want me to leave?

HARPAGON: Just the sort of question one would expect from a lout such as you. Get out, and get out now before I kick you out with my own two feet.

LA FLÈCHE: What have I ever done to you?

HARPAGON: You have done more than enough, so get out and get out now!

LA FLÈCHE: But my master, your own son, has ordered me to wait.

HARPAGON: Then go and wait for him out in the street, but do not stay in this house, spying on me, watching everything that is going on, and using it against me. No one is going to spy on me in my own home, particularly a wretch such as you who covets all I own, watches my every little action, and sneaks about to see if he can find something to steal.

FIGURE 8.7 *The Miser* by Molière. Wayne State University, directed by
Robert T. Hazzard.

LA FLÈCHE: How could anyone even find something to steal from you, when
you lock up everything you own and keep guard over it day and night?

HARPAGON: I will lock up anything I want to, and I will guard it as long as it
suits me. This is a pretty kettle of fish, when spies lurk around you all the
time. (*Quitely, aside*) I tremble if he should even suspect anything about my
money. (*Aloud*) So! you are probably just the kind of person who would go
around telling everyone about the money hidden in my house.

LA FLÈCHE: You have money hidden in this house?

HARPAGON: No! No! No! I never said that, you rascal. (*To himself*) I am going to
explode with rage! (*Aloud*) I simply asked if you would spread the story
about because of your bad manners and the ill will you bear me.

LA FLÈCHE: What? What does it matter to anyone if you think you have money
or not; the important thing is, do you really have some?

HARPAGON: (*About to strike La Flèche in the face*) Stop arguing with me. I'll slap
your nose, and mouth and ears, and then you can think about it. I say
again, get out of here.

LA FLÈCHE: Very well, I am leaving!

HARPAGON: Just a moment! You are not taking anything with you, are you?

LA FLÈCHE: And what would I take from you?

HARPAGON: Who knows? I have to look first! Let me see your hands.

LA FLÈCHE: Here they are.

HARPAGON: And the others?

LA FLÈCHE: (*Puzzled*) The other what?

HARPAGON: That's right, the other whats.

LA FLÈCHE: Here, look for yourself. (*Showing him his legs*)

HARPAGON: (*Pointing to La Flèche's breeches*) You have nothing hidden in there, you lout?

LA FLÈCHE: How would you like to look for yourself?

HARPAGON: (*Feeling La Flèche's pockets*) Those wide breeches of yours are purposely designed to hide things in them. You think you are very clever, don't you?

LA FLÈCHE: (*Aside*) Ah! How a man such as this deserves whatever happens to him—and what a pleasure I would have in robbing him!

HARPAGON: Eh!

LA FLÈCHE: What?

HARPAGON: What did I hear you mutter about robbing me?

LA FLÈCHE: I said if you feel carefully, you can tell if I have robbed you!

HARPAGON: That is just what I intend to do! (*Harpagon sticks his hands in La Flèche's pockets*)

LA FLÈCHE: (*Aside*) May the plague take him and all misers like him.

HARPAGON: What's that? What did you say?

LA FLÈCHE: What did I say?

HARPAGON: Yes, what did you say about misers, eh?

LA FLÈCHE: I said may the plague take all misers and people who act like misers.

HARPAGON: Were you speaking about someone in particular?

LA FLÈCHE: Just about misers.

HARPAGON: And who are these misers you were referring to?

LA FLÈCHE: Moneygrubbers and pennypinchers.

HARPAGON: And who did you have in mind? (*His hands are still in La Flèche's pockets*)

LA FLÈCHE: Why are you so concerned about it?

HARPAGON: I am concerned about what concerns me.

LA FLÈCHE: Did you think I was talking about you?

HARPAGON: I'll think whatever I want to think! I want you to tell me who you were talking about when you said that!

LA FLÈCHE: I am talking to—I am talking to my hat!

HARPAGON: And I am talking to the head beneath that particular hat.

LA FLÈCHE: Do you mean to say I am not permitted to curse pennypinchers?

HARPAGON: No—but not in this house. Stop whimpering and being insulting. Keep your tongue to yourself.

LA FLÈCHE: I didn't mention any names.

HARPAGON: I'll beat you within an inch of your life if you say another word.

LA FLÈCHE: If the shoe fits, one had better wear it.

HARPAGON: Will you keep your tongue in place?

LA FLÈCHE: Yes, but only against my will.

HARPAGON: Ah ha—So—So that's it!

LA FLÈCHE: Look here—(*showing Harpagon a pocket in his doublet*) Here's one you missed! Satisfied?

HARPAGON: Very well—you had better give me what is mine without my having to search you!

LA FLÈCHE: What did you say?

HARPAGON: What have you taken from me?

LA FLÈCHE: I have taken nothing at all from you.

HARPAGON: You swear it?

LA FLÈCHE: Of course!

HARPAGON: Goodbye, then, and you know where you can go!

LA FLÈCHE: (*Aside*) What a delightful and charming way to dismiss someone. (*He starts to leave*)

HARPAGON: (*Calling after him*) I shall leave you to your own conscience, to rob a poor, old, helpless, and generous man such as myself!

3. *The Doctor in Spite of Himself,* by Molière (translated and adapted by Stanley Kahan)
   From Act I

Scene: For two men, one woman
Characters: SGANARELLE, a drunken woodcutter
MARTINE, his wife
MONSIEUR ROBERT, a gentleman
Setting: A forest in France.
Time: A day during the mid-seventeenth century.
Situation: This is the opening scene of the play. Sganarelle and Martine are carrying on an argument that they started off-stage. They are low-comedy characters, endowed with little of the "gentility" found among the other characters in the play. Their speech and actions highlight the generally farcical knockabout nature of broad comedic acting.

(*Sganarelle and Martine appear on the stage quarreling*)

SGANARELLE: Absolutely not. I tell you I will do nothing of the kind. It is up to me to decide when to speak, and I will be master here.

MARTINE: And I am telling you that I will live as I wish, and I am not married to you to put up with all of your foolishness.

SGANARELLE: Good grief . . . what a pain in the . . . to have a wife! Aristotle was perfectly right in stating that a woman is worse than the devil.

MARTINE: Look at Mister Smart-Aleck—and his Greek friend Aristotle.

SGANARELLE: That's right. Mister Smart-Aleck. You go and find a better wood chopper who can debate the way I can.—I, who have served a great physician for six years, and who, when only a little boy, knew his grammar by heart!

MARTINE: A plague on this idiot!

SGANARELLE: A plague on this slut of a wife.

MARTINE: Cursed be the hour and the day when I took it in my poor head to say yes to this lout!

FIGURE 8.8 *The Doctor in Spite of Himself* by Molière. Wayne State University, directed by Robert T. Hazzard.

SGANARELLE: Cursed be the notary who made me put my mark on that vile contract.

MARTINE: So . . . it is very nice of you to complain about that matter. Shouldn't you rather thank Heaven every second you breathe that you have me for a wife? How did you ever deserve a woman like me?

SGANARELLE: Oh, my sweet, you are much too kind—and I must admit I have had occasions to remember our wedding night with great warmth! Heavens!—Don't make me open my mouth too wide. I might say certain things I shouldn't.

MARTINE: Eh! What? Say? What could you say?

SGANARELLE: Enough of that! Let us drop the matter. It is enough that we know what we know, and that you were very fortunate to meet me at all.

MARTINE: What do you mean—fortunate to meet you. A slob who will send me to a hospital?—a drunken, lying wretch who gobbles up every penny I have?

SGANARELLE: That is a lie: I don't gobble—I drink every penny of it!

MARTINE: A wretch who sells all the furniture in the house?

SGANARELLE: That is called living off one's means.

MARTINE: A fiend who has taken the very bed from under me?

SGANARELLE: That is simply to help you get up earlier in the morning.

MARTINE: An idiot who doesn't leave a stick of furniture in the house.

SGANARELLE: It is just a way to make moving that much easier.

MARTINE: A lout who does nothing from morning till night but gamble and drink.

SGANARELLE: I do that simply to keep from becoming too depressed.

MARTINE: And what am I supposed to do with our family?

SGANARELLE: You can do whatever you like.

MARTINE: I have four poor children on my hands.

SGANARELLE: Then drop them.

MARTINE: They keep asking for a little bread!

SGANARELLE: So then—beat them. When I've had enough to eat and drink, everyone in the house should be satisfied.

MARTINE: Do you mean to tell me, you drunken sot, that things can go on as they have been all this time?

SGANARELLE: My dear wife, let us not get excited, pretty-please?

MARTINE: And that I must bear forever your drunkenness and insults?

SGANARELLE: Let us not get upset, my little pigeon.

MARTINE: And that I don't know how to bring you back to a sense of responsibility?

SGANARELLE: My little canary—you know I am not a patient man—and my arm is beginning to get a little excited!

MARTINE: I give that for your threats. (*snaps her fingers*)

SGANARELLE: My bird, my parrot, my canary—your skin is itching for a good hiding!

MARTINE: You had better observe that I couldn't care less for your threats!

SGANARELLE: My dear little rib—you have set your heart upon a good beating.

MARTINE: Do you think I am frightened of all your talk?

SGANARELLE: Sweet little barbecued chop, I shall belt you in the ears.

MARTINE: Drunken lout!

SGANARELLE: I'll beat you!

MARTINE: Walking wine-cask.

SGANARELLE: I'll pummel you.

MARTINE: Infamous wretch.

SGANARELLE: I'll tan your hide so that you won't forget it.

MARTINE: Lout! villian! scoundrel! drunkard! wretch! dog's meat! horse's tail! liar! deceiver! . . .

SGANARELLE: So you really want it, eh? Very well then. (*He picks up a stick and starts to beat her*)

MARTINE: (*Yelling*) Help! Oh, help! Please help! Help!

SGANARELLE: And this my pet is the best way to shut you up!

M. ROBERT: Hello there! I say, Hello. Good Heavens. What is this? How revolting. The plague take this villian for beating the poor woman so.

MARTINE: (*Her arms crossed, she speaks to M. Robert, forcing him back, and then slaps him across the face*) Maybe I enjoy him beating me. In fact, I do!

M. ROBERT: Really! If that is the case, please continue.

MARTINE: Why are you interfering?

M. Robert: I must be wrong.—Pray forgive me.

Martine: Is this any of your business?

M. Robert: You are absolutely correct!

Martine: Look at this fancy peacock, who wants to stop a husband from beating his poor wife.

M. Robert: I said I was sorry!

Martine: What do you have to say about it—eh?

M. Robert: Not another word!

Martine: Who asked you to stick your nose in this business?

M. Robert: Mum's the word! I won't say anything else!

Martine: Mind your own business.

M. Robert: I'll be quiet as the grave!

Martine: I enjoy being beaten.

M. Robert: Good for you.

Martine: It doesn't hurt you, does it?

M. Robert: You are right. It doesn't.

Martine: And you are a first-class ass, who interferes in matters that don't concern you.

M. Robert: (*to Sganarelle*) My good friend, I earnestly beg your pardon. Go ahead and beat your wife as much as you wish. As a matter of fact, if you like, I'll lend a hand. Two hands are better than one! (*He moves over to Sganarelle who begins to beat him with the stick he has been using on Martine*)

Sganarelle: No thank you, I'm quite able to do the job by myself.

M. Robert: Ah—Well then, that is quite a different matter.

Sganarelle: If I feel like beating her, I'll beat her; and if I don't feel like it, I won't.

M. Robert: That's wonderful.

Sganarelle: She happens to be my wife, not yours!

M. Robert: I am certainly pleased about that!

Sganarelle: No one told you to tell me how to deal with my wife.

M. Robert: Quite right.

Sganarelle: I can beat her without your help, understand!

M. Robert: Evidently.

Sganarelle: And it is just your busy-body attitude that makes you meddle in other people's business. Remember what Cicero said: Between the tree and the finger you must not place the bark. (*He beats him and drives him off-stage. He returns to his wife and takes her hand*) Come my dear, let us make up. Let us shake hands.

Martine: That's fine now, after you have beaten me!

Sganarelle: That doesn't bother me. Let's shake hands.

Martine: I won't shake hands.

Sganarelle: What?

Martine: No!

Sganarelle: Come, my little canary.

Martine: I won't shake hands.

Sganarelle: Come, my little porcupine, let's shake hands.

Martine: I will do nothing of the kind!

Sganarelle: Come, now. Come, come on.

Martine: I have said no, and I mean it.

SGANARELLE: It's just a trifle. Please do, my little mackerel.

MARTINE: Leave me alone.

SGANARELLE: I said ''Shake hands!''

MARTINE: You have treated me too cruelly.

SGANARELLE: All right then! I beg your pardon; put your hand right there.

MARTINE: I forgive you. (*aside, very softly*) I shall see that you pay tenfold for this little escapade.

SGANARELLE: You are silly to take this matter too seriously. These are minor matters that are necessary now and then to show that we love each other. Five or six solid blows only strengthen our bond of affection. There—that's done. Now I'm going into the woods, and I promise that I will return with several full loads today.

4.   *Elizabeth the Queen,* by Maxwell Anderson
     From Act II, Scene 3

     Scene: For one man, one woman
Characters: QUEEN ELIZABETH OF ENGLAND
                LORD ESSEX
   Setting: The council chamber in the palace at Whitehall, London.
      Time: The late sixteenth century.
 Situation: The relationship between Queen Elizabeth and Lord Essex is more than that of queen and subject; they are deeply in love despite the fact that Elizabeth is many years older than Essex. In order to quell the Irish rebellion, Elizabeth sends Essex to Ireland with a military force. Essex returns to England at the head of a rebellion to unseat Elizabeth. His army is in London awaiting his orders. This confrontation between Essex and Elizabeth immediately follows Essex's arrival in London. Both Elizabeth and Essex here face a choice between love and power.

ELIZABETH: What did you write me?

ESSEX: I wrote you my love—for I thought you loved me then—
     And then I pled with you not to bring me home
     In the midst of my mission—and then at last angrily—
     For I had not heard—but always to say I loved you—
     Always.

ELIZABETH: But is this true?

ESSEX: Would I lie?

ELIZABETH: Some one
     Has lied and will pay with his life if this is true!—
     Before God and hell—some one will pay for this.

ESSEX: What did you write me?

ELIZABETH: I wrote—my love—
     God keep you safe—I know not—and then, not hearing,
     I wrote God knows what madness—as to a rebel—
     Thinking you no longer mine—faithless!
     Thinking—

ESSEX: I would I had known—I was in torment—
    I—forgive me—
ELIZABETH: You should never have gone away.
    God, how I've hated you!—
ESSEX: No!
ELIZABETH: Planned to put you to torture!
ESSEX: I have been in torture!
    (*He steps toward her.*)
ELIZABETH: Not yet—I can't breathe yet—I can't breathe—
    Or think or believe—
ESSEX: Nor I.
ELIZABETH: Can we ever—
    Believe again? Can it be as it used to be?
ESSEX: We can make it so.
ELIZABETH: Come, kill me if you will. Put your arms round me—
    If you love me. Do you still love me?
ESSEX: Yes.
ELIZABETH: Yes, yes—
    If this were false, then, then truly—then I should die.
    I thought because I was older—you see—someone else—
ESSEX: No one—never a breath—
ELIZABETH: Is it all, all as before?
ESSEX: We have not changed.
ELIZABETH: No. Yes, a little, perhaps. They have changed us a little.
ESSEX: Not I. I have not changed.
ELIZABETH: Can I trust you now?
ESSEX: Sweet, think back, all those months,
    All those hideous months! No word, no love.
    And then word did come, it was to make me prisoner!
    Christ, I have pride!
    And though I came here in defiance, I came truly to find you
    Who have been lost from me.
ELIZABETH: Do you ask forgiveness?
    It is all forgiven.
ESSEX: Then, why then, hell's vanished—
    And here's heaven risen out of it, a heaven of years
    In the midst of desolate centuries.
ELIZABETH: We have so few years.
    Let us make them doubly sweet, these years we have,
    Be gracious with each other, sway a little
    To left or right if we must to stay together—
    Never distrust each other—nay, distrust
    All others, when they whisper. Let us make this our pact
    Now, for the fates are desperate to part us
    And the very gods envy this happiness
    We pluck out of loss and death.
ESSEX: If two stand shoulder to shoulder against the gods,
    Happy together, the gods themselves are helpless
    Against them, while they stand so.

ELIZABETH: Love, I will be
    Your servant. Command me. What would you have?
ESSEX: Why nothing—
ELIZABETH: Take this my world, my present in your hands!
    You shall stand back of my chair and together we
    Shall build an England to make the old world wonder
    And the new world worship!—What is this doubt in your brow?
ESSEX: I am troubled to be dishonest. I have brought my army
    Here to the palace—and though it's all true that we've said—
    No letters—utter agony over long months—
    It is something in myself that has made me do this,
    Not Cecil—nor anyone. No one but myself.
    The rest is all excuse.
ELIZABETH: Speak what you will.
ESSEX: If you had but shown anger I could have spoken
    Easily. It's not easy now, but speak I must!
    Oh, I've thought much about this
    On lonely marches and in distant tents,
    Thinking of you and me. I say this now
    Without rancor—in all friendliness and love—
    The throne is yours by right of descent and by
    Possession—but if this were a freer time,
    And there were election, I should carry the country before me,
    And this being true, and we being equal in love,
    Should we not be equal in power as well?
ELIZABETH: We are equal.
    I have made you so.
ESSEX: Yes, but still it's all yours—
    Yours to grant me now or take away.
ELIZABETH: How could this well be otherwise?
ESSEX: Am I not—and I say this too in all love—
    As worthy to be king as you to be queen?
    Must you be sovereign alone?
ELIZABETH: You are young in policy,
    My Essex, if you do not see that if I
    Should grant high place to you now it would show ill to the kingdom—
    It would be believed that you had forced this on me,
    Would be called a revolution. It would undermine
    All confidence. What is built up for years
    In people's minds blows away like thistledown
    When such things get abroad.
ESSEX: But is this your reason
    Or have you another? Would you trust me as King?
ELIZABETH: No.
ESSEX: And are you still reluctant to give up
    Your prerogatives?
ELIZABETH: Yes.
ESSEX: Then now, when the country is mine, the court in my hands,
    You my prisoner, I must send my men away,

Disband my army, give back your kingdom to you,
And know I have been king for a moment only
And never will be again?
ELIZABETH: I am your prisoner?
ESSEX: The palace and the city are in my hands.
This England is mine now for the taking—
ELIZABETH: This is your friendship! This is your love!
ESSEX: As water finds its level, so power goes
To him who can use it, and soon or late the name
Of king follows where power is.
ELIZABETH: Oh, my Essex,
You are a child in war as you are in council.
Why all this talk of power? No army opposed you
When your troops came the road from Ireland.
    No guard was set
To stop your entrance with your thousand halberds.
Shall I tell you why? Because I wished to keep
A semblance of peace between us. And for that,
I am your prisoner!
ESSEX: Yes. My dear prisoner.
ELIZABETH: Now I do know at least
What it was you wanted. You wanted my kingdom.
    You have it.
Make the best of it. And so shall I.
What are your plans?
ESSEX: I have none.
ELIZABETH: The Tower, the block—
You could hardly take a queen prisoner and have no thought
Of her destiny. I am my mother's daughter,
I too can walk the path my mother walked.
ESSEX: These are heroics. You know you are free as air.
ELIZABETH: If I do as you ask.
ESSEX: Is it so hard to share your power with your love?
I could have all—and I offer to share with you.
ELIZABETH: Let's have no more pretending.
I'd have given all—but you came with an army, demanding—
In short, you don't love—nor trust me—no—nor want me—
ESSEX: God knows I have wanted you. I have wanted power—
Believed myself fitted to hold it—but not without you.
ELIZABETH: If you had wanted me would you rise and strike
At me with an army? Never, never! You'd have come
To me quietly, and we'd have talked of it together
As lovers should—and we'd both have our way—
And no one the wiser. But now, to take the palace,
Hold me prisoner—no—what you wanted you've taken—
And that is all you shall have. This is your kingdom—
But I—I am not yours.
ESSEX: But I am yours
And have been.

266

ELIZABETH: Who will believe that? Not the world,
>No, and not I. I'd rather go to the Tower
>Than share my place on terms like these.
> Put me where I
>Will do least harm.
ESSEX: I cannot, could not, will not.
ELIZABETH: If I could have given freely—
>But not now. Not surrendering. Not to a victor.
ESSEX: I am no victor if I lose you. The only gift
>That I could take from you is that we are equals.
ELIZABETH: Yes, but not now.
ESSEX: I ask one word from you.
>Give me this word—this one word—and these soldiers
>Shall leave, and you shall be free.
ELIZABETH: I'll believe that
>When it happens.
ESSEX: I'll believe you when you promise.
ELIZABETH: Then you have my promise.
>You shall share the realm with me. As I am queen,
>I promise it.
ESSEX: Then this is my answer.
> (*He kisses her, then calls*)
>Marvel!—Marvel!
> (MARVEL *enters.*)
>Carry out the order of release. Dismiss my guard—
>Return the palace into the queen's hands.
>Retire with all our forces to the Strand.
>Release all prisoners. Release the queen's guard
>And send them to their stations.
> (MARVEL *goes out.*)
>The palace will be
>Returned as quickly as taken. This is our last quarrel.
ELIZABETH: Yes—our last.

5. *Mary of Scotland,* by Maxwell Anderson
    From Act III

  Scene: For two women
Characters: MARY STUART
          ELIZABETH TUDOR
  Setting: A prison room in Carlisle Castle, in England. There are two windows,
          both barred.
  Time: An evening in the mid-sixteenth century.
Situation: *Mary of Scotland* is Maxwell Anderson's version of the historic conflict
          between the two queens Mary and Elizabeth. This conflict, both political
          and personal, was based in part on religion. Mary had been raised in
          France as a Catholic, and Elizabeth, daughter of Henry VIII, was raised

as a Protestant. Through her own errors and through the political machinations of Elizabeth and her supporters, Mary has become Elizabeth's prisoner. Elizabeth offers Mary freedom if she will abdicate her throne. The alternative Mary faces is remaining for the rest of her life in prison, "darkened from news and from the sun." Mary's proud spirit, however, does not break, and she wins a moral victory in this, the final scene from the play. This scene is also the first and only meeting between the two characters.

The actress will find it of interest to compare the portrait Anderson paints of Elizabeth in this play and the Elizabeth in his earlier play, *Elizabeth the Queen* (see p. 263).

ELIZABETH: You came here by your own road.
MARY: I see how I came.
    Back, back, each step the wrong way, and each sign followed
    As you'd have me go, till the skein picks up and we stand
    Face to face here. It was you forced Bothwell from me—
    You there, and always. Oh, I'm to blame in this, too!
    I should have seen your hand!
ELIZABETH: It has not been my use
    To speak much or spend my time—
MARY: How could I have been
    Mistaken in you for an instant?
ELIZABETH: You were not mistaken.
    I am all women I must be. One's a young girl,
    Young and harrowed as you are—one who could weep
    To see you here—and one's a bitterness
    At what I have lost and can never have, and one's
    The basilisk you saw. This last stands guard
    And I obey it. Lady, you came to Scotland
    A fixed and subtle enemy, more dangerous
    To me than you've ever known. This could not be borne,
    And I set myself to cull you out and down,
    And down you are.
MARY: When was I your enemy?
ELIZABETH: Your life was a threat to mine, your throne to my throne,
    Your policy a threat.
MARY: How? Why?
ELIZABETH: It was you
    Or I. Do you know that? The one of us must win
    And I must always win. Suppose one lad
    With a knife in his hand, a Romish lad who planted
    That knife between my shoulders—my kingdom was yours.
    It was too easy. You might not have wished it.
    But you'd take it if it came.
MARY: And you'd take my life
    And love to avoid this threat?
ELIZABETH: Nay, keep your life.

And your love, too. The lords have brought a parchment
For you to sign. Sign it and live.
MARY: If I sign it
Do I live where I please? Go free?
ELIZABETH: Nay, I would you might,
But you'd go to Bothwell, and between you two
You might be too much for Moray. You'll live with me
In London. There are other loves, my dear.
You'll find amusement there in the court. I assure you
It's better than a cell.
MARY: And if I will not sign
This abdication?
ELIZABETH: You've tasted prison. Try
A diet of it.
MARY: And so I will.
ELIZABETH: I can wait.
MARY: And I can wait. I can better wait than you.
Bothwell will fight free again. Kirkaldy
Will fight beside him, and others will spring up
From these dragon's teeth you've sown. Each week that passes
I'll be stronger, and Moray weaker.
ELIZABETH: And do you fancy
They'll rescue you from an English prison? Why,
Let them try it.
MARY: Even that they may do. I wait for Bothwell—
And wait for him here.
ELIZABETH: Where you will wait, bear in mind,
Is for me to say. Give up Bothwell, give up your throne
If you'd have a life worth living.
MARY: I will not.
ELIZABETH: I can wait.
MARY: And will not because you play to lose. This trespass
Against God's right will be known. The nations will know it,
Mine and yours. They will see you as I see you
And pull you down.
ELIZABETH: Child, child, I've studied this gambit
Before I play it. I will send each year
This paper to you. Not signing, you will step
From one cell to another, step lower always,
Till you reach the last, forgotten, forgotten of men,
Forgotten among causes, a wraith that cries
To fallen gods in another generation
That's lost your name. Wait then for Bothwell's rescue.
It will never come.
MARY: I may never see him?
ELIZABETH: Never.
It would not be wise.
MARY: And suppose indeed you won
Within our life-time, still looking down from the heavens

269

And up from men around us, God's spies that watch
The fall of great and little, they will find you out—
I will wait for that, wait longer than a life,
Till men and the times unscroll you, study the tricks
You play, and laugh, as I shall laugh, being known
Your better, haunted by your demon, driven
To death, or exile by you, unjustly. Why,
When all's done, it's my name I care for, my name and heart,
To keep them clean. Win now, take your triumph now,
For I'll win men's hearts in the end—though the sifting takes
This hundred years—or a thousand.

ELIZABETH: Child, child, are you gulled
By what men write in histories, this or that,
And never true? I am careful of my name
As you are, for this day and longer. It's not what happens
That matters, no, not even what happens that's true,
But what men believe to have happened. They will believe
The worst of you, the best of me, and that
Will be true of you and me. I have seen to this.
What will be said about us in after-years
By men to come, I control that, being who I am.
It will be said of me that I governed well,
And wisely, but of you, cousin, that your life,
Shot through with ill-loves, battened on lechery, made you
An ensign of evil, that men tore down and trampled.
Shall I call for the lord's parchment?

MARY: This will be said—?
But who will say it? It's a lie—will be known as a lie!

ELIZABETH: You lived with Bothwell before Darnley died,
You and Bothwell murdered Darnley.

MARY: And that's a lie!

ELIZABETH: Your letters, my dear. Your letters to Bothwell prove it.
We have those letters.

MARY: Then they're forged and false!
For I never wrote them!

ELIZABETH: It may be they were forged.
But will that matter, Mary, if they're believed?
All history is forged.

MARY: You would do this?

ELIZABETH: It is already done.

MARY: And still I win.
A demon has no children, and you have none,
Will have none, can have none, perhaps. This crooked track
You've drawn me on, cover it, let it not be believed
That a woman was a fiend. Yes, cover it deep,
And heap my infamy over it, lest men peer
And catch sight of you as you were and are. In myself
I know you to be an eater of dust. Leave me here
And set me lower this year by year, as you promise,

Till the last is an oubliette, and my name inscribed
On the four winds. Still, STILL I win! I have been
A woman, and I have loved as a woman loves,
Lost as a woman loses. I have borne a son,
And he will rule Scotland—and England. You have no heir!
A devil has no children.

ELIZABETH: By God, you shall suffer
For this, but slowly.

MARY: And that I can do. A woman
Can do that. Come, turn the key. I have a hell
For you in mind, where you will burn and feel it,
Live where you like, and softly.

ELIZABETH: Once more I ask you,
And patiently. Give up your throne.

MARY: No, devil.
My pride is stronger than yours, and my heart beats blood
Such as yours has never known. And in this dungeon,
I win here, alone.

ELIZABETH: (*turning*)
Goodnight, then.

MARY: Aye, goodnight.
(ELIZABETH *goes to the door, which opens before her. She goes out slowly. As the door begins to close upon her* MARY *calls*)
Beaton.

ELIZABETH: (*turning*)
You will not see your maids again,
I think. It's said they bring you news from the north.

MARY: I thank you for all kindness.
[ELIZABETH *goes out.* MARY *stands for a moment in thought, then walks to the wall and lays her hand against the stone, pushing outward. The stone is cold, and she shudders. Going to the window she sits again in her old place and looks out into the darkness.*]

6.   *Private Lives,* by Noel Coward
     From Act III

     Scene: For two men
Characters: ELYOT CHASE
               VICTOR PRYNNE
   Setting: An attractive flat in Paris.
     Time: Morning. Sometime between the two World Wars.
Situation: After an exciting but stormy marriage, Elyot and Amanda were divorced. Each remarried a mate who was totally different from their former spouses. Coincidentally, both Amanda and Elyot were honeymooning on the Riviera at the same time, in the same hotel, and in adjoining rooms. When they met, they discovered that they were still very much attracted to each other, and they fled to Paris to resume their loving and fighting.

Amanda's stuffy second husband, Victor, is disturbed by this strange behavior. He traces the pair to Paris, and the scene begins as Victor confronts Elyot. Victor soon discovers, however, that Elyot is decidedly his intellectual superior.

See another scene from *Private Lives* (p. 148), which occurs earlier in the play.

VICTOR: (*belligerently*) Now then!

ELYOT: Now then what?

VICTOR: Are you going to take back those things you said to Amanda?

ELYOT: Certainly, I'll take back anything, if only you'll stop bellowing at me.

VICTOR: (*contemptuously*) You're a coward, too.

ELYOT: They want us to fight, don't you see?

VICTOR: No, I don't; why should they?

ELYOT: Primitive feminine instincts—warring males—very enjoyable.

VICTOR: You think you're very clever, don't you?

ELYOT: I think I'm a bit cleverer than you, but apparently that's not saying much.

VICTOR: (*violently*) What?

ELYOT: Oh, do sit down.

VICTOR: I will not.

ELYOT: Well, if you'll excuse me, I will, I'm extremely tired. (*He sits down.*)

VICTOR: Oh, for God's sake, behave like a man.

ELYOT: (*patiently*) Listen a minute, all this belligerency is very right and proper and highly traditional, but if only you'll think for a moment, you'll see that it won't get us very far.

VICTOR: To hell with all that.

ELYOT: I should like to explain that if you hit me, I shall certainly hit you, probably equally hard, if not harder. I'm just as strong as you I should imagine. Then you'd hit me again, and I'd hit you again, and we'd go on until one or the other was knocked out. Now if you'll explain to me satisfactorily how all that can possibly improve the situation, I'll tear off my coat, and we'll go at one another hammer and tongs, immediately.

VICTOR: It would ease my mind.

ELYOT: Only if you won.

VICTOR: I should win all right.

ELYOT: Want to try?

VICTOR: Yes.

ELYOT: (*jumping up*) Here goes then—(*He tears off his coat.*)

VICTOR: Just a moment.

ELYOT: Well?

VICTOR: What did you mean about them wanting us to fight?

ELYOT: It would be balm to their vanity.

VICTOR: Do you love Amanda?

ELYOT: Is this a battle or a discussion? If it's the latter I shall put on my coat again, I don't want to catch a chill.

VICTOR: Answer my question, please.

ELYOT: Have a cigarette?

VICTOR: (*stormily*) Answer my question.

ELYOT: If you analyze it, it's rather a silly question.

VICTOR: Do you love Amanda?

ELYOT: (*confidentially*) Not very much this morning; to be perfectly frank, I'd like to wring her neck. Do you love her?

VICTOR: That's beside the point.

ELYOT: On the contrary, it's the crux of the whole affair. If you do love her still, you can forgive her, and live with her in peace and harmony until you're ninety-eight.

VICTOR: You're apparently even more of a cad than I thought you were.

ELYOT: You are completely in the right over the whole business—don't imagine I'm not perfectly conscious of that.

VICTOR: I'm glad.

ELYOT: It's all very unfortunate.

VICTOR: Unfortunate! My God!

ELYOT: It might have been worse.

VICTOR: I'm glad you think so.

ELYOT: I do wish you'd stop being so glad about everything.

VICTOR: What do you intend to do? That's what I want to know. What do you intend to do?

ELYOT: (*suddenly serious*) I don't know, I don't care.

VICTOR: I suppose you realize that you've broken that poor little woman's heart?

ELYOT: Which poor little woman?

VICTOR: Sibyl, of course.

ELYOT: Oh, come now, not as bad as that. She'll get over it, and forget all about me.

VICTOR: I sincerely hope so . . . for her sake.

ELYOT: Amanda will forget all about me too. Everybody will forget all about me. I might just as well lie down and die in fearful pain and suffering, nobody would care.

VICTOR: Don't talk such rot.

ELYOT: You must forgive me for taking rather a gloomy view of everything but the fact is, I suddenly feel slightly depressed.

VICTOR: I intend to divorce Amanda naming you as co-respondent.

ELYOT: Very well.

VICTOR: And Sibyl will divorce you for Amanda. It would be foolish of either of you to attempt any defense.

ELYOT: Quite.

VICTOR: And the sooner you marry Amanda again, the better.

ELYOT: I'm not going to marry Amanda.

VICTOR: What?

ELYOT: She's a vile-tempered wicked woman.

VICTOR: You should have thought of that before.

ELYOT: I did think of it before.

VICTOR: (*firmly*) You've got to marry her.

ELYOT: I'd rather marry a ravening leopard.

VICTOR: (*angrily*) Now look here. I'm sick of all this shilly-shallying. You're getting off a good deal more lightly than you deserve; you can consider yourself damned lucky I didn't shoot you.

ELYOT: (*with sudden vehemence*) Well, if you'd had a spark of manliness in you, you would have shot me. You're all fuss and fume, one of these cotton-wool Englishmen. I despise you.

VICTOR: (*through clenched teeth*) You despise me?

ELYOT: Yes, utterly. You're nothing but a rampaging gas bag!

[*He goes off into his room and slams the door, leaving* VICTOR *speechless with fury.*]

7. *Macbeth*, by William Shakespeare
   From Act II, Scene 2

    Scene: For one man, one woman
Characters: MACBETH, a Scottish nobleman, later King of Scotland
           LADY MACBETH, his wife
   Setting: A courtyard of Macbeth's castle at Inverness, Scotland.
     Time: An evening in the eleventh century.
Situation: Macbeth, a Scottish nobleman, stands on the threshold of seizing the crown of Scotland. Earlier in the evening, King Duncan and his retinue paid a visit to Macbeth's castle. Duncan has now retired and is guarded by only two grooms. Macbeth and his wife have decided to take this opportunity to murder him. Lady Macbeth has drugged the drinks of Duncan's two guards so that Macbeth's path to Duncan's bedside will be clear. But despite their ambition and their preparations, the enormity of their deed weighs heavily on them. As the scene opens, Lady Macbeth enters the courtyard to wait for Macbeth, who has just left for Duncan's bedchamber to commit the murder.

[*Enter* LADY MACBETH.]

LADY MACBETH: That which hath made them drunk hath made me bold;
What hath quench'd them hath given me fire. Hark! Peace!
It was the owl that shriek'd, the fatal bellman,
Which gives the stern'st good-night. He is about it:
The doors are open; and the surfeited grooms
Do mock their charge with snores: I have drugg'd their possets,
That death and nature do contend about them,
Whether they live or die.

MACBETH: (*within*)
                  Who's there? what, ho!

LADY MACBETH: Alack, I am afraid they have awaked,
And 'tis not done. The attempt and not the deed
Confounds us. Hark! I laid their daggers ready;
He could not miss 'em. Had he not resembled
My father as he slept, I had done 't.

[*Enter* MACBETH.]
                  My husband!

MACBETH: I have done the deed. Didst thou not hear a noise?

LADY MACBETH: I heard the owl scream and the crickets cry.
Did not you speak?

MACBETH: When?

LADY MACBETH: Now.
MACBETH: As I descended?
LADY MACBETH: Aye.
MACBETH: Hark!
    Who lies i' the second chamber?
LADY MACBETH: Donalbain.
MACBETH: This a sorry sight.
    (*looking on his hands*)
LADY MACBETH: A foolish thought, to say a sorry sight.
MACBETH: There's one did laugh in's sleep, and one cried "Murder!"
    That they did wake each other: I stood and heard them:
    But they did say their prayers, and address'd them
    Again to sleep.
LADY MACBETH: There are two lodged together.
MACBETH: One cried "God bless us!" and "Amen" the other;
    As they had seen me with these hangman's hands.
    Listening their fear, I could not say "Amen,"
    When they did say "God bless us!"
LADY MACBETH: Consider it not so deeply.
MACBETH: But wherefore could not I pronounce "Amen"?
    I had most need of blessing, and "Amen"
    Stuck in my throat.
LADY MACBETH: These deeds must not be thought
    After these ways; so, it will make us mad.
MACBETH: Methought I heard a voice cry "Sleep no more!
    Macbeth does murder sleep," the innocent sleep,
    Sleep that knits up the ravell'd sleave of care,
    The death of each day's life, sore labour's bath,
    Balm of hurt minds, great nature's second course,
    Chief nourisher in life's feast—
LADY MACBETH: What do you mean?
MACBETH: Still it cried "Sleep no more!" to all the house:
    "Glamis hath murder'd sleep, and therefore Cawdor
    Shall sleep no more; Macbeth shall sleep no more."
LADY MACBETH: Who was it that thus cried? Why, worthy thane,
    You do unbend your noble strength, to think
    So brainsickly of things. Go get some water,
    And wash this filthy witness from your hand.
    Why did you bring these daggers from the place?
    They must lie there: go carry them; and smear
    The sleepy grooms with blood.
MACBETH: I'll go no more:
    I am afraid to think what I have done;
    Look on 't again I dare not.
LADY MACBETH: Infirm of purpose!
    Give me the daggers: the sleeping and the dead
    Are but as pictures: 'tis the eye of childhood
    That fears a painted devil. If he do bleed,
    I'll gild the faces of the grooms withal;

For it must seem their guilt.
   [*Exit. Knocking within*]
MACBETH: Whence is that knocking?
How is 't with me, when every noise appals me?
What hands are here? Ha! they pluck out mine eyes.
Will all great Neptune's ocean wash this blood
Clean from my hand? No, this my hand will rather
The multitudinous seas incarnadine,
Making the green one red.
   [*Re-enter* LADY MACBETH.]
LADY MACBETH: My hands are of your colour; but I shame
To wear a heart so white.
   (*knocking within*)
                            I hear a knocking
At the south entry: retire we to our chamber:
A little water clears us of this deed:
How easy is it, then! Your constancy
Hath left you unattended.
   (*knocking within*)
                            Hark! more knocking.
Get on your nightgown, lest occasion call us,
And show us to be watchers. Be not lost
So poorly in your thoughts.
MACBETH: To know my deed, 'twere best not know myself.
   (*knocking within*)
Wake Duncan with thy knocking! I would thou couldst!
   [*Exeunt.*]

8.   *Blithe Spirit,* by Noel Coward
    From Act II, Scene 2

    Scene: For one man, two women
Characters: CHARLES CONDOMINE
             RUTH CONDOMINE, his second wife
             The ghost of ELVIRA CONDOMINE, his first wife
    Setting: The living room of Charles Condomine's house in Kent, England.
      Time: A summer morning. The present.
Situation: See the earlier scene from *Blithe Spirit* on p. 144.
             Madame Arcati, a spiritualist, has brought Charles Condomine's
first wife Elvira back from the spirit world. This state of affairs naturally
upsets his second wife, Ruth, who understands that Elvira is on the
premises but, unlike Charles, Elvira cannot see her. At the moment,
they are trying to work out some type of domestic life while also attempting to solve their dilemma.

CHARLES: What on earth was Madame Arcati doing here?
RUTH: She came to tea.
CHARLES: Did you ask her?

FIGURE 8.9 *Blithe Spirit* by Noel Coward. California State University, Long Beach, directed by W. David Sievers.

RUTH: Of course I did.

CHARLES: You never told me you were going to.

RUTH: You never told me you were going to ask Elvira to live with us.

CHARLES: I didn't.

ELVIRA: (*sauntering over to the tea table*) Oh, yes, you did, darling—it was your subconscious.

CHARLES: What was the old girl so cross about? She practically cut me dead.

RUTH: I told her the truth about why we invited her the other night.

CHARLES: That was quite unnecessary and most unkind.

RUTH: She needed taking down a bit, she was blowing herself out like a pouter pigeon.

CHARLES: Why did you ask her to tea?

ELVIRA: To get me exorcised, of course. Oh dear, I wish I could have a cucumber sandwich—I did love them so.

CHARLES: Is that true, Ruth?

RUTH: Is what true?

CHARLES: What Elvira said.

RUTH: You know perfectly well I can't hear what Elvira says.

CHARLES: She said that you got Madame Arcati here to try to get her exorcised. Is that true?

RUTH: We discussed the possibilities.

ELVIRA: There's a snake in the grass for you.

CHARLES: You had no right to do such a thing without consulting me.

RUTH: I have every right—this situation is absolutely impossible and you know it.

CHARLES: If only you'd make an effort and try to be a little more friendly to Elvira we might all have quite a jolly time.

RUTH: I have no wish to have a jolly time with Elvira.

ELVIRA: She's certainly very bad tempered, isn't she? I can't think why you married her.

CHARLES: She's naturally a bit upset—we must make allowances.

ELVIRA: I was never bad tempered though, was I, darling? Not even when you were beastly to me—

CHARLES: I was never beastly to you.

RUTH: (*exasperated*) Where is Elvira at the moment?

CHARLES: In the chair, by the table.

RUTH: Now look here, Elvira—I shall have to call you Elvira, shan't I? I can't very well go on saying Mrs. Condomine all the time, it would sound too silly—

ELVIRA: I don't see why not.

RUTH: Did she say anything?

CHARLES: She said she'd like nothing better.

ELVIRA: (*giggling*) You really are sweet, Charles darling—I worship you.

RUTH: I wish to be absolutely honest with you, Elvira—

ELVIRA: Hold on to your hats, boys!

RUTH: I admit I did ask Madame Arcati here with a view to getting you exorcised and I think that if you were in my position you'd have done exactly the same thing—wouldn't you?

ELVIRA: I shouldn't have done it so obviously.

RUTH: What did she say?

CHARLES: Nothing—she just nodded and smiled.

RUTH: (*with a forced smile*) Thank you, Elvira—that's generous of you. I really would so much rather that there were no misunderstandings between us—

CHARLES: That's very sensible, Ruth—I agree entirely.

RUTH: (*to* ELVIRA) I want, before we go any further, to ask you a frank question. Why did you really come here? I don't see that you could have hoped to have achieved anything by it beyond the immediate joke of making Charles into a sort of astral bigamist.

ELVIRA: I came because the power of Charles's love tugged and tugged and tugged at me. Didn't it, my sweet?

RUTH: What did she say?

CHARLES: She said that she came because she wanted to see me again.

RUTH: Well, she's done that now, hasn't she?

CHARLES: We can't be inhospitable, Ruth.

RUTH: I have no wish to be inhospitable, but I should like to have just an idea of how long you intend to stay, Elvira?

ELVIRA: I don't know—I really don't know! (*She giggles.*) Isn't it awful?

CHARLES: She says she doesn't know.

RUTH: Surely that's a little inconsiderate?

ELVIRA: Didn't the old spiritualist have any constructive ideas about getting rid of me?

CHARLES: What did Madame Arcati say?

RUTH: She said she couldn't do a thing.

ELVIRA: (*moving gaily over to the window*) Hurray!

CHARLES: Don't be upset, Ruth dear—we shall soon adjust ourselves, you know—you must admit it's a unique experience—I can see no valid reason why we shouldn't get a great deal of fun out of it.

RUTH: Fun? Charles, how can you—you must be out of your mind!

CHARLES: Not at all—I thought I was at first—but now I must say I'm beginning to enjoy myself.

RUTH: (*bursting into tears*) Oh, Charles—Charles—

ELVIRA: She's off again.

CHARLES: You really must not be so callous, Elvira—try to see her point a little—

RUTH: I suppose she said something insulting—

CHARLES: No dear, she didn't do anything of the sort.

RUTH: Now look here, Elvira—

CHARLES: She's over by the window now.

RUTH: Why the hell can't she stay in the same place!

ELVIRA: Temper again—my poor Charles, what a terrible life you must lead.

CHARLES: Do shut up, darling, you'll only make everything worse.

RUTH: Who was that "darling" addressed to—her or me?

CHARLES: Both of you.

RUTH: (*rises, stamping her foot*) This is intolerable!

CHARLES: For heaven's sake don't get into another state—

9. *The Taming of the Shrew,* by William Shakespeare
    From Act II, Scene 1

     Scene: For one man, one woman

Characters: PETRUCHIO, a rich gentleman from Verona
          KATHARINA, a shrewish young woman, daughter of Baptista

   Setting: A room in Baptista's house in Padua, Italy.

     Time: The sixteenth century.

Situation: Baptista, an elderly gentleman of Padua, has two daughters of marriageable age. The older of the two, Katharina, is a shrew, and no suitor has been able to tame her. More than one suitor has felt the sharpness of her tongue and nails. A young gentleman from Verona, Petruchio, has arrived in Padua in order "haply to wive and thrive as best I may." After settling financial arrangements with Baptista, Petruchio sets out to win Katharina for his wife. He finds it no easy task, but he turns out to be a bit more than the shrewish young woman bargained for. This is a lusty scene, both verbally *and* physically, as each tries to gain the upper hand.

PETRUCHIO: Good morrow, Kate; for that's your name, I hear.

KATHARINA: Well have you heard, but something hard of hearing: They call me Katharine that do talk of me.

PETRUCHIO: You lie, in faith, for you are called plain Kate.
And bonny Kate, and sometimes Kate the Curst;

But Kate, the prettiest Kate in Christendom,
Kate of Kate-Hall, my superdainty Kate,
For dainties are all Kates—and therefore, Kate,
Take this of me, Kate of my consolation:
Hearing thy mildness praised in every town,
Thy virtues spoke of, and thy beauty sounded,
Yet not so deeply as to thee belongs,
Myself am moved to woo thee for my wife.

KATHARINA: Moved! in good time. Let him that moved you hither
Remove you hence. I knew you at the first
You were a movable.

PETRUCHIO: Why, what's a movable?

KATHARINA: A joined stool.

PETRUCHIO: Thou hast hit it. Come, sit on me.

KATHARINA: Asses are made to bear, and so are you.

PETRUCHIO: Women are made to bear, and so are you.

KATHARINA: No such jade as you, if me you mean.

PETRUCHIO: Alas, good Kate, I will not burden thee!
For, knowing thee to be but young and light—

KATHARINA: Too light for such a swain as you to catch,
And yet as heavy as my weight should be.

PETRUCHIO: Should be! should—buzz!

KATHARINA: Well ta'en, and like a buzzard.

PETRUCHIO: O slow-winged turtle! shall a buzzard take thee?

KATHARINA: Ay, for a turtle, as he takes a buzzard.

PETRUCHIO: Come, come, you wasp. I' faith, you are too angry.

KATHARINA: If I be waspish, best beware my sting.

PETRUCHIO: My remedy is then to pluck it out.

KATHARINA: Aye, if the fool could find it where it lies.

PETRUCHIO: Who knows not where a wasp does wear his sting? In his tail.

KATHARINA: In his tongue.

PETRUCHIO: Whose tongue?

KATHARINA: Yours, if you talk of tails; and so farewell.

PETRUCHIO: What, with my tongue in your tail? nay, come again,
Good Kate, I am a gentleman.

KATHARINA: That I'll try.
(*She strikes him.*)

PETRUCHIO: I swear I'll cuff you if you strike again.

KATHARINA: So may you lose your arms.
If you strike me, you are no gentleman,
And if no gentleman, why then no arms.

PETRUCHIO: A herald, Kate? O, put me in thy books!

KATHARINA: What is your crest? a coxcomb?

PETRUCHIO: A combless cock, so Kate will be my hen.

KATHARINA: No cock of mine. You crow too like a craven.

PETRUCHIO: Nay, come, Kate, come. You must not look so sour.

KATHARINA: It is my fashion when I see a crab.

PETRUCHIO: Why, here's no crab, and therefore look not sour.

KATHARINA: There is, there is.

PETRUCHIO: Then show it me.
KATHARINA: Had I a glass, I would.
PETRUCHIO: What, you mean my face?
KATHARINA: Well aimed of such a young one.
PETRUCHIO: Now, by Saint George, I am too young for you.
KATHARINA: Yet you are withered.
PETRUCHIO: 'Tis with cares.
KATHARINA: I care not.
PETRUCHIO: Nay, hear you, Kate. In sooth you scape not so.
KATHARINA: I chafe you, if I tarry. Let me go.
PETRUCHIO: No, not a whit. I find you passing gentle.
   'Twas told me you were rough and coy and sullen,
   And now I find report a very liar;
   For thou are pleasant, gamesome, passing courteous,
   But slow in speech, yet sweet as springtime flowers.
   Thou canst not frown, thou canst not look askance,
   Nor bite the lip, as angry wenches will,
   Nor hast thou pleasure to be cross in talk,
   But thou with mildness entertain'st thy wooers,
   With gentle conference, soft and affable.
   Why does the world report that Kate doth limp?
   O slanderous world! Kate like the hazel twig
   Is straight and slender, and as brown in hue
   As hazel nuts, and sweeter than the kernels.
   O, let me see thee walk. Thou dost not halt.
KATHARINA: Go, fool, and whom thou keep'st command.
PETRUCHIO: Did ever Dian so become a grove
   As Kate this chamber with her princely gait?
   O, be thou Dian, and let her be Kate,
   And then let Kate be chaste and Dian sportful!
KATHARINA: Where did you study all this goodly speech?
PETRUCHIO: It is extempore, from my mother wit.
KATHARINA: A witty mother! Witless else her son.
PETRUCHIO: Am I not wise?
KATHARINA: Yes. Keep you warm.
PETRUCHIO: Marry, so I mean, sweet Katharine, in thy bed.
   And therefore, setting all this chat aside,
   Thus in plain terms: Your father hath consented
   That you shall be my wife, your dowry 'greed on,
   And, will you, nill you, I will marry you.
   Now Kate, I am a husband for your turn.
   For, by this light whereby I see thy beauty,
   Thy beauty, that doth make me like thee well,
   Thou must be married to no man but me;
   For I am he am born to tame you Kate,
   And bring you from a wild Kate to a Kate
   Conformable as other household Kates.
   Here comes your father. Never make denial.
   I must and will have Katharine to my wife.

CHAPTER NINE

Stage Fright

Stage fright has been examined by psychologists, as well as by teachers and students of acting and public speaking, from almost every conceivable viewpoint. It remains, however, one of the most common afflictions of those who work before the public. Stage fright besets actors in both the amateur and the professional theatre. Although experience with audiences gradually reduces the problem, one of the most helpful means of easing the discomfort of stage fright is to understand it. Even if it cannot be entirely eliminated, the actor should try to turn it to advantage. It is with this ultimate goal in mind that we should read the following pages.

What Is Stage Fright?

Stage fright is not difficult to describe. Almost everybody at some time or another in life experiences the symptoms, although not everyone reacts to the tensions of a given situation in the same way. The athlete about to compete in an important contest would probably describe the same symptoms as the actor waiting in the wings for his or her first entrance. The student waiting to see the dean of the college on academic or disciplinary matters might describe the tensions of the situation in the same way as would the prospective employee waiting for an interview for an important job or the salesperson planning the approach to an important client. Each will undergo many of the symptoms that the actor may feel belong to acting alone.

Although the symptoms will vary from one person to another, it is usually not difficult to recognize the more common manifestations of stage fright. Some people find that they have suddenly hatched a horde of co- coons in their stomachs and that butterflies are beating wings within; some people's legs may become uncomfortably weak and shaky, and indeed would be capable of a continual rhythmic dance if given the chance; the muscles may become tense and refuse to obey; and the mouth may seem uncommonly dry, if not suddenly filled with cotton. Some people wonder if they have been suddenly stricken by some rare disease which causes heavy perspiration even though the hands seem cold and clammy. Stage fright, like seasickness, may be unpleasant for the victim, but it is hardly fatal.

Some Suggested Causes

As we learn more about what motivates us as human beings, we have discovered a good deal about our psychological motivations and "hang- ups." As we continue to learn more, we may be able to speak with greater certainty about the probable factors that induce stage fright.

The first and most important thing to remember is that stage fright is not pathological. It does not indicate in itself any personality deficiency, mental ineptitude, or neurotic tendencies. The great number of successful actors and public speakers who suffer from stage fright presents convincing evidence that such conclusions are nonsense. We might clarify the problem by reminding ourselves that stage fright is not simply a mental state. In our account of the symptoms of stage fright a variety of disorganized physical activities were noted. This disorganized behavior is caused by the overac- tivity of the endocrine system, set into high gear by a tension-laden situa- tion. Adrenalin and glycogen are secreted into the blood stream to help cope with demanding emergencies. These secretions produce recognizable results: the heart beats faster; the respiratory system may become affected and cause gasping for breath; blood is drawn away from the organs and sent to the muscles in the arms and legs; a sinking feeling in the pit of the stomach may be experienced. *Unless the excess energy is used,* the symptoms may linger for a considerable period of time.

There are two explanations for the triggering of these physiological reactions in the acting situation. One is that *stage fright is learned behavior.* It has been suggested that stage fright is an individual's reaction to a set of circumstances that produced unpleasant effects earlier in that person's life. The origin may be as obvious as having once been embarrassed before a large group of people or having watched *someone else* in a relatively poor performance before an assembly or audience. Any unpleasant experience related to a large group may transfer itself as a fear of audiences in general. Well-meaning parents or friends may have caused apprehension by commenting: "Now, Mary, don't be afraid. You won't forget to say and do everything properly," at one's first social engagement or contact with an audience. Or a parent may have chided an active youngster who is possibly too prone to "performing" before company: "Behave yourself, Andrew. No one is paying any attention to you." Such events may no longer be a conscious memory, but when a new situation with any circumstances similar to that of the original experience is faced, some psychologists hold that the past experience may reassert itself and bring on stage fright.

Another explanation is that *stage fright is caused by inadequacy in meeting a new situation.*[1] Within the limits of our environment and range of experiences we are able to deal with our daily problems successfully and with few difficulties. As a result of past experiences under certain conditions, we have developed *patterns of response* (or behavior) which we adapt to situations of a similar nature. However, when new situations arise for which we have no experience, we have no patterned response that can be adapted to this new situation. Therefore, a response of uncertainty and fear may result. For example, we have a number of experiences in meeting people every day, particularly in informal situations, and we have set up a response pattern for such situations. But one day we may be presented to a high government official. Having had no past experience of this kind, we have no pattern of behavior to call on, and we become nervous and afraid of doing the wrong thing.

The actor about to go on the stage for the first time is likely to experience this reaction; the salesperson meeting a *new client* undergoes some emotional stress, and the experienced actor, facing a *new audience*, or appearing in a *new show*, may very well fall victim to the same fears that relatively inexperienced actors seem to think they alone suffer.

Do Experienced Actors Have Stage Fright?

The answer to the question of whether or not experienced actors suffer stage fright has already been suggested earlier in this chapter. Not only do successful actors experience stage fright, but they are not hesitant about ad-

---

1. See C. W. Lomas, "The Psychology of Stage Fright," *Quarterly Journal of Speech* 23 (February 1937): 35–44.

mitting it. It may be of some comfort to the student actor to realize that many of the most experienced actors, both in our time and in the past, have faced stage performances with less than equanimity. Edmund Kean, on the eve of his debut in London at Drury Lane, told his wife, "I wish I was going to be shot." After his successful debut as Shylock in *The Merchant of Venice*, he was now to appear again as Richard III. He was aware of what was expected of him and felt "so frightened, that my acting will be almost dumb-show tonight." Of course, he was magnificent on both occasions.

There is also a story of the great tenor Enrico Caruso, who was waiting in the wings one night before his performance in *A Masked Ball*. A young soprano, Edith Mason, was nervous at the prospect of going on stage and observed Caruso shaking like a leaf in the wind. "You, Caruso, are afraid?" asked the soprano in disbelief. "When you sing, Mason," he replied, "the audience expects 100 percent. But when Caruso sings they expect 150 percent." He continued to tremble until the moment of his entrance, after which the glorious voice filled the Metropolitan Opera House with unforgettable sound.

Noel Coward was one of the most successful actors, composers, and playwrights of our time. As an exponent of debonair wit and relaxed drawing-room comedy, he would seem an unlikely candidate for stage fright. Yet his autobiography describes an encounter with stage fright during the New York premiere of his own play, *The Vortex*.

> I paced up and down on a strip of coconut matting at the side of the stage and was told by the theatre fireman to put out my cigarette. At last it was near my time to go on, and I stood holding the door knob with a clammy hand, frowning in an effort to keep my face from twitching. My cue came and I made my entrance. There was a second's silence, and then a terrific burst of applause which seemed to me to last for ever. Fortunately the first thing I had to do was embrace Lilian [Braithwaite], which I did with such fervour that her bones cracked. The applause continued, and there we stood locked in each other's arms until I felt her give me a little reassuring pat on the back, and I broke out of the clinch and managed, in a strangulated voice, to speak my first line.[2]

Lauren Bacall has candidly commented about her stage fright in her delightful biography. Recalling the first day of shooting in *To Have and Have Not* with Humphrey Bogart, she remembered that:

> My hand was shaking—my head was shaking—the cigarette was shaking. The harder I tried to stop, the more I shook. . . . What must Bogart be thinking. . . . I was in such pain.[3]

---

2. Noel Coward, *Present Indicative* (New York: Doubleday, Doran and Co., Inc., 1937), p. 223.

3. Lauren Bacall, *Lauren Bacall By Myself* (New York: Ballantine Books, 1980), p. 123.

Even some time later her description of an overseas broadcast with Bing Crosby and Bob Hope brought on the same trembling.

> There was a large audience, and I remember Bing standing next to me with his arm lightly around my waist, knowing my nerves and letting me know he was there helping—and Bob Hope doing handstands in front of us.[4]

Other actors tell essentially the same tale. Eva Le Gallienne, upon being asked after her thousandth performance in repertory whether she had stage fright, replied, "Yes. And it gets worse every year." Yet audiences usually are not able to discern stage fright in the experienced actor. When all the excess energy is directed to the business at hand, the stage fright invariably disappears after the entrance on stage. Most stage fright occurs in the anticipation rather than in the execution of the performance. The very inexperienced actor, however, who is lacking in training or rehearsal time, may, on occasion, find that it will carry over to the performance. Lionel Barrymore has left us an amusing description of his first adventure on stage, in a minor role in Sheridan's comedy *The Rivals*.

> The horrible afternoon of my debut finally arrived and I was a wretched and frightened boy. . . . I crept on stage in an apathy of embarrassment and muttered my words like an automaton that needed the oil can. The scene was too much for me, as indeed, any scene would have been too much for me at that time.[5]

We find an interesting clue in Barrymore's remarks that "any scene would have been too much for me at that time." Certainly Barrymore's later performances belied the feebleness of his first efforts. The knowledge that he knew what he was doing kept his performances free of the chaos that marred his maiden effort. Although pre-performance jitters may not have disappeared entirely, once he stepped before an audience or camera his excess emotional energy was channeled in the proper direction. It is interesting to note that after two performances as Thomas in *The Rivals*, his scene was dropped from the production. Barrymore commented: "Since my debut, most performances of *The Rivals* have gone on without the front scene. I seem to have killed it for good, or perhaps directors have been worried lest I come back and play the part again."

---

4. Ibid., p. 185.
5. Lionel Barrymore, *We Barrymores* (New York: Appleton-Century-Crofts, Inc., 1951), p. 38.

What Can Be Done About It?

Must we accept stage fright as an inevitable outcome of public performance, or can we begin to do something about it? Many of the difficulties already described can be lessened to a considerable degree by four means: understanding, progression and experience, concentration, and making use of stage fright.

Understanding. In the preceding pages we have discussed the causes of stage fright as well as its extent. Understanding it is the first important step in dealing with stage fright. As long as it remains a baffling mystery and the actor believes that he or she is afflicted with it to a unique degree, there is little likelihood that progress can be made. But by understanding it the actor has already taken a great step forward; stage fright is no longer seen simply as a terrifying accompaniment to one's own performances but as a not unnatural reaction experienced by many who are truly accomplished actors.

Progression and Experience. Lionel Barrymore's early stage fright was due to inexperience and an inability to deal with a situation which at that time was overwhelming. Subsequent exposures to acting did not produce a repetition of this early difficulty. As he grew in experience and accustomed himself to difficult assignments, he was able to cope with the problem during performances. His great difficulty, in that first venture, was being asked to perform with a highly competent, professional company before a critical audience.

If the actor's experience can grow by degrees from relatively simple to complex stage assignments, the difficulty is usually eased. With this in mind, it should be easy to see that the exercises performed in acting class are an excellent means of exposing the problem in a relatively low-powered situation. As experience grows and the variety of roles increases, the actor discovers that stage fright during the performance becomes less and less of a problem.

Concentration. "If you are doing a good job of acting, you'll be too busy to worry about stage fright." This is one of the soundest maxims for the actor to learn. When the actor concentrates on the character and what he or she is doing, and on the projection of vitality and validity in the role, the engulfing emotion will not be the petty disturbances of fear and worry but a desire to do the best job possible. This does not necessarily mean that the actor must completely "live the role," but it does suggest that attention to the details of performance will leave no room for the entering wedge of stage fright.

In the discussion of concentration in Chapter 7, we noted that attention may be focused either on the details of the performance or on objects and other actors. The proper focusing of attention will serve to combat, if not entirely eliminate, stage fright during the stage performance. The busy actor simply will not have time for it.

Making Use of Stage Fright.   If we remember that the tensions and excitement that grip the actor are in part the body's means of preparing for a challenging situation, then it is clear that the person under tension is actually better equipped to handle the exacting demands of acting. Acting requires a tremendous output of energy. In helping the actor to meet the stringent requirements of public performance, the endocrine system is performing an important function. The excess energy is not wasted in the disorganized activity of stage fright, however, if it is applied by the actor to the demands of the performance. Without it, most performances would be lifeless and rather dull. With it, a merely competent performance can turn into an exciting and memorable one. The "case of nerves" that many great actors experience *before* each performance is turned to their advantage when they make their entrance and the extra energy is needed. Helen Hayes undergoes such nervousness before each performance. Yet in spite of it, or perhaps *because of it,* her acting is considered by many to be truly inspired, with a high level of consistency night after night.

The late American actor Richard Mansfield was acutely afflicted by stage fright, and opening nights particularly were hard on him. In his explanation, however, of why he refused to let it hamper him, we may see something of that unspoken determination that motivates all fine actors.

> The excitement of a first night is actual suffering; the nervousness actual torture. Yet as I walk . . . to the theatre . . . and note the impassive, imperturbable faces of the passersby, I must confess to myself that I would not change places with them—no, not for worlds. I have something that is filling my life brimful of interest. . . . It's like a battle. I shall win or die. . . .[6]

No matter how nervous the actor may be before or during a performance, the worst fears are seldom realized. This thought often sustains the actor in his or her worst moments. Yet sometimes more drastic measures than we have discussed are used to eliminate stage fright. On this point, we shall close with an anecdote often told about Alfred Hitchcock, the film director. During the filming of a sequence, a nervous actor kept muffing his lines. "Calm down," Hitchcock advised him, "Only your whole career depends on this scene."

---

6. Richard Mansfield, "The Story of a Production," *Harper's Weekly,* May 24, 1890, p. 408.

CHAPTER
TEN

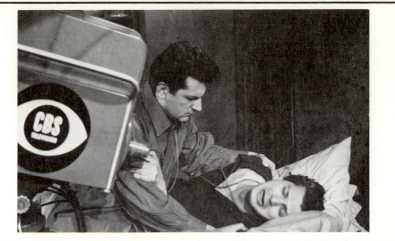

Television Acting

Television and film have become Everyman's theatre. Millions of people who have never seen a professional or amateur stage production are regularly exposed to a great variety of comic and dramatic programs. Television particularly includes soap operas, westerns, detective and spy programs, "sitcoms" (situation comedies), historical dramatization, long-running series extending over several years, mini-series, and one-shot specials. Many of the current stars of television have had equally successful careers in the theatre and film; still others have become famous through television alone.

In the early days of television, a variety of styles were evolved for broadcasting television programs. Since the early 1950s, however, film has played the major role in broadcast-television drama. With the development of videotape editing and easily portable recording units, greater diversity and speed in filming programs has become possible. The new tools have also helped to limit the ever-rising costs related to filming dramas.

Shooting the Television Drama

Today there are a large number of ways to "film" the television drama. To a great extent, television and cinema have become almost indistinguishable, and we must recognize their great similarity. Some distinctions, however, are worth looking at.

Single-Camera Filming.   Traditional movie-filming has utilized one camera, which makes it necessary to start and stop, shoot the drama out of sequence due to the availability of sets, and reshoot a scene several times until it is absolutely right. Much of the critical work in finally putting the program before the audience is the responsibility of the film editor, working long *after* the shooting of the scenes has actually taken place. This type of filming and editing permits attention to little details and the correction of any error, which is not possible in live television. Single-camera filming is also expensive and likely to be used only in a high-budget prestige television production.

Multi-Camera Filming.   More and more television programs have begun to use multi-camera shooting, a technique, incidentally, that was first used in the movies in order to ensure continuity and avoid "mismatches." By having more than one angle on a scene, it was possible to ensure against any later problems of showing the actor using the correct hand when picking up a book, having to show the *precise moment* when the actor put on a coat, or even more significantly, emotional mismatches, in which the level or intensity of a scene might vary from one shooting sequence to another.

Many television dramas today are shot on videotape, with all of the images of each video camera recorded, and the whole tape later edited by the editor and director. Some programs, particularly situation comedies, may be shot twice or three times through, with a multi-camera setup before a live audience in a single evening. Often a sequence will be shot from commercial to commercial, or through one entire setting. *All in the Family* (later *Archie Bunker's Place*) used this technique, which permits a high degree of spontaneity on the part of the performers and a freshness not always found in more carefully edited and repeated performances. Other comedies recorded on videotape have been shot without an audience, with up to four cameras each recording a short sequence. Each short sequence is repeated again and again, and the cast and crew do not go on to the next unit until the director is satisfied with the scene. Sometimes close to fifty hours of videotape will be shot in order to put together a single half-hour show.

Television and the Theatre

When we look at the demands placed upon the actor working in the television medium, we should note that certain factors differentiate the theatre and television. Most of all we must remember that television is seen and heard in the home, rather than in a theatre together with the members of an audience. Some of these general distinctions between a play in the theatre and a play on the picture tube lead to important considerations for the actor.

The Attention of the Audience Is Easily Diverted. This problem has required sweeping alterations in the structure, character development, and pacing of most television drama. In contrast to his or her behavior in the theatre, the member of the television audience may converse freely with those in the room; attention may be diverted by any number of distractions; and the viewer may change stations if dissatisfied with the play at any point. These circumstances lead to necessarily fast character development, a plot that is developed rapidly, and tension-packed situations which retain audience attention, usually at the expense of the more leisurely exposition found in the theatre.

The Audience Is Broken Down into Small Units or May Consist of One Person. At a play or in a movie theatre, many hundreds of people come together for the joint appreciation of the production. An individual cannot help being affected by the reactions of other people in the audience. Their laughter adds to the enjoyment of the comedy, and their tears will make tragedy more moving than it would have been had the person witnessed the play alone. This well-known psychological concept operates wherever large groups assemble. It ceases to be an important factor, however, in the transmission of drama to the home television audience which consists of relatively few people, often only one viewer.

In the early 1950s, the *I Love Lucy* sitcom dealt with this difficulty by putting recorded or "canned" laughter on the sound track in order to bring to the home viewer the illusion of being a member of a larger audience. The practice is still carried on today. This device not only permitted the use of comic timing similar to that used in the theatre but gave the home viewer a sense of audience participation. Today, those shows recorded before a live audience are able to deal with the problem of the isolated viewer by incorporating real audience response, although the laugh levels may still be monitored and adjusted by sound engineers for maximum effect.

The Audience Is Greater and More Diversified. Although the audience unit is smaller, the cumulative size of that audience is much greater than any attending a theatre or movie at one particular time. Only a few hundred people may attend the production of a new play, but several million can watch a television show in their homes. In addition, this home audience is not so selective in its tastes as the one that comes together in the theatre. The members of the theatre audience have attended by choice, because there is a specific play that they wish to see. This audience is united by a common interest even before the play begins. In any one home, and from one home to another, the television audience will be composed of individuals of varying ages, interests, and backgrounds. A television audience may include all the members of a family, ranging from the grandparents to the grandchildren, with each member having different program interests. Some may be habitual theatregoers with sophisticated tastes in the theatre, whereas others may never have attended a stage production and have no desire to do so.

Television Drama Is Usually Severely Restricted by Time. In the theatre, time becomes a crucial factor only when a drama begins to lose the attention of the audience. If a scene may profit from a slow and deliberate pace, the director and actors need not consider whether they will have sufficient time to finish the play. The televised play, however, is usually presented within a prescribed half-hour or hour period. The program must adhere exactly to its allotted time so that the next program, which the audience expects to be broadcast at a specific time, will begin as scheduled. Programs are also broken up into segments of fifteen or twenty minutes or less, separated by numerous announcements and commercials which tend to destroy continuity. With the recent expansion of ''pay cable,'' we may be seeing some changes in these traditional practices.

The Audience Sees the Actor Differently. In addition to the general differences just noted, there are unique problems for the actor. In the theatre an audience will view the performance from one fixed position, and the production is planned to make the action and dialogue meaningful for the stationary spectator. In television, the viewer sees the production through the eyes of many cameras, which are mobile. Thus the audience views the actor not only in a variety of positions but also in different sizes—in a long shot, medium shot, or closeup. Furthermore, the camera may move about the playing area during the production, creating differences in composition, balance, and emphasis without any need for the actor to make such changes.

Television Acting

Working before the camera, whether it be a multi-camera, multi-tapedeck, or a single camera, requires major mental and physical reorientation by the actor. Warren Beatty recalls his disappointment upon seeing his early films, and comments:

I realized that if I had done the same parts on the stage I would have had the opportunity to come back and do them again, in a better way, trying to find new meanings in them.[1]

The actor's ability to get the most out of the filmed performance, which can never be repeated again, requires an acute awareness of his or her instrument and the way it can most effectively be used in each medium. Nevertheless, the sensitive actor should be able to function successfully in both media. Bruce Dern is quite precise on this point:

> People who work in one medium to the exclusion of the other are going to have trouble making the adjustment. But if they're really good actors, they can survive it. The bottom line is that if you're good, you're good.[2]

It will be useful to examine some of the problems unique to television acting, from both the standpoint of multi- and single-camera work.

The Actor As a Unit

During a production the audience views the actor from various distances and angles. Most of this variety is achieved by the movement and refocusing of the television camera, all carefully planned by the director.

The actor is seen within the frame of the television screen. The television director usually works within a range of certain types of shots in relation to the actor's body. The most important of these are:

1. Extreme closeup
2. Closeup
3. Medium closeup
4. Shoulder shot
5. Full figure
6. Two-shot
7. Small group
8. Larger group

Additionally the camera may pan around a group, zoom in and out of a closeup, and constantly change the relationship of the actor to the frame in which the actor is appearing. It is important, therefore, that the actor accept the fact that he or she is one unit in a coordinated production scheme that

---

1. Warren Beatty, quoted in Lillian Ross and Helen Ross, *The Player: A Profile of an Art* (New York: Simon and Schuster, 1962), p. 192.
2. Bruce Dern, quoted in Joanmarie Kalter, *Actors on Acting* (New York: Sterling Publishing Co., Inc., 1979), p. 191.

FIGURE 10.1a Camera shots:
Extreme closeup.

includes the actor, camera, microphone, and lights, each carefully manipu-
lated by the director according to a preset plan. The intricacy of this coor-
dination will probably be greater than any the actor has experienced in the
theatre. Just as each unit must be in a specific place at a certain time, so too
the actor must accept stage movement and position as fixed elements in the
total design of the composition and organization of a scene.

Hitting the Mark.   In order to preset the location and movement of the actor
and equipment, positions are often carefully marked on the floor of the
studio. This procedure is almost universally followed during the rehearsal
period, when chalk marks are used to define the actor's exact position. It is

FIGURE 10.1b   Camera shots: Closeup.

FIGURE 10.1c Camera shots: Medium closeup.

imperative during rehearsals, and later during performance, particularly if it is a through take, as in multi-camera tapings, that when these marks may no longer be visible, the actor find the predetermined position. The slightest error off the mark will seriously disturb the planned effect of a scene. Television lighting is keyed to a certain spot on the studio floor, and if the actor is off the mark, the facial lighting may significantly alter the effect intended by the director and lighting designer. Furthermore, at no time should the audience ever get the impression that the actor is groping for the right position. The actor must work to make these exact movements as naturally as possible.

FIGURE 10.1d Camera shots: Shoulder shot.

FIGURE 10.1e Camera shots: Full figure.

Extraneous Stage Movement. The relative freedom of the theatre does not exist in television. Once the actor has hit the mark, it is necessary to remain fixed in the position without making any extraneous movement. This requires a high degree of control and restraint. After the exact position has been taken, any unspecified movement during certain camera shots, as in a closeup, may completely unbalance the prescribed emphasis of the scene, if not actually remove the actor from the picture. Sometimes such demands may call for strangely unorthodox techniques. Hume Cronyn, the versatile stage and film actor, faced just such an experience during his early career when working in a film sequence. He reported:

FIGURE 10.1f Camera shots: Two shot.

FIGURE 10.1g Camera shots: Four shot (small group).

A move which would be utterly false on stage, which goes directly against every reasonable impulse, may be camera-wise effective and necessary . . . During the meal, I said something upsetting to the character played by Teresa Wright. She turned to me with unexpected violence. I stood up in embarrassment and surprise and automatically took a step backward. However, at the point of the rise, the camera moved in to hold us in a close two-shot, and to accommodate it—that is, to stay in the frame—it became necessary for me to change that instinctive movement so that when I got up from the chair, *I took a step toward the person from whom I was retreating.* . . . I was convinced that the action would look idiotic on the screen, but I was

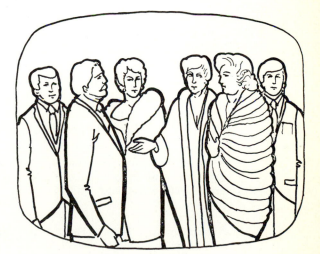

FIGURE 10.1h Camera shots: Group (larger group).

wrong. . . . I had to admit that the occasion passed almost unnoticed even by me.[3]

It is possible that a position assumed by the actor, as when playing in a two-character closeup, may seem uncomfortable and awkward, but the consideration of comfort must be disregarded in these sequences. Awkwardness is relative to the audience's view of the characters, as Hume Cronyn has clearly illustrated. It is the actor's responsibility to avoid any movement during performance, no matter how slight, that has not been previously planned and approved.

Playing Alone

In single-camera shooting, it is not unusual for the actor to be playing a scene alone, although he or she is supposedly speaking to another character. Scenes frequently begin or end with two characters in conversation, but only one character may actually be within the setting, being filmed or taped. The second character may be making a change of costume or moving to or from an adjacent setting. The camera, in closeup, will show only the character speaking, and the audience will naturally assume that the other character is present and listening. Solo work of this kind requires that the actor use a great deal of imagination to make these sequences convincing.

Subtlety and Intimacy

Although staging techniques are generally alike in television and the theatre, the intimacy of television imposes a number of modifications on the actor's projection of a role. Television acting most resembles central-stage acting, in which the same problems of intimacy and multiple focus are brought to the fore. After having worked in productions utilizing central staging, the actor will discover that the "level" of playing is much more similar to that required in television. If the actor's experience has been solely in large proscenium theatres, the necessary alterations will be somewhat more extensive. Bruce Dern reminds us again that in the theatre

you can be flamboyant, you can take off in different directions, you can hide certain faults, and yet you can't do that in film [and television] because the camera picks up *everything*.[4]

---

3. Hume Cronyn, "Notes on Film Acting," *Theatre Arts*, June 1949, p. 46.
4. Bruce Dern, quoted in Kalter, op. cit., p. 191.

The skills that the actor can transfer to television from experience in a relatively large theatre are proficient memorization of dialogue, imaginative analysis and development of character, and the sustaining of a role physically and vocally throughout a performance. Transposing a stage characterization directly to television, however, without modifications, is likely to make the actor appear inadequate. Such difficulties are usually caused by a misunderstanding of the nature of the medium.

Any observation of the silent films made during the formative years of cinema technique should prove highly instructive. In their early efforts the film pioneers used all the devices of the contemporary theatre. They were unaware that the new medium required a style and technique of its own. If we could watch a succession of films representative of succeeding decades, paying special attention to the acting, we would be aware of a decided change, a definite trend through the years toward naturalism in the performances. This change was fostered not by any notable trends in the theatre but by a growing understanding of the subtlety of the screen. The advent of sound in the late 1920s made further demands for subtlety in film acting. Since the cinema and television have much in common, the television industry has learned much from cinema techniques and experimentation. As a result, the development of fundamental techniques has been less prolonged and haphazard than the development of film techniques.

The ensuing comments about the use of the voice and body in television are directly concerned with the demands of subtlety and intimacy inherent in the television medium. One point should be emphasized at once. *The audience sits no more than five to ten feet away from the actor during a performance.* If this fact is kept in mind, much of what we shall discover about television acting will fall logically into place.

Subtlety in Vocal Acting

One of the common pitfalls that beset the actor in television is overemphasis. On the stage, confronted with the problem of projection over a considerable distance, the actor must be conscious of volume, clarity, and proper body position. Key lines or phrases must be carefully pointed and emphasized so that important information is not lost by the audience, even in the last row of the auditorium. Such delivery in television, magnified even further by the microphone, will seem grotesque and distorted, not at all suited to the intimate nature of the medium. The recognition of this principle has developed, in both the film and television, a manner of line reading and projection distinct from that used on the stage.

The most discernible element in this new style of reading dramatic dialogue is the attempt to suggest naturalness of expression. Although television drama is not entirely restricted to the realistic play, this type is prevalent—probably because the medium can best accommodate it. Plays

299

that were conceived in a nonrealistic mode have been conspicuously absent from the television screen, and when they are produced, as in the case of Shakespeare, they are drastically altered in playing style.

One of the most memorable film productions of one of Shakespeare's plays was Laurence Olivier's production of *Hamlet,* in which there was a unique treatment of the great soliloquies. The soliloquy is far removed from the naturalistic concept of drama, but in the film these speeches were superpersonalized to the point where Hamlet's lips did not move at all, the words simply being heard on the sound track as the camera seemed to scan the mind of the young prince. The same techniques are being used and refined in the BBC series of all of Shakespeare's plays, which began airing in the United States in 1978.

This is good cinematographic technique but hardly compatible with stage speech. This device has been carried over to television productions as well, and although some may object to it from an aesthetic standpoint, it clearly takes advantage of the great intimacy of the medium. What, indeed, could be *more* intimate than lodging ourselves in the secret compartments of the character's mind and intruding on his or her thoughts? This example is but one illustration of how the intimacy of the television medium has brought about new means of naturalizing standard theatre procedure.

In deciding on the proper means of modifying stage speech for television, two rules should be observed:

1. The low projection level used in radio is appropriate for television acting as well. Although the actor in television is not able to take the optimum microphone position as in radio, members of the studio crew will see to it that the microphone is no more than a few inches away from the actor, in a good pickup position, and out of the view of the television camera. (See the discussion of projection for radio acting in Chapter 11, all of which applies to television.)
2. The style of reading will be dictated by the style of the play; thus no one style of reading should be arbitrarily suggested. However, as a general rule, except when working in period plays which require a particular style of expression, the actor should adopt a conversational style of delivery.

Subtlety in Physical Acting

The intimacy of television calls for naturalness in bodily action. Two factors of proximity urge upon the actor important modifications of physical projection associated with the stage. These are the *proximity of the audience* and the *proximity of other actors.*

We have already indicated that the *proximity of the audience* is an essential consideration in all television work. The restraint needed to tone down the projection of physical action is derived from the same conditions of intimacy that bring about the lowered level of vocal projection. When the audience is no longer situated several hundred feet from the actor, the codified system of physical expression normally used on stage must give way to a style that is more intimate and simplified.

The actor in a television production often works only inches away from other actors. Whenever two or more characters are involved in any one scene, the dimensions of the television screen make it essential that they perform in close proximity. Working so closely with other actors prevents the use of expansive gestures and broadly conceived pieces of business. It requires close attention to details and subtle physical shadings to make the same point one would make broadly in the theatre. Lynn Redgrave reminds us that

> You have to have figured out your blocking, of course, you have to know where you're going to sit, where you're going to stand, where the director wants you, where the lighting man needs you to be, your mark, all those technical things.[5]

Leslie Howard once humorously remarked that such closeups in film, in which actors had to watch their positions, attend to details, and avoid casting shadows on other actors, accounted for the apparently alarming number of cross-eyed actors seen on the screen.

It would be erroneous to conclude that proximity forces the actor to be static, expressionless, and wooden. Expressiveness is extremely important and is most effective in television in a form we have not hitherto discussed.

Because the screen is relatively small, television is compelled to make extensive use of the closeup—in fact, even greater use than does the cinema. Such closeups provide the actor with an unusual opportunity to act "from the neck up." It means that the competent television actor should have a face that is flexible, sensitive, and above all, expressive. Here is the real key to expressiveness in television acting, but, in keeping with the requirements of subtlety and intimacy, facial expression must be handled with finesse. The smallest quivering of a lip in anger, the raising of an eyebrow in surprise, will be as meaningful in television as an expansive and broadly defined gesture or action is on stage. A little facial acting in television is capable of transmitting a great deal. Hume Cronyn has noted:

> In a "close-up" very little becomes much; a whole new range of expression is opened up to the actor . . . a glance, a contraction of a muscle in a manner that would be lost on stage. The camera will often reflect what a man thinks, without the degree of demonstration required in the theatre.[6]

---

5. Lynn Redgrave, quoted in Kalter, op. cit., p. 82.
6. Hume Cronyn, op. cit., p. 46.

Although facial expression is capable of suggesting essential facets of a characterization when used with taste and restraint, the danger exists that if it is not under perfect control it may seriously distort or hamper the actor's performance. Many of us are guilty of little idiosyncracies that go almost unnoticed by friends who are accustomed to seeing us daily. We are seldom aware of these habits and often surprised when they are brought to our attention. Such minor habits, exaggerated in a closeup and seemingly part of our characterization, will be detrimental to the performance. All distracting facial mannerisms should be eliminated if the actor hopes to work successfully in television drama. Common habits of this type include biting the lips, frowning, furrowing the forehead, blinking the eyes, tightening the mouth, and so on.

The power of television to convey even the most subtle emotional responses or "subtext" is so apparent that many politicians, including presidents of the United States, have videotaped their "spontaneous" talks before making the actual live delivery, in order to eliminate unwanted emphases in certain spots or any nervous mannerisms. Self-scrutiny and daily work in front of a mirror by the performer will help to reveal unsuspected habits. Such practice will not only aid in eliminating some of these distracting facial mannerisms but should also help the actor appraise his or her ability to communicate meaningfully by the face alone.

Action and Reaction

An expressive face is nowhere more effective than when it serves to comment on a scene by a series of carefully planned *reactions*. The cinema and television have developed a potent means of heightening the development of a scene by focusing attention on reactions rather than on actions. An effective device often used in a scene between two or more characters is to show not the character who is speaking but to film a closeup of the reactions of the listener or listeners. The following brief scene will illustrate how this principle can make the action of a scene more vivid by focusing on the characters' reactions. Let us take a sequence from a hypothetical mystery drama in which five persons, one of them a detective, are seated around a table. The detective knows that one of the other four in the room is guilty of murder. We will assume the scene is being shot on videotape with multiple cameras. The scene might be handled in the following manner:

Dialogue	Camera
DETECTIVE BARNES: Very well, we're not leaving this room until I discover which one of you turned the trick. You all had a motive and the opportunity, but the question is, which one of you got to him first?	*(A pan shot of entire group, moving finally to Barnes.)*

Dialogue	Camera
Was it you, John Flush?—He cheated you out of $50,000, you couldn't forgive him for that, could you?	(*Closeup of Barnes, as he points his finger at each suspect.*)
Or was it you, Hubert Hiebert? He knew a good deal about your illegal gambling operation. He was blackmailing you, wasn't he?	
And you, Claire Voyent, what was your motive? Jealousy? Perhaps his papers will tell the story.	
You needn't look so satisfied, Lord Upjohn, I'm just getting to you. There is a good deal in his diary you would like to get your hands on, isn't there?	
Well, we'll just sit here all night until one of you cracks.	(*Long shot of entire group.*)

Now, this not uncommon scene from any typical crime melodrama might be handled with the camera shots indicated above. They encompass the entire action of the scene and help propel the story forward. Yet this is not the most effective use of the camera in telling the story. Imaginative camera work on reactions would be more to the point and be of greater value in carrying along the action and heightening the suspense. Let us examine the scene again with a different set of camera directions.

Dialogue	Camera
DETECTIVE BARNES: Very well, we're not leaving this room until I discover which one of you turned the trick. You all had a motive and the opportunity, but the question is, which one of you got to him first?	(*A pan shot of entire group, moving finally to closeup of Barnes.*)
Was it you, John Flush?—He cheated you out of $50,000, you couldn't forgive him for that, could you?	(*Closeup of Flush nervously rubbing his chin.*)
Or was it you, Hubert Hiebert? He knew a good deal about your illegal gambling operation. He was blackmailing you, wasn't he?	(*Closeup of Hiebert mopping his perspiring brow.*)
And you, Claire Voyent, what was your motive? Jealousy? Perhaps his papers will tell the story.	(*Closeup of Voyent, coolly manicuring her nails.*)
You needn't look so satisfied, Lord Upjohn, I'm just getting to you. There is a good deal in his diary you would like to get your hands on, isn't there?	(*Closeup of Upjohn, hastily swallowing an aspirin tablet.*)

Dialogue	Camera
Well, we'll just sit here all night until one of you cracks.	(*Long shot of entire group.*)

This scene is certainly somewhat exaggerated, but the point should be clear. Reaction to the dialogue by each character is more meaningful than the action of the individual who is speaking. All the characters are acting during the sequence, in the television sense of reacting, as the camera searches out each character in turn.

Critic Dudley Nichols holds strongly to the concept that *reaction* is the key to all successful acting before the camera. His reference in the following comment is to the cinema and specifically to sequences from *In Which We Serve,* directed by Noel Coward and David Lean, but it is also directly applicable to television acting.

> At any emotional crisis of a film, when a character is saying something which profoundly affects another, it is to this second character that the camera instinctively roves, perhaps in close-up . . . If anyone doubts this let him study his own emotions when viewing a good film; . . . I recently did this with some lay friends after a showing of Noel Coward's *In Which We Serve,* and it was illuminating to find out that they had been most deeply moved by reactions, almost never by actions: the figure of a woman who gets news her husband has been lost at sea, the face of an officer when told his wife has died. . . . In the same film one of the most affecting scenes was the final one where the captain bids good-bye to the remainder of his crew; and while this appears to be action, the camera shrewdly presented it as reaction: It is the faces of the men, as they file past, that we watch, reaction to the whole experience even in their laconic voices and in the weary figure of the captain.[7]

The foregoing illustrations relating reaction to action are indicative of this most important distinction concerning television acting. The actor experienced only in the theatre correctly holds that although reaction is important, it is the projection of the action that is his or her dominant responsibility on stage. Something of an about-face is required to accept reaction as an equal if not superior means of communicating to a television audience.

Reviewing the Rules

It will be helpful to review the most important modifications imposed upon the actor by television. Although each of these rules may be broken in certain circumstances, they are the important operating principles that should guide the actor when making the transition from theatre to television acting:

---

7. Dudley Nichols, ''The Writer and the Film,'' in *Twenty Best Film Plays,* eds. John Gassner and Dudley Nichols (New York: Crown Publishers, Inc., 1943), pp. xxxiii–xxxiv.

1. Accept movement and position as an element to be coordinated with lights, camera, and microphone.
2. Be sure to hit the marked position preset during rehearsals.
3. Avoid all extraneous movement.
4. Do not look at the camera unless ordered to do so by the director.
5. Adopt a conversational level and style for line reading.
6. Keep planned business and movement simple and keyed to the intimate nature of television.
7. Do not overlook the importance of the face in expressing emotions.
8. Reaction to the events of the drama is frequently more important than executing the business or action of the play.

EXERCISES

1. Watch any half-hour program, filmed specifically for television. Count the number of closeups used during the program. Watch a telecast of a movie originally produced for showing in a large theatre. Count the number of closeups used during a half-hour segment. Compare your results.
2. Use a videotape recorder. If this is not available, work with a mirror. React facially to each of the following situations for a closeup and for a long shot. Note the differences required for each.
   (a) You *see* the following and then react: (1) a spider crawling up your arm, (2) a building on fire, (3) a new automobile given to you as a gift, (4) an automobile accident, and (5) a gun pointed at you by a madman.
   (b) You *hear* the following and then react: (1) a loud scream in the next room, (2) a long and boring speech, (3) a falling bomb coming nearer and nearer, and (4) someone sneaking up behind you.
   (c) You *touch* the following and then react: (1) a slimy snake, (2) a hot stove, (3) a broken heirloom, and (4) a mink coat.
3. Perform each of the exercises above before the class and ask them to identify each facial expression in turn.
4. Invent three facial reactions of your own for *sight, sound,* and *touch.* Perform them before the class and have the class try to identify them as closely as possible.
5. Choose any of the monologues from the exercise section in Chapter 1. Perform them *seated,* without any movement, as if in a closeup for television. Use the conversational and projection level required for a television closeup. Using a videotape recorder, record the monologue. If one is not available, perform the monologue live before the class. Have the class evaluate your performance in terms of a televised closeup. Compare it to the same selection prepared for a stage production.
6. Choose any three improvisations, including character, locale, and situation, listed in Chapter 3, *Using Improvisation.* Adapt them for use in a television production. Explain after each improvisation how you adapted them for television production and how they differ from an improvisation designed to be viewed on stage.

CHAPTER ELEVEN

Radio Acting

Not too many years ago it seemed as if radio drama had disappeared completely from the American commercial-broadcasting scene. With the rapid development of television during the 1950s and 1960s, radio, which had been the dominant form of commercial home entertainment for over thirty years, was reduced primarily to transmitting news and different varieties of music. However, during the past few years there were signs of a resurgence of interest in, and production of, radio drama. Regular production of original scripts by the "Mutual Radio Theater," "CBS Radio Mystery Theater," and other series that broadcast adaptations of classic works pointed to a renewed interest in radio as a medium for dramatic activity. Radio drama still thrives in colleges and universities and in the broadcast programming of other English-speaking nations, particularly Canada and the United Kingdom.

Whether or not we shall see a total revival of professional American radio drama is a moot question. One point is unmistakably clear: radio acting is an exciting and stimulating experience. This chapter will explore the basic techniques that must be utilized by the actor in order to function effectively in radio drama. This chapter is not complete in itself. Rather it is built upon the groundwork laid in the earlier chapters. Acting is acting, and the fundamental rules of imagination, good vocal habits, and the three V's of good acting are as applicable to radio as they are to theatre. We shall examine here how theatre techniques need to be adjusted for radio acting and also discuss the few additional problems peculiar to this medium.

Radio Drama

Many differences, discernible even to the most casual observer, distinguish the radio play from the stage drama. The most obvious difference is that although we only hear radio drama, we both see and hear the stage play. From this difference stems a series of distinctions that clearly separate the two forms. We need only close our eyes during the performance of a stage play to realize that the elimination of sight alone does not make radio drama. If we were to make such an experiment, we would miss many details of the plot and characterization, and for long stretches the play would be meaningless.

Because radio must depend solely on sound, certain conventions have developed to make radio drama meaningful without dependence on sight. No settings can be used to suggest locale, there is no lighting to develop mood or to enhance the production, and there are no costumes or makeup to help the actor project age or character. The actor simply stands in front of a microphone with script in hand, and, with the aid of a narrator, some sound effects, and music, must be able to suggest all the elements that in the theatre are presented by more literal means.

Such differences do not really constitute any great disadvantage for radio drama. It possesses a great degree of flexibility, not being restricted to specific stage settings, to a limited number of scenes, or to the physical confines of the stage itself. It may achieve effects impossible to match in the theatre. It is able to create from the merest suggestion a setting more intricate and exciting than can be duplicated on any stage.

The same element of suggestion applies equally to the actor. The radio audience will create its own image of a character entirely by what he or she says, by what others say about the character, and by the sound of the person's voice. Other physical qualities are of no importance to the actor in radio. The rich, resonant voice will suggest a character of stature and strength; the thin, sharp voice will suggest a person of relatively small size or strength. Such vocal characteristics may bear absolutely no relation to the physical identity of the actor. One interesting illustration of this phenomenon is the common practice of having women play small boys in radio dramas. The actor who would be quite believable as a certain character in the theatre with the aid of costume and makeup might present a totally unsatisfactory characterization on radio. Obviously the reverse will be true as well. Such firmly held theatre notions as physical typecasting naturally need revision in the context of radio drama.

The most important quality of radio drama is its great potential to stimulate the imagination of the audience. The sound of chirping birds becomes a forest in the springtime; the honking of a few automobile horns suggests a busy street in a large metropolitan area. Music will create a variety of moods: it can prepare the setting for a scene, comment on it as it proceeds, or punctuate it when it is over. So, too, the imagination of the listener will be stimulated by the actor's voice, by a change in inflection, or by the insertion of a meaningful pause. Most actors find radio drama not only simpler than working in the theatre but actually more concentrated in its requirements. It is an exhilarating challenge for the actor to direct his or her energies to the communication of a role within the scope of the voice alone.

Radio Production

Because of the factors that differentiate radio and theatre—the home audience, the aural nature of radio, and the limitations imposed by a restriction in playing time—a number of alterations in the form of the drama are necessary for broadcast purposes.

There is an unwritten rule in radio drama that the attention of the audience must be secured in the first minute or else it will be lost entirely. To this end material is compressed so that all extraneous elements are eliminated. The locale of the drama is established immediately by the use of a narrator or sound effects. Listening to E. G. Marshall as he opened the "CBS Radio Mystery Theatre" with an eerie "Good evening," followed by a creaking door and a brief excerpt from the drama, also indicates how an audience is put into a certain mood at the very outset of an approximately hour-long radio play.

Additional details suggestive of the setting or mood may be integrated within the program during the progression of the plot, but only if they do not interfere with the main thread of the story. Subplots or secondary story lines are rare in radio drama. They tend to be confusing, and time usually does not permit the development of more than one basic plot.

The actor will find that it is necessary to establish the character quickly, with little emphasis on subtleties and no more than basic variations of personality. Because long speeches and scenes cannot be diversified by movement, scenes are usually comparatively short, and passages of dialogue condensed.

These differences in style and organization of material may be reflected in the physical apparatus of the medium. Radio offers a distinctive set of working conditions within which the actor must function, and it is helpful to understand their relation to the creative process. We shall deal briefly with these now.

Studios and Microphones

The studio in which the radio drama is produced is radically different from the theatre used in play production or the television and film studio. In the early days of radio, experiments were made in broadcasting actual performances in the theatre. Insurmountable problems arose regarding not only microphone placement and acoustics but also the confusion of the broadcast audience because of radio's inability to transmit visual action. Today the Saturday afternoon broadcasts of the Metropolitan Opera Company during its winter season represent the only continuing effort to broadcast live "drama" from the theatre. The radio drama is now rehearsed, produced, and transmitted from modern studios especially equipped for this purpose.

Radio studios usually vary in size, depending on their specific function. The small studio is used for interviews, discussions, news broadcasts, and announcements of various kinds. The larger studio is devoted to broadcasts involving large pieces of equipment and sound effects, musical instruments, or a substantial number of people. Studios are so arranged and located that they are isolated from any extraneous and unwanted noise which might intrude during the broadcast. Careful attention is paid to the acoustical design of the studio in order to condition the sound before it actually goes out over the air.

One of the problems of studio design is reverberation. When there is a good deal of reverberation (that is, when a sound is still being reflected by the surface of the studio after the next sound is produced), we are likely to hear an effect that may be described as hollow, not unlike an echo. This can be very disturbing, if not actually confusing. Reverberation may be found in an extremely "live" studio, whereas no reverberation exists in a "dead" studio. For use in producing radio drama, the dead studio is more desirable. There are occasions when a certain amount of reverberation will be required to suggest a large chamber, a tunnel, a tomb, or certain ethereal effects. Such effects may be produced electronically, but many studios are equipped with drapes and movable panels permitting adjustments to be made in the acoustics.

The most important piece of equipment to be found in the studio is the microphone. Around this impersonal instrument the actors congregate in order to project their characterizations to the unseen audience. The function of the microphone is to convert the mechanical energy of the voice, music, or sound effect into electrical energy.

The microphones used in the studio may vary in the means by which they are mounted and in their pickup pattern. Microphones may be mounted (1) on a desk stand, (2) on a floor stand, or (3) on an overhead boom. Of the three mountings, the microphone on the desk stand is least likely to be used in radio drama. The microphone mounted on a floor stand will require the actor to hold the script in hand. The microphone on a boom is occasionally used with a reading stand that holds the actor's script.

In addition to their mounting and placement in the studio, microphones may be differentiated by the directional pattern of the sound they are able to receive. *Nondirectional* microphones will pick up sound equally from all directions. *Bidirectional* microphones are live on two opposite sides. Thus they are very useful for radio drama; it is relatively simple to achieve the effect of dimension in depth when the actor moves slightly "off mike." This type of microphone is the most likely to be encountered by the radio actor. *Unidirectional* microphones are live on only one side, shutting sound off from other directions. They are useful in suppressing unwanted sound such as the noise of a studio audience. *All-purpose microphones* can be adjusted to provide a variety of directional characteristics, including those described above.

Filter microphones are used to create a special effect, such as a voice speaking over a telephone. The filter microphone causes the voice to sound thin and somewhat distorted by eliminating certain frequencies that help to give the voice its distinctive quality.

Studio microphones should be used with care because they are expensive and highly sensitive to dust, loud noises, and sudden changes in air pressure. More than one good microphone has been ruined by a well-meaning actor blowing into it and then yelling, "Testing!"

Sound Effects

Some studios contain a certain amount of equipment that resembles a disorganized accumulation of junk. This is the collection of manual sound effects. When we remember that sound alone is the basic ingredient of radio, it should not be difficult to understand how a pair of coconut shells tapped on a hard surface suggest a galloping horse. Dried peas rattled in a pan will suggest a hail storm; crinkled cellophane will give the impression of a four-alarm fire. Other sound effects may be produced in the studio by records played on a sound console. This instrument has a number of turntables mounted on a wooden frame and is usually mobile. Here the sound engineer may play background or bridge music, or recordings of sound effects too difficult to achieve by manual means. Sound effects, which add immeasurably to the production of the radio drama, are produced by a specialist trained in their use, thus permitting the actor to devote full attention to projection of the character.

Microphone Techniques

Acting in front of a microphone rather than before an audience is usually the most important adjustment that the actor must make when performing in radio. The microphone must be used properly in order to realize optimum success with the characterization. Actually good microphone technique is relatively simple to achieve and requires few real adjustments for the actor trained in the techniques of the theatre.

Because most radio productions today use the bidirectional microphone (one that is live on two sides), our ensuing comments will be most directly related to this type.

Establishing the Proper Position

The director and audio engineer are best able to determine, on the basis of the pickup pattern of the microphone, the acoustical design of the studio, and each actor's vocal quality, the position of the actor in front of the microphone. Under normal conditions the actor should stand twelve to eighteen inches from the microphone. From this position—known as the *on-mike* position—words will be transmitted with the greatest effectiveness. An *on-mike* position, then, places the actor at the proper distance and *on the beam* with the microphone. *On the beam* means that the actor is on a straight line with the live portion of the microphone, no matter what the distance happens to be.

It is important to remember, however, that the distance from the microphone may be dictated by the vocal characteristics of other actors. The engineer can use only one control to balance the voices of two or more actors sharing one microphone. When an actor has a voice weaker or stronger than his or her partner's, adjustments may be made by having one of the two stand nearer to or farther away from the microphone. It is essential that, once the proper balance is established for work in a scene with another actor (and no acoustical changes are planned), the preset position be maintained throughout the entire scene. If the actor weaves back and forth before the microphone or shifts weight from foot to foot, the microphone will pick up the voice at rising and falling volume levels. This proves to be most distracting for any audience. There are, of course, a few notable exceptions to this rule, the most signficant being deliberate changes in aural perspective, which we will now consider.

Altering the Position

The actor *on-mike* may be compared to the actor in the theatre standing full front in the stage-center position. The audience will focus its attention on the actor in this, the most dominant position. Any movement away from the microphone, or to an *off-mike* position, results in the creation of depth and perspective. For instance an actor saying, ''I am leaving now,'' would read the line while moving away from the microphone. Such movement in relation to the microphone provides depth, which in the theatre finds its parallel in composition and stage movement.

Four fundamental positions and movements in relation to the microphone are used in radio acting: *on-mike*, with the actor twelve to eighteen inches from the microphone and on the beam, is the most common microphone position; the audience is oriented so that they feel as if they are ''with the actor.'' In the *off-mike* position, the actor is usually about eight to ten feet from the microphone, either on the beam or in a dead area, depending upon the sense of perspective and distance required. In a scene in which one character calls to another in the next room, the audience would be with the character on-mike, and the reply, from the next room, would come from off-mike. *Fading in* involves moving from an off-mike to an on-mike position while speaking. It is used primarily for making entrances; the parallel to the actor making an entrance in the theatre is obvious. *Fading off* is the opposite of fading in; the actor moves from an on-mike to an off-mike position.

Projection

The best voice level for radio performance is that used in everyday conversation. The difficulties in projection are exactly the reverse of those we find in the theatre. It is not uncommon for actors new to radio to project at the same level they would use in a large auditorium. This may not be merely a carryover of good theatre habits; many radio projection problems are caused by a consciousness of listeners located at a considerable distance from the studio—just as the person making a long-distance telephone call tends to shout in order to be heard over the distance.

The volume level required in radio acting, then, is considerably less than that used in the theatre, both in proscenium and in central staging. When on-mike the actor need not use a level greater than that which will permit the voice to be heard by another actor five or six feet away. Certain practical reasons necessitate this normal projection level. When the projection level is too high, the engineer at the control board will have to ''ride the gain'' carefully, often keeping the gain level extremely low. Such riding will have a deleterious effect on the quality of the voice, eliminating much of its tone coloring and causing it to sound flat. In addition, the conversational level will permit the actor to make use of nuances and shades of meaning not always possible in a large theatre. As the radio playwright and director Arch Oboler has pointed out:

> Where the very mechanics of the theatre make it necessary to project one's voice sufficiently to be heard in the last row, in the medium of radio every listener is standing right before the actor and there must be an under-emphasis in both the coloring and the projection of speech. There . . . is the basic prerogative of acting for the radio medium: the continued recognition of the fact that one is performing in an intimate medium to an audience of one whose loudspeaker is as close to you as you are to the microphone.[1]

Scenes that involve a highly emotional outburst or debate and argument pose special problems. The needs of the radio medium are best served if the actor can increase the level of intensity and vitality instead of raising the volume level. If increased volume cannot be avoided, as in shouts and screams, the actor should move in a diagonal line away from the microphone to a position that is both off-mike and off the beam. Aside from deliberate changes in depth, this is the major exception to the rule regarding the maintenance of the preset position at all times.

Microphone Behavior

Because of the demands for silence, order, and split-second timing in the studio during performance, the following procedure should be followed in a radio production. The actor should:

1. remain seated when not in a scene;
2. follow the script carefully until his or her scene arrives;
3. move into position about five lines before the first speech;
4. be careful not to rattle the chair when rising;
5. never pass between the microphone and an actor involved in a scene;
6. remain in the preset position during the entire scene (except for movements demanded by microphone technique);
7. remain in position after finishing speaking, as long as there are lines directed to the actor in the scene;
8. sit down again when the actor's scene is finished;
9. refrain from handling any of the equipment, especially the microphone;
10. *be absolutely quiet when not reading in the play.*

---

1. Arch Oboler, *This Freedom* (New York: Random House, 1942), pp. xiv–xv.

Working with a Script

Unlike the stage performer, the radio actor is closely bound to the printed script during an actual performance. The actor accustomed to working only in the environment of the theatre must not let the script prove to be an impediment. The beginning actor often assumes that it is not permitted to divert attention from the script at any time during the performance. This is not quite true. Actually, the radio actor must focus alternately on the script, the microphone, and the director. Indeed, it is essential that the actor keep an eye on the control room in order to receive all directions relating to his or her performance.

Marking the Script

Because the rehearsal period for a radio drama is considerably shorter than that for a stage play, the director and a carefully marked script are the constant aids upon which the actor must rely during a performance. Just as a good memory is a requisite of the successful actor in the theatre, a well-marked script is the hallmark of the intelligent radio actor. Arch Oboler strongly holds this view:

> The definite indication of an amateur actor, to a director, is to see a script page which, after hours of rehearsal, is as free of notations as a blank check. Every possible marking should be used as a sign-post to a good performance.[2]

The actor should mark the script with all the pertinent instructions given by the director during the rehearsal period. These notes will be of incalculable value in helping to execute the intent of the director as closely as possible during performance. The actor should guard against missed cues by circling the name of the character in the margin whenever he or she has a speech. This is the radio actor's substitute for memorized cues in the theatre.

Such marking of the script does not, and should not, imply that the actor must resort to a mechanical performance without concern for imagination and the three V's of good acting. However, the intricate demands of the radio production and the comparative short time available for character development make the intelligent use of such notations a practical necessity.

Handling the Script

The actor should hold the script in one hand, to the side of the microphone. Under no circumstances should it be held between the face and the mi-

---

2. Ibid., p. xv.

crophone. If the script is held at eye level, either to the left or right of the microphone, the dialogue may easily be read without interfering with the microphone.

One of the principal mechanical problems arising from acting with a script is to avoid the noise made by turning pages. It takes no more than a slight rattling of pages to remind the audience that they are not listening to a group of interesting characters but merely to actors reading a script before a microphone. The first step in preparing to read a script on mike is to remove the staple or paper clip. Noise is unavoidable if an attempt is made to turn pages while they are still attached. Some radio actors drop the pages quietly to the floor as the performance proceeds, but this creates another problem: actors moving into position may rattle the papers littering the floor.

The best solution is for the actor to slip each page, after it has been read, in back of the script. The actor should not wait until the bottom line is reached before moving the page; it should be quietly lifted and separated from the body of the script before all the speeches are finished so that the lines on the next page are visible. Thus there is no need to flip the page quickly to maintain the continuity of the dialogue. The page should be held apart until all the dialogue on it has been read and the next page *begun*. Then it may be quickly slipped behind the script.

The Elements of the Radio Performance

Preparing a Characterization

The conscientious actor is aware that it takes time and hard work to work out a characterization in any dramatic medium. Furthermore, many actors in the theatre find that they are not really able to bite into a role and project the full meaning of their lines until they are free of the script. The radio actor is never permitted such a luxury. He must be able to cut to the heart of the dialogue quickly, extract the meaning, and communicate it effectively. The following example of a typical rehearsal schedule for a half-hour drama program illustrates the type of pressure that the radio actor constantly faces.

Rehearsal	Activity	Average Time (in minutes)
1	Dry run—cast reads the script, usually around a table. Director gives general comments, and the script is cut and checked for time.	45
2	Two run-throughs of the script on mike, without music or sound effects. Additional cuts may be made. Director will give specific comments.	90

Rehearsal	Activity	Average Time *(in minutes)*
3	Run-through to coordinate music and sound effects. Check for final cuts or additions.	45
4*	Special check on scenes that may need detailed work.	30
5	Complete run-through (dress rehearsal).	30

With this type of rehearsal schedule, there is no question that a glib reader is likely to be more successful in radio than in the theatre; this does not imply, however, that the actor should be satisfied with a superficial performance. It has been proven over and over again that the better prepared an actor is for theatre work, the more easily he or she will be able to move into radio drama. Analysis, imagination, integrity, concentration, and the three V's of good acting apply equally to the radio characterization. The key to a successful transition is *compression*. Condensing the work into a shorter period of time requires the actor to expend energy and intelligence with care, but it should prove to be no insurmountable barrier. This condensation will take the form of concentrating on the most salient aspects usually covered in a more leisurely manner during the rehearsal period of the stage play.

The following procedure is suggested as a means of developing a meaningful characterization, even under the restrictions of the radio rehearsal schedule:

1. Read the script carefully the *first time* through, to determine the prevailing mood and theme of the play.
2. Determine clearly the character's age, social status, temperament, and education.
3. Find the character's dominant trait and work on it. (The radio character, by necessity, is simpler than the stage character.)
4. Search for a prevailing viewpoint that the character maintains throughout the script.
5. Decide upon the character's attitude toward each individual with whom he or she shares a scene, and make notes to this effect *in* the script.

Vocal Individuality

The burden of a good radio performance rests on the actor's voice. This may seem obvious, but it is the core of all radio acting. Many misconceptions prevail about the voice and voice technique in radio. The belief that the

---

*Optional

radio actor must possess a beautiful or attractive voice is not necessarily true. The most important attributes of a good radio voice are *expressiveness* and *adequate articulation*.

In the theatre, audiences are able to discern much about a character from choice of costume, makeup, posture, movement, and gesture. The radio actor must create a believable character without any of these elements, presenting a character to the audience by the voice alone. Because of this requirement, and because the radio drama is shorter than the stage play, radio characters are simpler and less fully developed than in the theatre. These circumstances impose two requirements upon the actor: first, the voice must be easily distinguishable from the other characters so that audiences will *immediately* recognize it. Hence the radio actor should strive for individuality rather than attractiveness in using the voice. Secondly, the voice must in some way indicate the personality of the character. This need is highlighted in the third step of the preparatory period: the search for the character's dominant characteristic.

Jon Eisenson, noting the link between voice and personality, has written:

> The way a voice affects us is not entirely a hit-or-miss affair. Radio performers present themselves as *kinds of personalities* by their voices . . . voices which communicate themselves almost immediately as personalities to be liked or disliked, to be responded to pleasantly or unpleasantly. We can be expected to recognize the average villain or hero the moment we hear him. The sweetness of the heroine comes to us through her voice. So does the staunchness, dependability, and unselfishness of the ever-available, good but somewhat past-middle-aged friend.[3]

Proper articulation is important in all phases of acting, and especially in radio. Poor articulation in radio is usually caused by slovenliness or tension. However, if the actor is aware that he or she has an articulation difficulty, it will help to work mechanically on the sounds that give trouble until the actor can improve upon them. The microphone is merciless in pointing up errors, but it is a two-edged sword. Overarticulated speech on the air will sound affected and unbelievable. Although the actor should devote time to working on troublesome sounds, it is incorrect to *over*articulate when broadcasting.

As important in radio acting as crisp articulation is a meaningful and stimulating delivery. The actor who overarticulates or whose voice is falsely resonant will call attention only to the voice, rather than to the matter being communicated. The key question the radio actor should ask in assessing his or her voice prior to performance is not how attractive the voice is but how effectively it will reveal the personality the actor wishes it to reveal.

---

3. Jon Eisenson, *Basic Speech* (New York: Macmillan Co., 1950), p. 147.

Reacting to Other Characters' Lines

The importance of listening to other characters on stage has already been emphasized. Listening is an integral part of the work done by every good actor not only in the theatre but also in radio. Although the radio audience cannot *see* the actor listening and reacting to other characters in the studio, they may easily sense it by the manner in which the actor's responding lines are read. It is important that the actor read lines not simply because they come next in the script but rather because they grow naturally out of the interaction of the characters.

Artificiality in script reading is a common fault even among actors who have no such difficulties in reading memorized lines in the theatre. It is not just a matter of not having had time to digest the material. Such artificiality is most frequently caused by the actor's concentrating *only* on his or her own dialogue and thus being unable to relate it to the context of the scene. Line reading is always improved by listening to all the dialogue of the scene or, in radio, by following it in the script. In other words, the radio actor *listens by reading* the dialogue as it is spoken.

It may also help the actor to play to the other characters as frequently as possible. This certainly does not mean moving off-mike but directing at least some attention to the action as it is projected by all the participants in a scene. To avoid losing the place in the script, the actor may use the simple expedient of following the dialogue with a finger as the dialogue proceeds.

Above all, the actor must remain in character all the time he or she is on-mike, even during long stretches when the character has no dialogue. It is true that the audience cannot see the actor, but the first fitful and poorly read lines of a new speech will be ample evidence that somewhere between speeches the character has ceased to exist.

Physical Action

Of what possible use, one may ask, is physical action in radio, especially in view of the repeated emphasis on the voice? The fact is that radio acting is not simply vocal acting. Although it is true that the radio actor communicates exclusively by voice, physical acting remains an important factor in the work.

Good acting in every medium requires a total bodily response by the actor. It is impossible to divorce vocal expression from physical expression. Try to read the line, ''I hate you, I'm going to kill you,'' in a tense, excited voice while remaining completely relaxed. Of course, it is next to impossible. However, as the physical attitude implied by the sentence is approximated, the vocal responsiveness will improve.

The implications for the radio actor should be clear. It is necessary to react physically through bodily action and facial expression while reading the script, regardless of the fact that no audience will see the performance. This procedure will have a decided effect on the vocal interpretation. Too many beginning radio actors stand numbly in front of the microphone and wonder why they are not able to project the tension and excitement of which they are capable on stage.

Physical action in radio, however, does not mean performing the same business demanded on stage. Clearly the demands of microphone behavior forbid this. Let us assume that an actor is reading a speech during which the character is supposed to be lifting a heavy crate of books. The actor cannot put down the script and lift a crate in order to achieve the appropriate vocal response. What is possible is to use the muscle tension associated with such heavy physical exertion while holding the script and reading the lines. This muscle tension will inevitably be communicated by the actor's voice.

Suggestions for the Radio Actor

Many minor problems arise in the performance of a radio drama. Some of these have their counterparts in the theatre, whereas others are peculiar to radio. The first type of problem the intelligent actor may anticipate or handle effectively by drawing on his or her stage experience. The second type is often more difficult to assess beforehand, and only experience will provide satisfactory solutions.

The following suggestions may be useful in helping the actor to anticipate and circumvent some of the difficulties of radio acting:

1. *Overacting.* Subtlety is the key to good radio acting. The radio actor does not have to bridge the distance between the actor and the audience that exists in the theatre.
2. *Diction.* The actor must be careful about diction. Slovenliness is greatly magnified by the impersonal microphone.
3. *Speed.* The actor must take time to extract the full meaning from each sentence and word and avoid the common error of begining radio actors, who often stumble over their words because of excessive speed.
4. *Care of the microphone.* The actor should not strike, handle, or hold the microphone and under no circumstances cough, sneeze, or whistle into it.
5. *Sharing the microphone.* Don't be a "mike hog." If someone else is standing on your side of the microphone, be sure to give the other person ample room.
6. *Picking up cues.* The dialogue should flow naturally, without awkward and unnecessary pauses between lines.
7. *Fear of a meaningful pause.* Although cues should be picked up, a mean-

ingful pause, or "dead air," at a significant moment in the dialogue may be tremendously effective. The actor need not be afraid of using this when it has a purpose.

8. *Avoiding monotony.* Reading from a script may produce a steady pattern of delivery that the actor would never use if the lines were memorized. The actor must guard against this by remembering the importance of variety.

9. *Breathing.* The actor must be careful not to breathe heavily near the mike. A sudden inhalation or exhalation will sound like a loud whistle on microphone. It is necessary to breathe deeply—but silently.

10. *Watching the director for signals and cues.* The director is the coordinator of the entire production and is the only person who knows how all the pieces of the puzzle fit together. Unlike the stage director, the director is there to guide the actors *during* the performance.

The Director's Signals

Because the actors must rely on the judgment of the radio director during performances as well as during rehearsal, a system of communication signals is essential, since the director obviously cannot *tell* the actors what to do when they are on the air. The director's language, then, is a set of visual symbols by which to communicate freely, in silence, from the control room to the studio. Every radio actor should know these signals and be able to respond accordingly.

1. *Stand by; your cue is coming.* The hand is held up, with the palm outward, warning the actor to wait for a cue. This signal usually comes at the beginning of the show. It may also be used to tell the actor to hold an extremely long dramatic pause or to hold for a music bridge before the lines are to begin again.

2. *It's your cue.* The forefinger is pointed directly at the actor who has a cue. At this signal the actor should respond immediately.

3. *Slow down; you are reading too rapidly.* With the fingers together, the hands are pulled apart slowly as if an imaginary rubber band were being stretched. It warns the actor to take more time in reading the lines.

4. *Speed up; you are reading too slowly.* The forefinger is extended and turned rapidly in a clockwise motion. It warns the actor to pick up the pace.

5. *Lower your volume.* The palm of the hand is moved downward. The common gesture of placing the forefinger to the lips may also be used. It directs the actor to lower the volume but may also indicate that there are unwanted noises in the studio. The director will clarify which message is intended by pointing to the actor in question.

6. *Bring up the volume.* The hands are raised, palms up. If the volume is not

cue 1

cue 2

cue 3

cue 4

cue 5

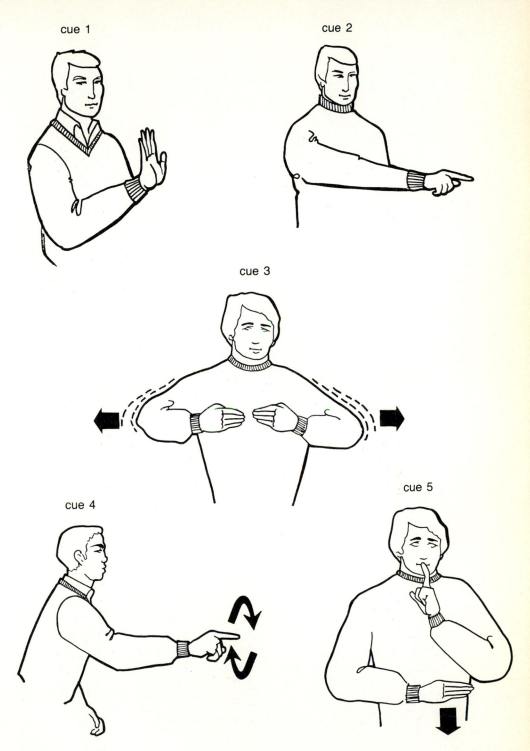

cue 6

cue 7

brought up to a satisfactory level, the hand may make short move-ments, quickly repeating the gesture. This indicates that the actor is speaking below the desired level.

7. *Move closer to the microphone.* The hands are moved together with palms facing each other. The speed and distance of the movement will indicate to the actor whether to make a slight or an extensive adjustment.

8. *You are too near the microphone; move back.* The reverse of the action above is used. Again the speed and distance of the movement will indicate the extent of the adjustment.

cue 8

cue 9

cue 10   cue 11

9. *The show is on time.* The forefinger is placed on the tip of the nose.
10. *Everything is O.K.* The hand is held up with the thumb and forefinger forming a circle and the other fingers extended. This may mean a scene went well, the performance is fine, keep up the same level of vitality, and so on. It's the most encouraging sign to come out of the control room.
11. *Cut.* The finger is drawn across the throat. It may indicate the end of the show or be an order *immediately* to stop a speech, a sound effect, a musical bridge, and so on.

EXERCISES

1. (a) Assume the posture of someone who is angry and tense, and read the line ''If you come one step nearer, I'll strike you.'' Note the amount of tenseness and rigidity in the torso and neck.
    (b) Take a position as if you were standing in front of a microphone, holding a script in one hand. Read the line again, once in the tensed posture, the next time relaxed. Note whether there is any difference.
    (c) Record this line of dialogue with a tape or cassette recorder, using both the tense and relaxed positions. Judge your reading as a listener would hear it, and listen carefully for any differences in the reading.
    (d) Choose a line for each of several emotional states, such as weariness, exultation, or terror. Read each line completely relaxed and then with the appropriate physical state accompanying the reading. Again try to note any differences in your reading.
2. In order to promote facility in sight reading, pick up a book or magazine and without studying it, read a selection aloud into a tape or cassette recorder. Play it back and consider how you may improve the level of your reading.

3. Each member of the class should tape-record the following line: "The day is sunny and warm, and the earth is in all her glory." Read the line as it would be read by each of the following characters, but choose your own order of reading: (a) a cynic, (b) a happy young boy or girl, (c) an old man or woman, (d) a business man or woman, (e) a poet, and (f) a condemned prisoner facing execution. Play back your reading to the class. They should attempt to identify each of the characters by listening to the recording alone.

4. Adapt any of the following short exercises in this book for a radio broadcast: *Private Lives* (Chapter 5), *The Fourposter* (Chapter 4), *The Diary of Anne Frank* (Chapter 6), *Death of a Salesman* (Chapter 7), *The Miser* (Chapter 8), *California Suite* (Chapter 4), or *Butterflies are Free* (Chapter 6). If practicable, tape-record the sequence. After the class or group has listened to these sequences, the following questions should be discussed:
   (a) What additions or deletions would make the scenes entirely intelligible to a radio audience?
   (b) Compare the characterizations of the radio production with those of the stage version.

A Radio Drama

The following half-hour radio play, from the so-called "golden age of radio," provides an interesting diversity of roles, although they are basically character types rather than individuals. Such characters, however, are typical of most radio dramas.

One sequence in the play that should be of particular interest to the student of radio acting illustrates clearly the great flexibility of radio drama. This is the *montage sequence*, or the rapid change of scenes, from the barber shop to a beauty parlor, a men's store, a dress shop, the opera, a gambling house, a city street, an airplane, Florida, and finally to the Empire State Building. The rhythm of this aural montage may be aided by a musical bridge after each short sequence. The actors playing the roles of John and Stella will have to be especially careful to suggest the different emotional responses of the characters during each brief sequence.

This exercise may be used in any of the following ways:

1. Short sequences that are complete in themselves may be used, with class members cast in several roles.
2. The entire play may be read without any of the accompanying musical or sound effects.
3. The play may be produced in class with all the production material integrated. For this purpose, a list of suggested sound effects is given at the end of the play. Although the radio actor is not responsible for producing these effects, they may be performed by a "sound person" chosen from the group. In this way the script may be produced with the greatest possible fidelity to its potential as "drama for the ear."

The Clinic, by Ted Key.[4]

Characters: John Libbey   Dr. Bethume
              Stella Libbey   Dr. Beems
              Harry, co-worker of John Libbey   Clerk
              Molly, a stenographer   Doris, a hospital typist
              Mr. Carlin   Orderly
              Dr. Seidel   Nurse

Scattered Voices: barber, beauty-parlor operator, croupier, anonymous voices, organ grinder, elevator captain, elevator boy, elderly lady, three bed-patients.

(A *cystoscopy,* mentioned in the script, is an examination of the kidneys or bladder.)

MUSIC: *Up to abrupt stop.*
CLERK: (*feminine*) Let me have your slip, please.
LIBBEY: I was here about a year ago. They said downstairs you had my record.
CLERK: John Libbey. What month?
LIBBEY: April.
CLERK: April—yes. Doris, type this for me a moment. You had an operation.
LIBBEY: Yes.
SOUND: *Typing in background.*
CLERK: I remember you. Remember him, Doris? He was in the clinic last year.
DORIS: (*typing stops*) Sure, I remember him. How you feeling?
LIBBEY: Not so well.
SOUND: *Typing continues in background.*
CLERK: Wait in there, Mr. Libbey.
LIBBEY: (*fading*) All right.
CLERK: He's married.
DORIS: He's the one who chewed gum all the time.
CLERK: Orderly, give Dr. Fineman this chart. This man's been here before.
ORDERLY: (*fading*) Dr. Fineman's on a cystoscopy.
CLERK: Dr. Bethume—he'll know about it! You can't tell that guy anything. Where's Libbey? Libbey!
LIBBEY: (*coming toward mike*) Yes?
CLERK: Did they see you downstairs about charges?
LIBBEY: Well, I saw them, and they said to come up here . . .
CLERK: About finances, though . . .
LIBBEY: I can't afford any more than I could last time. (*Typing stops.*)
CLERK: I'm no prophet. What do they expect me to go on?
LIBBEY: Shall I see them now?
CLERK: Wait till the examination. What's the matter with you?
LIBBEY: I don't know, I just have these aches sometimes on this side.
CLERK: Adhesions, probably.

---

4. *The Clinic,* by Ted Key. Copyright 1940 by the National Broadcasting Company, Inc. Reprinted by permission of the National Broadcasting Company, Inc.

LIBBEY: Adhesions should be on the other side. This side wasn't operated on.
CLERK: Well, you'd better sit down and wait till the doctor's ready.
LIBBEY: (*fading*) All right.
CLERK: How old do you think he is?
DORIS: I dunno. How old? Forty?
CLERK: He's thirty-eight.
DORIS: He looks more'n forty.
CLERK: He's thirty-eight.
ORDERLY: (*coming toward mike*) Dr. Bethume can see him now.
CLERK: Mr. Libbey.
LIBBEY: (*coming toward mike*) Yes?
CLERK: You want to follow the orderly? Take your hat and coat with you.
ORDERLY: This way, please. Dr. Bethume wants to see you.
LIBBEY: Bethume?
ORDERLY: Step in here.
SOUND: *Door closing.*
ORDERLY: (*turning from mike*) The doctor's reading your chart.
LIBBEY: Thank you.
SOUND: *Door opening and closing.*
DR. PHIL SEIDEL: (*voice muffled, behind door and some distance away*) Now still, hold your breath. (*Silence for three seconds.*)
SOUND: *Buzzing of X-ray machine.*
SEIDEL: (*muffled, far off*) Breathe again . . .
SOUND: *Door opening and closing.*
BETHUME: Are you Mr. Libbey?
LIBBEY: Yes, doctor.
BETHUME: What seems to be the trouble?
LIBBEY: I don't know, doctor. On this side every so often I have aches. Feels like something's wrong.
BETHUME: Take off your shirt.
LIBBEY: Yes, sir.
BETHUME: How often do you have these pains? Undershirt, too.
LIBBEY: I don't know, just recently, every so often. I was in the hospital last year.
BETHUME: Do you want to stand up straight, please—that's fine—fine.
LIBBEY: My heart's all right, I think.
BETHUME: Lean your head just slightly—that's it—want to look at your eyes. (*Silence*) Open your mouth. Open your mouth, please. (*Silence.*) Your right arm—just for blood pressure . . .
LIBBEY: I'm scared it might be something serious on the other side. I wouldn't want that, doctor.
BETHUME: Don't you worry about it too much.
SOUND: *Rubber bulb of blood pressure instrument.*
BETHUME: That's fine. Okay. Now when I ask you to cough—cough. Cough.
SOUND: *Cough.*
BETHUME: Again.
SOUND: *Cough.*
BETHUME: Again.
SOUND: *Cough.*

BETHUME: Again.

SOUND: *Cough.*

BETHUME: Sit up on the table.

LIBBEY: How am I, doctor?

BETHUME: Lungs all right. Blood pressure up a little but nothing to worry about. Over more. Lie back.

LIBBEY: You going to X-ray me?

BETHUME: I think so. The only way to tell anything. You'll have to lie still, Mr. Libbey.

SOUND: *Door opening.*

BETHUME: All right, nurse; come in, close the door.

SOUND: *Door closing.*

BETHUME: We're not going to try anything fancy on you, Mr. Libbey. You've had intravenous before.

LIBBEY: Sure.

BETHUME: Did you call Dr. Seidel?

NURSE 1: He's coming, doctor.

BETHUME: It's not going to hurt. Clench your fist. Let's see if we can find a vein here . . . fine . . . Okay, nurse . . .

LIBBEY: How much dye you using?

BETHUME: 20 cc.'s.

LIBBEY: Isn't that a lot?

SOUND: *Door opening and closing.*

SEIDEL: This the man?

BETHUME: Intravenous, Phil.

SEIDEL: He's not hurting, is he?

LIBBEY: No, I've had these before. As long as it's not a cystoscopy. (*Phil laughs.*)

BETHUME: That's all.

SEIDEL: I'm going to move you a little, Libbey. That's it. We've got to get you in line here.

LIBBEY: That stuff gets down fast enough, doesn't it?

SEIDEL: Sure does. I want you to take two deep breaths. Breathe through your mouth. I'll tell you when to hold it. Then lie perfectly still. I want you to lie perfectly still.

LIBBEY: Okay.

SEIDEL: (*off-mike*) Inhale.

SOUND: *Inhaling.*

SEIDEL: Exhale.

SOUND: *Exhaling.*

SEIDEL: Inhale.

SOUND: *Inhaling.*

SEIDEL: (*still off-mike*) Hold it. (*Silence for three seconds.*)

SOUND: *Off-mike, the chime of the bell, followed immediately by the tinkle of a typewriter bell and the usual patter of typing. Phone rings off-mike. Harry speaks into it, and sound of typing drops under.*

HARRY: Hub Auto Finance. Just one minute, please. (*to stenographer*) Make a little more noise, Molly, I'm talking on the telephone. (*Typing stops.*) Will you repeat that again; there was a little disturbance . . . oh, Mrs. Libbey, sure, sure. How are you, Mrs. Libbey? That's fine. I'll call him for you. Your wife, John!

LIBBEY: *(fading in)* She insists on calling at the office. *(into phone)* Hello, Stella.

STELLA: *(filter mike)* John, darling, what did they say at the hospital?

LIBBEY: I'll tell you when I get home, Stella.

STELLA: *(filter mike)* Tell me if it's serious, that's all.

LIBBEY: I'll tell you when I get home. Mr. C-A-R-L-I-N is in the office. He doesn't like pleasure on a business phone.

STELLA: I'm so worried. I been worried all day.

LIBBEY: There's no use worrying, Stella.

STELLA: Is it serious? At least you can tell me if it's serious.

LIBBEY: It's serious.

STELLA: Oh, God.

LIBBEY: You asked me. I told you.

STELLA: How serious? Who examined you, John?

LIBBEY: The regular doctors.

STELLA: The same you had last time?

LIBBEY: Darling, I got work to do. Wait till I get home. Can you wait till I get home? I'll tell you all about it when I get home.

SOUND: *Stella sobbing on filter mike.*

LIBBEY: Are you crying, Stella?

SOUND: *Click of receiver as Stella hangs up . . . silence . . . click of receiver as John hangs up.*

HARRY: I heard a good one last night. Charlie tell you, John?

MOLLY: Who was that lady I seen you with? Yeh, yeh, yeh!

HARRY: A great sense of humor, Molly, like an ox. Do you mind me tellin' John a joke? Like she never heard a joke in her life.

LIBBEY: I been thinking I'll take a vacation before I go to the hospital, Harry.

HARRY: That's a good idea. Listen to this, John. This gal . . .

LIBBEY: Just for maybe two weeks. You think he'll mind?

HARRY: If he minds or doesn't mind, take a vacation. Take it, and then tell him. If it was me, I'd take four weeks and with pay.

MOLLY: All your big ideas you give to other people.

HARRY: Listen now, Molly.

LIBBEY: Has he eaten?

HARRY: He's eatin'. You know what you gotta say to him, John? Like you was givin' *him* orders, not vice versa. Don't stand for a negative answer. And if he tries to say something, speak first.

LIBBEY: I deserve a vacation.

HARRY: Sure you do. I deserve one myself.

LIBBEY: I have a week coming to me from last year I didn't take. So it's only an extra week.

MOLLY: Who's gonna keep the books?

HARRY: You'll keep the books.

MOLLY: Ho! Listen to him, *me* keep the books. You think he wants to come back and find a mess a figures upside down and every which way? I'm not messin' John's books.

LIBBEY: I'm not coming back, so you don't have to worry about my books, Molly.

HARRY: Not coming back, what d'ye mean: You quitting?

LIBBEY: I don't think I'll come back, that's all.

HARRY: (*it dawns on him*) John, you're absolutely crazy! Get it out of your head once an' for all. Don't talk yourself into it! Are you crazy? That's no mental condition to be in! How you like it, a guy with his brains lettin' himself go like that. Why, there's millions a guys with operations every day an' what happens to 'em? You think they have that attitude? Where would they be if they had that attitude? Okay, you're feelin' bad; you just come from the doctor's; now you take a nice long rest . . .

MOLLY: Don't think such things, John. You mustn't think such things.

HARRY: He's all right, Molly, don't worry. And when he comes out, I'm gonna throw him a party. Get your mind off the whole business, John. Don't take it so serious. Ask him for a vacation. Have a good time. Molly will take care of the books while you're gone.

MOLLY: I'll take care of the books, John.

LIBBEY: (*fading*) I'll see what he says.

HARRY: You understand me, don't you, John? (*Silence.*) How you like the guy? (*fading*) Operations are three-fourths mental condition an' how you like him?

SOUND: *Soft rapping on door.*

CARLIN: (*muffled as if from behind door*) Come in.

SOUND: *Door opening.*

CARLIN: Come in, John. What is it?

SOUND: *Door closing.*

LIBBEY: I'd like to speak to you a minute if you're not busy, Mr. Carlin.

CARLIN: Well, I'm always busy, John, but sit down. I understand you went to the hospital this morning.

LIBBEY: I had these aches in my side and . . .

CARLIN: Oh, now, John, you needn't apologize for going. A thing like that must be seen to and the sooner you do it the better for all concerned.

LIBBEY: That's true.

CARLIN: I don't believe in tampering with nature; nature has her own laws. But a thing like yours . . . well, I want my people healthy. Health first, I say. Health first, always, never stint on health. You've been with us fifteen years; you know how I feel about that.

LIBBEY: Sixteen years.

CARLIN: Sixteen years should tell you that, John. If there's anything we can do for you, I want you to say it.

LIBBEY: Well, you can do something for me, Mr. Carlin.

CARLIN: All right, John?

LIBBEY: I'd like to have my vacation now.

CARLIN: Then later you're having this operation, is that it?

LIBBEY: Yes, Mr. Carlin.

CARLIN: How long do you think it will take, John, speaking conservatively, say.

LIBBEY: Oh, I don't know. These things you can't tell. Depends on what they do, Mr. Carlin.

CARLIN: Last year you were out about five weeks, weren't you, John?

LIBBEY: Yes, sir.

CARLIN: You understand why we didn't allow the vacation you speak of. Under normal circumstances, you would have had your vacation like the rest of them.

LIBBEY: I know that, sir, but usually there's one week with pay.

CARLIN: John, weren't you *paid?*

LIBBEY: No, sir.

CARLIN: How did that happen? You were never paid?

LIBBEY: No, sir.

CARLIN: Oh, now, there must be some mistake. There must be some mistake. That's never happened here before, has it, John?

LIBBEY: I don't believe so.

CARLIN: I'm sure it hasn't. Well! Well! Suppose you take your two weeks' vacation, John, and we'll see about that pay business when you return. How is that? Suppose we do that, John; and meanwhile you take good care of yourself, and let's have you back with us soon.

LIBBEY: All right, Mr. Carlin. Thanks.

CARLIN: Good luck, John, and take good care of yourself.

LIBBEY: Yes, sir. Good-by, Mr. Carlin.

CARLIN: Yes. Good-by, John.

SOUND: *Door opening and closing . . . Dead air . . . Key turning in keyhole . . . Door opening and closing.*

STELLA: *(far off-mike)* John?

LIBBEY: *(wearily)* Yes.

STELLA: *(fading in)* Give me your things.

LIBBEY: I'll put them away, Stella.

STELLA: I have some hot tea for you. Dinner's on the stove. Give me your things.

LIBBEY: I'm all right.

STELLA: *(fading)* Go in, dear, and sit by the table now.

LIBBEY: You don't have to baby me, Stella. I don't need babying.

STELLA: *(fading in)* Sit down now, sit down.

LIBBEY: Well, Stella, this has been a long day.

STELLA: Yes, of course it has. The tea is hot and I'll give you some lemon.

SOUND: *Tea pouring into cups behind voices.*

STELLA: Tea is nice no matter how you feel.

LIBBEY: I have to have another operation, Stella.

STELLA: *(after a time)* Cut me a piece of lemon with the knife, John . . .

LIBBEY: Don't get nervous, and don't cry, Stella. I don't want you to cry. It's nothing to cry about.

STELLA: I'm not crying, John.

LIBBEY: Let's talk sensibly like two human beings. I don't like crying.

STELLA: I know you don't, John.

LIBBEY: They showed me the plates. I took X-rays, and there were two white spots in the right kidney. That's the only good side left, Stella.

STELLA: Maybe they'll dissolve.

LIBBEY: They won't. They're too big.

STELLA: Is that what they said?

LIBBEY: I saw them myself. They're too big.

STELLA: Maybe they're not stones, John.

LIBBEY: They're stones.

STELLA: You feel all right now?

LIBBEY: I feel okay. They wanted me immediately, tomorrow or Thursday, but I said no. I think I'll wait a couple weeks. They have to give me a cystoscopy and more X-rays for further examination. So I'll go in on a Tuesday, and they'll operate on a Thursday or Friday.

STELLA: You're not afraid, are you, John?

LIBBEY: Yes, I am, Stella.

STELLA: I'm afraid too, John, I'm afraid. (*fading*) Something's in the kitchen.

LIBBEY: (*off-mike*) Smells good.

SOUND: *Frying in background, continuing under.*

STELLA: (*full*) Your specialty with onions.

LIBBEY: (*fading in*) I spoke to Mr. Carlin; and he's giving me two weeks off, so we'll have a vacation before I go.

STELLA: That's good, John. A vacation won't hurt you.

LIBBEY: Don't make the onions so brown.

STELLA: You need a rest.

LIBBEY: I don't need a rest. That's all I been doing. I been resting. I been dieting. I been following all their instructions. So what? Now I'm sick again.

STELLA: We'll go someplace where there's fresh air, and then afterwards, when it's over, you'll get better quickly. (*Frying ceases.*)

LIBBEY: Should I slice the bread?

STELLA: Dinner's ready. Sit down; I'll slice it.

LIBBEY: (*off-mike*) Any mail today, Stella?

STELLA: No mail, dear. Sit down.

SOUND: *Dishes being placed on the table.*

STELLA: Don't stare at me that way, John.

LIBBEY: I didn't mean to stare, Stella. Was I staring?

STELLA: Eat the beets. They're good for you.

LIBBEY: I checked up on the insurance policy today. It's all right.

STELLA: I don't wanna hear about the insurance policy.

LIBBEY: Those things have to be checked on and it's all right. There's $5,000 coming, and it's in order. These things have to be talked about.

STELLA: All right, we talked about it.

LIBBEY: All right. It just had to be said. When the time comes, you know where it is. (*Silence.*) It's fortunate I . . .

STELLA: I don't wanna hear about the insurance policy!

LIBBEY: Okay. I didn't say a word. Okay.

STELLA: Like you were gonna die, don't talk like that. (*Silence.*)

LIBBEY: I am going to die, Stella.

STELLA: John, no, John, you're not. You're not. You mustn't say it when you're not.

LIBBEY: (*Stella sobs behind his voice*) Please, Stella. (*hardly audible*) You mustn't even think about it. Sure, you think I don't know how you feel, but I know very well, Stella. I got ten times the pain thinking about it as from the pain itself.

STELLA: No, John, no, John.

LIBBEY: Well, I'm no different from anybody else. I realize that.

STELLA: You're not going to leave me. I'll be all alone. You won't leave me, will you, John?

LIBBEY: I don't wanna die.

STELLA: I'll die, too.

LIBBEY: Let's not talk about it. There's lots pleasanter things to talk about.

STELLA: John, you won't, will you? You won't?

LIBBEY: How can I say, Stella?

STELLA: Say you're not gonna die. Tell me like you meant it. (*Pause.*)

LIBBEY: Here's my wallet, Stella. Open it, and take what you see there.

STELLA: Why don't you answer me? There's ten one-hundred-dollar bills and two five-hundred-dollar bills. Two thousand. (*Pause.*) What is it? Where did you get the money, John?

LIBBEY: Pick it up, Stella. Have you ever seen a five hundred dollar bill before?

STELLA: Where did you get it, John?

LIBBEY: We're spending it on ourselves. I decided for both of us. Anything you see or want, we'll buy. Like you always wanted to go to the opera. We'll go to the opera. We'll buy some clothes and we'll go to the opera, and we'll do everything we've always wanted to do. That's what the money's for.

STELLA: We never had $2,000 in our life.

LIBBEY: I borrowed it from Mr. Carlin.

STELLA: He gave it to you?

LIBBEY: I didn't ask him.

STELLA: How—you took it?

LIBBEY: He'll get it back.

STELLA: Get it back? How's he getting it back if you're spending it?

LIBBEY: The money you're getting from the insurance, Stella. You'll pay him back. Don't look like that, Stella. It's no crime.

STELLA: There won't be any insurance.

LIBBEY: You'll have $5,000; and after you pay Mr. Carlin, you'll have $3,000 left. Why say there won't be any?

STELLA: So you're already figuring on it. Your mind's made up.

LIBBEY: Stella, all my life I've been broke. I never had a dime that wasn't somebody's soon's I got it. What's wrong then? Just because I'm doing what I always had a mind to? And now I can do it. I'm borrowing from you, but there'll be lots left. You won't feel sorry for the pleasure, Stella. We'll have that together, Stella.

STELLA: You coulda borrowed off the insurance, John.

LIBBEY: How long we had the policy—five years. What is there to borrow?

STELLA: Like money was the only thing in the world. Like it was the only . . .

LIBBEY: It's not the only thing in the world. I know it's not. I want some fun, Stella, that's all. Isn't that what we've always been talking about? Someday, we said. If we can't afford it now, when, then? When, then? Answer me. We've been living in this same place, this same apartment for years.

STELLA: I don't mind that.

LIBBEY: I mind it. I'm sick of it. Why don't you say you're sick of it? You are. I get sixty-five dollars a week so's you can wash and cook and take care of the home day after day, listen to the radio, and look at the furniture day after day after day, and that's not all. Don't tell me how you feel, Stella.

STELLA: I haven't complained about it.

LIBBEY: And I'm sick of your not complaining about it.

STELLA: What did you want me to do? I tried to make the best of things, didn't I, John?

LIBBEY: Making the best of things, all the time being brave. Denying and scrimping and saving and making ends meet. It adds up to nothing. That's what it adds up to Stella, nothing.

STELLA: (*a moment . . . then*) Put the money away, John, I'll give you some more tea.

LIBBEY: We'll use it then?

STELLA: We'll use it.

LIBBEY: You're not feeling bad. Please don't feel bad. That's not why I took it.

STELLA: I'm all right, John.

LIBBEY: Show me by smiling. See? It's not stealing. It's nothing like stealing, Stella. He'll get it back soon. We'll be very happy.

STELLA: The tea is still hot, John, if you'll pour me some. And you haven't eaten much, John.

LIBBEY: I'm full just thinking. I can't eat.

STELLA: You have to eat something.

LIBBEY: (*silence . . . then*) What are you thinking about? About me? And what about me?

STELLA: I'm not thinking anything at all, John.

LIBBEY: Do you hate me?

STELLA: I love you, John.

LIBBEY: Maybe afterwards you'd hate me?

STELLA: If I love you now, what's the sense of hating you later? I could ask you to change your mind, but you won't do that; for it's made up, and I can't argue things like that away. That's all I don't like about it, your scaring me and your thinking of what's coming and the fact maybe it's true.

MUSIC: *Descriptive music. Hold . . . then fade into background for this sequence:*

BARBER: Anything else besides the haircut?

LIBBEY: A shampoo and a scalp massage and tell the boy I want a shine. And put some of that smelly stuff on my hair and whatever else you can think of. Give me whatever you can think of.

MUSIC: *Same thread of music swells up . . . then fades behind.*

BEAUTY PARLOR OPERATOR: The manicurist will be with you in a jiffy.

STELLA: (*listlessly*) How long does this take? I'd like my hair washed and after the facial maybe a marcel.

MUSIC: *Swells up . . . then drops behind.*

LIBBEY: Look all right, Stella?

STELLA: It fits all right.

LIBBEY: How is it in the back? Is it all right there?

STELLA: How's it supposed to be? You never bought a suit with tails before. They just hang. They hang all right.

MUSIC: *Swells up . . . then drops under.*

STELLA: Well, John?

LIBBEY: I like it.

STELLA: Yes, but should I take it?

LIBBEY: I'd take it. It's the prettiest dress I ever seen on you, Stella.

MUSIC: *Swells up into operatic aria, sung by soprano voice . . . Hold . . . then fade down and into the roar of a fight crowd . . . Hold . . . then fade down under.*

VOICE: *(far off-mike)* The winner and still heavyweight champion of the world, Joe Louis!

SOUND: *Cheers sweep in . . . Hold . . . then fade down into the hum of voices in the background.*

CROUPIER: Eighteen on the red.

SOUND: *Chips . . . the whirl of the roulette wheel.*

CROUPIER: Bets, please.

SOUND: *The ball coming to a stop.*

CROUPIER: Twenty-two on the black.

MUSIC: *Fade in descriptive music; then fade into typical melody played by hand organ . . . Hold . . . then keep in background.*

LIBBEY: An organ-grinder, Stella.

STELLA: John, let him have something. Have you something?

ORGAN-GRINDER: *(after silence, far off-mike)* Grazias, grazias, signor, grazias!

STELLA: How much did you give him, John?

LIBBEY: Five dollars.

MUSIC: *Swells in . . . Hold . . . then fade behind.*

STELLA: John, you see it? Look 'way down there, see?

LIBBEY: A boat. It's about the size of . . . we must be going ten times as fast. Twenty times.

STELLA: How long will we stay in Florida? Long, John?

LIBBEY: As long as we feel like. Let's see what it's all about first. We'll stay as long as we feel like.

MUSIC: *Swells up . . . Hold . . . fades as sound of ocean waves sweeping on beach comes up strong . . . Hold . . . fade music behind sound of waves.*

STELLA: I could just lay here and lay here, the sand's so warm.

LIBBEY: We'll take one more swim tomorrow before we go. Listen to the ocean. You like the sound of the ocean?

STELLA: The sun's good for you, John. You've got a tan.

LIBBEY: Have I? So have you. Your face and your shoulders.

STELLA: I don't feel like going back. I'd like to stay here, John.

LIBBEY: Kiss me.

SOUND: *Soft kiss.*

STELLA: Do we have to go back, John?

MUSIC: *Descriptive music swells up . . . Hold . . . then fades out.*

ELEVATOR CAPTAIN: *(off-mike)* Those going to the tower take the elevator to the right.

SOUND: *Patter of feet, voices, all behind voice of*

ELEVATOR BOY: Going up. Step back, please.

SOUND: *Elevator door closing . . . hum of rising elevator as it rises swiftly . . . Stops . . . elevator door opening.*

ELDERLY LADY: Is this still the tallest building in the world, young man?

ELEVATOR BOY: Yes, ma'am. All out.

SOUND: *Voices of passengers up . . . then drop under and fade completely out.*

STELLA: You want to sign the book, John? Here's a book.

LIBBEY: Let's just look around. Where? We might as well sign first.

LIBBEY: (*slowly*) John Libbey, New York City. What's the date? Never mind. I see it, Stella. You sign.

STELLA: (*slowly*) Mrs. John Libbey—ditto.

LIBBEY: It's windy.

STELLA: Button up your coat, John.

LIBBEY: See everything from here—I'm all right, Stella. Don't button me.

STELLA: It's windy.

LIBBEY: There's Central Park, see?

STELLA: Over there.

LIBBEY: It's sure high up. Look straight down, Stella.

STELLA: They look like ants.

LIBBEY: Can you see where we live?

STELLA: Over there.

LIBBEY: Can't see it. There's buildings in the way. Pretty, isn't it, Stella? Big and far away. It gives me a funny feeling inside. We had a good time, didn't we, Stella?

STELLA: Yes, John.

LIBBEY: It's the prettiest scenery I ever seen.

STELLA: I'm not sorry, John.

LIBBEY: I have to be in the hospital by four. (*A moment . . . then*) You were good to me all the time, Stella.

STELLA: (*warmly, softly*) John.

LIBBEY: I'd better get rid of the nickels. Got the duffel-bag?

STELLA: Must you, John?

LIBBEY: I just wanna see what happens. We're too high up. (*fading*) Let's go down to the tenth floor.

MUSIC: *Fade in . . . Hold . . . then fade down.*

SOUND: *Muffled street noises . . . window opening and the street noises come up full . . . Hold . . . then keep behind.*

LIBBEY: Nobody will get hurt from here. You hand me the nickels, and I'll throw them out. Open the bag.

STELLA: Someone may see you.

LIBBEY: Hand them fast. There's only fifty dollars' worth. Unwrap them first, Stella. Anybody looking?

STELLA: Nobody's looking.

SOUND: *Jingling nickels.*

LIBBEY: Here goes.

STELLA: I can't see the sense to it, John.

LIBBEY: There isn't any sense to it.

STELLA: Throw them out fast.

SOUND: *Jingling nickels.*

LIBBEY: All my life I been making sense. Look at the people.

SOUND: *Jingling nickels.*

LIBBEY: People everywhere. Look at the people, Stella.

STELLA: Maybe they'll see you.

LIBBEY: I'm standing on the side here. They can't see me. Give me the rest quick.

SOUND: *Jingling nickels.*

LIBBEY: Don't it give you a thrill, Stella? All those people, and we're making them run. It's power. We have power. When you can afford to spend, Stella, it's power.

STELLA: We better go.

LIBBEY: Look at them, look.

STELLA: We better go, John.

LIBBEY: I never seen anything like that in my life.

SOUND: *Honking of car horns increases . . . Other street noises become louder . . . Hold . . . then fade out.*

MUSIC: *Fade in; then fade out.*

BED 1: *(off-mike)* Will you lower the blind while you're there?

BED 2: This one?

SOUND: *Adjusting blind . . . it stays under his voice.*

NURSE: *(fading in)* Here—what are we doing out of bed, Mr. Corroni?

BED 1: *(off-mike)* The light was in my eyes, nurse.

NURSE: All right, we'll fix it. Back in bed, Mr. Corroni. Some orange juice for you, Mr. Libbey.

LIBBEY: Thanks.

NURSE: Sleep well last night?

LIBBEY: Pretty well, thanks.

NURSE: You'll sleep better tonight. It's hard the first night. Dr. Beems will be here in a minute.

LIBBEY: The X-rays done?

NURSE: Oh, sure. You're down for surgery tomorrow, aren't you? Bed high enough?

LIBBEY: Yes.

NURSE: *(fading)* He'll be here in a minute.

BED 2: *(far off-mike)* See in the paper about all those nickels, Mr. Michaels?

BED 4: *(off-mike)* I didn't see the paper yet.

BED 2: *(far off-mike)* Someone threw a lot of nickels from the Empire State Building. They had a traffic jam a mile long.

BED 4: *(off-mike)* Nickels?

BED 2: *(far off-mike)* Two women fainted, and some guy had his fingers smashed.

DR. BEEMS: *(far off-mike)* Be right there, nurse. *(fading in)* Put on your bathrobe, and come with me, Mr. Libbey.

LIBBEY: Yes, sir.

DR. BEEMS: Slip on anything.

SOUND: *Shuffling slippers behind voices.*

LIBBEY: The cystoscopy X-rays, doctor?

BEEMS: Yes. We can see them here. *(Shuffling stops.)*

SOUND: *Click of electric switch.*

BEEMS: There. How does that look to you, Mr. Libbey?

LIBBEY: I can't tell. What do you mean?

BEEMS: There's nothing the matter with you, nothing that we can see, Mr. Libby. I'm going to give you a discharge. Have your wife call for you.

LIBBEY: But the other X-rays? There was something wrong.

BEEMS: Intravenous is not always dependable. The dye sometimes upsets the diagnosis. You're all right, Mr. Libbey. Go home whenever you feel like it. Have Mr. Libbey's clothes brought up, nurse.

NURSE: Yes, doctor.

BEEMS: The dressings in 10G for Baker?

NURSE: Yes, doctor.

BEEMS: (*fading*) Bring me his chart. (*off-mike and constant*) Ask Dr. Collins if I can see him. (*a little further off-mike and constant*) You're a very lucky man, Mr. Libbey.

MUSIC: *Very soft . . . Hold . . . musical curtain.*

The following means of producing the most important sound effects are included if you wish to integrate sound with the dialogue portions of the script. "Practical" refers to using the actual effect which is called for, as a typewriter for the typing effect, and so forth.

AIRPLANE: Use a recording or a vacuum cleaner turned on near the mike.

AUDIENCE APPLAUDING: Cast members should applaud off-mike.

BULB OF BLOOD PRESSURE INSTRUMENT: Squeeze an ear syringe bulb about two feet from the microphone.

CHIPS AND ROULETTE WHEEL: Use toy model.

CLOSING ELEVATOR DOOR: Push a roller skate across a table until it strikes a block of wood.

CROWD NOISE AT FIGHT: Cast members should choose ad-lib lines and mingle in a corner about fifteen feet from the mike.

DISHES BEING PLACED ON TABLE: Practical.

ELEVATOR: Use recording if possible.

FILTER EFFECT FOR PHONE CONVERSATION: If a filter microphone is not available, the actor should talk partly across a drinking glass and across the live side of the microphone.

FOOD FRYING IN BACKGROUND: Gently brush a whisk broom or crinkle cellophane near the microphone.

NEW YORK STREET NOISES: Cast may ad-lib off-mike and there may be the occasional sound of an automobile horn.

PHONE CLICK: Strike two pieces of metal (preferably lead) together.

TEA BEING POURED INTO CUPS: Cups and water.

TYPING: Practical.

WAVES: A drummer's metal brush may be swished softly on a cymbal.

A Glossary of Theatre Terms

Above: The general area farther away from the audience. The upstage area is *above* the downstage area.

Action: The progress of the play as made clear to the audience by dialogue, movement, and development of character and character relationships. In Method terminology, action refers to the inner motivation of the character, his or her reason for being on the stage. (In this context, see also **Intention**.)

Ad-Lib: (*ad libitum*—literally, at pleasure) Movement or dialogue inserted in the production that is not specified in the playscript; on occasion inserted during a performance to cover fluffs.

Antagonist: The character in the play most directly opposed to the main character, or protagonist.

Apron: The portion of the stage nearest to the audience and in front of the proscenium arch or house curtain.

Area: A portion of the stage that has been designated for use during the playing of a scene. The stage is divided into specific *areas*, such as down right, up left, etc.

Aside: A short speech intended only for the ears of the audience, and by convention not heard by other characters on stage. A typical device, for example, of nineteenth-century melodrama, it may be used to impart information or expose the secret thoughts of the speaker. (See also **Soliloquy**.)

Backdrop: Usually a large piece of canvas or other material behind the stage setting, sometimes with a detailed scene painted on it.

Backstage: The area in back or to the sides of the setting not seen by the audience.

Balance: The equalization of attention by bringing actors, properties, set pieces, and other elements into harmony so as to achieve the required physical equilibrium.

Beats: A term employed by Method actors meaning the distance from the beginning to the end of a continuing state of mind or intention of a character, whether or not it be explicitly stated in the dialogue.

Below: A position or area nearer to the audience. The downstage area is *below* the upstage area.

Bit Part: A role with few lines of dialogue.

Blackout: Throwing the playing area into complete darkness by the sudden turning off of all stage lights.

Blocking: The planned movement and stage composition of the production as developed during the early rehearsals.

Border: A curtain hanging behind but parallel to the proscenium to aid in masking lights, the working rigging, and the fly space.

Box Set: Interior setting consisting of three walls and often a ceiling as well. One of the most common of modern settings.

Build: The increase in energy, tension, or emotional key directed toward a climax, either in a specific scene or through the progress of the play.

Business: Detailed pieces of action developed to enhance characterization, establish mood, and so on. Not the same as the basic stage movement.

Call: The announcement that warns actors when they are to be ready for rehearsals, performances, or individual scenes.

Climax: The high point of interest and/or action in a play, act, scene, or speech. The climax of a play will invariably occur in the second half of the piece.

Close: To turn or adjust the body position so that the actor is turned away from the audience.

Closed Turn: A turn on stage in which the back of the actor is seen by the audience during the turn. (See also **Open Turn.**)

Comedy: (See Chapter 8.)

Company: The persons involved in the production of a play. May also refer to a permanent group involved in a succession of productions, as a "summer stock" company.

Counter: A shifting of position to compensate for the movement of another actor in order to reachieve a balanced and pleasing stage composition.

Cover: To hide from the view of the audience another actor, a property, or a piece of business. Often used deliberately so as not to make obvious the faking of an extremely difficult piece of business, as in a stage fight, stabbing, and so on.

Cross: A movement on stage from one area to another.

Cue: The action or dialogue that signals that the next line is to be spoken or certain business and movement is to take place.

Curtain Call: The receipt of applause by the cast as the curtain is raised at the end of the play.

Cyclorama (also **Cyc**): A backdrop surrounding the setting on three sides. Occasionally used to represent the sky, it is nonspecific in detail.

Dialogue: The words spoken by the actors in the play.

Downstage: The general stage area nearest to the audience.

Dress: (See **Counter**.)

Dress Rehearsal: A rehearsal prior to performance that unites all the elements of the production exactly as they will function during actual performance.

Emotional Memory: One of the most famous aspects of the Stanislavski system. By the development of a technique through arduous training the actor is able to evoke the memory of an emotion similar to the one the character on stage is to feel.

Emphasis: The highlighting or accenting of a particular portion or feature of the production. The actor may give emphasis to a specific action or to a key line and even to one word. (See also **Subordination.**)

Entrance: Coming on stage in view of the audience. May also refer to the opening in the setting that permits the actor to make his or her way on stage.

Exit: Leaving the playing area of the stage. It may also refer to the doorway or other opening in the setting through which the actor leaves.

Exposition: Material in the play that is included to give the audience the background required in order to understand the development of the story. Often refers to action that has occurred prior to the beginning of the play. Hence the exposition in a play is most likely to occur in the opening scenes.

Extras: Actors who appear in a play with no lines and little or no characterization. They are needed to perform a certain function in the play, as in the case of a member of a crowd scene. Also referred to as *supers*.

Farce: (See Chapter 8.)

Flat: A light wooden frame covered by canvas that constitutes the primary unit used to build such settings as the box set.

Flies: The area immediately over the stage where scenery may be raised by a system of pulleys and counterweights.

Floodlight: A large lighting unit used for illumination of broad portions of the stage, general rather than specific in the area it lights, as it cannot be focused.

Floor Plan: An outline drawing of the setting indicating only the design of the setting as it would be seen from above.

Fluff: A blunder during performance, such as a missed line or one that is garbled in its execution.

Focal Point: The point of greatest interest on stage during the playing of a scene.

Follow Spot: A spotlight that is not permanently focused on one position but may follow the movement of an actor about the playing area.

Footlights: Lights located in the stage floor at the edge of the forestage and permitting general illumination of the stage.

Forestage: (See **Apron.**)

Fourth Wall: The imaginary wall that separates the audience and the playing area. The term is used in reference to the realistic box setting which is comprised of three walls. The audience, by convention, is permitted to look at the action through the *fourth wall.*

Front: The auditorium and/or lobby, as distinguished from the stage. Used in such terms as *front of house* and *out front.*

Give Stage: To change stage position so as to permit greater emphasis to be focused on another actor.

Given Circumstance: A term utilized in the Stanislavski system referring to any dramatic occurrences that will affect the actor's playing of a scene. These may take place during the play or may have occurred before the beginning of the play. The death of Hamlet's father before the play begins is a *given circumstance.*

Green Room: Traditionally the gathering place for actors in the backstage area, often serving a social function as well.

Grid: (Gridiron) A framework of steel beams above the stage that supports the rigging required to fly scenery.

Heads Up!: A warning indicating that a piece of scenery or other object is falling or being lowered.

Hold: To stop the action of the play, whether movement or dialogue, usually because of applause or laughter.

House: The part of the theatre in front of the footlights, as opposed to the stage and backstage areas. Usually the auditorium, as in "How's the *house* tonight?" meaning "How many seats are filled?"

Improvisation: The performance of dialogue and/or pantomime without any determined plan from any source other than the actor's own creative spirit, often "on the spur of the moment."

In: To the center of the stage.

Intention: A term used in the Stanislavski system that refers to the actor's real reason for being in a scene, regardless of what he may be saying. If a character hates another character, but because of others present is required to speak pleasantly to that person, the proper *intention* of the relationship must still be conveyed by the actor. (See also **Subtext** and **Problems.**)

Kill: To spoil the planned effectiveness of a line, a movement, a piece of business, or a technical effect, usually by a miscalculation in timing.

Lines: Either (1) the speeches of the actors, or (2) the sets of ropes supported by the grid that are used to fly scenery.

Mask: To conceal from the view of the audience any area of the stage not intended to be seen.

Melodrama: A serious play in which the primary emphasis is on spectacle and contrived action rather than logical character development and relationships.

Method, The: An American school of acting that stresses internal development of the actor's resources for the purpose of properly motivating his or her acting. It has grown out of the system devised by the Russian actor-director, Constantin Stanislavski, although it is modified somewhat from the original.

Monologue: A long speech by one character without any interspersed dialogue by other characters.

Mood: The dominant atmosphere created by the various elements of the production.

Move On: A movement on the same plane toward the center of the stage, either from stage left or stage right.

Off Stage: The area of the stage not visible to the audience.

On Stage: The playing space of the stage intended to be visible to the audience.

Open: To turn or adjust the body position so that the actor may play more directly to the audience.

Open Turn: A turn on stage in which the front of the actor is seen by the audience during the turn. (See also **Closed Turn.**)

Out: A direction away from the center of the stage.

Overlap: To speak or move before the indicated cue, or before another speech or movement is completed.

Overplay: To give to a scene, dialogue, or action greater exaggeration and emphasis than is required.

Pace: Over-all rate of production, including reading of lines, picking up of cues, movement, etc.

Pantomime: The acting out of an incident or story without words.

Parallel Movement: The movement on stage of two or more characters in the same direction at the same time.

Pick Up: A command to increase the pace of the playing, often in reference to the shortening of the interval between the cue and the next line or action.

Places!: A command instructing the company that an act, in rehearsal or performance, is about to begin and each member is to take the proper position.

Plant: To call attention to an object or fact that will have special significance later in the play.

Play Script: The copy of the play including the dialogue and author's stage directions.

Play Up: To emphasize a key line, movement, or piece of business so that it will have greater significance. (Also **Plug.**)

Plot: The story of the play that is developed by the playwright in a logical sequence of events.

Plug: (See **Play Up.**)

Practical: A functioning prop which can actually be *used* by the actor rather than one that is ornamental and cannot be used, in the literal sense. A window that opens, a tap that runs water, is *practical*.

Precast: To choose actors for specific roles before the tryout period is held.

Presentational: (See Chapter 1.)

Problems: In Method terminology, the choice of certain small actions that will best help to project the intention of the character. (See also **Intention.**)

Production: All of the various elements that make up the finished play ready to be seen by an audience.

Project: To make dialogue or movement clear to the audience by proper accentuation and intensification.

Prompter: The person who aids a forgetful actor by reading aloud key words or lines (**Prompting**) from off stage, usually from the wings.

Props: (Properties) All the furniture, set pieces, and objects that are seen on stage. Large pieces, or props that are not used by the actors, are called *stage props*. Small props used by actors are called *hand props*. Props used only by one character and brought on stage by the actor are termed *personal props*.

Proscenium: The wall and arch that set off the stage area from the audience.

Protagonist: The central figure or hero of the play, from the Greek term meaning the first actor.

Ramp: A sloping platform used to serve the same functions as a step unit.

Rehearsal: The organized periods during which the cast prepares the play for production.

Representational: (See Chapter 1.)

Return: A flat set parallel to the footlights and at the downstage edge of the setting running off into the wings, just above the tormentor.

Routine: A specially rehearsed sequence of actions, as a dance or song number.

Run-Through: A rehearsal in which an entire scene or act is played without any interruptions.

Scene: Either (1) a portion of an act, which by the nature of the action, or some arbitrary division, is a distinct unit by itself; or (2) the locale indicated by the setting, as in: "The *scene* is set in a small living room."

Set: To make permanent the reading of lines or movement and business after a series of rehearsals. (Sometimes used as an abbreviation for **Setting.**)

Setting: The arrangement of the scenery and properties that designate the locale of the action.

Share: To take a position on stage so that equal emphasis is afforded two or more actors.

Sides: A typed script that includes only the speeches of one actor and the relevant cues.

Sight Lines: The visibility of the playing area from the audience, usually from the seats on the extreme right and left sides of the house.

Soliloquy: A monologue spoken by the actor as an extension of his or her thoughts and not directed to, or by convention overheard by, any other actor. It is longer than an aside, and usually the actor delivering the soliloquy is alone on stage.

Spine: (See **Superobjective.**)

Spotlight: A lighting unit used to light only a small section of the stage.

Stage Directions: Instructions in the playscript relative to movement, business, and so on.

Stage Left, Stage Right: To the left and right of the actor when facing the audience.

Static Scene: A scene with little or no movement and often having a slow pace.

Steal: The act of having one actor assume emphasis by drawing attention away from the character to whom it would normally be paid. The term is often used in a derogatory sense.

Step Unit: One group of several steps used in the stage setting.

Stock Company: A permanent group of actors that puts on a number of different plays during a comparatively brief period of time, as in a summer season.

Strong: Having high attention value, as in a strong position or area.

Subordination: To treat any element of the production as of minor or secondary importance so as to focus emphasis elsewhere.

Subtext: A term used in the Stanislavski system that refers to the real meaning underlying the dialogue—the purpose for which the words are spoken or their inner meaning. Hence, the lines are considered the text, the underlying meaning the subtext. (See also **Intention.**)

Superobjective: A term often utilized by Method actors and the Stanislavski system to describe the motivating idea or theme that pervades the entire play. Every major character has his or her own objective deriving from the *spine or superobjective* of the play.

Tag Line: The final line of a character when leaving the stage or just prior to the fall of the curtain.

Take Stage: To assume a more prominent body position or move to the most emphatic area so as to receive the focus of attention.

Teaser: A border drapery that masks the fly space and determines the height of the stage opening. It is located behind the house curtain and immediately in front of the tormentors.

Telescope: To have two or more actors overlap the reading of lines or execution of business.

Tempo: The impression the audience receives of the general rate of the production. Directly dependent upon pace.

Text: In Method terminology, the dialogue without reference to the underlying meaning of the lines. (See also **Intention, Subtext.**)

Throw Away: To underplay deliberately a line or business, often to achieve greater emphasis elsewhere in the scene or play.

Timing: The exact use of time, carefully planned to achieve maximum effectiveness in the reading of a line, execution of business or movement.

Top: To so emphasize a line or an action that it is more emphatic than the line or action that precedes it.

Tormentors: Two matching flats, usually black in color, located slightly upstage of the teaser and serving to mask the wings or to vary the size or width of the playing area. Together with the teaser, they effectively serve as a "picture frame" for the stage setting.

Tragedy: (See Chapter 8.)

Trap: An opening in the stage floor that may be used for the ascent or descent of characters or objects. Usually covered by a hinged, removable door.

Tryout: The auditioning of actors for roles in the forthcoming production.

Walk-On: A small role without any lines. (See also **Extras.**)

Weak: Having relatively low attention value, as in a weak position or area.

Wing Setting: Several hinged flats, often in matching pairs, set in sequence at stage right and stage left masking the offstage area. Most frequently used with a backdrop to enclose the playing area.

Wings: The offstage areas to the right and to the left of the playing space.

Index

Italicized page entries indicate photographs or illustrations in the text. Boldfaced page entries indicate a scene or exercise segment in the text.

Credits (continued from copyright page)